The very stones cry out for a tidal wave of justice. A painting by Barbara Paleczny SSND, based on her experience of campaigns within the garment industry.

Studies in Women and Religion /
Études sur les femmes et la religion : 6

Studies in Women and Religion / Études sur les femmes et la religion

Studies in Women and Religion is a series designed to serve the needs of established scholars in this new area, whose scholarship may not conform to the parameters of more traditional series with respect to content, perspective and/or methodology. The series will also endeavour to promote scholarship on women and religion by assisting new scholars in developing publishable manuscripts. Studies published in this series will reflect the wide range of disciplines in which the subject of women and religion is currently being studied, as well as the diversity of theoretical and methodological approaches that characterize contemporary women's studies. Books in English are published by Wilfrid Laurier University Press.

Inquiries should be directed to the series coordinator, Marilyn Legge, Emmanuel College, Victoria University, Toronto.

STUDIES IN WOMEN AND RELIGION /
ÉTUDES SUR LES FEMMES ET LA RELIGION

VOLUME 6

Clothed in Integrity
Weaving Just Cultural Relations and the Garment Industry

Barbara Paleczny

Published for the Canadian Corporation for Studies in Religion /
Corporation Canadienne des Sciences Religieuses
by Wilfrid Laurier University Press

2000

This book has been published with the help of a grant from the Humanities and Social Sciences Federation of Canada, using funds provided by the Social Sciences and Humanities Research Council of Canada. We acknowledge the support of the Canada Council for the Arts for our publishing program. We acknowledge the financial support of the Government of Canada through the Book Publishing Industry Development Program for our publishing activities.

Canadian Cataloguing in Publication Data

Paleczny, Barbara

Clothed in integrity : weaving just cultural relations and the garment industry

(Studies in women and religion;v.6)
Includes bibliographical references and index.
ISBN 0-88920-340-7

1. Clothing trade — Moral and ethical aspects. 2. Women clothing workers — Ontario — Toronto. 3. Home labor — Ontario — Toronto. 4. Christian ethics. 5. Feminist theology. I. Canadian Corporation for Studies in Religion. II. Title. III. Series: Studies in women and religion (Waterloo, Ont.);v.6.

HD6073.C62C3 2000   261.8′5   C99-932722-4

© 2000 Canadian Corporation for Studies in Religion/
          Corporation Canadienne des Sciences Religieuses

Cover design by Leslie Macredie, using "The Heart of Summer: My Summer Dress," by Sandra Woolfrey. Photograph courtesy of Pirak Studios.

Printed in Canada

Clothed in Integrity: Weaving Just Cultural Relations and the Garment Industry has been produced from a manuscript supplied in part in camera-ready form by the author.

Order from:
WILFRID LAURIER UNIVERSITY PRESS
Waterloo, Ontario, Canada N2L 3C5

For
Sister Ann Semel
and the large, wonderfully inclusive community of friends
who often gather at our home
to break bread and share red beans and rice New Orleans style!
We remember Sister Emiliana with fondness.

Why Do Spiders Eat the Sun?

Sun fed webs
Soft silk,
Strong, sturdy webs sticky silk
Webbed wisdom woven wisdom
              Sun fed threads
              Spiders eating spinning
              weaving waiting
              Webbed world

Quiet wisdom
Working, resting
Weaving wondering watching
Encasing, consuming fire
Sun solidarity
Sun spiders solidarity
       World webs
       World watch
       Soft strong silky sun
       Woven carefully
Sun fed spiders
          spinning power
            spinning soft power strong
weaving sticky silk sun
           into world webs
             webbed wisdom
               woven wisdom...

Carefully linked world watch
Sun fed threads
Sure strong power
Surrounding with silk sun.
Why wouldn't spiders eat the sun?

Contents

Part II: Constructing Feminist Socio-economic Ethics as Transformative Theology

Conclusion

Acknowledgements

Webbed Wisdom . . .

How grateful I am to all those who sew the clothes we wear and to those who work together in coalitions to bring fair wages and working conditions for them! Thank you to all those whose justice weaving drew me into collaborative research and campaigns. I note, in particular, The Homeworkers' Association, The Coalition for Fair Wages and Working Conditions, The Labour Behind the Label Coalition, UNITE, The Ecumenical Coalition for Economic Justice and its Women and Economic Justice Working Group, The Maquila Solidarity Network, The School Sisters of Notre Dame, Ten Days for Global Justice, The Toronto School of Theology and The Lonergan Institute.

With warm appreciation I thank those who critiqued numerous drafts, helped me integrate various aspects and trust God's power in the midst of the challenges of social engagement and research. These include Mary Ellen Sheehan IHM, Theresa O'Donovan, Sheila Kappler, Vicki Obedkoff, Michel Côté OP and Judy Engel OP. I am not forgetting all who read and responded to manuscripts along the way. You come from a wide range of backgrounds of activism and academia and I am deeply encouraged by your enthusiasm. The suggestions you made have found their way into the very fabric of this text.

Carroll Klein of Wilfrid Laurier Press has been an astute editor—always ready to collaborate for the best possible product and to do it in such a magnanimous, friendly way. It is so clear that Carroll loves her work and values mine. I am grateful.

To all who have critiqued, informed and supported, Thank You.
You trust and dare enough
to liberate with passion!

You risk your job
to speak and live the simple truth!

You welcome all
at the coalition table!

You eat with us
and help us to eat the sun!

Preface

Mrs. Cheung sews clothes at home for a Braemar contractor. Her average wage is $4 per hour. The legal minimum wage is $6.35. *She sews sleeves in a jacket that sells for more than $120 at Braemar.* She often works over seventy hours per week to meet the contractor's deadline demanded by Braemar.

Mrs. Cheung is owed over $22,000 in back wages, vacation pay and termination pay! Bravely, Mrs. Cheung filed a complaint with the Ministry of Labour to stop the violation of her basic employment rights.[1]

Dylex controls Braemar, Fairweather/Fashion Rack, Club Monaco, Harry Rosen, L.A. Express, Thriftys, Tip Top Tailors/Canadian Clothiers, BiWay and Drug World. Manufacturing and retailing men and women's clothing through fourteen chains operating 710 family clothing stores, Dylex tells customers, "We share your concern about the treatment of workers. That is why we try to provide some of the best working conditions and benefits to our employees in the industry today."[2]

The contradictions linking the accounts of the homeworker, Mrs. Cheung, and the retailer, Dylex, who sells what she sews are a source of my theological-ethical reflection. At stake in this interfacing of their positions is the meaning of current socio-economic relations. The underlying values these relations reveal are themselves essential to contemporary theological inquiry. Convinced that divine-human rela-

Notes to Preface are on pp. xxxii-xxxiv.

tions are simultaneously relations of social organization, meaning, values and decision making, I engage in women's concerns for economic justice to unmask structural causes of poverty as a theological-ethical issue.[3]

The process raises tough ethical issues since it involves examining the economic context in which the working poor grow poorer and co-exist with those who command increasing wealth and power. Complexities abound within an overall blatant discrepancy of winners and losers, haves and have-nots.

Why do many women earn so little when they work so hard? I explore this question in relation to Toronto women garment workers whose workplaces have shifted from factories to their homes. As a result of this growing trend, these women, known as homeworkers, are poorer and isolated. Many professionals, researchers and independent business personnel of both sexes prefer to work out of their homes. People need to have the choice of working at home or in factories where fair wages and working conditions prevail *in both*. Homeworking is not new in the garment industry. The new factors are the structure of the garment industry, its global nature and the explosion of homeworking as a low-wage strategy in garment production, in many other kinds of manufacturing and in services.

The "International Ladies' Garment Workers' Union 1993 Homeworkers' Study" found women's hourly wages as homeworkers were drastically reduced from their earlier factory incomes:

> On average, women made $4 less as a homeworker. Mrs. Chan made $8 per hour in a factory two years ago. Today she makes $3.50 per hour as a homeworker. Mrs. Young made $12 per hour in a factory one year ago. Now she makes $5.50 per hour at home.[4]

Not content to focus on description of their wages and working conditions, or the symptoms of their exploitation, I ask further questions: How is it that society allows such blatant abuse? Who benefits? At what cost? To whom? Who is responsible? How can we bring about transformation of the very system?

Homeworking provides an entry to explore how wages and working conditions are determined in the socio-economic and political domains beyond local decision making. I explore the actual, socially organized relation between the everyday experience of homeworkers and the social relations established by jobbers, manufacturers, retailers and consumers within the entire web of production. In other words, I examine structural causes of poverty of homeworkers and of unemployed garment factory workers and I proceed to unmask ethical implications of the current economic system for corporations, banks and faith communities.

Facing the structural causes of the poverty of homeworkers and of unemployed garment factory workers reaches down to the very nature of how formal economics functions today. Questions abound and this entire analysis sets the context for me to raise them, without claiming to deal with them comprehensively. What is the meaning and what are the implications of claims that economics is neutral and value free? What is regarded as value? How are basic human needs registered and obliterated in the market? How are effects of decision making and policy setting weighed and incorporated in economics? What do sourcing, production and trade relations have to do with a just practice of economics? Who are the essential players in policy setting by both corporations and governments? How are economic practices connected with real social and environmental costs? What are the long-term possibilities, responsibilities and essential ingredients of doing economics justly? Economics is not formally concerned with the causes of poverty, with the effects of the system on those excluded from sharing its benefits or with the well-being of those unable to engage in the system through consuming, borrowing or investing in significant ways. All of these issues concern the orientation of the economic system. They also point with urgency to the requirement that socio-economic ethics be incorporated as an *essential* part of doing economics.

Facing the structural causes of the poverty of homeworkers and of unemployed garment factory workers is an ethical issue that calls into scrutiny the protocol and practice of the large transnational corporations. Current global and domestic disparities warrant this investigation. They also make visible the pressing need for openly transparent, democratically shaped corporate ethical codes and independent monitoring of practice; of legislation to protect all those involved in any aspect of sourcing, production and trade related to each corporation; and of assessment of relevant environmental and social impacts.

The starting place for the formation of corporate ethics is with those most affected by corporate decision making, those suffering the effects of the system as a whole and of particular industries within it. The test of the authenticity of corporate protocol and practice is in the same group. If a corporation's brand name or label is on a product, the company is responsible. Being ethical on a corporate level goes far beyond the sincerity and generous donations of individual executive officers and owners, or even of companies. In fact, limiting focus to these features may be used to prevent dealing with extremely significant causes of poverty.

Corporate executives who are intent on *doing* justice have nothing to fear either from legislation or from this study. While still respecting the human worth of those who oppress, I am now interested in dialogue with those who really do care and are willing to translate their sleepless nights into fodder for devising structural solutions in a terribly broken world. We can celebrate what is in fact just and we can certainly discuss and change what is unfair. Perhaps past business practice covered over what is now being brought to light. The most-desired scenario would be that corporate executives, government officials, bankers, community groups and unions would collaborate effectively, with funding from more secure establishments, to finance groups whose budgetary restrictions would make negotiations prohibitive.[5]

Facing structural causes of the poverty of homeworkers and of unemployed garment factory workers is an ethical issue that spotlights governments. What kind of society and world do we choose? How can we shape our governments most effectively and ethically in order to provide for the well-being of all, especially the poorest and weakest? Although the question is far more extensive than this book, ethical issues of governing loom large as we consider questions of voluntary compliance, independent monitoring of implementation of codes and penalties for infringements. According to what principles and with whose participation are priorities set and budgetary allocations decided, regarding, for example, dependent care and environmental protection? How is the viability of an industry assessed? How can our governments be effective means to create a society that in practice protects the life and health of all people and the earth? These issues are a necessary part of my investigation and conclusions.

Even though my perspective is from the vantage point of homeworkers and of unemployed garment factory workers and those in solidarity with them, I do socio-economic ethics and theology with concern for scripture-inspired justice for all, including men and women who currently hold prestige, power and property. What does this mean in view of the economic and political issues I raise?

Serious Implications for Faith Communities

There is no expectation that readers share either my position of faith or my eco-feminist, liberationist theology. Facing the structural causes of the poverty of homeworkers and of unemployed garment factory workers has serious implications, however, for those who choose to belong to faith communities. Injustices challenge their values, their commitment to work for justice and even their ways of doing theological reflection. Theology involves examination of the conscious and unconscious interests, mystifications, values and meaning promoted in our culture in order to maintain existing exploitation.[6] Left unexamined, operative meanings and values could oppose the goals we claim to espouse. Much of this is also true for people who espouse no organized religion, and they may find these reflections significant as well. My point here is that, if groups claim to be Christian *of any denomination*, their theology needs to be informed and responsive to global crises. Indeed, response to current realities is a constitutive aspect of all faith that claims gospel foundations.

Through close ecumenical collaboration in interchurch justice coalitions over eleven years, I have discovered the complexities of referring to particular documents and policies. At the same time, I have been inspired by the gospel grounding we share. Many aspects of what I present have already been taken up by churches and other faith communities. This study and its conclusions may serve as a reflector to nuance and affirm analysis, to strengthen present resolve for solidarity, to deepen the spirituality required to understand the shifts in consciousness and to shape courageous, creative ways to implement what has been gleaned. Spirituality and ethics are intrinsically related throughout this book.[7]

Faith has social consequences and social realities have consequences for people who desire to live with faith and integrity. The latter is often lost. Certainly response to socio-economic injustice, domestically and globally, in concrete policies and practices, is the central issue on which the integrity of churches stands or falls. By standing with homeworkers, I expose the urgency of assuming responsibility for the social, economic and ethical systems which we as consumers and as sisters and brothers in the human community create and/or allow. Taking these responsibilities seriously means that doing theology becomes an engagement in personal and social transformation.

Ethics, whether claiming religious foundations or not, must be described in relational terms, beginning with those who are most adversely affected by policies and practices, focusing on both environmental and social costs and effects. Ethical criteria are rooted inherently in the profound, non-negotiable value of the human community within a healthy ecosphere. Given the interdependence of every aspect of our very beings with all of nature, with each other individually and in the world community, this is not too big a horizon. All ethical principles must be connected to the actual world.

These relational foundations need to be held in place when ethics is described in theological terms, by faith perspectives and underpinnings. Theological ethics goes further to reflect on conscious and unconscious religious attitudes and values that move us to hold particular beliefs and practices, to perpetuate injustice or to stand against injustice and create just relations. Such theological ethical reflection benefits, for example, from honesty in facing the operative images of divinity of various partners in any dialogue or conflict. When these are left unnamed and unconscious, unwarranted restrictions may destroy the ability to understand the issues, to see alternatives and to achieve transformation.

Since Christian theology mediates faith with contemporary cultural reality, I focus on traditional Judeo-Christian concerns of justice making, values, meaning and responsible decision making as they relate to the concrete situations of women homeworkers in the garment industry, to garment sourcing, production, retailing and consumption, to political responsibility and to faith communities' integrity. Deeply religious values such as wisdom, genuineness, courage, truthfulness, solidarity and love in their concrete expressions become crucial for transformative theory and practice.

In religious language, this study is a theological endeavour, from beginning to end. Exposing socio-economic injustice and establishing socio-economic justice are in themselves key theological and biblical issues. To know this and celebrate it offers occasion to transform justice doing into religious events. Doing justice theoretically and practically is an extremely grounded way of setting conditions for the possibility of knowing God. The path is well recognized in Judeo-Christian tradition.[8]

Theology is both an intellectual ministry to the faith community and a dimension of the community's ministry to society in particular situations.[9] This means that communities need to examine their beliefs and to question how unjust structures are held in place by unexamined attitudes and ways of relating. Doing theology involves both assessing the effectiveness of the practice of justice and shaping responses in ways commensurate with the problems at hand. Doing theology needs to involve individuals and to link communities in discerning what is healthy and helpful as well as what is destructive in specific cultures and faith traditions. It also challenges people to discover and live meanings and values deep enough to unmask injustice courageously and to call forth possibilities for transformation of social organization and relations.[10]

My Entry into the Problem

I am linked to the clothing chain as a consumer, citizen and sister in the struggle. My experience of God moves me to do justice, especially with and for those oppressed in present societal structures. As a white feminist, formally educated theologian and socio-economic ethicist, I approach this study in a gender-conscious, class-conscious, "race"-conscious way. As a member of an international Catholic women's religious community, the School Sisters of Notre Dame, I am committed to spirituality that values and celebrates all of creation, to research and action that counteracts structural causes of poverty globally, to solidarity particularly with/for women and youth and to a simple lifestyle so that we and all others may live life fully. Representing my community, I have been an administrative committee member of the Ecumenical Coalition for Economic Justice since 1986 and chairperson of its Women and Economic Justice committee. I represented the latter on the Coalition for Fair Wages and Working Conditions for Homeworkers.

My roots also inform my own entry into the problem. They tell a story that is part of a pattern of women's work in the history of Ontario. As a daughter of two factory garment workers who turned first to homeworking and then to start a small business, I find that statistics of long hours, low pay, family involvement and no benefits leap off the page to spark my memory. My mother, Florence Loughran, was a domestic worker, a factory garment worker and then homeworker-mother of nine children, of whom I am the third. Since her journey mirrors a trend in the industry, it is an appropriate introduction to the story of homeworking in Ontario.[11]

Daughter of a tailor and a seamstress, my mother, then Florence Missere, moved from Mildmay, Ontario, to Kitchener at the age of thirteen in 1930 to become a live-in domestic worker, caring for two children and assisting with the cooking and cleaning. She sent all her income of $13.50 a month to her mother, widowed with six children.[12] Several years later, Mom worked at Forsythe's shirt factory where she met my father, John Paleczny, a shirt cutter. In eleven hours of work each day, she sewed about eighty dozen backs of shirts onto the yokes at 4.75 cents a dozen. My father also worked at MacGregor Shirt factory in Hamilton and Balfour Shirt on Spadina Street in Toronto until he and my mother started cutting and sewing at home for stores such as Stanley and Bosworth, Eaton's and Tip Top Tailors. My mother always sewed collars, often until 2:30 a.m. My father cut and sewed in the basement, designing his own patterns. Both were very skilled. In fact, my mother's expertise and speed stands as a stark reminder to me of the socially constructed division of labour in which garment employers assign women's work as unskilled in contrast to men's skilled labour. By 1947, they developed a small custom-shirt business with five machines in the "dining room" and continued to supplement this endeavour by sewing for others as homeworkers.

We moved to Waterloo, Ontario, in 1953 and I learned only years later that my father had said, as we set out, that he had a wonderful wife, five healthy children and five dollars, and what more could he want! On that same trip, because I had commented about a shabby home along the way, they stressed that I should never look down on anyone who was poor. Getting no salary, having no time off either before or after childbirth, my mother laughs and says at least she had older children to care for the little ones. During all these years, my father usually held a part-time job in construction, sales or ladies' dress wear to supplement their low income. By the mid-fifties, they also rented space in Kitchener, Ontario, to make custom shirts and collars for Cluett-Peabody. Later they created pocket hankies to use scraps and to increase income. A cloth hanky was sewn at the top of a card used for advertising. Success led to sewing them for the dry cleaners as a giveaway to put in each suit. They employed homeworkers to sew shirts, the pocket hankies and some graduation gowns. My parents also bartered or did exchange purchasing with Richardson Shoes, Schneider's Meats and Zehrs grocery stores. Quilting bees in our living room were other income savers and important social events.

I remember my parents mainly at the sewing machines and cutting table, night and day. I never had to wonder where they were or what they were doing! It is not surprising to me that hanging laundry outside was an enjoyable break for my mother. My father helped with a fair amount of child care and grocery shopping. The division of labour was not too important for us because all worked at home and at whatever outside jobs our ages allowed. We contributed our earnings as bills needed to be paid.

After my father's sudden death in 1962 of a heart attack, my mother and older brother Raymond carried on the business for another five years. By then it had expanded to Niagara Falls, New York, especially to produce pocket hankies: eight million the year my father died.[13] It was the American business rather than work in Canada that provided the main source of my mother's income as a widow.

My questions arose early and remain. Why were they so poor when they worked so hard? They did not even drink or smoke. Was anyone profiting inappropriately from their work? My mother did not recall ever hearing any discussion of unionization. I marvel at my mother's buoyant spirit, energy, flexibility, generosity, joy and interest in world geography. She said simply that faith, love for each other and friends carried them through difficult times, and that a good dance now and then cures many problems! What I saw and heard at home, in fact all of the above, informs my analysis and inspires me with creativity to find solutions to socio-economic exploitation in the midst of very changed global relations.

Perspective and Purpose

A Designer label like Alfred Sung, through the corporate owner, ETAC Sales Ltd., uses homeworkers who are paid less than the minimum wage and are forced to work weekends if they want the work, while trying to look after their children. Homeworkers are paid as little as $4 for a jacket that sells for $375. Who gets the remaining $371?[14]

As I make visible the situation of homeworkers in the garment industry in Toronto, I have taken the side of homeworkers in pushing for fairness in corporate practice. It is of utmost importance to me that I relate the homeworkers' own accounts of their stories faithfully and adequately.[15] They have been largely invisible in the clothing industry. The presence and spoken experiences of these Toronto women raise a wide range of questions about the production of clothing, our capitalistic system and the relations of ruling that predominate. Engagement in socio-economic analysis exposes the mechanisms of the interlocking powers that control the garment industry. I analyze causes of women's poverty and investigate the relations of ruling in the web of production from a global perspective as they impact on these homeworkers. As one among many, this perspective of some women's work claims power by clarifying connections.[16]

Committed to foster *effective socio-economic change*, I repeat Leonardo Boff's question: "Everything must come to a point in praxis (love). But here the problem arises: which praxis *really* helps, and does not merely *seem* to do so?"[17] That is the challenge! Collaboration with many groups to form a broadly based social Coalition for Fair Wages and Working Conditions for Homeworkers (Homework Coalition), reflection on the coalition's campaign and priorities and related studies help me to deal with questions of what is needed for both short- and long-term change.

Exploring the social roots of the failure of justice for homeworkers, I investigate what patterns of institutional relations must be confronted and transformed in order to achieve right relations.[18] After examining interests, biases and myths that keep patterns of injustice in place, I suggest a preferred framework and constitutive elements for a transformed society, not as final solutions but as contributions for dialogue.[19] Of course I realize that the tasks of reorienting economics and theology, and of fleshing out implications within expanded blueprints for societal organization, extend well beyond this book. The work neither begins nor ends with the contribution of any one person. Nor does it happen in only one place. Revised views will be strengthened by the diversity of regional differences.

Time Frame

The time frame of this book is from late 1991 until early 1995, which covers the entire duration of the Coalition for Fair Wages and Working Conditions for Homeworkers. Note that the International Ladies' Garment Workers' Union, to which I refer throughout this book, amalgamated with the Amalgamated Clothing and Textile Workers' Union to form the Union of Needletrade and Industrial Textile Employees (UNITE) in 1995, just after the main time frame of this study. A new coalition, The Labour Behind the Label Coalition, was formed in 1997.

Method

This is not a book on capitalism in itself. Nor is it a critique of works of resource people like Nancy Folbre, Bernard Lonergan or Hazel Henderson. Nor is this a survey of all literature on any topic in the book. The material is selected from the perspective of solidarity with homeworkers according to what is helpful to sort out and to present truth as fairly as possible, as I construct my work. I do not hold opposing positions as normative, giving them priority of place because I would then be left needing to defend and persuade those who control the production of knowledge.

Also, unless readers know the literature being surveyed, they may become overly burdened by what is not familiar. The complexities and objectives of the themes, including the integration of significant aspects from a variety of disciplines, led me to present a manuscript in order to enter a dialogue of discussions and manuscripts. I offer it for dialogue and I welcome others' experience, research and contribution!

Relationships with the Homeworkers' Association (HWA), the Coalition for Fair Wages and Working Conditions for Homeworkers (Homework Coalition), the Ecumenical Coalition for Economic Justice (ECEJ) and its Women and Economic Justice Committee link me with concrete communities already sharing a vision of justice that brings bread and culture, work, meaning and celebration together. These communities offer economic analysis.

Engaged in praxis, I experience the venture as a journey moving forward in a horizontal spiraling motion in which I reweave themes introduced earlier to create an ever-expanding horizon. By praxis, I mean "the total complex of action, including all the reflection embedded in that action."[20] An image of my method is that of spiders spinning webs from different directions, linking strands and being strengthened in sunshine! Weaving a basis for creative collaboration, I keep homeworkers central in the context of the socio-economic system. The horizon is local and global, intercultural and interior, as I set the grounds, engage in explanatory analysis, steadily broaden the horizon and ask the next relevant question. Through this process, I am able to discover further implications and some avenues for transformation. The reader is invited to take up this study as a journey in action-reflection-integration. This often means holding unfinished aspects gently as other concerns emerge.

Grounding in praxis informs the entire study. "Part I: Identifying Relations of Ruling and of Solidarity" is both descriptive and explanatory. In chapters 1 to 3, I gather local and global facts as well as some of the historical context for the various webs of women's work and chains of production. These strands are linked in the analysis of the relations of ruling and, in chapter 4, in the relations of solidarity evident in the Coalition for Fair Wages and Working Conditions for Homeworkers. Being involved in this coalition was energizing, informative, enriching, hard work, time-consuming and fun! It was through this coalition that I met many homeworkers, gathered the data for chapter 1 and the motivation to research chapters 2 and 3. Chapter 4 is a story of the coalition itself from my perspective as a community partner.

"Part II: Constructing Feminist Socio-economic Ethics as Transformative Theology" is analytic and constructive. In chapter 5, I examine and question the horizon in which both exploitation of women, particularly black women and women of colour, and retailers' amassing of private wealth at women's expense have been generally accepted.[21] By foregrounding critiques gleaned from gender, "race" and wealth/empire analyses, I draw attention to biases that distort the capacity to establish just relations.[22] Difference and specificity are essential aspects of my interpretation. I relate the significance of family/kin/friendships as a lifelong immersion in fostering both autonomy and mutuality to analysis of the public/private split. By so doing, I make explicit the values that enable me to reveal and account for omissions and biases in social consciousness, in policy setting and in issues of agency and interdependence.

Chapter 6 continues the analysis of subjugation according to difference, as exploitation is perpetuated in the artificial public/private split. Since this split also legitimizes a capitalist mode of social organization, I consider foundational elements of an alternative societal framework. How such a framework is applied will vary as extensively as the communities who use it.

Remaining grounded in actual situations, in this case of women homeworkers, reveals the urgency of total transformation of every aspect of how we shape our social organization. When judged from the perspective of those who suffer the effects of systemic exclusion and exploitation, current theory and practice in all critical aspects of social organization, values and meaning are profoundly inadequate. Finding praxis, that is, both theory and action, inherently flawed, I take up the challenge of shaping some directions to counteract this blatant injustice. This does not involve imposing theological reflection on homeworkers or on those in solidarity with them. My concern is to indicate directions for the transformation of society that allows exploitation to continue. It will be achieved in praxis, not by books alone. The transformation is also my own as a feminist theologian who is challenged in praxis.

Conclusions from praxis about the socio-economic system and about method in ethics and theology are significant, for homeworkers eventually, for consumers, for corporate elites and certainly for people of faith. In chapter 7, I extend boundaries to pursue implications for constructing socio-economic ethics particularly in terms of meaning, values, collaboration and decision making. By identifying and analyzing socio-economic reality as a source of theology, I construct elements of social ethics.

Since I focus on societal values, vision and elements of socio-economic ethics, I need to comment on use of the theoretical. In the current context of unjust globalization of the economy and of power, pseudo-theory often masquerades as the only option and a dis-economy claims power as the best path to choose.[23] Theorizing involves understanding, judgement and decision making about experience. Even as I affirm the importance of theory in this research, I also find it imperative to ask who decides what is significant, essential and relevant and to inquire about criteria for decision making. In addition to local action, the extent of economic exploitation against women requires concerted social analysis in a search for the kind of truth making and justice doing commensurate with the problems at hand. It is, of course, *only in practice* that values and transformation are known and lived.

I explore five webs: first, the web of exploitative relations of international garment production; second, the web of collaborative coalition building; third, the web of myths and biases that keep many women and men invisible and poor; fourth, the web of relations or dialectics in our interdependent biosphere in which personal subjectivity and economics are parts, not the whole; and, finally, the web of just relations set forth by open dialogue, decision making and action to reorient theology and economics. And why the image of the web?

Importance of Images and Symbols

The image of the spider spinning her web came to me as I walked along the lakeshore integrating what I have learned in coalition work, through theological research, and in socio-economic ethics. The image took me by surprise with the question, "How does a spider eat the sun?" Only later did I learn that in Native American, African, Greek and Celtic mythology, the spider brings light and wisdom to knowledge and experience! I ponder how the spider transforms energy from the sun through the eco-chain into strong, silk strands and I wonder about our resources, our weaving, our ability to heal our predominantly unjust culture. Throughout the book, I include some indications of my personal experience, images and dreams that surfaced steadily in relation to the content itself. The personal is political.

Many have grasped the power and significance of the use of symbols and of the importance of such a holistic approach. These are crucial if we are serious about releasing corporate control over our collective unconscious and about cross-cultural solutions to global exploitation of women's work. Use of images and symbols include and carry us beyond the rational, strengthen us in solidarity and move us affectively to the extent that our ability to imagine alternatives can shift out of customary paralysis. Work in solidarity involves gathering information and making informed judgements and decisions, thinking clearly, feeling deeply, speaking courageously, acting effectively and celebrating these joyfully. Each of these is radical, prophetic and transformative! This book is *not just* about gaining regulatory changes in labour laws by a provincial government! I draw on different approaches and disciplines both in analyzing and in finding ways to transform and to contribute to the creation of a just culture. Hence the need to incorporate both long-term and short-term objectives, vision, facts, goals and alternatives. Cultural problems and initiatives extend far beyond what any one text or campaign can solve. Given that reality, I contribute some direction for current policy discussions and a range of solutions for the underlying causes.

Assumptions and Horizons

A note about ideology. As an important part of the data of consciousness, ideology shapes several aspects of method and conditions how we interpret issues. I accept Beverly Wildung Harrison's definition of ideology "as commitment to a world view or cultural gestalt or as a politically mystifying conception of society."[24] Accordingly, philosophical assumptions about moral reason and attitudes about gender, "race" and empire/wealth must correlate with our socio-historical, theological assumptions and accountabilities. Since an ideological position shapes the data we accept as factual when describing a moral issue and explaining causes and connections, openness about our ideological commitments helps us to see and hear accurately and to be fair to those with whom we disagree. Thus I attempt to achieve methodological coherence by consistently integrating awareness gleaned in the theological, anthropological, ethical and socio-economic perspectives I assume. I am particularly alert for hidden normative assumptions in praxis. Pre-thematic, pre-discursive convictions and loyalties affect approaches to concrete problem solving. I ask then what principles actually guide our imagination and decisions. The challenge lies before us as a society to choose values to direct our future.[25] In unmasking ideological blinders in relation to our socio-economic theory, I am aware of Beverly Wildung Harrison's observation that

> we tend to ignore precisely that contemporary theory that is most critical of our existing political economy.... The ideological constraints we have knowingly or unwittingly interjected into perceptions of our social world, its problems, and prospects, through the social theory we employ or fail to attend to, turn out to be dramatic indeed.[26]

My work is one of exposition, of explanation of causes and of relation of systems. It also points toward transformative alternatives. This, in fact, partly describes the horizon of the research.

The comprehensive horizon is, in fact, the interdependent biosphere in which principles of subjectivity, differentiation and communion sustain each part and the whole at all times and places.[27] Grasping the significance of having such a comprehensive horizon is utterly central to recognition of the importance of these three central principles as keys for transformation. Lived interdependence, responsible personal and group agency and respect for difference are crucial in word and in deed if we are to heal our broken world and unjust relations within it. Ignoring the depth and breadth of this horizon severely limits even our imagination when we consider both structural causes of exploitation and solutions to counteract them. Appreciating the beauty of people and all nature, the wonder of creation, we can know when we have *enough*. Such is the foundation for knowing what is abundant, superfluous or luxurious. Such is the foundation for facing obscene discrepancies of wealth and destitution in our global village. When those who have enough to live adequately grasp for more wealth and power, they are trying to quench a fire with grease.

Because of the controlling grip and ramifications of the sins of racism, sexism and wealthism, I hold that authentic socio-economic relations require transformation of our vision, our value systems, our definitions of what is meaningful and our expression of societal and cosmological relations. Such transformation calls for profound conversions which, for example, prompt some to surrender competition, power and privilege in social as well as personal relations and others to shift from deceptive inferiority and powerlessness to courage, collaboration, dialogue and decision for action. Reflecting may free us to discover that the solutions are right within us, especially in our collective wisdom.

Stories

So let the stories unfold! Stories of women's homework in the garment industry, stories of the emergence of current macroeconomic context, stories of the impact of all these on me and stories of analysis and construction. The story of my involvement, research and analysis may resonate with others' experiences and grappling. I present significant social and ethical perspectives mainly for social justice activists, academics, people in politics and business personnel committed to societal transformation to foster discussion of difficult issues and to strengthen our collaborative efforts to do justice. Political scientists, bureaucrats and other professionals can add their own expertise from within public systems to implement these. It is in interiority, dialogue and action in solidarity that peoples heal our broken world.

Notes

1 Coalition for Fair Wages and Working Conditions for Homeworkers, "Are These Clothes Clean or Made by EXPLOITED HOMEWORKERS?" (single-page handout, November 1993). The homeworker's name is changed for her protection.

2 Ibid., n.p. See also Rick Haliechuk, "Kay, Posluns Begin Court Battle for Control of Huge Dylex Empire," *The Toronto Star*, 26 May 1994, B1, 16. For the history of Dylex Ltd. acquisitions, sales of companies (or interests) and mergers, refer to "Dylex Ltd.," in *Moody's International Manual* (New York: Moody's Investors Service, December 1995), 1243-44. Dylex, for example, owns Nu-Mode Dress Co. and Tobias Kotzin Co. and has substantial interest in The John Forsythe Co. and in The Shoe Shoppe Ltd.

3 Beverly Wildung Harrison, *Making the Connections: Essays in Feminist Social Ethics*, ed. Carol Robb (Boston: Beacon Press, 1985), 56.

4 Jan Borowy and Fanny Yuen, *International Ladies' Garment Worker's Union 1993 Homeworkers' Study: An Investigation into Wages and Working Conditions of Chinese-Speaking Homeworkers in Metropolitan Toronto* (Toronto: ILGWU, 1994), 3. The names are fictitious; the facts are not. Unless specified otherwise, references to the ILGWU mean the ILGWU Ontario District.

5 The Labour Behind the Label Coalition, formed in 1997, has gathered corporate and individual endorsements of a petition to the federal government requesting that a task force be established to gather information and assess the entire garment industry in Canada, as well as labour practices related to offshore sourcing of garments imported.

6 As Robert Doran emphasizes, "The art of social diagnosis is thus an intrinsic and constitutive element of theological method." Robert Doran, *Theology and the Dialectics of History* (Toronto: University of Toronto Press, 1990), 424, including reference to Juan Luis Segundo, "Preface" to Alfred Hennelly, *Theologies in Conflict: The Challenge of Juan Luis Segundo* (Maryknoll, NY: Orbis Books, 1979), xiii-xviii.

7 I develop aspects of spirituality more fully in another work in progress.

8 In another book in progress, I focus on some scriptural foundations and on spirituality in an age of corporate rule.

9 Doran, *Theology and the Dialectics of History*, 356.

10 Doran explains some implications of this position: "A methodical theology grounded in the concrete but explanatory self-appropriation of the theologizing subject would provide foundations for a reorientation of the human sciences, an integral component in the movement from the present situation to an alternative state of affairs.... By a methodical theology, I mean one whose practitioners 'submit their cognitive, affective, moral, religious, and Christian consciousness to explanatory differentiation in the mode of interiority, thereby recovering with structural precision the path and the immanent intelligibility of their own search for direction in the movement of life, and ... ground their theology in the discoveries they have made and verified along that path'" (ibid., 356, quoting Robert Doran, *Psychic Conversion and Theological Foundations: Toward a Reorientation of the Human Sciences* [Chico, CA: Scholars Press for the American Academy of Religion, 1981], 5).

11 Interview with Florence Loughran, 28 December 1991, Waterloo, Ontario, regarding her work from 1930 to 1962. She died in 1998.

12 Environmental and workplace pollution claimed the lives of both my grandfathers when they were young parents, through typhoid fever and stone workers' consumption. My paternal grandmother was an immigrant garment factory worker who spoke six languages.

13 At that time, apparently no patent was permitted because of the change of advertisement with each order. The Smithsonian Institution in Washington, DC, exhibits one made for the J.F. Kennedy campaign.

14 Coalition for Fair Wages and Working Conditions for Homeworkers, Background Information Sheet, "Clean Clothes Test," Toronto, 1992. See also Virginia Galt, "$375 Jacket Stitched for $4, Conference Told: Protection for Homeworkers Promised as Union Seeks End to 'Exploitation,'" *The Globe and Mail*, 2 October 1992, A1, A8. Lida Baday, who employs homeworkers, was awarded the designer of the year award in 1992.

15 The International Ladies' Garment Workers' Union (ILGWU) conducted surveys in 1991 with thirty Toronto women, and in late 1993 with forty-five. Interviews in Chinese were at least two hours each.

16 Dorothy Smith, *The Everyday World as Problematic: A Feminist Sociology* (Boston: Northeastern University Press, 1987), 121, referring to Sandra Harding, *The Science Question in Feminism* (Ithaca, NY: Cornell University Press, 1986), 194.

17 Leonardo Boff, "The Contribution of Liberation Theology to a New Paradigm," in Hans Küng and David Tracy, eds., *Paradigm Change in Theology: A Symposium for the Future* (New York: Crossroad, 1989), 412.

18 Wildung Harrison, *Making the Connections*, 81.

19 I refer to myth as a "commonly held belief that is untrue, or without foundation," rather than as "an ancient traditional story, especially one offering an explanation of some fact or phenomenon" (*Chambers English Dictionary*, 7th ed. [Cambridge: Chambers and Cambridge University Press, 1988], s.v. "myth").

20 Wildung Harrison, *Making the Connections*, 248.

21 Linda Carty explains that "the term 'women of Colour' acknowledges our ethnic differences.... It indicates a common context, grounded in shared systemic discrimination" (Linda Carty, ed., *And Still We Rise: Feminist Political Mobilizing in Contemporary Canada* [Toronto: Women's Press, 1993], 8, n. 1). See also Michael Vannoy Adams, *The Multicultural Imagination: "Race," Color, and the Unconscious* (New York: Routledge, 1996).

22 Cornel West signals the importance of being alert to silences regarding fundamental categories of gender, "race" and empire. The modern world, he suggests, is primarily about big business and the empires constructed by transnational corporations. Refer to bell hooks and Cornel West, *Breaking Bread: Insurgent Black Intellectual Life* (Toronto: Between the Lines, 1991), 35, 45. Wealthism and wealth analysis are my terms.

23 I follow Jane Flax's assumption that "the most important characteristic of theory is that it is a *systematic, analytic* approach to everyday experience. This everybody does unconsciously. To theorize, then, is to bring this unconscious process to a conscious level so it can be developed and refined.... Theory makes those choices conscious and enables us to use them more efficiently" (Jane Flax, "Women Do Theory," in *Women and Values: Readings in Recent Feminist Philosophy*, ed. Marilyn Pearsall [Belmont, CA: Wadsworth Publishing, 1986], 3).

24 Wildung Harrison, *Making the Connections*, 56.

25 June O'Connor, "On Doing Religious Ethics," in *Women's Consciousness, Women's Conscience*, ed. Barbara Hilkert Andolsen, Christine Gudorf and Mary Pellauer (San Francisco: Harper & Row, 1985), 271.

26 Wildung Harrison, *Making the Connections*, 57.

27 Brian Swimme, *The Order of the Universe*, no. 4 in a twelve-part video series: *Canticle to the Cosmos* (San Francisco, CA: New Story Project/Tides Foundation, 1990).

Part I

Identifying Relations of Ruling and of Solidarity

1

Present Conditions of Garment Homeworking in Toronto: The Microeconomics of a Low-Wage Strategy

Spiders eating spinning
weaving waiting

While women's need to earn an income has increased within double- and single-parent families, public workplace jobs in Ontario in all sectors have decreased. Even service jobs are suffering loss because of the North American Free Trade Agreement.[1] Homeworking is being promoted as a key, corporate, flexible, lowest-wage-possible strategy. It is portrayed as a solution to multiple problems.

Three distinctively different categories of homeworkers exist: home-based employees; self-employed, home-based business owners; and unprotected labourers. Keeping them clear in our minds is extremely important if we are to sort out advantages and problems of each fairly. The home-based employee on a company payroll works in

Notes to chapter 1 are on pp. 12-16.

both the home and the office. A self-employed, home-based business owner actually is an independent contractor, consultant or proprietor. A third, more ambiguous, category is the unprotected labourer, one without a formal contract or benefits, expected to perform with limited control and autonomy, and without adequate compensation.[2] According to the Employment Standards Act, homeworkers are defined as employees and "Homework means doing any work in the manufacture, preparation, improvement, repair, alteration, assembly, or completion of any article or thing or any part thereof in premises occupied primarily as living accommodation."[3] Homeworkers depend on contractors to supply work and to pay them fair wages. Homeworkers do not sell the goods or services directly to the market, do not keep the profits and do not control work schedules. It is with workers in the third category, the unprotected employees, that my research is concerned. Meeting and hearing the stories of homeworkers, unemployed garment factory workers and those currently employed in factories but fearing loss of their jobs have jolted my understanding of garment production. It made me wonder about the source of some of the societal myths that support extensive malpractice.

A Story of Exploitation

Ming-Zhen sews a woman's jacket in one hour and earns $4.15. She receives no compensation for training time when new styles arrive. She must teach herself the new design. The jacket is sold at Eaton's for $275 to $375.[4] Poi-Yee makes $5 for sewing a dress in one hour, but she has had to buy the sewing machine and cover all operating costs such as hydro and heat. The dress is sold for $150 to $200 at a high-end retail boutique. A contractor often delivers work on Friday to Yen, who must complete it by Monday morning. She must care for her children while she sews at least ten hours a day all weekend. She is paid $3 to $3.25 for the forty minutes required to complete skirts which sell for $150 to $200 at the Hudson's Bay Company. In contrast to the inside factory worker with regular wages, benefits and overtime pay for overtime hours, homeworkers received none of these in the early 1990s. Their story and the story of legislative changes gained through a public campaign follows in chapter 4.

The examples cited involved Alfred Sung products which were sold at Eaton's, Hudson's Bay Company, Holt Renfrew and other popular retailers in Toronto. The Sung label was owned by ETAC Sales Ltd., which made over $2 million profits in 1991. Their revenues increased by 36 per cent from 1991 to 1993. Like many large manufacturers, they sent much of their actual production work out to subcontractors who then sent it to homeworkers.[5]

The current situation of homework in the garment industry in Canada has been described as "a story of exploitation."[6] This history is long in Canada, since homework has been used by garment manufacturers to depress wages and block unionization. But this technique has expanded. After the recession of 1981-82, there was rapid growth in subcontracting in the women's garment industry. This meant that employers used the cheap, unprotected labour of women in their homes to compete with producers in Thailand, the Philippines, Honduras, El Salvador and more recently with those in Poland, Hungary and the Czech and Slovak Republics.[7] Employers have adopted a lowest-possible-wage strategy domestically to deal with cheap labour competition. But, as Alexandra Dagg, Manager, Ontario District of the International Ladies' Garment Workers' Union (ILGWU), says, "Low wages are no way to make us competitive. We can never, never compete with $1 a day wages in Guatemala."[8] Furthermore, the union has no desire to compete with other women around the globe for subsistence or less than subsistence wages, for their well-being and our own. It should also be emphasized that although imported clothes cost the retailer less because women and children work for extremely low wages in poor working conditions, the cheaper prices are not passed on to the consumer.[9] Consumers pay the same price as for Canadian-made and imported garments. Retailers maximize profits.[10]

In 1993, the ILGWU, Ontario District, estimated that there were 2,000 to 4,000 homeworkers in Metropolitan Toronto, calculating from the number of plant closures and the increase in contracting shops since 1986.[11] There was no strong evidence of a cutback in the industry itself to correspond with the plant closures.[12] Nor was there any outstanding technological innovation to account for the difference in labour productivity. Restructuring in the garment industry means increased use of homeworkers who must work at a greater speed.

Although Ontario homeworkers were covered by Employment Standards protections related to minimum wages and permits, in-depth two-hour interviews with thirty Chinese-speaking Metropolitan Toronto homeworkers showed that Ontario's Employment Standards legislation was routinely violated.[13] Even a year later, in 1992, only seventy-seven employers obtained the permits required by the Ontario government to hire homeworkers.[14] Wages were well below minimum requirements

($5.90 at that time). The average hourly rate of those interviewed was $4.64, and some did not even dream of earning minimum wage since they now received as little as $1 or $2.50 an hour. Only one was given her allotted vacation pay. Only one said her employer had the permit required to employ homeworkers. New machines cost $2,500 to $3,800. All workers provided their own, usually second-hand, machines paid through savings. They also covered the cost of work space and of energy use despite their low wages. Nearly all simply had to accept the pay scale unilaterally determined by the employer. Several told they were informed of the amount to be given only after the completion of work. Twelve reported difficulty getting employers to pay them for completed work. Twenty-one were employed by subcontractors, nine for factories and all but four worked for more than one employer. Many children and/or spouses helped with the work, folding and cutting threads, ironing and picking up or delivering finished products without extra remuneration.[15]

The Ontario Employment Standards Act of 1990 explicitly excluded homeworkers from the protections of maximum hours of work, overtime pay and public holidays.[16] The same regulation stipulated, "No written authorization of an employee shall entitle an employer to set off against, deduct from, retain, claim or accept wages for faulty workmanship." Homeworkers who were interviewed worked longer hours than were permitted under the Industrial Standards Act which regulates factory work in the garment industry. Work fluctuated according to the demands of the employer, averaging forty-six hours a week, ranging from a low of sixteen hours a week to a high of eighty-two hours a week, with no overtime pay. Busy seasons brought an average of seventy hours weekly. The range was from thirty-six to one hundred hours per week without overtime rates. Such sporadic employment meant that workers lacked secure income and the ability to manage their time and other commitments. The survey revealed that, contrary to promotional arguments encouraging homework, homeworkers did not have the independence to determine their own pace of work.

There was no job security and no real protection from employers who defaulted or went bankrupt. The responsibility for formal complaint lay with the individual workers who lacked time, resources and bargaining power to pursue enforcement. Several had contacted the provincial government for help in asserting their rights, to no avail. It should also be noted that employers made no contributions to the Canada Pension Plan or to Unemployment Insurance premiums on homeworkers' behalf.

Exposing Some Myths

Little has changed *in practice* within the time frame of this book. Myths serve to maintain the system. A myth that is being promoted by some in the media is that homeworking provides an opportunity for women to combine child and/or elder care while earning a bit of extra money on the side. It is true that women are combining child care with waged work. The reality for homeworkers in the Toronto garment industry, however, is very different from the popular illusion of women working according to their convenience in conditions under their control and to their liking. The vast majority of homeworkers in the Toronto garment industry are female with young children. Lack of affordable, quality child care is the most important reason they do homework.[17] Twenty-eight of the thirty women interviewed in 1991 had economically dependent children, one was a grandmother caring for the children and one was disabled (deaf) with no children. The almost unanimous reason for leaving a garment factory job was pregnancy; they continue to work inside the home only because of lack of child care. Twenty-seven of the twenty-eight women with children said they would happily take a factory job if they had a choice.[18] "So now they are doing the same work, sometimes for the same employer, for less money in their homes. The double day of factory work and family care becomes the endless day of homework and family care."[19] Most women extended their work day deep into the night and found that it took a toll on their relationships with their husbands and their children. Furthermore, they preferred working at home only to not working for income at all.[20]

As the Homework Coalition's brief to the Ontario Government, *Fair Wages and Working Conditions for Homeworkers*, explained, "the majority of women doing homework lack English language skills and are often characterized as 'immigrant women.' The category 'immigrant,' however, often connotes a culture and a relationship to the labour market as much as the length of time in Canada."[21] The 1991 survey of the thirty Chinese-speaking homeworkers, for example, found that twenty-four were Canadian citizens, five required more time before applying and one could not afford the time to attend citizenship classes. Sixteen have been in Canada more than ten years. Although literate in Chinese, all but one could not converse in English. Their formal education varied, with half having completed grade eight or less, thirteen with grade twelve or less, one with nurses' training from a college and one with a law school degree.

Health and safety problems arise in garment home production, first of all, from allergy to the dust from fabrics, as twenty-seven of the thirty attested in 1991. This is not surprising in view of the predominant and relatively recent creation of synthetic materials such as polyesters, acrylics, acetates and rayon made from chemical fibres throughout the petrochemicals and textile industry.[22] Second, most emphasized that they experienced much stress resulting from employers' pressure to finish work quickly and from family members who expected full attention and service from a wife/mother still at home, and who resented the steady noise and use of already limited space for this work.[23] Over half suffered from back problems. Other frequent problems included sore shoulders, myopia and migraine headaches. Third, homeworkers were explicitly excluded from the Ontario Workers' Compensation Act, and the Ontario Occupational Health and Safety Act bypassed homeworkers by defining "factory" to exclude their workplace: home.[24] Two thirds of garment homeworkers sewed in the basement, most in cramped space and often with poor ventilation.

The *International Ladies' Garment Workers' Union 1993 Homeworkers' Study* investigated wages and working conditions of forty-five Chinese-speaking homeworkers in Metropolitan Toronto.[25] Results confirmed the 1991 findings. In 1993, for example, 80 per cent were Canadian citizens, 16 per cent were sole income earners for their family, 96 per cent had economically dependent children. Sixty-two per cent reported hourly wages below the provincial minimum ($6.70 as of 1 January 1994). Wages ranged from $3 to a high of $8 an hour received by only one worker. Fifty-six per cent reported that piece rates have been reduced by contractors. Twenty-nine per cent have earned the same pay only by working more hours. None received benefits or overtime pay even though 13 per cent averaged working fifty to fifty-nine hours a week, but sixty-one to seventy-five hours per week in their busiest time. Six per cent worked more than one hundred hours per week in the busy season. High numbers reported stress and strain: an overwhelming 95 per cent suffered back strain and 86 per cent added eye strain. Ninety-one per cent identified stress about finishing work, 89 per cent stress related to the pressures of working at home and 78 per cent stress concerning fulfilling their role as worker and mother. Only one reported receiving help with child care from a relative. Ninety-one per cent said they became homeworkers because they needed child care. All took care of their children while working.

Other major questions arise, such as the status of the employee, the precarious nature of this work, the responsibility of related employers and whether wages and working conditions for these homeworkers may be included in a union's collective bargaining process, a question which will be taken up in the third chapter.[26] At this point, I reflect further on myths about homeworking.

Societal myths promote a glorified view of family and homeworking that set a context in which many women become locked into low-wage work at home. Most basically,

> the view that [the] sexual division of labour takes place within a nuclear family unit of a conjugal pair with dependent children dominates both the social-science literature and common-sense views of the world. These perspectives together not only ignore the statistical realities of household composition and women's economic activity but also obscure the most important aspects of the relations between production and reproduction, as these constrain women.[27]

The differential bases on which women and men become integrated into production are tied to women's unpaid work in the home and the relative absence from such work for the majority of men. With strong pressure to engage in paid work, women must simultaneously do "all the time-consuming, laborious, caring work of reproduction and their paid work as well. Therefore, the sexually segregated labour market both reflects and causes the limited options open to women. This is particularly evident in the case of homeworking."[28]

The fact is that homework isolates workers and, with the present lack of protective measures, allows for some of the most exploited labour in Toronto, held in place by powerful myths such as the claim that women's place is in the home where they are to create a safe haven from a hostile world.[29] Even questioning health and safety factors is incomprehensible to some; it shatters this myth of the home as a separate, hallowed sanctuary.

Another double-edged myth suggests that women who are at home full-time do not work but that they exercise significant power and influence in the world. Suggesting that a homeworker is largely her own boss ignores the demands experienced by women in their being wives, mothers and homemakers with the inherent difficulties of setting limits to their availability, especially if they are on site. In addition, the design, performance of work tasks and quantity accepted are rarely part of a worker's choice.[30] Meeting production targets is assumed to be a responsibility of the homeworker, even if it involves overtime and night or weekend labour. It shatters the illusion that homeworkers have a great deal of autonomy. The reality is that the supplier controls the amount and timing of work with consequent insecurity for workers regarding reliable income. Realities of homeworking explode the myths.[31]

Women's bargaining positions for waged work both in and outside the home are affected by their weak positions of being almost solely responsible for housework and child care.[32] Regarding child care only as private life and a matter of individual responsibility to be solved in individual homes keeps it out of the public eye and concern.

> The lack of affordable child care was the single most important reason given for women working in the home.
>
> Rather than originating in the free choice of women, homeworking is rooted in the economic vulnerability of women in industrial societies which do not provide the social services to support their full and equal participation in the workforce. The most fundamental of these services is affordable, quality child care. The other major factor confining workers to homework was the lack of English language skills and other job skills which would allow them to find work which paid enough so they may purchase child care services for their children.
>
> Child care services and training are government responsibilities. In failing to provide these services, governments contribute directly to the creation of a pool of labour which is highly vulnerable economically and available for exploitation by unscrupulous employers.[33]

Some employers use the circumstance of women's child-raising responsibilities to promote homework, thereby reducing overhead and keeping wages low. As part of the underground economy, these homeworkers are almost an invisible part of the labour force.

Protection of Homeworkers in Multiple Sectors

Homework and domestic labour are key lowest-possible-wage strategies for the 1990s, now characterized as years of "the lean workplace."[34] Homework has been expanded to become a multiple-sector trend. It includes assembling auto and electrical parts, taking phone orders, filling envelopes, preparing food and doing telework. Of central concern is that work is being reorganized to jeopardize worker rights.

Electronic homeworking or telework, for example, is at a crucial stage. The Public Service Alliance of Canada is a large, well-established union working to protect members and new workers' rights to have the status of employees with union membership as homeworkers. Collaboration with the ILGWU has increased their understanding of homeworking pitfalls to be avoided.[35]

Intercede, an organization of domestic workers, is a challenging and encouraging example that isolated workers can be brought together to protect workers. The Coalition for Fair Wages and Working Conditions for Homeworkers has supported the parallel development of a Homeworkers' Association. Societal attitudes about immigrant women, about work done at home (and domestic work done in public places like hotel laundries, the fast-food industry and department store work) and about child care directly impact both groups.[36] I will pick up the focus on racism, on attitudes about work-at-home and on care of children again.

Conclusion

Homeworking in Ontario has exploded as a low-wage strategy. Predominantly non-unionized workers make up a large, hidden, unprotected workforce for which employers evade responsibility. Home-based workers who complete one or more steps of a production process and are paid on a piecework basis are a growing class of the working poor. This trend reflects a global pattern. With the unrelenting increase of unemployment in large parts of the world, homework of many kinds has become an important means of earning some income.[37] This situation leads me to a number of observations.

First, homework has been regarded traditionally as outside the formal market and Canadian definition of economy. Taking the perspective of homeworkers challenges our very understanding and judgements about the nature of the economy we choose.

Second, a critical area to be developed is that of relevant legislative change, including the benefits of broader-based bargaining, contract negotiations and central registries.[38] The data presented here provide the grounds for such lobbying.[39] A trend to explain homeworking by focusing exclusively on characteristics of the homeworkers and domestic workers themselves would involve at least an underlying assumption that they want and cause the situation for their own benefit. "It becomes the statistical equivalent of blaming-the-victim. Such data collection describes homework out of the context of the chain of production."[40]

A third implication of the homeworking trend is that workers now in middle-level-income jobs may well find themselves sliding down to poverty-line (or lower) incomes. The already large class of the working poor in Canada is on the verge of exploding. Governments, corporations and workers together have the power to choose a better basis than competition for our economy. The challenge of how we use technology, for well-being or for exploitation, remains.[41]

Finally, gathering this data establishes the importance of the criteria of bringing forward the truth of how a system or process affects people. It also calls for the elimination of inauthentic myths in making judgements and decisions as well as in deriving categories for ethical reflection. Authentic immersion in the issue with homeworkers themselves and with people committed to them makes genuine objectivity possible.[42] The data as presented so far, however, are incomplete. In order to make satisfactory judgements, further information is needed. Analysis, judgements and decision making about homeworking require understanding of both the international web and the pyramidal structure of the chain of production of which it is a part. These are the basis of the next chapter.

Notes

1 Ontario Women's Directorate, *The North American Free Trade Agreement: Implications for Women* (Toronto: Ontario Women's Directorate, 1993), 2-5. Refer also to National Action Committee on the Status of Women, "NAC Brief to the Sub-Committee on International Trade," presented by Judy Rebick, Monique Simard and Hari Dimitrakopoulou-Ashton, 10 February 1993: 4; Marjorie Griffin Cohen, "Americanizing Services: U.S. Firms Eager to Run Our Institutions—for a Profit," in *The Facts of Free Trade: Canada, Don't Trade It Away*, ed. Canadian Union of Public Employees (Ottawa, 1988), 63-67; GATT-Fly (Ecumenical Coalition for Economic Justice), "Free Trade in Services: The Multinationals' Agenda," *Pro-Canada Dossier* 21 (18 September 1989): 13-15; Linda McQuaig, *The Quick and the Dead: Brian Mulroney, Big Business and the Seduction of Canada* (Toronto: Viking Press, 1991), 52, 53, 55; Isabella Bakker, "Pay Equity and Economic Restructuring: The Polarization of Policy?" and Judy Fudge and Patricia McDermott, "Pay Equity in a Declining Economy: The Challenge Ahead," both in *Just Wages: A Feminist Assessment of Pay Equity*, ed. Judy Fudge and Patricia McDermott (Toronto: University of Toronto Press, 1991), 254-80 and 281-88.

2 See Kathleen Christensen, "Home-Based Clerical Work: No Simple Truth, No Single Reality," in *Homework: Historical and Contemporary Perspectives on Paid Labour at Home*, ed. Eileen Boris and Cynthia Daniels (Chicago: University of Illinois Press, 1989), 183.

3 Employment Standards Act, in *Revised Statutes of Ontario 1990*, chapter E14, article 1. This definition is retained in the 1994 publication in which amendments relevant to homeworkers are made.

4 Homework Coalition, "Backgrounder 2" (single sheet handout): "Canada's Most Prestigious Label—Alfred Sung—Made by Homeworkers for Less than Minimum Wage" (October 1992). For their protection, the homeworkers' names are fictitious; their stories are true. A workshop participant told me that it is impossible to sew a jacket in an hour. If it also took Ming-Zhen longer, she actually received less than $4.15 per hour.
5 Homework Coalition, "Backgrounder 2." See chapter 3 for more of the ETAC and Alfred Sung story.
6 Laura Johnson and Robert Johnson, *The Seam Allowance: Industrial Home Sewing in Canada* (Toronto: Women's Press, 1982), 59.
7 Michel Chossudovsky, *The Globalisation of Poverty: Impacts of IMF and World Bank Reforms* (Atlantic Highlands, NJ: Zed Books, 1997), 81.
8 Michele Landsberg, "Home Can Be a Sweatshop in Low-Paying Garment Trade," *The Toronto Star*, 9 November 1991, K1.
9 Homework Coalition, "Backgrounder 1."
10 Derek Ferguson, "Mexican-Made Bras Don't Hold Up, Garment Workers Tell Trade Hearing," *The Toronto Star*, 10 April 1993, A6. Mexican workers earned about fifty cents an hour for sewing Vogue bras which retailed for $19.50 here in contrast to a Canadian-made $20.50 bra for which Cambridge factory workers received $8 an hour before the company closed in January 1992 to move to Mexico. "Clearly, Canadian workers are not benefiting, Mexican workers are not benefiting and consumers are not seeing any savings." ILGWU concern is for consumers and workers.
11 Intercede and International Ladies' Garment Workers' Union, Ontario District Council, *Meeting the Needs of Vulnerable Workers: Proposals for Improved Employment Legislation and Access to Collective Bargaining for Domestic Workers and Industrial Workers* (Toronto, 1993), 16.
12 Ecumenical Coalition for Economic Justice (ECEJ), "Not by Choice—The Growing Phenomena of Homework," *Economic Justice Report* 3, 1 (January 1992): 2.
13 Barbara Cameron and research assistant Teresa Mak interviewed thirty Chinese-Canadian women in 1991 as the basis for the report, *Chinese-Speaking Homeworkers in Toronto: Summary of Results of a Survey Conducted by the International Ladies' Garment Workers' Union* (Toronto: ILGWU, 1991). Follow-up interviews with another thirty confirmed results of the original study.
14 Ontario Ministry of Labour, "The Employment Standards Act and the Protection of Homeworkers, Consultation Paper," Toronto, August 1993, 2.
15 Cameron and Mak, *Chinese-Speaking Homeworkers in Toronto*, 3-6.
16 Employment Standards Act, in *Revised Statutes of Ontario 1990*, "General" Regulation 325, articles 4f, 6e, 7d and 14.2 regarding deductions. See chapter 4 for regulatory changes made by the Ontario cabinet in 1994 in response to lobbying by the Coalition for Fair Wages and Working Conditions for Homeworkers.
17 Margaret Oldfield, "The Electronic Cottage—Boon or Bane for Mothers?" in *Proceedings of the Conference on Women, Work and Computerization, Helsinki, Finland, 30 June-2 July, 1991* (Helsinki: Ministry of Social Affairs and Health, 1991). For information about Oldfield's telephone survey and

interviews of clerical workers, refer to Audrey Ho and Laura Johnson, *Home Sweat Home: Regulation of Industrial Homework in Ontario* (Toronto: Social Planning Council of Metropolitan Toronto, 1982).

18 Cameron and Mak, *Chinese-Speaking Homeworkers in Toronto*, 5. Fifteen also supported dependents other than children, usually living outside of Canada. Twenty-seven had at least one other income earner in the family, most often a husband.

19 Homework Coalition, "Backgrounder 1."

20 Christensen found similar results among American women. See Christensen, "Home-Based Clerical Work," 193.

21 Coalition for Fair Wages and Working Conditions for Homeworkers, *Fair Wages and Working Conditions for Homeworkers: A Revised Brief to the Government of Ontario* (Toronto, February 1993), 4.

22 See Frederick Clairmonte and John Cavanagh, *The World in Their Web* (London: Zed Press, 1981), 100-64, particularly 102 and 111 on petrochemicals and chemical fibres. The high cost of pollution control in producing these fibres has led fraudulent producers to countries such as Mexico where regulations are either not in place or are not enforced.

23 "Life of Homeworkers—Suffering in Silence," *World Journal Daily News* (Toronto Chinese newspaper), 16 November 1991. See also Johnson and Johnson (*The Seam Allowance*, 59-83) about working conditions, wages and stress.

24 Oldfield, "The Electronic Cottage," 43.

25 Borowy and Yuen, *International Ladies' Garment Workers' Union 1993 Homeworkers' Study*, 2-5, released 14 February 1994 at a press conference by the Homework Coalition at Queen's Park, Toronto.

26 Related employers would be those at the top of the clothing production pyramid. They control the prices and timelines set for manufacturers and subcontractors below them.

27 Sheila Allen and Carol Wolowitz, *Homeworking: Myths and Realities* (London: Macmillan Education, 1987), 274.

28 Ibid., 275.

29 Meg Luxton, Harriet Rosenberg and Sedef Arat-Koç, *Through the Kitchen Window: The Politics of Home and Family* (Toronto: Garamond Press, 1990), 31-32, 34, 57, 86, 136.

30 Allen and Wolowitz, *Homeworking: Myths and Realities*, 112-25. The ILGWU *Revised Brief* (1993) showed that 82 per cent of homeworkers said they must adapt their schedule to employer demands, compared with 66 per cent in 1991.

31 "Popular images of working at home—flexible working hours, more time to spend with one's children, a reduction of work pressure, a less stressful day—have nothing to do with the experience of homeworking.... It intensifies the pressures of both waged work and unpaid domestic labour" (ibid., 134).

32 Kathleen Christensen, ed., *Women and Home-Based Work: The Unspoken Contract* (New York: Henry Holt, 1988), 7-68.

33 Coalition for Fair Wages and Working Conditions for Homeworkers, *Fair Wages and Working Conditions for Homeworkers: A Revised Brief*, 5.

34 A conference sponsored by the Centre for Research on Work and Society, McMaster University Labour Studies Program, Canadian Auto Workers, Canadian Union of Public Employees, International Ladies' Garment Workers' Union and the Ontario Public Service Employees Union focused on "The Lean Workplace: Labour's Response to the New Managerial Agenda," 30 September-3 October 1993, Port Elgin, ON.

35 Refer to Jan Borowy and Theresa Johnson, "Unions Confront Work Reorganization and the Rise of Precarious Employment: Home-Based Work in the Garment Industry and the Federal Public Service," in *Re-shaping Work: Union Response to Technological Change*, ed. Christopher Schenk and John Anderson (Don Mills, ON: Technology Adjustment Research Programme, Ontario Federation of Labour, 1995), 29-47. See also Jane Stinson, "Home Truths: Federal Government Teleworkers," *Our Times* 12, 1 (1993): 39, and Human Resources Development Council (HRDC), "Telework Pilot Program in the Public Service" (Ottawa 1992). For a Public Service Alliance of Canada (PSAC) response to telework in the federal public service, see *Go Home ... And Stay There?* (Ottawa: PSAC, 1993), and Virginia Galt, "Oh, Give Me a Home...," *The Globe and Mail*, 19 September 1992, A6. In February 1995, federal Finance Minister Paul Martin announced that 45,000 public service jobs would be cut.

36 Makeda Silvera, "Immigrant Domestic Workers: Whose Dirty Laundry?" *Fireweed* 9 (1981): 53-58; Makeda Silvera, *Silenced: Talks with Working Class West Indian Women about Their Lives and Struggles as Domestic Workers in Canada* (Toronto: Sister Vision Press, 1989); Luxton, Rosenberg and Arat-Koç, *Through the Kitchen Window*; and research by Intercede: "Domestics Sweep the World," *Wages for Housework Campaign Bulletin* 5 (Spring 1981): 1; *Know Your Rights: A Guide for Domestic Workers in Ontario* (Toronto, October 1987); and Sedef Arat-Koç and Fely Villasin, *Report and Recommendations on the Foreign Domestic Movement Program* (Toronto: Intercede). See also Veronica Strong-Boag, "Discovering the Home: The Last 150 Years of Domestic Work in Canada," in *Women's Paid and Unpaid Work: Historical and Contemporary Perspectives*, ed. Paula Bourne (Toronto: New Hogtown Press, 1985), 35-60. Note especially Wenona Giles and Sedef Arat-Koç, eds., *Maid in the Market: Women's Paid Domestic Labour* (Halifax: Fernwood Publishing, 1994).

37 International Labour Organization, *Conditions of Work Digest: Homework* (International Labour Office, Geneva) 8, 2 (1989): 1-9.

38 Intercede and ILGWU, *Meeting the Needs of Vulnerable Workers*, 14.

39 Ibid., 16.

40 Ibid., 17.

41 A poem popular among Japanese workers, "Japanese Women Organize," expresses the problem:

> Computer drives out women.
> As if it were a friend of women
> It drives out women.
> Computer is an enemy of women.
> Though it glitters and looks clean
> It makes a woman cry.

Oh computer,
Women have long been waiting for you,
Hoping that you help us to have more free time
And yet you, computer,
You have helped us to shed more tears.

Committee for the Protection of Women in the Computer World, Japanese Women's Council (Tokyo, 1983), in Swasti Mitter, *Common Fate, Common Bond: Women in the Global Economy* (London: Pluto Press, 1986), 147.

42 Refer to Bernard Lonergan, *Method in Theology* (Minneapolis: Seabury Press, 1972), 292, on objectivity.

2

The Macroeconomics of Garment Homeworking: Homework in Its Historical Context

---

World webs
World watch

My parents' story as garment workers reflects work trends in the province and stands as a reminder that homeworking is not new. Garment homeworking is particularly significant in the story of women's work. Why are these women so poor when they work so hard? The story is intimately bound up with changes in the political, social and economic trends. These in turn demonstrate the nature of capitalism as multifaceted and fluctuating. In this chapter, therefore, I briefly indicate some historical factors and then focus on contemporary aspects of the relationship between homeworking and the political economy, provincially in Ontario and federally. Understanding and interpretation of both the context and defining influences on women's garment production are essential groundwork for my later focus on choices for solidarity and on ethical decision making.

Notes to chapter 2 are on pp. 46-55.

Homeworking in the Context of Expanding Capitalism

The current reality of precarious work for women, of corporate influence over government decision making and of capitalist expansion have deep historical roots. Since the root system is connected and since features of emerging patterns become evident at different times, naming phases can vary widely. I refer to women's evolving role in garment production in four interrelated phases as Pre-Industrial Women's Work, Domestic Service and Sweatshops, Classification: Unskilled and Contracted Out. I set these in the context of some of the economic interests that shaped Canadian politics and name these overlapping phases as toiler production and mercantile capitalism, industrial capitalism, monopoly capitalism, Canadian state monopoly capitalism, globalization and financial capitalism.[1] Intrinsic to all phases of capitalistic development are the competitive process of capital accumulation; acquiring surplus value through present and past labour, one's own and others; unpredictability for investment and outlook; and continuously self-generated change that arises from the inner workings of the system itself.[2] Capitalistic process presumes relations of dominance within roles, of distribution, of ownership and of control between unequal exchange partners so that one individual or corporate partner steadily gains while the other loses.[3] From the outset, I accept Nancy Folbre's assessment that "The nature and consequences of capital vary enormously among nations and are significantly affected by racial/ethnic divisions and class differences within countries."[4] Folbre proposes that the basic features conveyed by the term capitalism are best understood as

> combinations of structures of constraints based on nation, race, and class in which private property and market exchange play an important role. This implies that "capitalism" in the abstract really has no distinct "laws of motion," but allows [for] more historical analysis of social structures.[5]

She explains that a structure of constraint can be defined "as a set of assets, rules, norms and preferences that fosters group identity and creates common group interests."[6] I return to this in chapter 6.

Phase 1: Pre-Industrial Women's Work
Women's Work

Lower-class "toiler" production in the early nineteenth century was characterized by all-day and all-family work with mother-child production teams in the home; a wide range of skills and expertise learned by doing the work of child care, sewing and home/farm management; and low market productivity and commodity exchange. This home-based production, however, differs from current garment homework, as the Homework Coalition explains:

> A popular illusion about homeworking sees it as a variant of pre-industrial household production in which workers produced goods or services in the household for sale on the market using supplies which they provided under conditions which they controlled. In this period, the household was to some extent an autonomous unit of production.
>
> Homework does not date historically from this period. Rather, its historical origins lie in the period of the industrial revolution when much of production was transferred from the household to the factory. It is associated with the *subordination* of the household to a market dominated by employers.[7]

Home production is a class-specific term. Class differences were markedly distinct. Closely related to the way of life for the upper class, for example, was the maintenance of a servant class, not slave but expected to be subservient, with sex-based hierarchy even among servants. Bringing in women to be wives for early European settlers, and other immigrants to be servants, helped to root cultural imperialism and the sexual/racial division of labour. Adrienne Shadd points to large-scale black immigration of this time: "Blacks were one of the largest groups to enter the country during the 19th century when 40-60,000 fugitive slaves and free people of colour sought refuge in Canada West (Ontario) between 1815-1860."[8] Many became part of the servant class. In its present, unprotected form, domestic service may be an adaptation of indentured slavery, or at least of a servant class.

The Context: Toiler Production and Mercantile Capitalism

One early corporate development directly impacts homeworkers in the garment industry today—namely, with the foundation of the Hudson's Bay Company in 1670, First Nations were caught in economic wars between the French and the English, becoming dependent on them and subjugated to business interests in what in the long run became a losing relationship.[9] Seeking profits, forming a fur-trade monopoly and securing fur-bearing regions through firm possession of the colony (secured militarily) shaped this forerunner to Canada's textile/garment industry, even if it meant dominating a "race" of people to do it. This assessment overrides both individual and short-term benefits. Many native women, for example, apparently promoted the fur trade in order to gain access to European goods such as kettles, needles, knives and cloth, and because of widespread intermarriage between Indian women and incoming traders.[10]

Although the colonial economy under France was mercantilist in character, rapid change under British rule beginning in 1763 and lasting until 1821 brought the decline of mercantilism. It was replaced by competitive capitalism or economic liberalism. In 1821, the two rival fur-trading monopolies, the Hudson's Bay Company and the North West Company, merged to offset the negative impact of competition from Britain's textile manufacturers.[11]

Competition and subjugation of people to secure profits and control are part of history as companies ensured their dominance over fur trade and textile manufacturing.

Phase 2: Domestic Service and Sweatshops
Women's Work

Although 41 per cent of all women doing paid work in Canada in 1891 were employed in domestic service, by 1921 only 11 per cent remained in domestic service. Domestics tended to be young girls, often immigrants. They faced critical problems such as isolation, long hours, low pay, close supervision, sexual harassment and intimidation.[12]

Between 1871 and 1911, from 38 to 46 per cent of all employees in the three main textile sectors in Canada were women over sixteen years of age and 10 to 21 per cent were younger. The 1880s were the peak employment times with 45 per cent consisting of women, and girls as young as nine and ten comprising 18 per cent of all textile employees.[13] Women and children filled lower-income work categories and received less when doing the same jobs as men.

Even in 1895, in spite of poor working conditions, sweatshop work was considered an advance for women from work as domestics:

"Of course the work is hard, and they have to keep on the hustle." He [an overseer in one of Toronto's best workshops] wished he could pay better wages but it was not possible with the low prices paid by the wholesalers. It was all the fault of the sweaters, said this "contractor," as they are constantly undercutting the prices in order to get the work, and the wholesalers are continually playing one lot against the other.... The girls are paid by the piecework system; and how they worked! The machines could scarce move fast enough, as with stooped shoulders, heads bent forward, the rapid movement of hands and feet, with furtive and momentary glances in the direction where employer and stranger stood talking, the work rushed along as though life depended on every stitch made by the whirring machines.... "How can they possibly live on such wages?" was asked. "Well I'll tell you how it is," he replied, "their brothers or fathers, I suppose, have to help keep them." All these women were of adult age.

In the other place ... the wages were very low and the work very hard. But *that could not be avoided so long as the trade was conducted as it is under the present system.*[14]

Although working full time, women's low wages forced their economic dependency on men.

In this phase, female economic and social roles were subordinated to male economic relations. Men created and dominated the world of production. What women did, economically and socially, was shaped by the defining male relations—that is, by their husbands, brothers or fathers. Whereas male economic relations determined their social relations, female social relations determined their economic relations. With industrialization, however, paid work became available. Women and children could compete for work and for wages.

In 1884, Ontario passed its first laws to protect women and adolescents in industrial establishments. No laws protected waged labour in homes. Generally employed on piecework rates based on the output of the fastest workers, most women earned less than a living wage. In contrast to the male cutters, women who worked machines were considered unskilled and their pay reflected this bias.[15] Protest against harsh working conditions and low pay, however, generally was expressed in the transiency of workers among factories and to other jobs such as waitressing or fruit picking. This made any collective organization difficult.

Homework seems to have declined between 1900 and 1920 due to the economic and social effects of World War I and to the shortage of male factory labour. In 1919, an Ontario government report revealed some of the strains and working conditions of garment homeworking:

The work suits women because they can carry on household work at the same time; several women are mothers of families who eke out their husbands' wages in this way; others are obliged to be at home to care for aged or sick relatives.... The living conditions of the family are apt to be upset by the pressure of the mother and the older children to work; the price of work for shop workers is cut through this illegitimate competition; the long and irregular hours kept by homeworkers are ruinous to the health; workers suffering from disease often work where they would not be permitted to do so in a shop.[16]

Nevertheless, homework increased somewhat in the 1920s as the world economy sagged and as many men were hired in the new synthetics industry.[17]

In 1928, there were at least 64,000 women employed in the garment and textile industries in Canada. In spite of sweatshop working conditions, factory work was increasingly sought by white women. Dionne Brand presents the situation of black women:

> Since their arrival in Ontario, first as slaves then as fugitives from slavery in the early 1800s, Black women had worked on farms, in domestic service and at home. Indications are that not until 1940 or so did any significant number of them work at industrial labour. Certainly up to World War II at least 80 per cent of Black women in Canadian cities worked in domestic service. Industrialism did not have the overwhelming impact on Black women wage earners that it did on white women.[18]

Working conditions in factories became marked by pressures for increased productivity. By 1930 major industries, including the textiles, used professional consultant teams to manage production in a "scientific" way.[19] Developed by an American, Frederick Taylor, and implemented in the U.S. as early as 1922-23, the method of analyzing and breaking down tasks to "unskilled," repetitive work, assigning specific methods and controls, regulating timing to demand maximum output and, in effect, tying workers to their machines became known as scientific management or rationalization. Production and distribution processes were linked more closely to supply and demand. A new hierarchy of foremen and technicians controlled knowledge and power, preventing workers as a group from organizing the process. Using time studies to determine the most efficient method for a task, and requiring a production quota based on this faster method as well as on the speed of the most capable producers, employers set rates for piecework done both in factories and in homes. Rationalization accelerated what had been a growing practice in Canada's textile and garment industry.

Made up of hundreds of shops with twenty-five to two hundred workers, the Toronto garment industry was the largest employer in Toronto in this period. This labour-intensive industry struggled with a low profit margin with much competition and high bankruptcy rates.[20] In the midst of the Great Depression, owners tried to manage the crisis of the postwar overproduction boom and lack of internal and external markets by laying off workers, cutting wages and decreasing the gross value of goods produced, all in order to stabilize the rate of profit for the industry.[21]

Until 1930, women garment workers had little union organization.[22] A two-and-a-half-month strike by five hundred women of the International Ladies' Garment Workers' Union (ILGWU) in 1931 in Toronto was history making as a women's effort. Unfortunately, it still left them with a limited choice of unemployment, part-time work, piecework, homework or "unskilled" jobs in the labour-intensive garment industry.[23]

Industrial demand for a cheap, sporadic reserve labour pool of homeworkers prevailed over women's preference for factory work where they earned more and focused on one job. Employers had organized "a series of hierarchies, each with a corresponding limited function, scale of wages, and bargaining power. The strongest of these divisions of labour ... continued to be the oldest, the sexual division between men and women."[24] Dependent on low-wage female labour, employers were likely to regard solidarity between male and female workers as a real threat. Often they used "divide and conquer" tactics to offset effectiveness of strikes. Labour organization required time not available to married women because of their double workload. Furthermore, for many male unionists, their gender identity was linked with the brotherhood. Women were excluded from this fraternal socializing. Male workers feared that employment of women would worsen their job possibilities by allowing employers to undercut wages.[25]

The controlling male ideology that a woman's proper place is in the home, a man's castle, provided social roots for exclusion. Women also experienced widespread social pressure to be relatively passive and to obey the male employers. In response to these efforts to prevent women from being hired as competitors of jobs and/or to protect them from supposed moral and spiritual breakdown, certain tasks in both factory and office were designated as women's work with lower wages. Such segregation meant that women still provided a source of cheap labour without posing a threat as direct job competition. Societal hostility, family responsibilities and job insecurity made women's situations so precarious that they were in a weak bargaining position.

For Catherine Macleod, even "legislation to fix a minimum wage for women, which was intended to increase their job security and discourage their exploitation, seems to have had the opposite effect, especially in the garment industry."[26] In 1933, for example, the law required that only 60 per cent of piecework employees [in factories] be paid enough for them to earn the minimum weekly wage for a full week's work, but enforcement "would require a staff of inspectors many times greater than we now possess and would inflict undue hardship on a number of small employers who are doing the best they can under conditions over which they have no control."[27] When unionization was successful in obtaining better pay and improved working conditions for both men and women, employers fired women workers in a significant number of cases.[28] In these situations, equal pay meant that men were assured preference in hiring. Many women were rehired as home-based garment workers with lower wages.

Unemployment rates had escalated throughout the Great Depression from 2.9 per cent in 1929 to 11.4 per cent in 1939, bringing utter destitution since there was neither unemployment insurance nor any health and welfare system. Strong public outcry led the Canadian government to take steps to alleviate the suffering. This stage, to a limited extent, held the beginnings of the social welfare stage of industrial capitalism. Pressure from national trade unions led the state to increase regulation of hours and of salary, and to protect programs such as marketing boards. In 1914, Ontario passed the first compulsory social insurance legislation in Canada, the Workmen's Compensation Act, followed closely by a Dominion scheme of pensions and rehabilitation after World War I. Manitoba legislated the first mother's allowance scheme in 1916 and Saskatchewan the first temporary welfare relief, also in 1916. Ontario began its welfare program in 1920.[29] Large numbers of unemployed in the 1930s obtained more state intervention through the Dominion Unemployment Relief. The Unemployment Insurance Act was set in 1940.[30]

Ontario passed laws in 1936 and 1937 requiring employers to obtain permits from factory inspectors who could inspect payroll records and workshops. However, both federal and provincial governments also used force to repress strikes, exposing the contradiction between the needs of Canada's working people and a state which favoured monopoly capitalism and furthered the interests of finance capital.[31] I now sweep back to focus on the beginnings and unfolding of this phase of "Domestic Service and Sweatshops," this time to highlight some aspects of the corporate story in industrial capitalism and in monopoly capitalism.

The Context: Industrial Capitalism

What of the corporate story is relevant here? I suggest some basics. Economic diversification brought an expansion of capitalism, of wealthism and of economism, as well as the emergence of a Canadian working class in the late eighteenth and early nineteenth centuries.[32]

In 1826, the British government had decided to expand a proletarian working class in Canada by ending its policy of free land grants to working-class immigrants whom they were simultaneously encouraging to migrate here. By 1850, therefore, an increasing shortage of cheap land and large numbers of Irish immigrants created significant groups of labourers in cities such as Quebec, Montreal, Kingston, Toronto and Hamilton—enough to force competition for low-wage jobs.

This phase of industrialization in Canada is sometimes referred to as economic liberalism. Capital and technology each form a structure that conditions the economic, political and cultural functions of the time.[33] Capital was predominantly locally based with numerous competitive family firms. Production was labour intensive, austere and built on class conflict with minimal state interference in the market or protection for workers. Licence for the few in power was proclaimed as "freedom."

What characterized use of capital and technology in this phase? First of all, localized capital meant that benevolent managers who paid the full social costs of production, that is, gave decent wages, had to market their goods at higher prices. They were at a disadvantage alongside exploitative managers who required long work hours for low pay in unsanitary and dangerous working conditions. Trade unions were repressed and women and children's underpaid labour were used to deflate men's wages. Second, use of labour-intensive technology meant that not enough goods were produced to create a consumer society.

British bestowal of "responsible government" to the colony and the twelve years of reciprocity or free trade with the U.S., 1854 to 1866, "eventually made Canada and the U.S. each other's largest trading partner and ... geared a large part of the Canadian economy to supplying the U.S. market with raw and semi-processed materials, much to Canada's long-term disadvantage."[34] The Canadian capitalist class increased control over the state, with the policy of forming closer economic relations with the U.S., to secure profits.

Closer trading ties raised the issue of independence. Remembering the aggressive, American manifest destiny policy, the War of 1812 and, in 1848, the loss of half of Mexico's territory to the U.S., government and corporate leaders collaborated to build railways and establish the Canadian state through Confederation in 1867. When, for example, the Hudson's Bay Company refused to co-operate with Canadian political vision for the West, it was purchased by E.W. Watkin, president of the

Grand Trunk Railway, and others interested in achieving Confederation and western expansion.[35] They later sold the Hudson's Bay Company and the entire Hudson's Bay watershed, Rupert's Land and the Northwest Territories to the government in 1869, ignoring the fact that this land was already settled by the region's native peoples.

It becomes apparent that early conservative emphasis on British connections arose not only from a desire to be linked with what were roots for many, but also as "protection against the powerful drift of continentalist forces that always threatened to draw Canada into the American orb."[36] Similarly, the National Policy was designed to protect the Canadian market from foreign competition and to substitute Canadian-made products for imports. In the textile industry, which made up about 30 per cent of Canada's imports, for example, tariff rates of up to 30 per cent were introduced.

The importance of these policies in terms of homeworkers is the development not only of a powerful business class but also of early business control of government. The state stimulated the formation of monopolies, adopting a policy of combining massive financial assistance with the encouragement and concentration of capital. In this phase, I note that the shift to industrial capitalism left the home unrecognized as a productive workplace. The family became less acknowledged as a unit of production.

Male and female labour was separated by task and location. Both industries and occupations were divided along gender, "race" and class lines. Women's unpaid labour for family consumption was not regarded as a contribution to capital formation. Theoretical division was created between publicly accepted economic activity and privately needed work for survival.[37]

Public control was increasingly taken by businessmen. Women's maintenance of the home and family made possible men's waged labour. These relations paved the way for later problems of work segregation, "creation of the housewife" and devaluation of women's work.[38] Women gained access to markets to sell home-produced goods and to do waged work only with the expansion of the industrial economy and of transportation systems.

Shift in Context: Monopoly Capitalism

Monopoly capitalism emerged early within the industrial context. With the necessary infrastructure set in place by laissez-faire practice, Canadian business took advantage of the international economic boom which took hold in the last third of the nineteenth century.[39]

Canada has always relied on imported or foreign capital. Steady expansion of such investment separated the ownership and activity of capital. Although capital investment was needed, the effects of the long-term drain of surplus capital became more evident as job production was stifled and community responsibility evaded. The context is a global one as transnational investment largely determines global exchange relations, specialization and the division of labour.

In Ontario, expansion of industrial and finance capital, improved technology, economies of scale in some industries and the growth of the world market all facilitated economic concentration. Production in the textile industry more than doubled.[40] Mergers occurred first of all in the financial sector, followed by those of leading oil refineries as early as 1880, of cotton companies in 1891 and of four major textile companies in 1904 to form Dominion Textiles which was then taken over by Royal Trust.[41] The desire to lessen vigorous competition and to maximize profit led owners to focus on large-scale production, control of pricing policies and patents, domination of the market, horizontal and vertical mergers and integration of the marketing and distribution network. While horizontal mergers happened between companies with similar products, vertical ones integrated buyer-seller relationships—for example, those of textile manufacturers and apparel retailers. They tested the effectiveness of cutting prices in one locality to beat local competition while recouping profits in another, maintaining façades of independent concerns and securing rebates and preferential agreements.

Capital was concentrated in monopolized national corporations, with controlled amounts of foreign "national investment." Improved technology meant that there were more goods for bargaining, laying the foundation for a consumer society and, therefore, increasing demand for both labour and productivity. Characterized as benevolent, at least in some years for some people, this stage is noted as bringing opportunity for many: "prosperity became the basic trend even though not all shared in it."[42] Certainly it was not shared by women generally, nor by blacks and people of colour generally.

The first legislative provision for homeworkers in Ontario in 1936 established a double permit system, one for the employer and one for the homeworker.[43] By the 1940s, however, many North American trade unionists thought that the exploitative conditions of long hours and low wages in the industrial homework of the garment industry had been ended. They believed that the steady diminishment of the homework system would lead to its complete disappearance.[44] But it did not disappear. It only became less visible.

In contrast to the American formal ban on the most common forms of homework, provincial regulations in Canada were instituted to protect homeworkers from unfair employment practices. A particular directive—that a permit, issued by the chief inspector, was required to employ a homeworker—was included in the Industrial Safety Act, 1964, and then within the Employment Standards Act, 1968. The latter amended the requirement of obtaining permits to employers only, not homeworkers.[45] The permit required every employer to keep a register of the name and address of every homeworker to whom the employer gives work and the wages paid for it. As noted earlier, it was also at this time that homeworkers were included in minimum-wage legislation.

Homeworkers have never been independent producers. Instead, they have been the poorest and most vulnerable employees at the bottom of the economic ladder. This points to the fact that women's needs forced them to accept even ill-paid work. Clearly the issue is complex and analysis of the total chain of production and profit making needs to be in the foreground of strategizing.

In the pre-capitalist, toiler society, then, the family formed a basic unit of production and reproduction of both goods and labour power. Women farmed, made garments, cleaned, nursed, took care of the children, husband and elderly relatives, all as part of the total family production. The modern family emerged under early laissez-faire capitalism with its labour split into two separate spheres with mainly men doing commodity production in industry and mainly women doing unwaged productive and reproductive work at home. These forms of women's work were not formally recognized as economic production. Adding waged work in the home in the form of domestic service or garment homework combines the most exploitative practices of the workplace and societal oppression of women. The labour is invisible and unprotected.

Phase 3: Classification: Unskilled
Women's Work

With the concentration of jobs, industry and people into cities came the ironic atomization and alienation of everyday life for individuals and for families. The private sphere of housewives was radically altered. The fact that most aspects of women's lives were integrated into capitalist commodity production means that "even the most personal parts of our social relationships have been reduced to commodities, to be bought and sold."[46] With new products, appliances and services, the structure of domestic labour changed. Commodification meant that more money was required to purchase what were becoming necessities even as the alternative means of achieving these tasks and skills were disappearing. Gradually most aspects of living were subjected to commodity forms. Simultaneously, "women's jobs in the labour market expanded as women searching for paid employment competed with each other for work in trade and in the private service sector where training periods and skill requirements were minimal."[47] I emphasize that early instruction gave many women the required skills, giving them the advantage of needing little formal training.

Context: Canadian State Monopoly Capitalism

From the perspective of corporate expansion, this phase is still monopoly capitalism, marked by consolidation of state involvement in corporate power. The state itself became a centralized corporate power. While governing in ways that assisted capital accumulation, the government intervened at least minimally to protect workers.

The structure for a transnational phase is also becoming visible. The elimination of many firms during the crisis of the 1930s set the stage for consolidation, for concentration of related production and services in large monopolistic corporations, for parallel growth of the state and for continual restructuring of the labour force.[48] Pressure from all sides for varying reasons led to expansion of public ownership and massive state intervention in social and economic affairs. By the end of World War II, Canada had consolidated state-monopoly capitalism.[49] The government was pressured by American government objectives toward Canada during the Cold War period which were

> to assure that Canada is closely tied to the United States through a series of military treaties, with the Canadian armed forces under the general direction of the U.S. military command system [and] to gain access to Canada's storehouse of strategic raw materials including energy resources.[50]

Groundwork for continental economic restructuring was being laid under American hegemony.

The ensuing technological explosion and political agreements revolutionized world trade and investment, control of international production, finance and commerce. They also altered the global corporate process. Advances from 1948 to the mid-1960s in containerized shipping, satellite engineering, instantaneous data processing and global air networks were paralleled by international corporate takeovers of control of banking decisions and of the advertising media. An expansionist view considered raw materials cheap and plentiful.

The 1960s witnessed a quantitatively new dimension in the scale of operations of the transnational corporation.[51] Mergers left a concentrated industry and productivity was central. The dominant Canadian textile companies, principally Celanese and Dominion Textile, for example, had significantly reordered industrial capacity in all but the knitting division.

International agreements regulating trade became increasingly imperative. After World War II, one of the many institutions which the "developed" capitalist economies (DCEs) set up to protect their interests was the General Agreement on Trade and Tariffs (GATT). At first only in textiles (early 1960s), the U.S., Europe and Japan controlled global trade generally to their advantage, often creating what they regarded as "orderly" or "voluntary" marketing agreements with "undeveloped" capitalist economies (UCEs) to "resolve" their conflicts. These conflicts find their greatest institutional expression in GATT's Multi-Fibre Arrangement (MFA). Starting in 1962 with regulation of cotton goods, the MFA broadened control in 1973 and 1974 to include all categories of textiles and clothing.[52] The MFA is a trade policy to facilitate transition to liberalization by protecting both importing and exporting countries from disruptive effects in both markets and production lines. I shall focus on the MFA again in terms of liberalization of the textile and garment industry and its relation to the free-trade agreements.

A reform that accorded status to collective bargaining in the late 1940s radically changed much of industrial society since principal wages would not be determined only by the market. Workers and unions gained new standing in the workplace and influence in state policy making. Their achievement shifted competitive capitalism to a somewhat more regulated capitalism.[53] Although workers gained some rights, governments did not regulate restructuring processes in favour of workers. In fact, they actively assisted those accumulating capital. Several accounts show the underlying trend.

In a study of the period from 1950 to 1971, Rianne Mahon observes, first, that woven fabric and low-cost clothing imports depressed prices and contributed to a lower-than-expected return rate of investments in new plants and acquisitions, and, second, that a simultaneous increase of labour bargaining power raised wages.

The clothing industry, though located in large urban centres like Montreal and Toronto, could avoid some of this pressure, since it *benefited* from the relatively open immigration policy of that period. Immigrants from lower-wage countries, such as Portugal and Greece, *especially the women immigrants employed in the clothing industry, could be paid at well under the minimum wage.*[54]

This description portrays the clothing industry as belonging to the investors and points to exploitation based on racism and sexism as an apparently acceptable practice among employers.

M. Webber and S. Tonkin present a detailed analysis of the technical changes and the rate of profit in the Canadian textile, knitting and clothing industries in a time frame that overlaps with the last cited, from 1952 to 1981. They drew some important conclusions. First, although profit increases have been similar to other manufacturing as a whole, the growth rate of output in the clothing industry fell from 4.8 per cent per annum between 1974 and 1979 to –6.2 per cent per annum between 1979 and 1981.[55] Second, during the 1950s and 1960s the rate of profit increased in the textile, knitting and clothing industries, in contrast to the steadily falling rate (about 1 per cent per annum) in other Canadian manufacturing.[56] Third, they note that, in spite of competitive weakness and slow rates of capital accumulation, rates of profit in the knitting and clothing industries in 1988 are markedly high.[57] Accordingly, these two authors question the causes of various forms of restructuring in these industries.

Surveys conducted by the Micro Economic Analysis Branch of Industry, Trade and Commerce in 1977 and 1978 showed that, in spite of collective bargaining possibilities, workers bore the costs of industrial restructuring. One third of the 2,664 textile workers and nearly two fifths of 753 clothing workers who were laid off between 1974 and 1976 had not yet found other jobs. Of those who did, 30 per cent took a cut in pay, which is significant considering that average textile hourly wages are 73 per cent and clothing hourly wages only 66 per cent of the average manufacturing wage. Over half the workers, therefore, suffered the effects of restructuring and "these statistics provide only a superficial measure of the hardship encountered by displaced textile and clothing workers."[58] Rianne Mahon argues that neither the Adjustment Assistance Benefit program nor the broader employment programs of the federal government addressed the problem of job destruction resulting from destructuring the textile and clothing industries. This failure, she claims, is related to the relative weakness of organized labour in Canada.[59]

Within a broader corporate horizon, as a result of two major merger movements beginning in 1968 and 1977, the number of companies with assets over $1 billion and the size of those assets grew rapidly. From 1975 to 1980, for example, Canada's wealthiest men and largest conglomerates "expanded the book value of their assets from $25 billion to $52 billion, ... 40 per cent of this through takeovers."[60] These corporations could deduct interest on finances for the takeovers from their taxes and offer shareholders more shares instead of cash in order to avoid the capital gains tax. All of these companies rely on their own holding, management and investment firms to control their internal capital resources. What is most important is that the key wealth-producing assets are in the hands of a minority of people in Canadian society with little or no open, public accountability regarding community responsibility. Many are able to use even recessions to their advantage, as the following American data suggests:

> A detailed study of five postwar United States recessions found conglomerates exercising a direct and harmful impact on unemployment and inflation. In highly concentrated industries, conglomerates managed to induce price mark-ups as high as 14 per cent during recessions.... Inflation is not only a systemic emanation of oligopolistic capitalism but also reinforces oligopolistic structures by driving out small firms. To the extent that large corporations tend to have lower labour, utility, and raw materials costs as a percentage of aggregate sales than smaller firms, they are less adversely affected by the batterings of inflation.[61]

But wealthy individuals were not content to risk the insecurities of a volatile system without acting for their own short- and long-term advantage.

Following the example of the 196 top American corporate leaders who in 1994 formed the Business Roundtable to engage in direct lobbying campaigns, chief executive officers of 150 leading corporations in Canada formed the Business Council on National Issues (BCNI) in 1976.[62] The Canadian Labour Congress had recommended collaboration with business and government leaders in what they called social corporatism and the Liberal government led by Prime Minister Pierre Trudeau had held meetings with both groups to try to form consensus about follow-up to the compulsory wage and price controls of 1975. The members of the new BCNI wanted to promote corporate concerns with government and labour in tripartite economic management. Their initiative was designed to strengthen their ability to shape national priorities and public policies more efficiently, to improve Canadian standards of living and to make the state more accountable to special interests of the private sector. More than a third of its members are foreign—mainly U.S.—owned, and include some of the most powerful transnational corporations in the world."[63]

In this phase, therefore, consolidation of state involvement with corporate power laid the groundwork for continental restructuring. Economic integration and dependence on the U.S. economy augmented concentration of wealth, maximization of profits and mobilization of capital. Corporate control of the economy provided broad power for lobbying business interests within the government. Increasingly government and law are directed by and for the interests of the wealthy. Culturally, freedom means security for the few. The gap between corporate owners and homeworkers became a chasm.

Phase 4: Traded Away and Contracted Out
Garment Work

A maze of contradictions sharply divides both descriptions of reality and solutions to socio-economic crises affecting both garment workers and consumers in the Greater Toronto Area. The closure of unionized factories like Nike's York Manufacturing in 1994 and Numode in 1995 leaves many garment factories hollow.[64] Since the late 1980s, there has been a dramatic increase in garment homeworking and contracting shops.

As the federal government promoted the Free Trade Agreement (FTA) and the North American Free Trade Agreement (NAFTA), it argued that garment production was dying in Canada, that it was in fact a "sunset industry." Employment figures before the agreements reveal a different story.

> Between 1971 and 1988 employment in the garment industry actually rose by 11,000—at a time the industry was supposedly in decline. It was not until the late 1980s and the signing of the Free Trade Agreement that the garment industry began to face massive job loss. Employment dropped a full third from 95,000 in 1988 to an estimated 62,000 in 1992. In Metro Toronto alone there were 24,711 workers in 1988, but in 1991 that number had fallen to 14,328.[65]

The ILGWU emphasizes that "there is nothing 'inherent' or 'natural' about the garment industry that suggests clothes should be produced in low-wage countries. Low-wage countries do not 'naturally' have a comparative advantage in the garment industry. Rather, the federal government has made clear choices."[66] It is important to examine some of these choices, particularly as evident in the trade agreements involving the textile and garment industries.

In the context of widespread structural unemployment and low-wage strategies, women who have stated clearly that they do not want to be homeworkers are forced to be, in corporate language, flexible.[67] Low-wage strategies for industrial and electronic homeworking and for domestic labour are directly linked to the exploding capital and power that now control global economics and exert strong pressure over governments. The corporate agenda is evident: in globalization, in financial policies which involve the creation of export-processing zones around the world, in the FTA and NAFTA and in Canadian industrial policy for the garment sector. More on the structure and restructuring of the garment industry globally, federally and provincially later!

Context: Globalization

As noted previously, transnational corporations were entrenched as the dominant force in the world economy by the 1960s. The 1967 to 1969 rapid mergers into stateless, conglomerate corporations were repeated in Canada from 1988 to 1992. A few giant corporate enterprises dominate sectors, maximizing profits by using economic and political power to determine prices and output. Corporate executives are able to use profits from prosperous sectors to subsidize temporarily depressed lines and to shift resources to whatever is most profitable at the time. They are also able to transfer their large cash reserves between currencies to protect themselves against devaluation or inflation earning maximum interest payments. The corporate agenda driving the present relationship between markets and states can be summed up in the term globalization which is marked by: (1) integrating national markets into more extensive trading zones; (2) increasing financial speculation and capital mobility; (3) the flexibility of production systems; (4) competing for lowest-wage strategies; (5) decreasing world market prices for resources; (6) deteriorating terms of trade for most countries; (7) cumulative indebtedness for nations and the poor; and (8) unequal division of labour and corporate control of specialization. High interest rates, cuts to social spending and rampant unemployment all flow from the corporate agenda.

These aspects characterize the resurgence of belief in unfettered market liberalism, that is, the belief that the structure and rules of market relationships somehow define themselves and do so most efficiently when left to their own dynamic.[68] Such lack of planning has led to a general crisis of the world capitalist economy, evident in chronic overproduction and intensified competition without adequate consumer purchasing power. In the 1970s the International Monetary Fund and the World Bank required countries caught in a debt crisis to shift to export-led development instead of focusing on industries to serve the needs of their own people. Export-processing or free-trade zones were established to attract transnational corporations by exempting them from taxes and tariffs on the importation of materials and on exports of the finished product, from corporate income and profit taxes and from labour laws such as minimum wage and the right to organize a union. Companies there can hire and fire with minimal compensation. According to Susan Joekes and Roxana Moayedi, textile and clothing and electronics industries are the most important manufacturing areas of activity for foreign investors. Such outward processing is usually done in an offshore, global assembly line. Available jobs are usually unskilled, dead end, poorly paid and done mostly by women.[69] At issue here is the fact that the IMF and World Bank have dictated policies which set women around the globe in competition with each other for the lowest wages.

The major effect of such economic restructuring, as Maria Mies explains, is that less economically powerful countries use most labour time, raw materials, skills and technical development toward export-oriented production of consumer goods to meet the demands of rich countries. The latter become areas of consumption while the needs of those in the producer countries are neglected to an unprecedented degree.[70]

Corporate control has led to a crippling socio-economic dependency for many with no way, as Drache and Gertler put it, "to redress for the fundamental inequality in the transfer of power and wealth that results when private property is made sovereign.... In a low-wage economy, the working poor subsidize managers' incomes and owners' profits."[71] In this context, global capitalists set the market trends suitable for corporations to gain sufficient power to establish product prices, wage rates and returns on investment, and to obtain governmental backing for free-trade agreements which promote their financial gain. This lasting structural crisis of the world economy leaves nations vulnerable before corporate power.[72]

The impact of this recession is magnified by the steady dismantling of social programs.[73] For example, by linking social services, post-secondary education and health care from the Established Program Financing and the Canada Assistance Plan into one block-funding grant to the provinces in the Canada Social Transfer, and by slashing $4.1 billion in spending in the 1995-96 budget, the government is surrendering its ability to protect national standards in these areas. By 1999, federal program spending diminished to 12.6 per cent of the GDP.[74] Communities within all provinces are forced to divide smaller transfer payments among health care, education and social services. Equalization payments cause provinces with greater social assistance needs to strain education and health care budgets.[75]

Cuts in social spending are made in the name of minimizing inflation and cutting government deficit and long-term debt.[76] While the Canadian Centre for Policy Alternatives and Choices: A Coalition for Social Justice accepts the government's target of deficit reduction to 3 per cent of the GDP by 1996-97 and also pursues the goal of stabilizing the debt, particularly the foreign-held portion, it chooses different means to achieve these goals. Its proposal offers a serious alternative to the government's budget which, it claims, will have great difficulty reaching its targets "because of the negative impact of expenditure cuts themselves on GDP, job growth, and therefore on tax revenue, and because of the impact of recent interest rate increases on debt servicing costs and expected real growth."[77]

Context: Trade Agreements

Overproduction and decreasing purchasing power have led to an insecurity among capital owners to the extent that it has triggered the formation of a new economic and political agenda.[78] As John Warnock notes, "In Canada it has taken the form of the rise of the New Right in politics and economics ... and the promotion of a free trade agreement with the United States."[79] Organized labour was not strong enough to shape the "free-trade" agreements, at least in part because the great recession of 1981-82 and other aspects of the globalized economy brought such high levels of unemployment. Previous gains were lost to the corporate sector. The story of the agreements reveals struggles and surrender that undermine the Canadian garment industry.

The Multi-Fibre Agreement, as previously noted, is in principle based on multilateral agreements to deal with the international textile and garment trade. Its actual workings, however, rely on bilateralism and global ceilings. In fact, the export quotas of Taiwan, Korea, Hong Kong and India have been severely slashed and allocated to other countries. As a result they are forced either to reduce textile and clothing output or to shift to other products or markets. These regulations intensify competition within the UCEs. To bypass enforcement, some countries use others' labels and quotas or classify power-loom products as hand-loom. The MFA principle of "special and differential treatment for less developed countries" has given way to the transnational corporate agenda favouring deregulated global markets for goods, services and investment capital. GATT members agreed at the Uruguay Round in 1994 to phase out the MFA by 2006. It is being replaced by the World Trade Organization (WTO) with free trade in clothing and textiles, favouring transnational corporate control. The roots of the crisis remain. The objective of the struggle is clear—namely, to retain and increase global markets.[80] As the ILGWU signals,

> The MFA rollback is a significant change since it removes more than fifty years of "special status" for textiles and clothing. Without MFA and with no social clauses in the new system, the World Trade Organization, large retailers and manufacturers can move trade of textiles and clothing in an environment free from control.[81]

The ILGWU is not, however, endorsing the MFA as the best means to control production between Canada and DCEs. In fact, the union critiques the MFA as unsuccessful in managing international trade fairly, weak in regulating "surges" from low-wage areas, partial to the U.S. over DCEs and ineffective in regulating production locations for textiles and garments.

The liberalized direction set by the GATT and by the MFA sheds light on the decisions made regarding the garment and textile trade in the FTA and NAFTA. These agreements signal the end of a protection era and lead to the imminent global deregulation of this sector under the World Trade Organization. FTA and NAFTA are also attempts to intensify Canada's relations with the U.S. Canadian manufacturers were directly competing with the 807 regulations of the U.S. government which, in 1984, allowed American garment manufacturers to cut garments in their own country, and then ship them to Latin America or the Caribbean basin where women would sew them for low wages.[82]

Although limited in scope, the bilateral FTA set important precedents for the NAFTA which overrides both the FTA and the MFA. According to Leah Vosko, the significant areas of NAFTA for garment and textile industries are the rules of origin, the triple transformation issue, fabrics in short supply, tariff rate quotas and the redefinition of wool.[83] The triple transformation rule of origin defines when a good is considered to originate with Canada, the U.S. or Mexico. In the FTA, apparel made from fabrics woven in Canada or the U.S. from yarns or fibres produced in other countries is eligible for duty-free treatment.

Although garments sewn from fabrics produced offshore were not eligible for duty-free status under the FTA, special tariff rates were established to allow a quota of such Canadian garments to be allotted a special rate of duty.

Even the FTA brought a major setback for the Canadian garment industry. Canada is internationally recognized for cutting, sewing and finishing high-quality apparel, often constructed from European fabrics. Classed as non-originating, such Canadian-made apparel goods received new export quotas. The further restriction in NAFTA that requires yarn production, cutting and sewing (triple transformation) in order for garments to qualify as duty free will bolster U.S. industries while penalizing Canadian industries.[84] Although rules concerning fabrics that are in seriously short supply may be adjusted, the U.S. has already restricted a list drawn up by Canadian retailers, importers and apparel manufacturers of 117 such fabrics to only 8, the number insisted upon by U.S. textile manufacturers.[85]

The annual quota for wool places a stiff limit on Canada's most competitive export. Even the 2 per cent increase in tariff preference levels is reduced to 1 per cent for wool. Canadian manufacturers are forced to compete for the right to use this amount. In addition, although Canada wanted to maintain definitions that required the fabric to be 50 per cent wool to be classed as a wool good, the U.S. preference was 36 per cent for woven apparel and 23 per cent for knitted or crocheted apparel.[86] Since this stipulation drastically increases the garments that are now classified as wool, these levels force Canadian manufacturers to sacrifice quality by decreasing wool content. Leah Vosko claims that the redefinition of wool "represents the most serious concession in the apparel good trade. [It] could potentially eradicate quality apparel production in Canada.... The wool tariff rate quota applied to Canada becomes unjustly restrictive."[87] Furthermore, Vosko concludes that in the Textile and Apparel Goods Chapter of the legal NAFTA text, "There is no illusion of a level playing field.... Canada is the clear loser in this chapter."[88] The excessive job loss and regional concentration created by the FTA indicate the direction set by the more stringent continental harmonization in the NAFTA. The availability of cheap Mexican labour, the "yarn forward"/triple transformation rules of origin and export restraints placed on Canadian apparel goods all become ominous threats against union efforts to maintain labour standards and to organize both homeworkers and factory workers. This industry "is generally regarded as the biggest loser in NAFTA."[89]

Both the FTA and the NAFTA legislate Canada's dependence on foreign corporations and create a common market in social and economic policy controlled by the foreign investment criteria.[90] A viable Canadian industry is being destroyed in agreements which in practice are a North American "bill of rights for business." American retail chains, such as The Gap, Talbots and Nordstrom, and large Canadian retailers have promoted free-trade agreements either to bypass Canadian manufacturers or to enter into integrated supply arrangements with American producers. Previous efforts to bypass the Multi-Fibre Agreement and similar restraint levels through use of outward processing are now legitimized in the NAFTA.[91] American and Mexican businesses are granted the right of national treatment and national presence.

Within Canada, the force behind the agreements is the Business Council on National Issues. As in the United States,

> neo-conservatism in Canada is also identified with nineteenth-century liberal individualism. This is best illustrated in the publications of the Fraser Institute, the "think tank" for Canadian big business.... They take the view that legislation to protect women, minority and ethnic groups actually harms them. They oppose equal pay for work of equal value and any form of preferential treatment for minorities.... Lower wages for women should be permitted because "the right to discriminate" is a fundamental individual right. Is there any wonder that women are skeptical about the neo-conservative agenda and, what is essentially tied to it, free trade with the United States?[92]

The corporate drive for North American free trade and for its hemispheric expansion in the Enterprise of the Americas are directly related to the distribution of economic power. If any form of economic democracy is to be achieved, trade relations must be reframed on the basis of a clear understanding of productive, marketing, social and reproductive relations.

Industrial Policy for the Garment Sector

In view of global impacts, it is time to focus on federal and then provincial policy for the domestic garment industry.

Federal Policy: The ILGWU reports that since 1989,

> through Industry Science and Technology Canada, the Federal government supported a new fashion apparel sector strategy—called "Fashioning the Future." ... The strategy rightly points out that the apparel sector is the fifth largest employer and 14th in terms of shipments in Canada.[93]

It is evident that the garment sector is significant. This new strategy forms the main Canadian industrial policy for apparel. It relies on export-led industrialization, free trade, the possibility of creating a Canadian-based design image and improved marketing. This means that the sector would expand to higher-end, higher-value-added products, encourage high product quality, encourage imaginative fashion orientation and require flexible manufacturing plants.[94] A six-million-dollar campaign to implement these strategies included several aspects. Numerous studies provided data for manufacturers. Working groups were created around marketing; management and technical skills in computer-aided design and computer-aided manufacturing (CAD/CAM); the importance of a fashion-oriented textile industry to support a high-end niche of apparel production; and increased designer linkages with manufacturers. Firms are expected to produce more efficiently in less time by upgrading their technology. The federal government has financially supported an industry federation and linkages among design, textile, apparel and retail firms. Finally, if the main consumer information program, the CA number program, regarding who is responsible for garments purchased is privatized, as recommended, it means that a monitoring program for consumer interests will be changed to a registration program for manufacturers.

Taking the perspective of garment workers, the ILGWU offers significant critique of "Fashioning the Future" as a sectoral strategy. With no mention of sewing machine operators and other workers in the documents, "It is as if the entire industry, one of the country's most labour intensive, was workerless."[95] Only design and marketing are considered "value-added components." Workers' roles in adding value to production are dismissed. It follows that the government also omits the need for adjustment policies related to free trade and to technological change. The silence about production and work organization leaves untouched questions about who produces garments, how they are produced, under what conditions and with what skills. Unions were not even consulted.

Reducing the sector to fashion means that the federal government is excluding other significant areas such as workwear, uniforms and household items from its strategy. By directing manufacturers to focus on higher quality and styles for more affluent customers, the government is limiting the industry to small niche markets. This direction has been set without adequate statistics regarding various product levels within both Canadian and international markets which means that it is difficult to determine the market potential for fashion products themselves. The inadequacies of federal strategy centre on its exclusion of workers and unions, the complete reliance on liberalized, non-interventionary policies and the collapse of the garment sector into high-end fashion apparel.

Ontario Policy: According to the ILGWU, the provincial government placed little emphasis on the garment industry in the 1980s. Through the Ontario Development Corporation (ODC), the provincial government provided a $100-million manufacturing recovery program for working capital loans. The ILGWU found that this initiative is inadequate in the amount required and in its inability to respond quickly to a company's financial crisis.[96] Provincial criteria focus on extremely short-term rather than long-term aspects for economic development. Lacking sectoral strategy, it decides each firm's situation independently, using narrow business criteria. Broader strategic and social needs, as well as the employment of mainly women/immigrant workers are relative to market principles which are determined without the participation of the garment unions and workers.

Although the provincial government established an industrial policy framework for sectors to develop into "higher-value activities," it was not until early 1994 that a sectoral fund process for the garment industry was put in place.[97] Labour and management were encouraged to co-operate to develop common strategies with task forces on specific topics. The ILGWU found, however, that the sectoral partnership fund process is too labour-intensive for a small union which lacked resources for research, for development of a work plan and for participation on the task forces. By early 1995, differing interests and goals of labour and management led to an impasse: "Specifically, the union was not supported by management in developing a small program of worker-centred research. Any attempts to develop autonomous research capacity were not supported by management."[98] The union was committed to develop an alternative strategy from a workers' perspective. They found that both worker-centred proposals, like ensuring daycare, and attempts to challenge the focus on marketing as the key strategic development issues for the industry were ignored. Union representatives soon realized that they were expected to be present at meetings and accept alternatives as designed by management representatives. It was painfully clear that labour and management were not equals at the table and that "using a labour-management approach where the government does not intervene, in effect, creates a power imbalance between workers and management."[99]

By ensuring a stronger voice for labour, the provincial government could have furthered their own objective of moving to a higher-value-added sector by recognizing the value of labour in production. A basic issue then is what forms the starting point for sectoral strategies and what value various goals and strategies have in the well-being of workers, consumers and business. The ILGWU is clear in its call for more active government intervention in reshaping sectoral strategies in the Ontario garment industry and in the international global assembly line of apparel production.

In the phase of globalization, the free market system has exploded and the merging of corporate, bank and government power has changed the context in which homeworkers struggle to obtain even minimum wages. The corporate agenda relies on competition and low-wage strategies for profit and on the global division of labour and state intervention to support business interests. The place of homeworkers stands in a relation of stark contrast. Their voices are unheard. Homeworkers must mount campaigns even to have their existence and concerns recognized.

Shift in Context: Financial Capitalism

Globalization of the free market system is most apparent in the emergence of an integrated world financial system. Financial transactions have exploded to an unprecedented seventy-two times the amount of merchandise trade. The speculative economy is even greater, "When the markets for currencies, stocks, bonds and commodity futures are taken together, *daily transactions total some US$4 trillion*. Most of these transactions are speculative; they are not in and of themselves necessary to finance the production or trade of goods and services."[100] By exchanging hot cybermoney on computer screens, investors use money to make money, without investing in production of goods or in services. Like the aboriginal peoples who wrote of the sixteenth-century invaders, "All that is of value was counted as nothing," we as a people can lament today that investment in much-needed production of basic necessities and services for peoples in Canada and globally is tied up in valueless speculation.[101] Social and environmental costs are ignored. As Dillon and the Ecumenical Coalition for Economic Justice (ECEJ) explains,

> For the high rollers of world finance, people are becoming less important—both as producers and as consumers. Latin Americans no longer speak about the millions who live in absolute poverty as the "marginalized," since this term implies that sooner or later they might be incorporated into the mainstream of society. Instead they now speak about "the excluded" masses

who neither produce for the world economy nor consume from it. In Colombia the excluded have even been described as "the disposable ones."[102]

In stark contrast, only 358 persons owned fortunes worth US$762 billion in 1994. As Xabier Gorostiaga points out, the wealth of these billionaires equaled the income of the poorest 45 per cent of the world's population, 2.3 billion people.[103]

The Bretton Woods system has collapsed.[104] When President Nixon unilaterally announced in a televised speech on 15 August 1971 that the U.S. dollar would no longer be redeemable for gold, the Bretton Woods era ended and a new era of speculative or financial capitalism began.[105] That decision meant that American dollars deposited around the world were unregulated and that banks could create new money without any reserve requirement.

Corporate owners can finance their production through their own investment companies and accumulate more capital through speculation than through job creation in goods and services. While a minority grow wealthy from this new economy, the majority pay for it and do work that supports it.

This structural shift in the Canadian economy was supported by federal and provincial policies and entrenched by "a made-at-the-Bank-of-Canada recession in 1990" from which we have not yet emerged.[106] The bank's policy of making even zero inflation a top priority and using high interest rates and high unemployment to achieve it reflects the financial world's pressure to protect its own capital accumulation. Banking channels facilitate capital export for super-profit. They also repatriate and accumulate excess capital nationally and internationally for the elite. Corporate involvement in banking decisions and government policies entrenches financial capitalism.[107]

The Royal Bank of Canada, with profits exceeding a billion dollars in 1995, is a major decision maker of plant closures and garment workers' jobs. A well-documented example is the closure of the Great Sewing Exchange (GSE) in 1992. With the GSE financial data before them, and considering the initiatives of new management and the recent acquisition of the Harley Davidson licence, the International Ladies' Garment Workers' Union was convinced the business was viable. Deeper issues were revealed when the bank was requested to allow more time for management and the union to find a solution to the problem. A former finance manager of GSE reported the bank's loan officers were instructed to get out of textiles and the garment industry. Royal Bank president John Cleghorn made this position clear:

We're hearing advice from the street and our own consultants that we should be looking at it [credit quality] not only account by account but also from a macro point of view. Rather than wondering whether we can get by with this account until next year or the year after, we're standing back and saying, "Wait a minute. There's something affecting the whole industry, so let's try and get this behind us now."[108]

As the ILGWU points out, banks call this process "sectoral provisioning." In spite of the thousands of jobs in garment manufacturing, the evidence strongly suggests that since the FTA (or because of the FTA) banks and government have written off the industry. Although government officials speak to union representatives of the need to be more proactive, the province did not even include the garment industry in the fifteen key sectors which it identified for developing sectoral strategies. Costs to individuals and to society because of massive layoffs and closure of a whole sector are not counted.

The Personal Is Political

I am becoming aware just how transformative and therefore responsible it is to speak in the light what we hear in the dark. As I gathered the data that became the first two chapters, I sensed that despair about possibilities of socio-economic transformation and of ecclesial participation in such transformation was mounting within me. It is abundantly evident to me that economically we are in an overall process of societal decline, similar to the historical exploitation of Third World areas. Younger and less populated, Canada hides its poverty. During a private retreat, I expressed my lament and grief by painting. I describe these because they are significant to me and, I am quite convinced, to society and churches collectively. The first was one of my images of God, as a woman in shackles with her mouth bound and her eyes open. I saw this image as portraying that God wants to be loving and just in our lives but we shackle divine power in our midst through racism, sexism and wealthism. I hold that, to the extent that we tolerate violence against women and against nature, we cannot know the living God, her power and healing love.[109] The second painting, *After*, expresses a way I stand with those who have suffered abuse, rape, torture, harassment, discrimination and exclusion. The third focuses on a woman who weeps over the disappearance of a loved one, with the Toronto skyline and globe in the background. I call this, *Woman spirit rising up to lament the destruction of our planet and to stand against the corporate agenda.*

After doing these three paintings of lament, I dreamt of a young, very beautiful woman and my eight-year-old niece, Michelle, singing more sweetly than I had ever known, a song that to my knowledge I had never heard before. The next week, on Holy Thursday, I heard it on the radio! The Cambridge choir was singing "All Things Bright and Wonderful" by John Rutter. The next part of my dream was filled with exhilaration, joy, new life, surprise and deep peace as horses kept coming up out of the sea onto the shore, prancing and frisking there in the sun. I painted the horses.

What I had experienced in such a profound way was that pouring out lament and grief is a foundation for hope. In a culture of injustice where exploitation is the norm, unmasking false ideologies and critiquing causes of racism, of sexism, of wealthism, of the international division of labour and of pollution of the earth create room for hope. Lament and critique are foundational to hope and to partnership with the divine mystery in just relations. They are one part of the process of solidarity and transformation, of bringing justice in fact, not merely seeming to do so and not merely talking about possibilities for it.

Conclusion

Even this brief focus on the history of women's work in garment production records a pattern that reinforces devaluation of their work. Garment workers in the homes and factories are excluded from decision making about sectoral strategies, wages, working conditions and alternatives. There is an increasing chasm between corporate-bank-governmental control in public realms and female labour and poverty in both production and the private sphere of the home.

Identification and ways of naming the overlapping contexts and phases of history vary according to perspective and interpretation of the author. My concern was not to limit categories but to see what is going forward and what is declining in historical well-being, as well as to glimpse why our particular current reality is shaped as it is. Such an approach allows us to locate causes and to understand where changes may be introduced. I turn now to the global web of production in the garment industry, all the while gathering data for ethical decision making and responsible action.

Notes

1 I expand the analysis of Gerry Van Houten's phases in *Corporate Canada: An Historical Outline* (Toronto: Progress Books, 1991). Analysis in the early 1970s showed that major structural changes occurred within distinct periods in political economy. Colonial Canada moved from almost complete dominance by the British government in all areas: (a) to responsible, semi-colonial government with autonomy in local affairs; (b) to the British non-interference in governmental affairs but with nearly total, neocolonial dependence on England and United States in economic concerns; (c) neo-colonialism continues in current relations which subject government, finance, trade and commerce to stateless, conglomerate corporations. Refer to Leo Johnson, "The Political Economy of Ontario Women in the Nineteenth Century," in *Women at Work, Ontario, 1850-1930*, ed. Janice Acton, Penny Goldsmith and Bonnie Shepard (Toronto: Canadian Women's Educational Press, 1974), 13-31. See Gary Teeple, "The Development of Class in Canada in the Twentieth Century," in *Capitalism and the National Question*, ed. Gary Teeple (Toronto: University of Toronto Press, 1972).

2 See Robert Heilbroner, *Twenty-first Century Capitalism* (Concord, ON: Anansi Press, 1992), 19-20, 26, 104.

3 Refer to Tamás Szentes, *The Transformation of the World Economy: New Directions and New Interests* (London: Zed Books, 1988), 3, 34, 90.

4 Nancy Folbre, *Who Pays for the Kids? Gender and the Structures of Constraint* (New York: Routledge Books, 1994), 59.

5 Ibid., 60.

6 Ibid., 57.

7 Coalition for Fair Wages and Working Conditions for Homeworkers (which includes International Ladies' Garment Workers' Union, Workers' Information and Action Centre of Toronto, Chinese Workers' Association, Parkdale Community Legal Services, Ontario Coalition of Visible Minority Women, Ontario Coalition for Better Child Care, Trinity/Spadina New Democratic Party Riding Association, the Ecumenical Coalition for Economic Justice, National Action Council on the Status of Women, Labour Council of Metropolitan Toronto and York Region, School Sisters of Notre Dame, Workers' Educational Association), *Fair Wages and Working Conditions for Homeworkers: A Brief to the Government of Ontario* (Toronto, December 1991), 4.

8 Adrienne Shadd, "Institutionalized Racism and Canadian History: Notes of a Black Canadian," in *Racism in Canada*, ed. Ormond McKague (Saskatoon: Fifth House, 1991), 3. Chinese and Japanese also came in the nineteenth century.

9 Van Houten, *Corporate Canada*, 6-7, 13-15, regarding 1670-1763, from the foundation of the Hudson's Bay Company to the signing of the Treaty of Paris which marked the beginning of British rule. The company was incorporated under Royal charter in England in 1670, and moved its domicile and head office from London, England, to Winnipeg, Manitoba, in 1970, subject to Canadian supplemental charter and laws. Refer to "Hudson's Bay Company," in *Moody's International Manual*, 1333.

10 See Sylvia Van Kirk, "The Role of Native Women in the Fur Trade Society of Western Canada, 1670-1830," in *Perspectives on Canadian Economic Development: Class, Staples, Gender and Elites*, ed. Gordon Laxer (Toronto: Oxford University Press, 1991), 353.

11 James P. Catty, "Canada's Most Significant Merger," *CA Magazine* (September 1983): 48-51.

12 Linda Briskin and Lynda Yanz, eds., *Union Sisters: Women in the Labour Movement* (Toronto: Women's Press, 1983), 46.

13 Alan B. McCullough, *The Primary Textile Industry in Canada: History and Heritage* (Ottawa: Environment Canada, 1992), 95-96. Women comprised 34 per cent of the industrial labour force in Toronto in 1871 (Alison Prentice and S. Trofimenkoff, eds., *The Neglected Majority*, vol. 1 [Toronto: McClelland and Stewart, 1977], 125). Refer to Marjorie Griffin Cohen, *Women's Work: Markets and Economic Development in Nineteenth-Century Ontario* (Toronto: University of Toronto Press, 1988), 131-34, regarding homework and child labour in the garment industry, 1850-1911.

14 K[night] of L[abour], "Where Labor Is Not a Prayer," *Walsh's Magazine* (Toronto, 1895-96): 112, reprinted in "How the Sweatshop System Began: 'Homework' in Toronto," in *The Canadian Worker in the Twentieth Century*, ed. I. Abella and D. Millar (Toronto: Oxford University Press, 1978), 154-56. Emphasis is mine. This analysis represents the heart of today's debate and challenge.

15 See Ruth Frager, "No Proper Deal: Women Workers and the Canadian Labour Movement, 1870 to 1940," in *Union Sisters: Women in the Labour Movement*, ed. Linda Briskin and Lynda Yanz (Toronto: Women's Press, 1983), 44-45. Information on wages and statistics in the labour force is based on Canadian census data every ten years, starting in 1921.

16 Anonymous Report, "Information Regarding the Tailoring Trade in a Small District of Toronto," Deputy Minister of Labour files, 1916-20, in Archives of Ontario; referenced in Catherine Macleod, "Women in Production: The Toronto Dressmakers' Strike of 1931," in *Women at Work, Ontario, 1850-1930*, ed. Janice Acton, Penny Goldsmith and Bonnie Shepard (Toronto: Canadian Women's Educational Press, 1974), 316.

17 Johnson and Johnson, *The Seam Allowance*, 50-51.

18 Dionne Brand, Lois De Shield and the Immigrant Women's Job Placement Centre, *No Burden to Carry: Narratives of Black Working Women in Ontario 1920s to 1950s* (Toronto: Women's Press, 1991), 15.

19 For example, in 1928, Canada Cotton Ltd. hired the Textile Development Company Ltd. of Boston to reorganize their entire Hamilton plant. "The 'science' consisted of analyzing the way the workers had organized production on the shop floor, and inventing methods to destroy it." See Dorothy Kidd, "Women's Organization: Learning from Yesterday," in *Women at Work, Ontario, 1850-1930*, ed. Janice Acton, Penny Goldsmith and Bonnie Shepard (Toronto: Canadian Women's Educational Press, 1974), 351.

20 Ibid., 339-40.

21 Ibid., 326-28, fn. 11. During the 1930s, 17 per cent lost their jobs and the others were cut about one third of their wages (ibid., 315).

22 The cloak industry had first organized in the early 1900s, the dress industry in the 1930s and, more recently, the sportswear industries (Charlene Gannagé,

"Changing Dimensions of Control and Resistance: The Toronto Garment Industry," *Journal of Canadian Studies* 24, 4 [Winter 1989-90]: 59, fn. 22).

23 Catherine Macleod, "Women in Production: The Toronto Dressmakers' Strike of 1931," in *Women at Work, Ontario, 1850-1930*, ed. Janice Acton, Penny Goldsmith and Bonnie Shepard (Toronto: Canadian Women's Educational Press, 1974), 310.

24 Kidd, "Women's Organization," 336.

25 Frager, "No Proper Deal," 48.

26 Macleod, "Women in Production," 317-19.

27 Macleod, "Women in Production," 318, quoting Deputy Minister of Labour files, in Archives of Ontario. Only in 1968, however, was the Minimum Wage Act of Ontario rewritten to include homeworkers (Johnson and Johnson, *The Seam Allowance*, 51-52).

28 Frager, "No Proper Deal," 47, 52, 53.

29 The current General Welfare Assistance Act was passed in 1959 and the Family Benefits Act in 1967. The federal Canada Assistance Plan, which pays part of provincial welfare costs, was passed in 1966 replacing a number of other programs aimed at assisting particular groups such as seniors and the disabled.

30 See Laurie Monsebraaten, "Evolution of the Dole: Unemployment Insurance, A Capsule History," *The Toronto Star*, 5 November 1994, B1, 6.

31 Van Houten, *Corporate Canada*, 82.

32 By economism, I mean the group bias that selects economic principles for an elite quite separate both from the needs of the majority and from a balanced positioning of economics as a subsystem within society. At the heart of capitalism is the drive to accumulate capital. By wealthism, I mean the distortion of assuming power and prestige on the basis of ownership and inequality. Capitalistic power relies on wealth as its strength in the marketplace, but values it mainly for its use to maximize profits and increase both capital and power. Refer to Heilbroner, *Twenty-first Century Capitalism*, 26-32.

33 Joe Holland and Peter Henriot, *Social Analysis: Linking Faith and Justice* (Washington: Center of Concern, 1980), 28-29. This analysis is from an American perspective with little comment about exploitation of the two-thirds world and nothing about Canadian development. It is, however, helpful in analyzing the contexts and changes of the global market and influences/threats to Canadian values.

34 Van Houten, *Corporate Canada*, 51. See also John Warnock, *Free Trade and the New Right Agenda* (Vancouver: New Star Books, 1988), 80-90, for a history of free trade between Canada and the U.S. In 1910 the U.S. proposed a new reciprocity agreement which, as President W.H. Taft declared in an election campaign a year later, was "the first step towards bringing Canada into the U.S. federal union." Canadian rejection of it signaled a will to remain independent (ibid., 83).

35 Van Houten, *Corporate Canada*, 52, 54.

36 McQuaig, *The Quick and the Dead*, 242.

37 Refer to Marjorie Griffin Cohen (*Women's Work*, 9, 16-22) regarding this process in Britain and assessment of the impact of industrialization on women in Upper Canada.

38 Pat Armstrong and Hugh Armstrong, *The Double Ghetto: Canadian Women and Their Segregated Work* (Toronto: McClelland and Stewart, 1978), 58. See Maria Mies, *Patriarchy and Accumulation on a World Scale: Women in the International Division of Labour* (London: Zed Books, 1986), 112-44.

39 Szentes, *The Transformation of the World Economy*, 43.

40 Van Houten, *Corporate Canada*, 69.

41 Ibid., 71. From 1909 to 1912 and 1925 to 1930 there were two major merger movements.

42 Holland and Henriot, *Social Analysis*, 32.

43 *Employment Standards Policy and Interpretation Manual*, vol. 1, no. 5.2, listing legislative history regarding homeworkers and referring to the Factory, Shop and Office Building Amendment Act, 1936, S.O. 1936, c. 21.

44 Johnson and Johnson, *The Seam Allowance*, 9.

45 Industrial Safety Act, 1964, S.O. 1964, c. 45, and the Employment Standards Act, 1986, S.O. 1968, c. 35.

46 Kidd, "Women's Organization," 342.

47 Armstrong and Armstrong, *The Double Ghetto*, 56.

48 Pat Armstrong, *Labour Pains: Women's Work in Crisis* (Toronto: Women's Press, 1984), 49. See also Szentes, *The Transformation of the World Economy*, 43, and Heilbroner, *Twenty-first Century Capitalism*, 38, 61-62.

49 Van Houten, *Corporate Canada*, 83-84; see also 159-76. Examples include the founding of the Canadian Broadcasting Corporation in 1932 and Air Canada (Trans-Canada Airlines) in 1937, nationalizing of the Bank of Canada in 1938 and Eldorado Mining and Refining Ltd., passing the Unemployment Insurance Act in 1940, Central Mortgage and Housing Company in 1945 and founding Polymer (later Polysar) Corporation and Canadian Arsenals Ltd. in 1942 and 1945.

50 Warnock, *Free Trade and the New Right Agenda*, 86: "Canada and underdeveloped countries were advised to concentrate on their natural 'competitive advantage.' They were encouraged to borrow capital to develop an infrastructure necessary to extract and to export their resources [and] to rely on foreign, particularly American, investment. This basic objective has been a regular part of U.S. policy towards Canada since the onset of the Cold War and is central to proposals for trade liberalization, whether through the GATT or on a Canada/U.S. bilateral basis." Canada and Mexico both increased their dependency on the U.S. at this time.

51 Clairmonte and Cavanagh, *The World in Their Web*, 5-7.

52 Ibid., 188. Chinese products are now overtaking Korean and Hong Kong products in Japanese markets and have rapidly gained a global place.

53 Daniel Drache and Meric Gertler, *The New Era of Global Competition: State Policy and Market Power* (Montreal and Kingston: McGill-Queen's University Press, 1991), xiv.

54 Rianne Mahon, *The Politics of Industrial Restructuring: Canadian Textiles* (Toronto: University of Toronto Press, 1984), 55-56. Emphasis is mine. Mahon's account is particularly helpful in its detailed description of political influences and manoeuvres in Canadian textile history. Charlene Gannagé also focuses on the vital role played by immigrant women in the garment industry, Canada's third largest manufacturing sector (Charlene

Gannagé, *Double Day, Double Bind: Women Garment Workers* [Toronto: Women's Press, 1986], 14).
55 M. Webber and S. Tonkin, "Technical Changes and the Rate of Profit in the Canadian Textile, Knitting and Clothing Industries," *Environment and Planning A* 20 (1988): 1489.
56 Ibid., 1489-1500. Well above the Canadian average, the rate of profit in the clothing industry "rose from an early 1950s level of 65 per cent per annum to a high of 85 per cent in 1981" (ibid., 1497). While prices were kept low by competition from imports, real wages and the value composition of capital were relatively low compared with other industries. The value rate of profit actually rose in all three industries, but it was most marked in the clothing sector: by 80.9 per cent from 148.47 per cent to 229.37 per cent in the thirty years considered. Value composition (technical change) had in fact declined (in itself providing a 51.7 per cent increase in the rate of profit) and the rate of exploitation exceeded the negative effect (-27.6 per cent) of the increasing turnover time. This contrasts usual expectations regarding technical change and the effects of prices. Increase of plant machinery has been almost negligible in the clothing industry but the rate at which materials are processed per hour increased. In all three industries, capacity utilization rates increased.
57 Ibid., 1503-1504: "Technical change in the clothing industry has been minimal: there has been little increase in either plant and equipment per worker or in the rate at which raw materials are processed. Thus, as the value of constant capital inputs has fallen, the value composition of capital has also tended to fall. The effect of this fall and of the sharp effect of the rise in the rate of exploitation have combined and have driven the value rate of profit upwards. Despite a negative trend in the implicit price of the surplus, the value rate of profit has carried the price rate of profit up with it."
58 Mahon, *The Politics of Industrial Restructuring*, 127. "The state's orientation to clothing capital implicitly recognized the latter's class power. Clothing capital's active consent to the terms of the policy is critical if the sector is to become internationally competitive, because capital controls the investment process. In this sense political action is less important than class position, at least when labour is unable to act collectively in its own name" (ibid., 128).
59 Ibid., 125.
60 Van Houten, *Corporate Canada*, 94, 101-102, 104-105. Although the Irving and Eaton families are among the wealthiest in personal wealth, they own their corporations outright as private companies with no shares offered to the public on the stock exchange. Canadian media giant Kenneth Thomson is listed by *Forbes* magazine as tied for seventh among the world's richest people ($8.9 billion U.S.). Refer to "What's a Billion? These People Know," *The Toronto Star*, 5 July 1995, B1. The International Thomson Organization owns The Hudson's Bay Company, Zellers, Simpsons, Robinsons and Fields. Refer to information sheet 2, "General Pyramid Structure of Canada's Garment Industry," prepared by Jan Borowy for an ILGWU conference in Port Elgin, ON, August 1992.

61 Van Houten, *Corporate Canada*, 20, referring for the first part to United States Senate, *Mergers and Industrial Concentration: Hearings Before the Subcommittee on Antitrust and Monopoly of the Senate Judiciary Committee*, Washington, DC, 12 May, 27 and 28 July and 21 September 1978, 126. These were the findings of Howard Wachtel.

62 David Langille, "The Business Council on National Issues and the Canadian State," *Studies in Political Economy* 24 (Autumn 1987): 42-47.

63 Maude Barlow and Bruce Campbell, *Take Back the Nation* (Toronto: Key Porter Books, 1991), 11. See also David Langille, "The BCNI Calls the Shots: Big Corporations Are Pulling the Canada-U.S. Trade Strings," in *The Facts on Free Trade: Canada, Don't Trade It Away*, edited by Canadian Union of Public Employees (Ottawa, 1988), 102: "The BCNI is composed of the chief executive officers of the 150 largest corporations operating in Canada. They control assets of over $700 billion dollars, earn annual revenues of $250 billion, and employ over 1-1/2 million Canadians."

64 ILGWU Nike campaign. One hundred and twenty-five women lost permanent jobs because Nike ended its licensing agreement with York manufacturing in March 1994. They sewed cotton sweatsuits, shorts and T-shirts. Nike's global corporate strategy is to rely on independent contractors and, in the case of York Manufacturing, to shift production out of Canada. Benefiting from NAFTA, Nike will ship goods here from a giant distribution centre in Memphis, Tennessee. In November 1999 Nike agreed to disclose information about 41 of its 541 factories.

65 Jan Borowy, Shelly Gordon, Gayle Lebans, "Are These Clothes Clean? The Campaign for Fair Wages and Working Conditions for Homeworkers," in *And Still We Rise: Feminist Political Mobilizing in Contemporary Canada*, ed. Linda Carty (Toronto: Women's Press, 1993), 301, referring to Statistics Canada, *Employment, Earnings and Hours: Catalogue 72-002* (Ottawa: Government of Canada, 1992).

66 International Ladies' Garment Workers' Union (ILGWU), Ontario District Council, *Designing the Future for Garment Workers*, Researcher: Janet Borowy (Toronto: Ontario Federation of Labour's Technology Adjustment Research Program, 1995), 23.

67 Ibid., 316.

68 Drache and Gertler, *The New Era of Global Competition*, xii. Maude Barlow and Bruce Campbell summarize the Conservative/corporate agenda in *Take Back the Nation*, 12-15. John Warnock analyzes the development of the new business agenda, the ideology of free trade and continental integration (*Free Trade and the New Right Agenda*, 60-92). Karl Polanyi opposed this theory, saying that "the road to the free market was opened and kept open by an enormous increase in continuous, centrally organized and controlled interventionism.... *Laissez-faire* was planned; planning was not" (Drache and Gertler, *The New Era of Global Competition*, xv, quoting Karl Polanyi, *The Great Transformation* [Boston: Beacon Press, 1957], 140).

69 Susan Joekes with Roxana Moayedi, *Women and Export Manufacturing: A Review of the Issues and Aid Policy* (Washington: International Center for Research on Women, 1987), 19, 24. They recommend "measures to improve quality of work life and job satisfaction which reward workers

during their period of employment ... and interventions directed at improving women's prospects for productive activity after they leave the export manufacturing sector" (ibid., 42-43).

70 Mies, *Patriarchy and Accumulation on a World Scale*, 114.

71 Daniel Drache and Meric Gertler, *The New Era of Global Competition*, xv-xvi, xviii.

72 Szentes, *The Transformation of the World Economy*, 79-80.

73 Refer to the Ecumenical Coalition for Economic Justice, *Reweaving Canada's Social Programs: From Shredded Safety Net to Social Solidarity* (Toronto: ECEJ, 1993), 30-46, for an analysis of these claims.

74 Social and Economic Policy Department of the Canadian Labour Congress, *Mr. Martin's Budget vs. the Alternative Federal Budget* (Ottawa: CLC, February 1999), 1.

75 Paul Leduc Browne, "Under the Guise of Fairness, the Federal Budget Hurts Canadians in Need," Canadian Centre for Policy Alternatives, 22 February 1999, http://www.policyalternatives.ca. Minimal increases in transfers for health care in 1999 were not adequate to offset real cuts from previous years or facilitate health care restructuring. Refer to John Loxley, "The Great Money Trick: The 1999-2000 Liberal Budget versus the Alternative Federal Budget," Department of Economics, University of Manitoba, http://www.policyalternatives.ca.

76 Linda McQuaig sees the debt obsession as part of a corporate agenda which facilitates private capital accumulation, maintains a flexible work force, restrains government spending and autonomy and shapes the tax system to favour the investors. Refer to Linda McQuaig, "The Debt Obsessions," *The Toronto Star*, 18 February 1995, C1, 4, and Linda McQuaig, "Who Cashes in on High Interest Rates," *The Toronto Star*, 19 February 1995, C4.

77 Canadian Centre for Policy Alternatives and Cho!ces: A Coalition for Social Justice, *Alternative Federal Budget 1995* (Ottawa: CCPA, 1994). Specifically, they introduce an alternative budget based on Canadian establishment of monetary policy that includes a 1 per cent lower interest rate, tax reforms that reduce taxes for low-income Canadians, increased taxes for high-income earners and profitable companies and elimination of all unjustifiable tax loopholes and subsidies. Its foundational principles include a commitment to full employment and a more equitable distribution of income and wealth.

78 William Cline, for example, in *The Future of World Trade in Textiles and Apparel* (Washington: Institute for International Economics, 1987), presents three alternatives for the future of the textile and apparel industry: (a) increase protections immediately and decisively; (b) renew the Multi-Fibre Agreement constantly; and (c) set up a timetable to liberalize the industry. Favouring the latter, he includes adjustment to foreign competition through revitalization and by downsizing employment. In so doing, he sets job loss encountered under liberalized methods against both "the extremely high and distributionally regressive consumer costs" of protecting domestic industry and "the poor record of adjustment despite more than a quarter century of protection." He is convinced, however, that the apparel industry will survive, given the "record of relatively high apparel profits, the evidence on broad compensation of lower foreign wages by

lower foreign productivity." Refer to ibid., 1, 5, 19-22, and all of chapters 1 and 11. This stance is clearly from the corporate perspective and contrary to the position assumed by the Homework Coalition.

79 Warnock, *Free Trade and the New Right Agenda*, 40.

80 Ecumenical Coalition for Economic Justice (ECEJ), "Notes on the Globalization of the Economic and Political System" (Toronto, 31 March 1993), 4 (unpublished), and Ecumenical Coalition for Economic Justice (ECEJ), "Phase Out of Multifibre Arrangement Benefits Transnationals," *Economic Justice Report* 5, 1 (April 1994): 5.

81 ILGWU, *Designing the Future for Garment Workers*, 17.

82 Ibid., 18-19.

83 Leah Vosko, *The Last Thread: An Analysis of the Apparel Goods Provisions in the North American Free Trade Agreement and the Impact on Women* (Ottawa: Canadian Centre for Policy Alternatives, 1993), 3-10.

84 "U.S. Seeking Compromise with Canada on Rules of Origin for NAFTA Textiles," *Inside U.S. Trade*, 17 April 1992, 17-18. Refer also to Canadian Centre for Policy Alternatives in co-operation with Common Frontiers and the Action Canada Network, *Which Way for the Americas: Analysis of NAFTA Proposals and the Impact on Canada* (Ottawa, 1992), 52-54.

85 James Bovard, "NAFTA's Protectionist Bent," *The Globe and Mail*, 15 August 1992, B1, 3.

86 Vosko, *The Last Thread*, 9, referring to External Affairs Canada, *The North America Free Trade Agreement* (legal text) (Ottawa: External Affairs Canada, 1992), sec. 10, 3-B10.

87 Vosko, *The Last Thread*, 10.

88 Ibid., 9.

89 Barrie McKenna, "NAFTA: Day 1. Threat Won't Force Change," *The Toronto Star*, 1 January 1994, B1, 5. See Canadian Centre for Policy Alternatives, *Which Way for the Americas*, 117.

90 Daniel Drache, "Corporate Canada's Dream: Deal Makes Economic Continentalism a Political Reality," in *The Facts on Free Trade: Canada, Don't Trade It Away*, ed. Canadian Union of Public Employees (Ottawa, 1988), 35.

91 Annie Phizacklea, *Unpacking the Fashion Industry: Gender, Racism and Class in Production* (New York: Routledge, 1990), 40; for example, under tariff item 807, producers using outward processing pay duty only on the value added to the garment abroad. "Duties on some clothing items between Canada and the U.S. under the free-trade pact will be eliminated by 1994 and the rest by 1999."

92 Warnock, *Free Trade and the New Right Agenda*, 194. David Langille refers to *neo-conservatism* as promoting traditional values of patriotism, the family and religion, and *neo-liberalism* as actively establishing free market individualism. Although both require strong state intervention to promote their special interests, both camouflage their campaigns in a call for less government. See Langille, "The Business Council on National Issues and the Canadian State," 44. Also refer to the Ecumenical Coalition for Economic Justice, *Reweaving Canada's Social Programs*, 28, 31.

93 ILGWU, *Designing the Future for Garment Workers*, 10.

94 Ibid.
95 Ibid., 12.
96 Ibid., 20.
97 Ibid., 21. The sectoral partnership fund was designed to help each sector innovate, improve skill levels, increase technological capabilities, establish an Ontario home base, develop new networks and build international capabilities. The fund is to assist new technological capabilities, sectoral marketing, knowledge-sharing infrastructure development and upgraded programming.
98 Ibid., 21-22.
99 Ibid., 22.
100 John Dillon and the Ecumenical Coalition for Economic Justice (ECEJ), *Turning the Tide: Confronting the Money Traders* (Ottawa: Canadian Centre for Policy Alternatives, 1997), 2.
101 An annual artist's garden in front of York Quay Centre at the Toronto harbourfront displays and lists plants of the Americas along with this quotation.
102 Ibid., 6.
103 Xabier Gorostiaga, "The New Consensus: A Civilization Based on Harmony and Simplicity," presented to a New Development Options Conference in Oslo, Sweden, 1995, as referenced by Dillon and the ECEJ, *Turning the Tide*, 6.
104 The Ecumenical Coalition for Economic Justice (ECEJ) has published extensively on reasons for this, the effects and alternative means for reconstruction of economic justice. Refer to ECEJ publications: *Debt Bondage or Self-Reliance: A Popular Perspective on the Global Debt Crisis* (Toronto: GATT-Fly, 1985); *Recolonization or Liberation: The Bonds of Structural Adjustment and Struggles for Emancipation* (Toronto: ECEJ, 1990); *Reweaving Canada's Social Programs*; and Dillon and the ECEJ, *Turning the Tide*. Numerous ECEJ *Economic Justice Reports* focus on these as well.
105 Dillon and the ECEJ, *Turning the Tide*, 91.
106 Arthur Donner, "Recession, Recovery, and Redistribution: The Three R's of the Canadian State Macro-policy in the 1980s," in *The New Era of Global Competition: State Policy and Market Power*, edited by Daniel Drache and Meric Gertler (Montreal and Kingston: McGill-Queen's University Press, 1991), 27-47; Jonathan Ferguson and John Deverell, "Rate Hike Fuels Fear of New Recession," *The Toronto Star*, 22 June 1994, E1; and Roy Culpepper, "New Debt Crisis on Horizon," *The Toronto Star*, 22 June 1994, A19.
107 The Royal Bank of Canada has assets tripling those of the largest privately owned industrial corporation, Bell Canada (1974-89). The Bank Act (1967) had limited company or individual ownership of a chartered bank to 10 per cent and bank ownership of other companies to 10 per cent. When the conservative government under Brian Mulroney liberalized ownership rules, however, banks bought into large investment-dealing companies, making chartered banks the collective property of the monopoly capitalist class without state ownership. State intervention in fact set the rules to protect the collective interests of big business and the Bank Act codified the practices of their economic world in law. In 1995, for example, earnings of

Canada's six largest banks amounted to $6.2 billion. Business volumes and profitability of personal and commercial banks have grown strongly. The Bank of Canada is the major fiscal agent of the federal government. It controls the economy in many ways, including managing the public debt, issuing notes for circulation and controlling interest rates. Refer to Van Houten, *Corporate Canada*, 96, 174; Virginia Galt, "Federal Policies Common Thread in Protest: Garment Workers Demonstrate Over Job Losses as Bank Liquidates Upscale Firm," *The Globe and Mail*, 9 January 1991, A6; Marjorie Griffin Cohen, *Women and Economic Structures: A Feminist Perspective on the Canadian Economy* (Ottawa: Canadian Centre for Policy Alternatives, 1991), 9-11.

108 *The Globe and Mail*, 6 November 1993, as referenced by the International Ladies' Garment Workers' Union (ILGWU), Ontario District Council, *When One Door Closes ... Another Opens? A Follow-up Study on the Closure of the Great Sewing Exchange*, Researcher: Joan Atlin (Toronto: ILGWU, 1994), 19-20.

109 I painted a picture of a statue in Alameda Park in Mexico City. It had left a lasting impression on me from a visit when I represented churches against free trade in 1990.

3

The Macroeconomics of Garment Homeworking: The International Web of Production and Feminist Analysis of the Relations of Ruling

Webbed world

G arment production in Toronto happens within a global web with interlaced chains of processes and controls. I critique the relations of ruling which underline the international web of production as they affect garment homeworkers. The processes hidden behind purchases of clothing are global. They are also as local as each homeworker and each consumer.

Notes to chapter 3 are on pp. 82-87.

The International Web of Production in the Garment Industry

Why do homeworkers earn so little when they work so hard? Who benefits? Questions about the creation and appropriation of economic surplus are essential to determine structural causes of the devaluation of homeworkers' production and to locate present sources of power. This involves going beyond idealized economic theory to the reality of processing and marketing chains and to the international division of labour. Configurations of corporate power operate at each stage of commodity output. Confining analysis to any single commodity or working group is inadequate in view of the generalized process of global accumulation in the hands of an elite who interlace multi-commodity flows through the political, economic and marketing mechanisms of corporate expansion.

The textile industry is comprised of two basic integrated and overlapping marketing chains: first, the cotton/yarn/textile/clothing/textile machinery chain; second, the petroleum and natural gas/petrochemicals/chemical fibres chain. I name and, in some cases, briefly develop the links in these interconnected chains in the textile/garment industry in order to situate garment production in shifting global structures.

The First Chain: The Cotton/Yarn/Textile/ Clothing/Textile Machinery Line

My concentration in this section is on the garment industry with only an indication of other links.

Link 1: Natural Fibre Production

Plant fibres have been used for garments for thousands of years: flax as early as 10,000 B.C. and cotton since 3,000 B.C. Hemp and linen are also plant fibres. Wool, silk, vicuna and spider silk are animal fibres. Cotton and wool production are the most commercially significant in the first chain. Cotton output is fragmented, involving landless labourers, tenants, landlords and independent farmers, all open to exploitation by the conglomerates at the next link.

Link 2: Fibre Trading

Natural fibres, except silk and flax, are relatively short staple or discontinuous fibres.[1] Multicommodity traders market cotton and wool to spinners controlled by transnational conglomerates.

Link 3: Processing

The next step involves processing, which begins with yarn preparation. A highly developed fibre science serves industry by studying the basic chemical and physical structure of organic polymers and quality of solvents as they interact with water.

As previously set forth, for apparel to be counted as North American and therefore eligible for preferential duty access, a garment would have to be made from North American woven textiles made from North American spun yarn. This is particularly problematic for Canada because of the need to import much yarn and because the quotas for preferential rates are very low. State intervention holds little power for the Canadian textile and apparel industries when foreign interests are at stake. The restrictive trade rule regarding origins could block Canadian imports from Peru, India and China, drive costs up by 50 per cent and cost 55,000 (half of) Canadian textile jobs because of inability to compete with low wages and production costs in Mexico.[2] Among other concerns, Mexico objected to the stipulation that provisions of NAFTA "shall prevail over those of the Multifibre Agreement or any other agreement applicable to textile products between the parties."[3] The concerns around this legislation become clearer when the advancements in fibre technology are considered.

Link 4: Textile Weaving, Knitting and Manufacturing

This is the most capital intensive and highly automated segment. Central concerns in fibre science at this stage are mechanical properties, compression, tenacity, strength for stretching, bending, twisting and time and temperature dependence. Important physical properties include optical and thermal properties, friction, electrical conductivity and static charge build-up.[4]

Strong competition from several underdeveloped capitalist economies has shifted this work dramatically away from developed capitalist economies.[5] Manufacturers are caught between two segments of the chain that provide less output but more control: the chemical fibres and the textile machinery oligopoly, which works on new fibre specification and the clothing producers, and wholesale/retailers, who specify fabric and fibre content. Massive automation and rationalization sharply curtail employment as the overall productive capacity outpaces demand.

These links involve the production of rapidly expanding woven, non-woven, knitted, natural and variously constructed fabrics, the specialized finishing systems, fabric preparation, dyeing, printing processes and final functional and aesthetic finishes.[6] High-touch microfibres may surpass natural silk, be irridescent or scented. Power fibres store solar energy and protein fabrics feel like human skin. Super high-performance and functional fibres serve life sciences with biocompatible and biodegradable materials—for example, heat-resistant and lightweight fibres for space, high strength in oceans, insulators for energy conservation and functional, organic optical fibres for information technology.[7] In view of the extensive properties and uses of textiles, it is not surprising that the textile industry accounts for 3 per cent of all world trade.

Link 5: Clothing Manufacturing and Retailing

The next concentration of the clothing industry is in manufacturing and retailing. The Canadian clothing industry is concentrated in Quebec (69.5 per cent), Ontario (21.7 per cent), Manitoba (4.3 per cent) and other provinces (4.5 per cent).[8] The 1988 total employment of 95,800 in the garment industry in Canada fell to 62,300 by 1992. Two major forces are reshaping the industry. First, the economic crisis has reduced demand for new housing/home furnishings and automobiles/tires. Second, clothing markets are globalized and oversaturated. Undeveloped capitalist economies have also transformed the world market with dramatic increases in exports of clothing to developed ones, second only to petroleum.

My present concern is the major textile end use: the garment industry. Since both retailers and manufacturers are seeking to lower costs and raise profits by increasing productivity and by decreasing production time, they have restructured the industry. They cause globalization as well as respond to it. Even a decade ago, I might have described manufacturing and then the subsequent step of retailing. Now the changed lines of hierarchical control, from the few retailers at the top to the multitude of homeworkers at the bottom, constitute a pyramid of production and sales (see fig. 1). This hollow pyramid with its interdependent processes has several tiers: a centralized tier of retailers, a tier of large super-label manufacturers and jobbers, a tier of contractors and subcontractors, a tier of factory workers and sweatshops, and a tier of homeworkers. The framework for my description is based on that of the ILGWU, although I name contracting and subcontracting as one tier, regard factory workers as a separate tier and set all on the foundation of consumer power.[9] Retailers, like Eaton's, The Hudson's Bay Company and Sears, and manufacturers like Alfred Sung source both here and abroad for their labels.

Figure 1
The Garment Pyramid

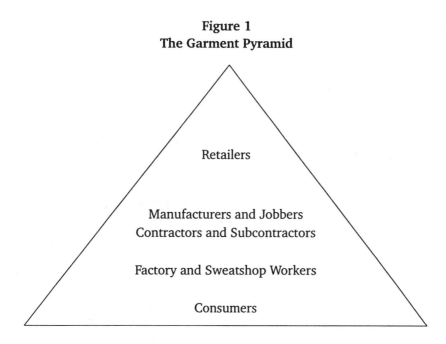

(a) *Retailers*. The economics of garment production has shifted because retailers control both production system and costs. In contrast to previous negotiations between the manufacturer and retailer to determine a selling price based on cost and profit, retailers now set the selling price unilaterally. Manufacturers must accept this or lose the contract. Retailers' markups now start at 100 per cent but are as high as 200 per cent for imported clothing. Clearly, retailers' gain is at the expense of others in the chain and at consumers' expense. Retailers' demands for lower prices mean that the only way for manufacturers to increase profits is to cut wages.[10] Nor have suppliers been able to counteract common practices of retailers who make unilateral decisions about stipulations and then deduct from manufacturers' invoicing if retail standards are not met. In 1993, for example, the National Apparel Bureau objected that the terms set by Hudson's Bay Company

> can only be viewed as an insult by these suppliers who serve you with integrity. Moreover, to attempt to burden your suppliers with your own regular operating costs and problems would constitute not only a contravention of fair trade policies established in our industry, but ... an unreasonable and unacceptable *"forced sharing"* of your own operational costs by suppliers.[11]

Since 1993, Eaton's obliged suppliers to comply with specific rules on packaging, prepricing, labeling and shipment accuracy. Their manual sets out the details and a system of penalties for non-compliance.[12] Having withdrawn from manufacturing, large retailers in Canada still set production demands in terms of time and quantity, requiring the firm to be fully "flexible."[13]

Use of private brands to replace producer trademarks gives retailers another lucrative opening for markups since it prevents consumer comparison of different clothing brand prices. Retailers such as the Gap, Benetton's and Dylex-owned Club Monaco control production of their own labels and the casual-wear market in Canada to the extent that they influence the way all clothes are produced.[14] Hudson's Bay, Eaton's and Dylex Ltd. pressure those all the way down the pyramid to lower costs in competition with low-wage imports. Cheaper imported clothing is sold at the same price as domestic products.

Increasingly retailers require manufacturers and subcontractors to carry the risks. In the late 1980s, for example, as retailers fought to retain profits in the midst of price competition and the recession, the Great Sewing Exchange, one of four major Toronto manufacturers of workwear and casual pants, met the demands of Mark's Work Wearhouse and Dylex-owned Harry Rosen for lower costs. Although retailers placed large orders, they would accept delivery of only a small portion at a time, dependent on sales. The manufacturer had both to wait increasingly long times for payments and to cover all costs of maintaining a large inventory. Cash flow was problematic. Sometimes manufacturers had to ship new orders even with previous retailer debts unpaid in order to obtain bank credit.[15]

A further example shows the impact of this requirement on homeworkers. The Bay's suppliers of women's clothing are subject to the Bay's electronic data interchange system, which allows the Bay to order specific demands without accumulating inventory, or at least to accept goods on consignment. The supplier, in turn, covers this added risk by reducing overhead. To achieve this, the manufacturer designs garments, buys textiles for them and then subcontracts the cutting and assembly operations to a jobber, who may in turn subcontract to still smaller contractors with sweatshops, and eventually to women working in their own homes. Total "jobbing," that is, contracting out the entire production, leads to empty factories or "hollow" corporations. Although retailers at the top of the pyramid do not hire homeworkers directly, they are related employers because they control the entire system of production timing and costs. According to the Coalition for Fair Wages and Working Conditions for Homeworkers, Dylex, Eaton's and the Hudson's Bay Company are related employers. They determine factors that control standards among other partners in garment production.[16] Examples of labels sewn by Toronto homeworkers who receive less than minimum wage are Braemar and Club Monaco of Dylex, Northern and Pursuits at Eaton's and Sensation and Global Casuals at the Bay.[17]

Retailers' reporting of "loss" raises serious questions about disclosure of information and camouflaging of information for the sake of maximizing profits. When representatives of Dylex, for example, reported a $55.4 million loss for 1991, the company said that "despite its disappointing 1991 results, 'Dylex maintained a strong balance sheet, with $117 million in cash on hand at year-end.' That figure does not include an additional $30.8 million raised in a share issue earlier this year."[18] Dylex operates about 1,300 stores in Canada and the United States.

Hudson's Bay Company profits in 1991 were $158.2 million from $4.6 billion sales.[19] Privately owned Eaton's sales totaled $2.3 billion.[20] As Heinzl notes, "Among department stores, Montreal-based Zellers Inc., the cash cow [sic] in the Toronto-based Hudson's Bay Company empire, opened fifty-eight stores. Meanwhile, Dylex's profitable BiWay unit added thirty-two locations."[21] Closing some stores and opening others is part of restructuring in which "expansion is key to the success."[22] In 1995, the Hudson's Bay Company controlled 40 per cent of all department store sales in Canada with 102 Bays, 296 Zellers and other banners amounting to nearly five hundred stores. Sales in 1994 rose to $5.8 billion, an overall increase of about 7 per cent. President George Kosich says of "the world's oldest corporation" that "we are pretty well everywhere we want to be."[23] The Bay steadily increased its purchases from the American suppliers who offered a lower price based on economies of scale.[24]

While proud of the Hudson's Bay Company's donation of 15 per cent of one day's sales from their annual United Way day, Kosich objects to the taxes charged in downtown Toronto and warns of the fate of stores there if these persist.[25] In the same month, the Metro Council threatened to cut grants to community groups such as Youthlink, a counseling group for street youth. This translated into a reduction for the second consecutive year of 9 to 10 per cent of Youthlink's $92,706 annual budget.[26] The issue of large retailers' rights to amass vast surplus while finding ways to evade substantial community responsibility needs public attention.

In 1995, Dylex filed for bankruptcy under the Companies' Creditors Arrangement Act but needed to alter plans because of landlords' opposition.[27] Investments in the U.S., especially in the chain NBO, brought loss and the company wanted to restructure. A unionized factory, Numode Dress, was particularly vulnerable since restructuring often involves closures of union plants and new contracts only with non-unionized firms.

In the midst of major corporate restructuring and in filing for bankruptcy, my reasonably well-grounded concern is that restructuring, bankruptcy and use of the term loss may sometimes be devices to maximize profits, to gain control of an administrative board and/or to confuse the public. These goals involve cutting staff, avoiding taxes, gaining tax credits, undermining the research set forth by citizens' groups and continuing exploitative practices under a new name or names. To the extent this scenario is actualized, the company masquerades the moral issues of responsibility and accountability to the community. In such circumstances, social immorality remains regardless of acceptable business practice or technicalities won through a legal system.

(b) *Jobbers and Manufacturers.* Some manufacturers may still control their own chain of production with their own labels. Others keep mainly high-end designer labels but simply organize production. As jobbers, their processing includes design, purchasing of textile and cutting the garments. From here, they shift production to contractors, sweatshops and homeworkers. The trend in manufacturing, however, is toward hollow corporations with all processes contracted out.

Three exclusive brand names, Jones New York, Liz Claiborne and Alfred Sung, dominate the women's clothing market in department stores. Liz Claiborne produces in forty-eight countries but not in Canada. Operating on quick response, these super labels produce a new fashion concept or new line of styles every six weeks with a new colour line every fifteen days. With federal and provincial funding, Toronto opened a new design centre in an effort to support specialization in the high-fashion niche.

Because of Alfred Sung's use of homeworkers at less than minimum wages and because this label involves an example of a hollow pyramid, its story is of particular interest here.[28] Alfred Sung started out in a unionized factory called Monaco Group which chose to follow

Benetton strategy, shifting design to a separate corporation called Alfred Sung Designs. After short-term involvement with many different corporations, they reorganized to create a company called Mimran Group Inc. Doing no production at all, Mimran Group Inc. owns the label and licenses parts of the Alfred Sung empire to various companies. After closing one of their unionized factories, they continued the label within a series of network firms, producing purses, bridal gowns, sunglasses and women's clothing.

From 1990 to 1993, ETAC Sales Ltd. was responsible for manufacturing and marketing all Alfred Sung ladies' wear in what was intended to be a fifty-year license. In addition, ETAC held rights to manufacture and market the Canadian labels of Ports International, Tabi International and Britches. It owned and operated Ports International, Tabi, Alfred and Alfred Sung stores and, in 1992, purchased Bretton's, a Canadian chain of department stores. Behind these retail stores and the Alfred Sung label were the small contracting shops and homeworkers who produced the clothing. By 1994, the ETAC chain had overextended its management capabilities, and lost on quick response because of production in China. It ended in bankruptcy. The Alfred Sung licence is still owned by the Mimran Group. In 1995, Alfred Sung women's wear was linked with Mr. Leonard clothing manufacturing.

The ILGWU describes three basic strategies created by manufacturers to stay competitive.[29] First, the quick-response system is designed to shorten turnaround time between design, production and availability in stores from at least twelve months to less than three weeks. On the positive side, quick-response goals encourage companies to remain in Ontario and in factories to lessen turnaround time. This system also reduces retailers' inventory. Introduced in the U.S. by Wal-Mart in 1984, this form of just-in-time production was taken up in Canada by Eaton's, then the Hudson's Bay Company and Dylex. Workers are employed on a short-term, as-needed basis.

A serious problem in the quick-response pipeline, however, is Canada's need to import textiles after federal government policies downsized and rationalized production of fashion garment fabrics in the 1980s. Introduction of the system is uneven in the garment industry and manufacturers are clear that they are submitting to retailers' new rules of holding all inventory, of completing all inventory preparation and of reducing production because, at the present, they think they have little power to change the way retailers operate. (What effect might organized strategic action achieve on manufacturers' part?)

According to ILGWU research in unionized factories, manufacturers' response is varied. It ranges from closing the factory, downsizing production lines and relying on imports even for 50 per cent of a line, increasing use of contractors, finding the lowest labour costs and reliance on retailers' private-label production for the majority of their work. The context of free trade, however, has relativized the value of licensing agreements.

The second strategy is the introduction of new technology which makes response to quick fashion demands possible. Information technology software packages facilitate instantaneous tracking of production and costs, as well as point-of-sale information. Electronic data interchange (EDI) between retailers and manufacturers, integrated statistical monitoring productivity and replacing piecework ticketing and inventory and bar coding packages all serve to monitor workflow and pace and to redesign inventory systems worldwide. Benetton, the Italian clothing firm, for example, operates a rapid, integrated response system globally.

Computer-aided design and computer-aided manufacturing (CAD/CAM) are now available in computer software format for pattern design, grading sizes and layout. One computer operator can run a cutting system guiding automated cutters to use motor-driven cutting knives. For manufacturers, this translates into speed, accuracy and fabric and labour savings, using one cutter instead of four or five. Jones New York, for example, cuts in its high-tech, computer-aided shops. From there, the work is dispersed to contracting shops and to homeworkers.

Two advances in sewing machines have been introduced. A dedicated or single-purpose machine completes only one operation, such as setting pockets or hemming pant legs. Programmable machines have timers which preset the length of time allotted for the operation and then increase the pace for repetition of the same operation. The machine records the number of pieces completed. It also cuts threads automatically. In practice, technological change is regarded as a limited option by manufacturers. Even investment in a new electronic data interchange system with a retailer provides no guarantee that the retailer will continue to rely on that supplier.

The third strategy to make the industry more competitive is to introduce work methods known as synchronous, flexible or modular manufacturing. The goal is to increase productivity in less time. Unit production systems were introduced in the early 1960s. By presenting and removing garments or pieces directly, these systems reduce labour costs and electronically monitor both the number completed and the time required. They shorten total production cycles from fifteen days to six days.[30] Modular manufacturing involves the formation of teams of employees who are responsible for all decisions regarding the performance of tasks. A team sews a complete garment by sharing measurable tasks in turn. Cross-trained, workers are expected to complete more tasks and eliminate all buffer time among themselves. Payment depends on team productivity.

To a great extent, Toronto garment firms have turned to homework production in lieu of technological advancement. The issue of increasing technology is fraught with contradictions and problems—for example, the impact on workers. Since machines such as those made by Gerber are designed for large shops, they are too heavy for the prevalent twenty-or-less-employee shops which are often located on second stories. Current efforts to reduce the size of machines will also reduce costs significantly.

Current manufacturing emphasis, therefore, centres on expectations and programs that are quick, flexible and capable of developing a whole new attitude. Their goal is to save labour costs and move production rapidly through the factory and/or subcontracting system. Small enterprises bear the risks and uncertainties of fluctuating sales.[31]

(c) *Contracting, Subcontracting and Sweatshops.* In the last chapter, I discussed outward processing and the creation of export-oriented production zones in undeveloped capitalist economies. For manufacturers, this means that costs are cut by designing and cutting in the home country, but contracting out the most labour-intensive apparel phases to countries with lower wage rates. They reimport even partially finished items for finishing and packaging.

Although the idea of this type of subcontracting system has changed little in the last hundred years, the system's spatial boundaries have expanded to global horizons. As already emphasized, power to dictate production requirements has shifted to the transnational retailers.[32] Large technologically advanced manufacturers based in Hong Kong or Korea, for example, supply major retailers and control subcontracting wherever they can obtain the cheapest labour and most favourable quota and tariff rates.[33] Along with North American-based companies, these Asian companies contract work in free-trade zones in China, Macao, Mauritius, Thailand and Malaysia and the entire Caribbean Basin.

Major cheap-labour production areas have emerged globally. Just as Canadian and American firms have relocated in the maquiladoras south of the Mexican border, German firms expanded to Poland, Hungary, Czech and Slovak republics, beyond the Oder-Neisse line and the former Berlin wall. Japan shifted much of its manufacturing to Thailand and the Philippines.[34]

The Canadian apparel market includes 45 per cent imports. Seventy-eight per cent of these are from low-wage countries.[35] The trend toward sweatshops and cheap labour is conspicuously present in Ontario as well.

> The restructuring in the garment industry is most apparent in the rise of both smaller workplaces and the emergence of a greater number of contracting shops. In 1971 only 22 per cent of the industry was made up of shops with fewer than twenty workers. By 1991 this picture had reversed itself so that 76 per cent of clothing production was in shops with fewer than twenty workers. The number of contracting shops in Ontario grew from only four in 1971 to over 116 in 1991. (In fact, we would argue, available statistics woefully underestimate the number of contractors in the province.) Contractors often run a fly-by-night operation, opening and closing with great rapidity.[36]

Contractors and subcontractors do little design or marketing. With the role of production alone, they are viciously competitive, especially in terms of labour costs and quick turnaround time in both small shops and homes, often avoiding minimum employment standards legislation. In fact, it was for accessibility and speed that the system of subcontracting arose in seasonal and fashion-led areas of production.[37]

(d) *Factory Workers*. Groups of garment factory workers and union personnel in Toronto identified central key issues for the ILGWU.[38] High unemployment and repeated plant closures cause fear of job loss and create a climate of hostility. Threats of further closures and contracting out curtail worker initiative. Pressures for increased productivity in shortened time translate into a hectic pace with unrelenting anxieties in the workplace in order to maximize profits for others. Workers and their unions are pressured to work faster for lower wages and to concede in tougher contract negotiations. Collective agreements, particularly regarding contracting-out clauses, are violated. New technology means deskilling, expectations for multitasking and job loss. Lay-offs are alternated with condensed work times. On-the-job harassment, particularly for those who do not speak English, is increasing. Health and safety questions are left unanswered. There is a steady shift to part-time, temporary jobs in factories and warehouses. The social costs and real working conditions for workers are increasingly ignored by those on higher tiers of the pyramid.

In short, quick response is a form of lean production that pressures workers in unionized factories to comply with whatever direction management desires. While retailers and management call for flexibility, workers are required to meet shortfalls in a production quota, to fill gaps in multiskilled production and to accept part-time work, wage concessions and piece rates. The core group of workers is reduced in the midst of a startling shift to non-standard work.[39] The ILGWU emphasizes the context of restructured work in the garment industry: precarious or non-standard work is one of the most rapidly expanding sectors of the economy.[40] Workers are being forced into isolated, unprotected work patterns in Canada and abroad.

As undeveloped capitalist economies increase industrial exports, have more job-cutting technological innovations, face economic stagnation and negotiate as debtors, they are particularly vulnerable to similar trends in the free market system.[41] Intense competition among thread-bare wage earners who cannot afford to purchase the goods they produce starkly contrasts the control by monopolies and oligopolies who increase profits exponentially. While the latter move unhindered around the globe in search of the cheapest labour costs, the workers tend to be held immobile within their home countries, like Mexico, or within the European Union.[42] The oversupply of production in depressed areas reduces factory prices and industrial profits. International traders and distributors appropriate the accruing surplus, even "adding value" not by labour but by transportation to and sale in the market. It has become abundantly clear that as the market and technology centralized, production became more and more fragmented and decentralized, reinforcing the international division of labour.[43] Drive for low-wage labour affects garment factory workers and homeworkers internationally:

> In Mexico City, the number of garment workers declined from 70,000 in 1981 to 45,000 in 1991. The destruction of the domestic industry in Mexico as a result of free trade policies parallels our experience in Canada. Jobs have shifted from large factories, to clandestine sweatshops and homework, with no enforceable standards. The garment jobs being created in the maquiladora free trade zones are still primarily along the border (but now also in and around Mexico City) where women workers labour long hours, six days a week for a wage of $5 a day. What's produced is for export only—

often re-imported into Mexico with "made in the U.S. labels" and available at cheaper prices than "domestic" products.[44]

About 70 per cent of the 500,000 workers in Mexico's 2,000 Maquila factories are women.[45]

Exploitation of labour happens interracially and intraracially. The drive for profits through neo-liberal policies such as free trade reveals the polarity that already exists along class and political lines.[46] The plight of homeworkers in Canada and Mexico is directly related to domination by stateless corporations.[47]

(e) *Homeworkers.* At the bottom of the pyramid are the home-workers who traditionally have held little bargaining power. In the quick-response system, contractors set work schedules, often over a weekend. A homeworker is expected to be available for work upon demand and may deal with several contractors in a month. With factory workers, home-workers assume the costs of production in their low wages, pressured working conditions and lack of benefits. These costs have been shifted downward from retailers to manufacturers, to contractors and subcon-tractors. Precarious, low-wage work is structured into the present system of garment production in increasingly oppressive ways.

Clothing sewn by Toronto homeworkers who are paid less than minimum wage is marketed under the labels Braemar, Braemar Petites, Daniel Hechter, Club Monaco, Northern Pursuits, Sensation, Global Casuals, Cotton Ginny, Lida Baday, Franco Mirabelli, Alfred Sung, Jones New York, Sunny Choi, Norma Peterson, Sally Fourney Associ-ates, Cleo, Elite, Select, Blouseworks, Peter Chan, Freda's, Zakura, Jethro Bodine, Athena, Dino Classic, Via Condotti, Bianca, Silhouettes and Action Sports.[48]

(f) *Consumers.* The largest group in the link of production and sales is comprised of all consumers who purchase textiles and clothing locally and globally. The market stands or falls on consumer prefer-ences, fads and fashions, needs and purchasing power. Consumer research shows that two thirds of Canadian shoppers would be more likely to shop in stores that advertise and promote ethical products and that shoppers would more likely be treated honestly and fairly there. Consumers explicitly link ethical retailing and good service. Shoppers' long-term needs are for fit, quality, durability, price and good service. Another significant observation of the researchers is that Canadians appear to want a viable base for the future. They note,

In particular this study has revealed that, perhaps as a reflection of the upheaval in the traditional expectations about the workplace, most Canadians are willing to, and indeed seem anxious to, purchase clothing made by workers in Canada who are treated fairly. Not only will they purchase such products, a majority of them will gladly pay more than for items made under "unethical" conditions.[49]

It seems that there is new market opportunity for manufacturers and retailers who are socially and environmentally responsible.

Link 6: The Textile Machine Industry

From the early spindles and the spinning jenny, the water-powered frame of 1769 shifted textile production to factory systems. Other inventions, like the spinning mule (1779) and heavy-duty wide looms (1823), prepared the way for steady improvements in machinery. In 1851, Isaac Singer of Boston, Massachusetts, produced the first practical domestic sewing machine.[50] In 1960, open-end spinning was developed in Czechoslovakia to produce high-quality yarn faster, and in the 1970s lasers were introduced to cut clothing in bulk processes.

The global machinery market for the production of both textiles and garments is controlled by a small number of transnational machinery producers. Although Singer, for example, has dominated sewing machine production, its profitable operations in power tools, electronics and credit expand their finance base far beyond the sewing sector. Billionaire James Ting of Markham, Ontario, is the chief executive officer of International Semi-Tech Microelectronics Inc., which has entered the Chinese consumer market in a joint venture with Singer Co. N.V. to build a plant in Shanghai and to establish China's first installment purchase plan.[51] With the Singer Credit Co. Ltd. in China and in Ho Chi Minh City, Vietnam, they expect growth comparable to Thailand and the Philippines. Singer's world headquarters is in Wanchai, Hong Kong, with a distribution network that spans over one hundred companies.[52] In addition to being the world's largest manufacturer, marketer and distributor of consumer and industrial sewing machines, Singer markets a wide range of consumer electronic products, home appliances and home furniture.

Toyota is one of the leading textile machinery corporations. Corporate aerospace laboratories, such as Hughes Aircraft, have made breakthroughs in computerized clothing machinery. Also to be noted here is the fact that new technology promotes use of chemical fibres because the speed of operations is incompatible with natural fibres. This strengthens the relations between the machine industry and the entire second chain.

As is evident globally, the clothing industry has relied historically on labour-intensive manual processes of marking, pattern-cutting, ironing, inspection, labeling and packing. But far-reaching innovations such as water-jet cutting are now being applied to cloth. Mass production cutting, however, is required to offset the high capital costs of improved die-cutting and laser-beam cutting. Innovations in sewing have been towards higher operating speeds. The main emphasis is on workplace engineering and automatic transfer to replace sewing altogether with textile bonding agents and meltable interlining fabrics. A device pioneered by the U.S. Cluett-Peabody, one of the "big clothing ten" with its own machinery company, can pick up a piece of fabric and position it for sewing, a breakthrough vital to replacing the sewing machine operator. New technologies include electronic and financial data interchange; computer-aided design, cutting, grading and marking; computer-controlled spreaders, hanging and sorting; auto serging, dart tucking, loop tacking, bag and sort; contour seaming; and bar coding. Ultrasonic sewing, in which high-frequency sound waves are used on materials with a high synthetic content to simulate stitching, creates a frictional bond between layers of thermoplastic cloth. Canadian manufacturers have implemented a low to moderate level of modernization.[53] Implementation is slow because of the capital intensity, complicated processes and lack of need as long as cheap labour keeps profits high.

Control of the world market requires a comprehensive marketing web with sales services, punctual delivery dates, meeting users' needs, provision for comprehensive training and systematic spare-parts flow. This marketing web is expensive and possible only for transnationals who are able to invest in research and therefore reap its benefits.[54] Without national loyalties, transnationals base their production sites where labour costs, markets and tariffs serve their demand for capital accumulation. Frequently, more automation holds neither promise of better remuneration nor more secure or fulfilling jobs for the workers.

Second Chain: Petroleum and Natural Gas/Petrochemicals/ Chemical Fibres
Link 1: Petroleum and Natural Gas Production

The U.S.A., Russia, the Middle East, Latin America and China are well known for their production of petroleum and natural gas. In 1960, the Organization of the Petroleum Exporting Countries (OPEC) was instituted to co-ordinate production and exporting policies of its Middle Eastern and Latin American member nations.[55]

The Near East Cultural and Educational Foundation of Canada revealed strategic international trade connections underlying the importance of this link:

> George Bush may have spoken the truth when he said that Iraq's seizure of Kuwait threatened "the American Way of Life." The short-term costs of blockading Iraq are enormous, not only for the U.S., but for many others as well, including Canada.... An indefinite U.S. military presence "for regional security" purposes would position the U.S. to secure favourable trading arrangements and to influence the price and flow of oil to Europe and Japan. It would secure a competitive edge for American business interests over European and Japanese businesses.
>
> Now that Canada is tied so closely to the U.S. economy through free trade, the health of that economy in the face of stiff European competition, is of prime concern to the government which engineered the free trade agreement.... Canadian involvement appears to be advantageous in the short-run and in the long-run as well.[56]

The petroleum industry, which includes production of petrochemicals and chemical fibres, is a central American "interest."

Link 2: Production of Chemical Fibres

In 1824, chemist Charles Mackintosh produced the first waterproof garments using rubber.[57] But it was not until 1892 that chemists created the first artificial fibre, rayon, from cellulose. In 1935, a Dupont chemist discovered nylon which, in 1948, was used to create velcro. The era of natural fibres such as cotton and wool lasted generally until the 1950s, when synthetic fibres like nylon and polyester appeared as a "second generation" of light, high-strength fibres. Processing petroleum and natural gas into petrochemicals supplies the primary feedstock for the development of chemical fibres.

In the early 1980s, general-purpose and specialty fibres were improved to become high-functional fibres. By combining fine spinning and fine processing using highly reliable technology, researchers have responded to demands for energy conservation, ocean/air developments from earth to outer space, requirements for transportation, sports and leisure. Since 1984 superfibres emerged as a chemical and technological triumph, "as a direct consequence of cellulose being re-evaluated world-wide as a renewable resource following the oil crisis."[58] The Japanese led in the creation of "high-touch" imitations of natural fur, silk, wool and leather. The stage is set for the replacement of metals by fibres marked for their tenacity and strength.

This second chain intersects the first one at the stage of textile manufacturing where corporate owners promoting chemical fibres are systematically and irreversibly eroding fibre end-uses that depend on cotton. Although the chemical fibre industry represents only a fragment of the total chemical industry, it yields the highest returns on investments.[59] U.S. firms maintain hegemony over the chemical oligopoly with over two thirds of carpets, clothing and tires, for example, having synthetic origins.

The outline of the links of the chains suggests how people use levels of automation and capital intensity to determine geographical location and to constitute the labour force for the generation of goods and services, creating the international division of labour. Maintaining advantage for some investors depended on the post-Second World War separation of colonial and semicolonial raw-material-producing countries from metropolitan manufacturing ones. Since then, however, corporate capital investors have established industrial sites around the world, a process clearly visible in the production and export of textiles, clothing and chemical fibres. Corporate drive is for lower-cost raw materials and labour inputs, for more lucrative investment outlets, potential industrial markets, free-trade zones, tax write-offs and lack of environmental regulations.

The extremes of the chains are, on the one hand, the landless labourers on cotton plantations and the homeworkers or sweatshop workers in the garment industry contrasted, on the other hand, with those who wield power in the strategic deployment of corporate chemical and petrochemical output with their marketing research expertise. Those who concentrate capital at the trading level gain global power as multicommodity, conglomerate corporations dominate the global scene.[60]

Feminist Analysis of the Relations of Ruling in the Garment Industry

By juxtaposing the actual situations of homeworkers in the garment industry together with their capitalist context in the previous chapters, and with the global web of production in this chapter, I have foregrounded power relations affecting homeworkers' everyday lives. I now turn to the specific question of the power relations, viewing these relations intentionally through a feminist lens, provided in part by the work of sociologist Dorothy Smith. This method also clarifies some of the fault lines which offer possibilities for transformation.

I take the term "relations of ruling" and its meaning from Dorothy Smith as an analytic category. Since I want to apply it and develop its relevance regarding my theme, I quote Smith at length. Relations of ruling involve

> identifying a complex of organized practices, including government, law, business and financial management, professional organization and educational institution as well as the discourses in texts that interpenetrate the multiple sites of power. A mode of ruling has become dominant that involves a continual transcription of the local and particular actualities of our lives into abstracted and generalized forms. It is an *extralocal* mode of ruling. Its characteristic modes of consciousness are objectified and impersonal; its relations are governed by organizational logics and exigencies. We are not ruled by powers that are essentially implicated in particularized ties of kinship, family and household, and anchored in relationships to particular patches of ground. We are ruled by forms of organization vested in and mediated by texts and documents, and constituted externally to particular individuals and their personal and familial relationships. The practice of ruling involves the ongoing representation of the local actualities of our worlds in the standardized and general forms of knowledge that enter them into the relations of ruling. It involves the construction of the world as texts, whether on paper or in computer, and the creation of a world in texts as a site of action. Forms of consciousness are created that are properties of organization or discourse rather than of individual subjects.[61]

Rational organization, which is supposedly objective, impersonal and universal, is paramount in determining and maintaining such relations of ruling. Although the gender subtext is invisible in its discourse, focus on historical practice serves to make gender relations explicit. Gender roles and relations are evident in the private life of sexuality, family and interpersonal relations, which are for the most part considered marginal, left unremunerated and regarded as informal economy by institutions of ruling. Introductory social analysis reveals that gender has been socially constructed with men representing the masculine, "neutral" principles. I address this point later.

The point to make here is that the subtext concealed beneath supposedly impersonal forms contains vested interests favouring men. It is integral to the system and it excludes women from sharing in power within textually mediated relations of ruling. As these exclusive modes of thinking became traditional, ideological positions solidified to defend the status quo. They legitimized and sanctioned the social order in which women had neither adequate time nor social and material means to participate in creating categories of analysis adequate to their experience or to define and raise social consciousness about their concerns.

These relations of ruling were organized historically as an intricate part of the construction of capitalism. Shifts of capital concentration from small-scale enterprises to local family firms to merged corporations changed property relations significantly. Managerial process became organizationally more technical, accounting more complex and analysis more comprehensive in assessing the economic environment, supply and demand. As management became more self-conscious of organizational process, it began to measure performance of different departments in relation to one another and in terms of the entire enterprise. Dorothy Smith observes that "social relations, organizations ... became conceptualized as discrete and self-conscious processes quite separable as such from the particular individuals who performed and brought them into being as concrete social activities."[62]

What is particularly significant is that the dominant extralocal viewpoint of society and social relations was not located in particular localities or in local social relations, other than those of a mainly male elite in corporations, banks, governments and churches. The separation of the formal economy and economic theory from the locus of the particular, from subjectivity and from local social relations was rapidly solidifying. Managers created an economy in which they were able to transform actualities into forms of thought which could then be used in an abstracted conceptual mode of ruling.

Economists gained confidence in organizing their concepts and evaluations into categories, observations and texts quite separate from the workers' realities and concrete material processes. The actual practices of economic relations were changed into labour relations, business confidence, categories of skilled and unskilled labour, quotas, minimum wages, supply and demand, interest rates and, later, maximization of profits, globalization, competition, privatization, deregulation, mobility of capital and restructuring. In this context, it was not too difficult to separate money from its material gold base, as American President Nixon did in 1971. Capital creation, wealth and power based on it escalate exponentially, as illusory cybermoney in the disconnection from the base of global, lived reality.[63] The new phase of speculative capitalism burst upon us.

People thus became organized in relation to the abstracted, conceptual mode of ruling. Economic consciousness became located in corporations distant from local communities and controlled by unknown elites. Such objectification contributes to a more pervasive reification of persons. Economic knowledge has meant that the knowers start already located outside themselves. Economic democracy steadily diminished as people lost the ability to think about choices, effects, social organization and action in terms of systems and of social processes external to the individuals themselves.

Traditional ruling establishes a mode of knowing, experiencing and acting that is based on the textual and beyond the body-space of ordinary living. Ironically, women at the base are needed to sustain these relations of ruling. By taking care of household chores, parenting, nursing, secretarial and cleaning jobs, routine computer work, as well as most primary education, women's work allows for this disconnected organization of consciousness. Women, and increasingly underemployed men, provide body-related logistics that permit others largely to bypass the bodily location of consciousness.

Many people came to expect that others will not only fill their needs without reciprocal service but justify their split consciousness and being out of touch with the ordinary with rationalizations such as "Time is money." Too often "the place of women, then, in relation to this mode of action is where the work is done to facilitate men's occupation of the conceptual mode of action.... At almost every point women mediate for men the relation between the conceptual mode of action and the actual concrete forms on which it depends."[64] A vicious circle is deepened as such work in turn protects too many men against the very grounding and being in touch that offers possibilities for healing. The two worlds are not simply the public and private but the split consciousness "with a world directly experienced from oneself as centre (in the body) on the one hand and a world organized in the abstracted conceptual mode, external to the local and particular places of one's bodily existence."[65]

Suppression of interest in local and material realities has been organized into a division of labour that accords to others—women, especially black women and women of colour and some men without power—the production and maintenance of the material aspects of a total process. The interests of transnational corporate rulers prey on the economic needs of the most vulnerable economic groups. Their power game to maximize profits regardless of the social costs, and often the environmental ones as well, dominates and fuels the system.

Social construction of labour segmentation includes personalization of the market so that its processes appear inevitable. Pat Armstrong critiques the surrender of responsibility implied in such language, evident in claims such as this: "The market has become the major source of power, of control, of change, and thus it sets the conditions in our society as well as the outlines of what is valued as work."[66] The organization of this division becomes visible from the base where people are most silenced, at least as long as fear controls them. The modes of action that suppress the concrete and material and, with them, the local, particular and material locus of consciousness depend on this silence to maintain the illusion that the conceptual alone is reality. The market is personalized and of ultimate value even as masses of people are disposable.

Feminist critique arises from outside these relations of ruling. The starting point for economic evaluation is not in the principles of economic theory, but within the working conditions and wages of the working poor, such as the homeworkers. In this case, the disjuncture is between the actual experience of homeworkers and the texts or theories which the government, bankers and retailers suggest as good economy. Homeworkers are invisible in such textual modes. At most they are present as objects, not as subjects giving their own standpoint.[67] The vocabulary, concepts, symbols, frames of reference, forms of thought and institutionalized structures of reference used in deciding economic priorities exclude these women. Corporate control ensures public acceptance of this system as an inevitable economy, social knowledge and practice.

Interests in capital accumulation have taken control of the production and dissemination of knowledge, influencing how people see, think and limit categories of imagining alternatives. As external relations expand within corporate domination, local input and participation in decision making diminish. This has the serious effect of establishing the differentiation between the public and the private as systemic structure. Functions of knowledge, judgement and will are transferred to governing processes of capitalistic enterprises, to bureaucratic administration, to extended social relations of textually mediated discourse and to the productive and market processes. It is not only democratic participation that is suffocated. The very confidence in the general public to consider itself capable of understanding the system is destroyed. Ironically, paralysis and withdrawal in the face of such bureaucracy may be "sane alienation from a sick system."[68] Yet this retreat has left control more firmly in the hands of those disconnected from the actualities of ordinary family and community life.

Figures 2a and 2b delineate the process. They are based on and expand the work of Dorothy Smith.[69]

Figure 2a

Capitalism

- new and constantly changing terrain: laissez faire, liberal, globalize, financial

  - external to the local

  - excludes participation of personally mediated economic and social relations

intimately linked with

Relations of Ruling

- their profit, organization and expansion

The Surrender of Local Democracy and of Sovereignty

Progressively massive shift:

As the external expands, the local diminishes:

Separation of the public

and private becomes part of societal structures.

Surrender personal and group agency and decision making.
Surrender ability to think,
    to claim own knowledge as valid,
    to judge,
    to choose governing process.
Surrender local democracy.

Rule by transnational corporate and financial elite who control bureaucratic governments.
Their texts and theories are the site of action and norm of legitimacy.

Figure 2b

Relations of Ruling

Realities: relationships, practicalities, organization, meaning and values

When realities
> are abstracted, generalized and objectified,

whether
> by governments, by corporations or by churches,

to become
> impersonal and rational,

the resulting discourse
> is apparently neutral

but it extensively excludes
> women of all "races" and many men.

Institutions Organize the Discourse

- governed by organizations' logic
- generally the standpoint of some men with power and/or wealth
- gender and "racial" subtexts
- gender and division of labour

Construction of the world with texts and theories as the sites of action

- creates forms of consciousness that are properties of organizations
- discourse does not include those outside the power structure's operative boundaries
- the excluded are labeled as special interest groups
- controls the production and dissemination of knowledge
- affects how both women and men think and feel, what horizons we hold and what kind of imagining and alternatives we allow

---

Conclusion

The macroeconomics of garment production, marketing and distribution shed light on the situations of homeworkers. Focus on global aspects of apparel production locates control of power and profit in the present structure, especially within socio-economic relations external to the local, everyday world of most work and the particularities of personally mediated relations. Feminist analysis of relations of ruling reveals how women's invisibility is maintained by apparently neutral, impersonal discourse. This analysis lays the groundwork for making judgements both of facts and of values.

If we are to achieve long-term economic justice for homeworkers, it is not enough just to describe their wages and working conditions. That is a necessary beginning. Their everyday world is not fully explicable within its own scope. Nor is it easily possible to observe the structures that impact on them. The reason is not only the size and complexity of the stateless corporations. It is also connected with corporate control, popular powerlessness and community stratification. The fundamental form of social organization has changed dramatically in this century, reversing, for example, traditional government control of the economy and institutions in favour of the present corporate agenda of governments and banks.

Since these changes did not arise out of a logic of organization within the local setting on which they are now being imposed, people tend to regard them as inevitable or at least too complex for them to have any possibility of influence over them.

Socially organized forms of living by which individuals and communities depend upon one another become externalized as a differentiated system of relations. People in the same community are stratified so that, although they live alongside one another, their social relations are organized by relations external to the area without their direct participation. Those controlling relations organize the processes of material and social organization which may be experienced as disorganization, incoherence and lack of sense at the local level. Nevertheless, corporations have managed to direct the actual material setting and social organization so extensively as to universalize their properties. Thus actual settings are conceptually substitutable as are different local and particular places readily substitutable.

Through macroeconomic analysis, I have continued to unmask roots of women's invisibility in society. Understanding the complexity of factors can facilitate the generation of options for organized short-

and long-term solutions to the current problems faced by homeworkers. I have focused on the implications of seeing the relations of
ruling from the perspective of a local reality. Complex, bureaucratic,
corporate protection secures and augments an international system
involving homeworkers. The task remains, of course, to go beyond and
underneath the structures to understand deeper causes of exploitation
as well as opportunities for transformation.

As oppressive as the situation is, I believe in a transformative possibility brought about in part by integrating the conceptual and the concrete. In chapter 4, I turn attention to another set of relations, a social
movement in which unions, homeworkers, community groups and
churches form a coalition intent on strategizing and acting for effective
change in the garment industry.

Notes

1 An average cotton fibre is approximately three centimetres long, while an
average wool fibre is about ten centimetres long.
2 Jonathan Ferguson, "Textile Firms Warn of Job Loss," *The Toronto Star*, 7
April 1992, A5.
3 "NAFTA Text on Textiles," *Inside U.S. Trade*, 27 March 1992, S1. "The
investment provisions would severely constrain the ability of Mexico or any
other less developed country that later joins the free trade zone to set rules
and conditions for foreign investors to foster national development. One
clause would prevent any heavily indebted Latin American or Caribbean
member country from declaring a moratorium on its onerous debt payments." Refer to "NAFTA Negotiating Text Exposes Hypocrisy of Mulroney
Government," *Continental Trade Alert* 6, 3 (24 March 1992): 2, note 3.
4 Steven Warner, *Fiber Science*. (Prentice Hall: Englewood Cliffs, NJ 1995),
Introduction, 6.
5 Developed Capitalist Economy: DCE; Underdeveloped Capitalist Economy:
UCE; and Centrally Planned Economy: CPE. This naming clarifies its intrinsically biased economic interests in reference to people of differing cultures. I
use it only to expose global production according to capitalistic relations.
6 Refer to Peyton Hudson, Anne Clapp and Darlene Kness, *Textile Science*, 6th
ed. (New York: Harcourt Brace College Publishers, 1993).
7 Tatsuya Hongu and Glyn Phillips, *New Fibres* (Toronto: Ellis Horwood,
1990), 47, 51-84.
8 Johnson and Johnson, *The Seam Allowance*, 20. Three quarters of Canadian
garment production is done in Montreal, Toronto and Winnipeg. According
to Statistics Canada, in 1975 there were 2,318 garment manufacturing
firms in Canada and approximately 120,000 workers.
9 ILGWU, *Designing the Future for Garment Workers*, 35-49.
10 International Ladies' Garment Workers' Union (ILGWU), Conference Notes
4, "Shift in the Economics of Garment Production," Port Elgin, ON, August
1992. A signature campaign and a press conference on 15 March 1994

protested the shutting down of York Manufacturing by Nike who, in spite of setting new records in revenues and net income for the sixth consecutive year with total sales of $3.9 billion and profits of $365 million in 1993, moved manufacturing to take advantage of lower labour standards, reduced tariffs and easy access to the Canadian market under the Canada-U.S. and North American Free Trade Agreements. Refer to ILGWU information sheet, 1994, which quoted the Nike 1993 Annual Report.

11 Letter from the National Apparel Bureau to the Hudson's Bay Company (Montreal, QC), 27 July 1993.

12 John Deverell, "Eaton's Warehouse Revolution: Retailer Aims to Move Goods In and Out of Its Big Distribution Centre in a Day," *The Toronto Star*, 10 April 1995, E3.

13 Phizacklea, *Unpacking the Fashion Industry*, 12.

14 Coalition for Fair Wages and Working Conditions for Homeworkers, Draft, single-sheet "Backgrounder," "How Are Those Hip Hop 'n Happenin' Clothes Made?" 9 May 1993.

15 ILGWU, *When One Door Closes ... Another One Opens?*, 6. Banks extended more credit on the basis of receivables (60-90 per cent of the dollar value) than on stock inventory (30-50 per cent).

16 Alexandra Dagg and Judy Fudge, "Sewing Pains: Homeworkers in the Garment Trade," *Our Times* (June 1992): 25. See also Coalition for Fair Wages and Working Conditions for Homeworkers, *Fair Wages and Working Conditions for Homeworkers: A Brief*, 5-6.

17 Borowy and Yuen, "International Ladies' Garment Workers' Union 1993 Homeworkers' Study, 9.

18 John Heinzl, "Dylex Posts $55.4-Million Loss: Discontinued Operations Account for Sizable Part of Year's Red Ink," *The Globe and Mail*, 9 April 1992, B9. Another *Globe and Mail* report states, "Operating profit at Zellers climbed to $91.1 million in 1987 from $61.7 million the year before. The Bay department stores, by comparison, saw a drop in operating profit to $60.9 million from $79.6 million. Overall, Hudson's Bay made a profit of $23.2 million last year on revenue of $4.3 billion. But after writing down its real estate interests, and including extraordinary items, the company posted a final loss of $96.5 million." Tax exemption is another major issue in assessing profits and "loss" (Karen Howlett, "Hudson's Bay Unit Sells 'Just Kids' Clothing Division," *The Globe and Mail*, 6 May 1988, B10). Again, "Despite a solid improvement in sales, retailing giant Dylex Ltd. lost $37.6 million in the six months to Aug. 3. Total retail sales ... climbed 5.8 per cent, compared with last year. Revenue for the six months was $823.2 million, compared with $780.1 million a year ago. The loss equates to 79 cents a share" (John Heinzl, "Big Loss for Dylex Despite More Sales," *The Globe and Mail*, 7 September 1991, B7. John Heinzl, "Town and Country Chain to Close All 162 Stores: Dylex Decision to Cut Losses Affects 1,300 Employees," *The Globe and Mail*, 30 November 1991, B4. Similarly: "Revenue rose to $1.29 billion from $1.23 billion.... Although Dylex's losses continue to widen amid a severe economic downturn in the retailing sector, analysts said the results were better than expected. Dylex class A shares *moved up* 10 cents to $3.25 on the Toronto Stock Exchange" (John Heinzl,

"Dylex Loss Deepens," *The Globe and Mail*, 7 December 1991, B5; emphasis mine). Dylex closed Suzy Shier and Big Steel in 1993.

19 Operating profit in 1995 was $161.3 million for the Hudson's Bay Company and $215.56 for Zellers. The Hudson's Bay Company acquired control of Henry Morgan & Co. in 1961, A.J. Freiman Ltd. in 1972, bought and/or sold interests between 1973 and 1990 in companies such as Siebans Oil and Gas Ltd., Markborough Properties Ltd., Roxy Petroleum, Northern Stores and Simpsons-Sears. The company acquired Towers in 1990 and Linmark, an overseas buying agency which operates thirteen offices in the Far East. In 1991, the company merged with Simpsons and, in 1993, with Woodward's Ltd., a department store operator in B.C. and Alberta. With a head office in Toronto, the company operates 505 stores in Canada (100 of these are Bay department stores and 292 are Zellers department stores). Refer to "Hudson's Bay Company," in *Moody's International Manual*, 1333.

20 ILGWU, information sheet 2: "General Pyramid Structure of Canada's Garment Industry."

21 John Heinzl, "Retailing Industry Still on the Rocks: Survival Name of Game," *The Globe and Mail*, 10 March 1992, B1, 10.

22 Ibid., B1, and Steven Chase, "Bargain Harold's Goes Bi-the-Way: Dylex Buying 25 of Bankrupt Retailer's Sites to Expand Its BiWay Chain," *The Globe and Mail*, 15 May 1992, B14.

23 John Deverell, "Jubilant Bay Chief Celebrates Record Year," *The Toronto Star*, 7 April 1995, C1. Kosich asked, "Do they think U.S. competition is new to us? Why is Woolco gone? Why do we make more money than Kmart? Why is Sears stalled? And I'm glad Wal-Mart finally came. Now they're here and they're naked."

24 Canadian Press, "Hudson's Bay Looks to U.S. Suppliers: Garment Makers Fear Loss of Business," *The Globe and Mail*, 2 November 1991, B3. "Hudson's Bay Company began courting U.S. suppliers recently by hosting a reception in New York and placing an ad in Women's Wear Daily with the headline 'Why Not Do Business with North America's 7th Largest Department Store? Eh?'" (Mark Evans, "Retailers Eye U.S. for Goods," *Financial Post*, 22 November 1991, 7).

25 Deverell, "Jubilant Bay Chief Celebrates Record Year," C3.

26 Jane Armstrong, "Tough Choices in 'Mean' Budget," *The Toronto Star*, 18 April 1995, A1.

27 Companies' Creditors Arrangement Act, *Dylex Ltd. and Twelve Other Corporations: Plan of Arrangement of Dylex Ltd., February 24, 1995* (Toronto: Government of Ontario, 1995). See 17 for a list of closures.

28 Based on the ILGWU account in *Designing the Future for Garment Workers*, 38, and on an interview with ILGWU researcher, Janet Borowy, 27 March 1995.

29 ILGWU, *Designing the Future for Garment Workers*, 25-33.

30 Ibid., 31. In early 1995, no ILGWU factory uses a unit production system.

31 Intercede and ILGWU, *Meeting the Needs of Vulnerable Workers*, 19, referring to Guy Standing, "Global Feminization through Flexible Labour," *World Development* 17 (July 1989): 1079.

32 Intercede and ILGWU, *Meeting the Needs of Vulnerable Workers*, 13, and Canada, Textile and Clothing Board, *Report on Textiles and Clothing, 1988*

(Ottawa: Ministry of Supply and Services, 1989), 30, tables 26, 58, 60. The clothing industry in the U.S. is notoriously fragmented but includes giants such as Gulf and Western, which rates as the largest American apparel manufacturer, after Levi and Blue Bell denims. Yet their clothing sales are only 17 per cent of their aggregate sales. See Phizacklea, *Unpacking the Fashion Industry*, 35.

33 International Ladies' Garment Workers' Union (ILGWU), Conference Notes 8, "The Global Assembly Line and the Issue of Competition: ... Myth 2: Internationally, Garments Are Produced by Small Contractors," Port Elgin, ON, August 1992. The Fang Brothers, for instance, are a Hong Kong-based international manufacturer for Liz Claibourne. They subcontract through-out Hong Kong, Thailand, Malaysia, Ireland and Panama, using low-wage labour.

34 Chossudovsky, *The Globalisation of Poverty*, 81.

35 ILGWU, Conference Notes 8, "The Global Assembly Line and the Issue of Competition."

36 Intercede and ILGWU, *Meeting the Needs of Vulnerable Workers*, 19.

37 Sheila Rowbotham, *Homeworkers Worldwide* (London: Merlin Press, 1993), 44.

38 ILGWU, *Designing the Future for Garment Workers*, 33, 44-45.

39 Daniel Drache, "The Systematic Search for Flexibility: National Competi-tiveness and New Work Relations," in *The New Era of Global Competition: State Power and Market Power*, ed. Daniel Drache and Meric Gertler (Mont-real and Kingston: McGill-Queen's University Press, 1991), 251-69. As the market and technology are centralized, production is fragmented and decentralized, reinforcing the international division of labour.

40 Non-standard work is any part-time, temporary or contract work, including short-term and own-account self-employed workers. See ILGWU, *Designing the Future for Garment Workers*, 48.

41 John Dillon, "Turning Mexico Inside Out," *Pro-Canada Dossier* 29 (March-April 1991): 21-23, and Scott Sinclair, "Free Trade: A Dead-End Develop-ment Strategy for Mexico," *Pro-Canada Dossier* 27 (August 1990): 16. "Employment in the *maquiladoras* mushroomed to over 430,000 in 1989, from just over 100,000 in 1982. Most of these jobs were created by trans-ferring work directly from manufacturing plants in the U.S. and Canada. Ironically, during the same period, manufacturing jobs were also being lost in the rest of the Mexican economy outside the *maquiladoras*. Between 1982 and 1987 over 700,000 jobs were lost, 450,000 of them in manufac-turing. This bloodletting, especially in the manufacturing sector, has contin-ued since 1987."

42 Chossudovsky, *The Globalisation of Poverty*, 82-89. Refer to tables on cost structures, distribution of earnings and comparative costs of labour in man-ufacturing in the garment industry (90-95).

43 More narrowly, this term often connotes the changing structure of global employment patterns, relocating jobs from higher-waged Western countries to low-wage newly industrialized countries in the Southern Hemisphere. Between 1971 and 1983, for example, 1.5 million workers, mostly women, lost their clothing and textile jobs in Europe and the U.S. while two million

or more women workers found clothing and textile jobs in the two-thirds world (Mitter, *Common Fate, Common Bond*, 9).

44 National Action Committee on the Status of Women. "NAC Brief to the Sub-Committee on International Trade," 11-12. Ignacio Peón Escalante reported that, after the 1985 earthquake destruction of many buildings used by clothing firms, work resumed in homes with women buying their own machines. "The worker remains without union protection or social security but she survives. The companies can make any number of deals and avoid many social expenditures. For the population entering the labour market, it's not so terrible an alternative as having no source of income." See Ignacio Peón Escalante "Savage Liberalism: A Case Study of the Clothing Industry in Mexico" (Mexico City, 1993), trans. Ecumenical Coalition for Economic Justice, Toronto (unpublished), 3. The savings for employers are substantial. *El Tiempo* (Ciudad Juarez, Mexico), 17 March 1988, reports, "An article that a maquiladora produces for a dollar, is produced in the 'pequenas maquiladoras' [minor subsidiary workers] for between 2 and 30 cents a piece."

45 Lynda Yanz, "Women's Maquila Network: Mexico to Central America," *Correspondencia* 16 (May 1994): 3.

46 Warnock, *Free Trade and the New Right Agenda*, 22.

47 In addition to wages and working conditions, Canadian social policies have eroded since the free-trade agreement came into effect in 1989: the Unemployment Insurance program has been cut back; universal family allowance has ended; a national child-care program is no longer a priority and decreased federal contributions to health and education costs cause provincial restructuring. See National Action Committee on the Status of Women. "NAC Brief to the Sub-Committee on International Trade," 7. Refer also to Jean Swanson, "Competing to Be Poor," *Pro-Canada Dossier* 30 (March-April 1991): 10-11, and Jonathan Ferguson, "Trade Pact a Step Back for Women, Rebick Says," *The Toronto Star*, 11 February 1993, A11. Refer to Neil Brooks, "We Can Save Social Programs," *Pro-Canada Dossier* 30 (March-April 1991): 11-12, regarding misallocation of resources.

48 Borowy and Yuen, *International Ladies' Garment Workers' Union 1993 Homeworkers' Study*, 9.

49 Fruitman Consulting Group, *An Exploration of the Feasibility of a "Clean Clothes" Programme in Canada: Consumer Research*, conducted for the Ontario District of UNITE (Union of Needle Trades, Industrial and Textile Employees) (Maple, ON, October 1995), 30.

50 *The Guinness Book of Answers* (London: Guinness Publishing 1991), 279-80.

51 Brian Banks, "One Billion Buyers, Easy Credit Terms," *Canadian Business* 67, 6 (June 1994): 33-36.

52 Canada has a management office but no manufacturing facilities. Refer to "Singer Companies," in *Moody's International Manual*, 5132-33, 6309 and 6860.

53 International Ladies' Garment Workers' Union (ILGWU), Conference Notes 15, "New Technologies: Worker-Centred Modernization," Port Elgin, ON, August 1992.

54 Refer to Phizacklea, *Unpacking the Fashion Industry*, 107: "Research on the

social relations of new technology illustrates the way in which it is effectively reproducing the traditional class, gender, and racial divisions of labour."

55 Algeria, Ecuador, Gabon, Indonesia, Iran, Iraq, Kuwait, Libya, Nigeria, Qatar, Saudi Arabia, United Arab Emirates and Venezuela are member countries. Refer to *The Guinness Book of Answers*, 487-88.

56 President's Corner, "Is a Devastating War in the Gulf and Perhaps Beyond Inevitable?" *The NECEF Report* 2, 3 (November-December 1990): 1-2. Short-term losses to business credibility of co-belligerence may be offset by enhanced short- and long-term business with Saudi Arabia and the Gulf States. Human costs seem not to factor. (NECEF is the Near East Cultural and Educational Foundation of Canada.)

57 *The Guinness Book of Answers*, 280.

58 Hongu and Phillips, *New Fibres*, 6.

59 Clairmonte and Cavanagh, *The World in Their Web*, 101. Polyamid, polyester and acrylic are built from six basic chemicals (benzene, toluene, xylene, ethylene, propylene and butadiene). Benzene is produced from coking coal; all the rest are obtained from crude oil and natural gas liquids through refining or petrochemical processes. Considering the competition among the U.S., Europe and Japan, the large scale of this multibillion dollar industry and both Europe and Japan's dependence on Iraq and Iran for oil and natural gas, one questions even further American motivation for its pressure on the U.N. for aggression in Iraq in 1991 (ibid., 104-109, 114-16, 156-57).

60 Marc Lee, "Global Alternatives and Future Negotiations," submission for the Ottawa-based Canadian Centre for Policy Alternatives to the Canadian Standing Committee on Foreign Affairs and International Trade, 26 April 1999: "According to the UNCTAD, one-third of global trade represents intra-firm transfers, while another third represents transactions involving one transnational corporation. The US Bureau of Economic Analysis states that one-third of US exports and more than two-fifths of US imports are intra-firm transfers."

61 Smith, *The Everyday World as Problematic*, 3.

62 Ibid., 76.

63 Refer to Dillon and the ECEJ, *Turning the Tide*, 91-93.

64 Ibid., 83. See also 213.

65 Ibid., 84.

66 Pat Armstrong, *Labour Pains*, 34.

67 Pressured by a sweatshop fashion show during provincial hearings regarding the Employment Standards Act, Woolworth Canada Inc. met with representatives of the Homeworkers' Association who sew garments for their labels Northern Reflections, Northern Spirit and Northern Get-Away in Toronto in December 1996. Although Woolworth agreed to investigate alleged violations of two of their subcontractors, they refused both to share their results and to compensate the workers. The Labour Behind the Label Coalition continued this campaign and intervened with another contractor improving practices and gaining contracts from other retailers.

68 Marilyn Waring, Public lecture sponsored by the Ontario Women's Directorate, Toronto, 1990.

69 Smith, *The Everyday World as Problematic*, 3-8, 81-100.

4

Transforming the Local Situation in Its Global Context

Sun fed spiders
spinning power
spinning soft power strong
weaving sticky silk sun
into world webs
webbed wisdom
woven wisdom

That homeworkers are exploited is abundantly clear. What is less obvious is how to change the relations of ruling within the pyramid structure of the garment industry in order to create just relations, especially for homeworkers at the bottom. The Coalition for Fair Wages and Working Conditions for Homeworkers (Homework Coalition) took up this challenge and launched a multifaceted campaign. It is an example of a transformative option and process. Engagement in broad-based solidarity also raises issues about how we collaborate.

Notes to chapter 4 are on pp. 123-29.

Fair Wages and Working Conditions for Homeworkers' Coalition Campaign in Ontario

Several recent historical processes coalesced in Toronto by 1991 to help set a new direction for the International Ladies' Garment Workers' Union (ILGWU) in the garment industry. In 1990, a "rank-and-file representatives' council" of the ILGWU in Ontario elected a feminist, Alexandra Dagg, "who knew that the fight to save the union was integrally related to industry restructuring and its impact on immigrant women."[1] The union also received Technology Adjustment Research Project funding, administered by the Ontario Federation of Labour for the Ministry of Labour. The feminist researchers for this project, Barbara Cameron and Teresa Mak, closely examined restructuring within the garment industry, its impact on labour and possibilities for effective industrial strategy to reverse the trend. Their initial investigation of the wages and working conditions for homeworkers included setting up a hotline, distributing educational pamphlets and holding interviews.

In 1991, the ILGWU invited many groups to form a campaign coalition. Members include the Workers' Information and Action Centre of Toronto, Chinese Workers' Association, Parkdale Community Legal Services, Ontario Coalition of Visible Minority Women, Ontario Coalition for Better Child Care, Workers' Educational Association, National Action Committee on the Status of Women, Centre for Research on Work and Society, Labour Council of Metropolitan Toronto and York Region, Ecumenical Coalition for Economic Justice, Women Working with Immigrant Women, School Sisters of Notre Dame and the Cross Cultural Communication Centre. Thus a new, though not isolated, incidence of an alliance between unions, social movements, community groups and churches was created.

Each member group has its own story leading to this new solidarity. The administrative committee of the Ecumenical Coalition for Economic Justice (ECEJ), for example, had agreed in 1990 to use the following as a guide to integrate a feminist perspective in all of its research and action programs:

> While accepting liberal feminism's goals of full participation and equal opportunity, ECEJ goes beyond these preliminary steps to espouse liberationist feminism. This can become a full-fledged Christian spirituality as it:
> 1) analyses the oppressive system of patriarchy, regarding it as the use of power and authority by sex, class, nation, race or hierarchy to dominate others even in the name of God;

2) develops an alternative, liberating vision. We stress praxis that incarnates the vision, inviting women and men to transform the oppressive system and establish justice for all.

In defining feminism, we fully support co-operation, full recognition and participation of all persons, the importance of networking and coalition-building, the interdependence of all life in the cosmos, and responsible action to ensure these in social cohesion. We assume opposition to subordination, not only of women to men, but also of any race to another, of colonies to master nations, of believers to clergy, of any social class to another.[2]

In 1991, ECEJ hired Lorraine Michael to research and network with women's groups for economic justice for women. Within this context, the 1991 invitation of the garment workers' union to churches to establish a broadly based coalition to respond to the crisis in homeworking was welcomed. I agreed to represent ECEJ on the Homework Coalition. The churches' coalition also initiated a Women for Economic Justice working group which collaborates with the Homework Coalition.[3]

The Homework Coalition's initial campaign objectives were: (a) to facilitate homeworkers' identification and fulfillment of their needs by organizing a homeworkers' association which could provide direct information and services to homeworkers and collectively advocate for their rights; (b) to counteract low-wage strategies throughout the garment industry, particularly through labour law reform and by raising long-term global economic issues underlying the increase in garment homeworking; (c) to support unionization and broader-based bargaining agreements which include homeworking and related employer clauses; (d) to provide public education about the current exploitation of homeworkers; and (e) to expand the coalition campaign by reaching out to community groups, labour organizations and activists.

A key approach for the entire campaign was collaboration within the broadly based coalition. While requiring much time on a regular basis, this process strengthened our resolve, and offered a range of expertise in advocacy, research and activist-educational techniques. It also offered a network for concerted response. Collaboration challenged participants to be thorough, to think out specific objectives carefully and to remain open to further insights. My experience was that an encouraging amount of esprit du corps enabled listening, clarification, critique and choice of options in a way that often gave rise to the synergy needed for the task at hand.

Our strategizing was also fraught with complexity because corporate bureaucracy has built up a pyramid structure of power and exploitation. But community collaboration helped us to understand the corporate process and to strategize in the face of tremendous opposition. It also offered a source of hope. As Janet Silman emphasized from her work with the Tobique women of New Brunswick,

> The key new component ... which facilitated the transition from "survival" to "insurrection" was the critical consciousness that social change was possible. Consciousness, then, is intrinsically spiritual in that it gives hope to people who have been oppressed. It enables people to see injustice, and to envision the possibility of justice prevailing. Critical consciousness offers an authentic horizon of hope.... The women's critical analysis was structural, beginning with the concrete situation; attending to the web of relational dynamics; and, through those dynamics, discerning the structures which determined the organization of social power....
>
> What they discovered about "truth-telling" was that it freed them from fear of the oppressor.... "The truth shall make you free" is the truth which liberates the oppressed from the power of the oppressor. The mobilization of those who had existed with no hope involved an "awakening," or conscientization, in which a vision of the *possibility* of justice was reborn. Conscientization itself is the lens through which the vision of liberation can be seen. Oppressed people then can claim their collective power to become moral agents of social change.[4]

Consciousness and vision were explicit sources of shared strength for coalition members and some garment homeworkers. Awareness among homeworkers is growing, through participation in events such as a series of workshops on leadership formation offered in 1994 by the Homeworkers' Association.

The Homeworkers' Association (HWA)

The Homeworkers' Association is an independent organization led by homeworkers to provide opportunities to meet each other, to form their own organization and to share planning for services suited to their own needs.[5] The HWA has one full-time worker, Holly Du (1992-94), followed by Fanny Yuen.[6] The salary for this position was funded by the Ontario Women's Directorate. It was also supported by the ILGWU and the Homework Coalition. The early 1992 decision to form an independent association linked to the ILGWU shifted the role of the Homework Coalition to be one of friendship, sharing of information and providing pamphlets, such as "Homeworkers Know Your Rights!"[7]

Organizing to promote and form the Homeworkers' Association required a strategy different from the factories' traditional workplace leafleting and restaurant gatherings. Early efforts brought almost no response. A turning point in organizational strategy came with the co-ordinator's realization that unless families are involved, homeworkers could not afford time away from production schedules for social activities. Lack of child care for initial events meant lack of presence of homeworkers themselves. Trips to a maple sugar bush, Niagara Falls, recreational parks, fruit picking and an overnight trip to Ottawa for a major Canadian Labour Congress and Action Canada Network demonstration have attracted workers and their families. Such occasions provided the opportunity, mainly within the Chinese and Vietnamese communities, to discuss homeworking, the Association, the ILGWU and workers' rights.[8] A solid base for a union local among homeworkers was growing.

Milestones multiplied. Mrs. Cheung was a homeworker delegate and speaker at the June 1992 Associate ILGWU Member (AIM) locals' convention in Miami.[9] She explained homeworkers' situations and association activities in a workshop for AIM and for delegates of the forty-first Convention of the International Ladies' Garment Workers' Union. Another Toronto homeworker became an executive member of AIM by 1994.

An educational weekend in Port Elgin in August 1992, sponsored by the ILGWU for its members, the Homeworkers' Association and the Homework Coalition enabled participants to resolve tensions about the impact of homeworking on union jobs and bargaining power. Unionized factory members gradually became convinced that organizing homeworkers would actually help reduce the wage differential between themselves and homeworkers.[10]

The coalition was not opposed to homeworking itself. The main focus of coalition strategy was to protect labour in factories, offices and homes, and to counteract unfair wages and exploitative working conditions. If a woman does choose to do homework in order to set her own schedule, have a familiar working environment and be her own boss, "it is imperative that she make the choice freely and that she have all the benefits of a worker doing similar work in the work place, whether those benefits are equal pay, job security, vacation pay or working conditions that are both safe and not injurious to her health."[11]

At the gathering, unionists learned about homeworkers' wages and working conditions. Factory workers spoke about significant differences in their production since the Canada-U.S. Free Trade Agreement was signed in 1989—for example, the major decrease of employees within factories, increased pressure for quantitative output, adding labels in the warehouse for retailers and, in some cases, handling imports exclusively. While factory and warehouse workers were very knowledgeable about the source and destination of the garments, homeworkers knew little of either. Need for solidarity to prevent bargaining against each other became clear.[12] All three groups walked together at the Toronto Labour Day parade in September 1992 and annually since then.

On 31 October 1992, the first associate local in Canada was certified with an annual general meeting and an elected executive of homeworkers. The New York Director of the AIM program presented the homeworkers with their official union charter as AIM Local 12. The coalition and ILGWU members were delighted to share this exhilarating moment. In view of the long history of attempts to ban homeworking—for example, by the ILGWU in the U.S., or to control it in Ontario simply by requiring employers to obtain permits and by dealing with grievances through individual employee complaints—these steps were history making in a very significant way.[13] The vision of women such as Alexandra Dagg, manager of the Ontario District Council of the ILGWU; Barbara Cameron, a research co-ordinator; Judy Fudge, law professor; and Shelly Gordon of the Workers' Information and Action Centre of Toronto had not only led them to call groups together to form a campaign coalition but also underlined for them the importance of protecting homeworkers in an organized way. With thirty-five members in October 1992 and 155 by October 1994, association participants have spoken up in legislative meetings, at conferences and in newspaper and magazine articles. The association facilitates development and use of focused leadership skills. New awareness of the possibility of change energized homeworkers, making them eager for concerted action even as the isolated nature of homework and fear of reprisal make the formation of an association particularly difficult.[14]

The advantages of belonging to the Homeworkers' Association for an annual fee of twelve dollars are evident in the extent of services they offer. These are listed in their English, Chinese and Spanish pamphlets:

LEGAL AND SOCIAL SERVICES
- free legal advice and referral on work-related issues.
- escort and interpretation for you at the Ministry of Labour.
- information on subsidized housing, UIC, social welfare, immigration.
- workshops on occupational health and safety, worker's rights.
- referrals to affordable income tax clinics.

ACTIVITIES
- recreational activities, i.e., trips, new year and holiday celebration.
- English as a second language class.
- improved sewing skill classes, pattern design class.

IN ADDITION YOU WILL RECEIVE ...
- $1,000.00 accidental death benefit at no extra cost when you join the Homeworkers' Association.[15]

The HWA is meeting homeworkers' expressed need for English-language classes, through assistance from the Toronto Board of Education. Sunday afternoon classes incorporate learning resources designed from the homeworkers' experience. With other community groups, the association regularly co-sponsors legal clinics and workshops on topics such as workers' rights, communication skills and parenting. A registry of homeworkers, domestic workers and their employers is being created.

Advocacy has successfully led to remuneration for unpaid back wages. Mrs. Tse lost $500 in wages owed her when a company closed in 1991 and $2,800 when her next employer also shut down.[16] With no formal documentation of her labour and not recognized as an employee, Mrs. Tse's plight was rejected by the Ontario Ministry of Labour until a concerted lobby by the association won a changed ruling. Mrs. Tse and others received back wages from Ontario's Wage Protection Fund in 1993.

Many workers' plights, however, remain unresolved. One employer gave Vivian only seventeen dollars for thirty hours work. Yen lost back wages in three plant closures. Another employer was to pay her a total of seventy dollars for sewing ten blouses but she was informed that her faulty sewing had cost him nine hundred dollars in lost revenue. As a "compassionate" man, "he offered to split the loss with Yen, charging her $50 for each blouse, for a total of $500!"[17]

Steadily, the HWA is expanding its membership, vision, confidence and solidarity links. Although the HWA reports its events and concerns at Homeworker Coalition meetings, they prefer to limit their representation to the co-ordinator. Several homeworkers have been active in government lobbying, demonstrations and press conferences. HWA is deciding if it will initiate action to obtain vacation pay and to extend their Association.

Labour Law Reform

Dylex stated their position on legislation regarding home-working for Ministry of Labour consultations:

> Voluntary action by retailers to encourage compliance by suppliers ... combined with the existing mechanisms in place by the Ministry of Labour are sufficient to ensure fairness in the treatment of homeworkers.[18]

By contrast, the Homework Coalition advocated labour law reform: (1) to ensure employee status for homeworkers with recognition by related employers who are responsible for employment practice, wages and working conditions, (2) to obtain enforcement of provincial standards through company audits and (3) to establish sectoral or broader-based bargaining, thereby recognizing homeworkers' right to form a union.

The Ontario Employment Standards Act still required that "No person shall employ a homeworker without a permit issued by the director of the Employment Standards Branch."[19] The register of the names and addresses of all homeworkers and their wages supplied through this annual permit system was to be made available for company audits and could be used to simplify enforcement through government auditing of employers on some regular basis, especially if a central registry or database were established. The information is also needed by the Homeworkers' Association. What prevents these regulations from being adequate protection? The permit system is ineffective for three reasons: insecure and isolated workers fear reprisal for speaking up, employers fail to request permits and the government does not provide effective audits or enforcement. As the ILGWU and Intercede explain,

> Not only is there a low monetary cost to violating the Act, the probability of detecting a violation is likely to be small given the small number of routine investigations. This is because the Employment Standards Branch relies almost exclusively on an individualized complaint model to detect violations.... Without the backing of either a strong government agency or a union, the burden of enforcing standards falls on the individual workers, who, precisely because of their vulnerability, are in the least favourable position to do so.[20]

A commonly used term, "illegal homeworkers" is actually a misnomer. In the surveys cited, homeworkers did not give exchange for anonymity as a reason for accepting substandard wages and working conditions. Since most employers do not report the use of homework labour to government authorities, it is they who violate employment standards legislation and, in some cases, collective agreements with unions. Fear of losing work prevents women from presenting this and other abuses to authorities. The Employment Practices Branch has no procedure to protect adequately the jobs of workers who file a complaint while still working for the employer.[21] Problems of lack of payment and of deduction of wages are severe but homeworkers had to remain anonymous as they shared their stories with an Employment Standards Working Group gathering evidence.[22] The Homework Coalition, therefore, is urging the government to conduct company audits instead of concentrating public resources on individual complaint investigations.

As Alexandra Dagg and Judy Fudge explain, merely imposing liability on a small contractor does not solve the problem.[23] As one business closes, another springs up in its place, sometimes run by the same person but as a different corporation. Enforcement mechanisms for minimum labour standards for homeworkers must be directed to the higher levels of the garment production pyramid where power and wealth are held, for example, with the owners of the Hudson's Bay Company, Eaton's and Dylex Ltd. As employers related to production, they would be held responsible for wages and working conditions throughout their entire subcontracting process. The problem lies in the fact that subcontracting chains in the garment industry have not been regarded as part of the related employer provision. Manufacturers and jobbers thus shift compliance with minimum-standards legislation on to subcontractors who then use homeworkers to avoid the legislation.

All legislative reforms must be based on recognition that our present homeworking system structures in the subordination of the household to the employer-dominated market. It is within the explicit recognition of this determinant that the coalition advocated changes to the Ontario Employment Standards Act (ESA) in order to provide homeworkers with equal and enforceable minimum labour standards. The coalition consistently urged the ESA to broaden the definition of homework to respond to its rapid expansion into new areas, such as electronic homework. Coalition members met with each of Ontario's three political parties in December 1991. Judy Fudge explained the coalition's position:

> The simplest and most effective means of ensuring compliance with minimum-standards legislation is to impose joint liability for minimum labour standards on the businesses at the top of the pyramid. Manufacturers and jobbers control the labour process, and they are economically stable. They

also set the terms which the contractors must comply with. To ensure that they will not be liable for any breaches of minimum standards, the manufacturers and jobbers could easily demand that their contractors meet minimum statutory obligations. In this way, wages and working conditions will not be subject to a constant downward pressure.[24]

The key issue is joint liability for subcontractors' payment of fair wages and working conditions if those at the top of the pyramid do not disclose names of their suppliers. The significance of this legislation lies in the perceptible change in international sourcing of garments in the 1980s when subcontractors became the focal point of the new pattern. Transnational corporations favour subcontracting to reduce visibility while maintaining strict control over market conditions and technology.[25] Subcontracting also provides flexibility for changes in market demand.

Some of the policies for homeworkers depend on the employment status designated to them by the Canadian and Ontario governments— that is, whether a homeworker is considered an employee working at home or an independent contractor. The latter, for example, must make government pension plan contributions from their own income tax returns instead of being covered by the employer, and they are ineligible for unemployment insurance. The distinction needs to be emphasized so that homeworkers, as home-based employees, will be covered by legislated programs such as Unemployment Insurance and the Canada Pension Plan.

Although homeworkers are defined as employees and are entitled to minimum wages and vacation pay in the ESA, they were excluded from several protective measures relating to the hours of work, statutory holidays and overtime pay.[26] The Ontario Federation of Labour (OFL) supported Homework Coalition lobbying to change this and resolved further: (1) to investigate the growth of "precarious" or nonstandard employment, such as contract work, part-time or casual work and homework, and (2) to campaign actively for an amendment to section 12 of the Act to clarify related employer status of corporations and those dependent on them.[27] The 1992 OFL women's conference, More than a Day's Work: Women in the Union at Home and on the Job, sponsored a homeworkers' lobby bringing four hundred participants together with each of the three Ontario political parties to press for these resolutions.[28] At the same meeting, Minister of Labour Robert Mackenzie, accompanied by two cabinet ministers and twelve members of the provincial parliament, promised to make amendments to the Employment Standards Act. Minister of Community and Social Services and Minister Responsible for Women's Issues Marion Boyd announced an $85,000 grant for Intercede and the ILGWU to facilitate organization and education of domestic workers and of homeworkers.

The recent shift to casualized employment meant that labour law had to address the needs of those in small workplaces or only marginally attached to an individual employer.[29] Since the Ontario Labour Relations Act required at least two workers in a bargaining unit for it to be certified, homeworkers and domestic workers were excluded. Their economically vulnerable positions prevented bargaining. There was an overwhelming inequality in bargaining power. Striking and walkouts were virtually impossible. Nor were there extensive resources to fund, organize and support numerous small locals with collective bargaining, processing grievances, memberships and strike support.

The Ontario District Council of the ILGWU and Intercede proposed sectoral regulation clearly designed to provide effective regulation of the live-in domestic and garment sectors and to lead toward effective self-organization and mandatory broader-based collective bargaining. The intent was to make domicile-based employment visible through registration, legislation and enforcement, thereby benefiting the workers, law-abiding employers and government officials committed to protect vulnerable workers. Such integration and structural reform would also be "a step towards identifying and valuing women's traditional work."[30] Other government-funded reforms were needed to institute a quality system of affordable child care on a priority basis and to provide training and language programs to allow homeworkers to choose to work outside the home if desired.

In December 1993, the Ontario government agreed to issue an order in cabinet, first, to delete regulations which excluded homeworkers from protective legislation in regard to the hours of work, public holidays and overtime pay.[31] Second, the order in cabinet adds a 10 per cent premium on the minimum wage to cover overhead costs normally borne by the employer. Third, it requires employers to provide homeworkers, in writing, with the particulars of their employment conditions, including piece and hourly rates, the nature and amount of work and the completion deadline. Finally, the order allows the ministry to charge a fee for homework permits to help finance the cost of improved enforcement of these new regulations. The Homework Coalition lauded this first step even as we pressed for legislative change covering an expanded definition of homework, joint liability and a central registry. We also pressed for sectoral collective bargaining.[32]

In April and May 1993, over fifty unions, churches and community organizations sent letters pressing for legislation. The Homework Coalition increased advocacy only to learn through leaked documents that homework legislation was a low priority.[33] In February 1994, the Homework Coalition held a press conference at Queen's Park to publicize the *ILGWU 1993 Homeworkers' Study*," an overview of campaign activities and a list of labels sewn by Toronto homeworkers.[34] The coalition asked the government, "What more do you want before you will legislate justice for homeworkers?" Postcards were distributed to be sent to Premier Bob Rae urging him to initiate legislation.

Public Education

Educational approaches varied. Coalition members took initiative to provide articles at every opportunity to daily newspapers and magazines.[35] Members spoke and gave workshops at the annual general meetings of the Canadian Labour Congress, the National Action Committee on the Status of Women and the Women's Interchurch Council of Canada.

Coalition information handouts described the campaign and its objectives, possibilities for future alternative directions in the garment industry, information on the pyramid structure of the industry and a "clean clothes card." The latter was an awareness-raising device to encourage consumers to question the source of clothing and the working conditions and wages of those involved in its production. A fact sheet explained the costs at the various stages of the "clothes line," particularly the salaries of homeworkers contrasted with the large profits of major Canadian retailers.

The coalition organized press conferences and an incremental series of action demonstrations with an educational purpose. A key strategy was to expose retailers' control of production and globalization that forces cheap labour and uses homeworkers. The 1993 Toronto International Women's Day rally included an address about homeworking followed by active protest. A thousand people marched to an Alfred Sung outlet in the Eaton Centre to oppose exploitation of homeworkers and to a Pizza Pizza outlet on Yonge Street to support the boycott there.[36] In 1994, a garment homeworker spoke at the International Women's Day rally in Toronto. It was organized by Women Working with Immigrant Women and drew a crowd of two thousand to proclaim a message of unity, which is crucial for the Homework Coalition as well. As co-organizer Judy Persad said, "The message is that we need to work together.... Our divisions make us less strong. We must not let anything divide us. For a movement to be successful, for its politics to be successful, it must include all women."[37] An Ontario Federation of Labour rally at the Eaton's Centre brought out four hundred to call for an end of exploitation of homeworkers.

In late 1992 and 1993, about three thousand people across Canada mailed Homework Coalition postcards to the ILGWU and to the presidents or chief financial officers of Canada's three largest retail chains, Eaton's, Dylex and Hudson's Bay Company. The message on all three was to "Stop the Exploitation of Homeworkers" and "Buy from Manufacturers Who Pay Workers Fair Wages and Working Conditions." Appropriate applications were added. For instance, "Your 'Buy Canada Campaign' doesn't mean that garments are made by workers who receive fair wages and working conditions" was sent to Mr. George Craig Eaton, president of T. Eaton Company of Canada. "Not only are we not doing any better, but neither are homeworkers, women garment workers who are compelled to work from their homes for low wages" was the message for Mr. George J. Kosich, then president of the Hudson's Bay Company. The Women's Missionary Society of the Presbyterian Church in Canada sent postcards and background information to every presbytery in Canada. Both the Canadian Labour Congress and the Canadian Religious Conference–Ontario distributed cards to members.

Coalition public education was built on the premise that knowledge of retailers' control in restructuring the industry to maximize their own profits while ignoring the socio-economic costs for the labourers is a public right, as are debates about responsibility for the present social construction. Organizational momentum relies on public awareness of alternative methods and fair labour practice.

Homeworking Conference

Another major part of the coalition campaign was an Ontario-based conference, From the Double Day to the Endless Day, that brought together 130 community activists, trade unionists, homeworkers, international resource people and researchers in order to share experiences, network and devise specific plans to organize and protect homeworkers.[38] Members of the Homeworkers Association participated in at least part of the weekend. Employer demands pressured them to stay home to sew.

This conference addressed industrial and electronic homeworking and noted other forms of homework such as packaging, assembling auto parts, phone ordering and food preparation. Themes included (1) linking community and labour concerns, coalition building, analyzing what legislative changes need to be made and how to do effective advocacy; (2) linking unions and homeworkers both by including homeworkers in the collective agreement and by reviewing the history of the trade union movement in tandem with the issue of homeworking; (3) analyzing the corporate agenda in its global context in terms of women's work, precarious forms of employment and the creation of homeworking; (4) challenging the myths of homeworking; discussing the connections between homework and racism, the needs of immigrant women and of the disabled; sorting out issues about health and safety, about child care and child labour, concerning racism, the trade union movement and homeworking; and regarding the Clean Clothes Campaign; and (5) networking and organizing internationally. International guests explained the extent of homeworking as a low-wage strategy and indicated some initiatives being taken to network throughout different regions of the globe. Guests included Jane Tate and Kuldeep Bajwa from the West Yorkshire Homeworkers' Unit in England, Berzabeth Corona from the September 19th Union in Mexico, Ligia Orozco from the Women's Secretariat of the Sandinista Workers' Central in Nicaragua and Kathleen Christensen from the U.S.

Conference action involved a rally to launch the Clean Clothes Campaign outside the Eaton's Centre, where information was handed out to Saturday shoppers who were then asked to mail in postcards to the presidents of Eaton's, Dylex and the Hudson's Bay Company. Together with participants from the Canadian Research Institute for the Advancement of Women international conference, Making the Links: Feminism and Anti-Racism, a united voice was formed.

From the Double Day to the Endless Day provided direction, insight, solidarity and energy for further initiatives in Ontario. Proceedings of the conference were published to provide a further educational tool.[39]

Expanding the Coalition

The strength of the coalition campaign arose from the solidarity of groups committed to its objectives. The HWA and the Homework Coalition value increased collaboration beyond the present Chinese/Vietnamese focus. A think tank was held with members of Latin American, Filipino, Southeast Asian and Chinese community groups regarding their interests, ideas and possibilities for involvement.[40] A support group for the HWA was reactivated.

Our extensively endorsed brief, *Fair Wages and Working Conditions for Homeworkers* was presented in November 1991 to the Ontario government, and again in a revised version in February 1993.

Core Issues Arising from Praxis

Through the experience of the coalition campaign in Ontario, coalition members realized that some issues were steadily gaining importance. Questions arose whether focus on legislation was an effective use of limited coalition resources, why homeworkers themselves were not at Homework Coalition meetings, how we might better support homeworkers to expand and strengthen their HWA and what form our coalition might take in order to welcome more extensive representation by women of all "racial"-ethnic origins. Usually the mix at meetings was about 30 per cent women of colour and 70 per cent white. Since I believe these questions can lead us to expand our horizon and increase solidarity in more inclusive, effective collaboration, I now reflect on some significant implications.

An underlying concern I had was why persistent political lobbying and such a major public campaign were needed at all. The changes sought were for minimum rights. Legislation for joint liability and implementation of a central registry are structural measures ensuring that retailers who control the pyramid and reap the profits are socially responsible. And if legislation is implemented, government audits and enforcement are still problematic. Did well-funded lobbying by major retailers dominate to the extent that campaign issues were not even raised in the Ontario legislature? What might have been achieved if Gordon Wilson, president of the OFL, had made this legislation one of the stipulations for OFL support of the NDP in the coming election?

Internal Government Views

Although interviews were requested from all Ontario political parties, I was able to obtain only two, both from the official government during our coalition's concerted lobbying, the New Democratic Party. From an internal government point of view, Frances Lankin, MPP, then Ontario minister of Economic Development, assured me that the cabinet committee on economic development was very supportive, with no opposition from within. The key concern was to assess the extent of what could be legislated and enforced. Under powerful lobbying from retailers, Lankin depended on the briefs, telephone calls and visits by the Homework Coalition to obtain alternative and more com-

plete information. Our lobbying helped her to argue more strongly
with some bureaucrats who backed retailers.[41]

Marion Boyd, MPP, who was the minister responsible for Women's
Issues during this entire campaign and minister of Community and
Social Services until she became attorney general early in 1993,
explained the government predicament and choices. Key aspects of the
interview follow.[42]

> Barbara Paleczny: Could the government have taken more time and passed
> legislation?
>
> Marion Boyd, MPP: During the course of a government, it is unusual for one
> ministry or one area to get more than two or three major pieces of legislation
> through. Labour had several great big pieces of legislation, like Bill 40, changes
> to the Workers' Compensation Act and issues with the construction trade and
> international unions, and it was very hard for Bob Mackenzie (minister of
> Labour) to persuade his colleagues that he should have even more air time.
>
> BP: And I understand that there was very heavy lobbying by retailers.
>
> MB: It wasn't discussed as the issue for us. It may well have been part of the
> decision not to have a strong recommendation to put that legislation at the
> top of the agenda. The issue [of our recommended legislation] was dis-
> cussed both in caucus and in cabinet because Bob [Premier Rae] was really
> crusading for this and because of those of us who were particularly worried
> about women's rights issues. There was quite a lot of discussion about how
> to fit it into the agenda and how to deal with the politics of the thing.
>
> And you may be right that there was a lot of direct pressure around
> saying "Why can't it be voluntary compliance?" My own approach is to get
> first a regime for voluntary compliance. Just as a general theory, where
> you've got a highly controversial and difficult area, like voluntary compli-
> ance, to show that it didn't work is often the way to pave the way to manda-
> tory legislation.
>
> BP: What have we had, if not voluntary compliance? It's not written but it is
> that.
>
> MB: It's unwritten but the issue for the industry is that the homeworkers
> haven't been included under the act in a way that was enforceable. Bob
> Mackenzie [minister of Labour] and I were hoping that we could strengthen
> the position of the homeworkers.
>
> BP: Would it have helped if there had been more pressure from a few big
> unions?
>
> MB: Maybe. But the real decision was whether to go into a huge revision of
> the Employment Standards Act where it would have been included. And
> because of the other big pieces, we didn't feel that we had time once we
> really got Bill 40 through to do the kind of job that really needed to be

done. We thought it had to be a second term's work to do that. So it might have made a difference but I don't really think so. The campaign was very important but it's the competition for legislative time. That's the issue.

The other issue was that we were getting very conflicting legal advice about the ability to do some of these things given free trade. So that is a really important issue. Exactly how we would do that without being seen to be contravening NAFTA. There were some who advised that it wouldn't make any difference at all and others who said we'd be called up in front of the commission. I don't think there's much chance of renegotiating NAFTA. I think the Liberals not only have just jumped on the wagon but they're driving it pretty fast because they obviously want to get into similar kinds of agreements with the Far East.

BP: Do you recall why you'd be called up before the commission?

MB: The proposal that had come forward for joint liability was where the real problem seemed to lie. How can you do a joint liability on a company that is not a Canadian company? The issue is whether or not we would have had the capacity to carry it through, given the international nature of the industry. And if we were only penalizing Canadian corporations, would we in fact be destroying that industry, given the competition issues that had already risen under free trade?

BP: Could the government have spent more days in the legislature during the last year to deal with further issues?

MB: The kind of hostility to the Labour Acts that we had already passed was extreme. We were starting to see the real efforts of big industry to see that we were defeated and to turn around what we had already accomplished, never mind anything new. They were putting a lot of their resources into making sure that we were defeated. And the first act, whether it had been of the conservatives or of the liberals, in my view, would have been a repeal of what we had done. So to expand collective bargaining again under these circumstances, and you remember that it was very difficult to try and find a formula that would really fit the requirements of an enforceable law and yet satisfy the homeworkers themselves, would have been another blow to the possibility of our forming another government the next time around.

BP: What do you think is most needed in terms of our campaign?

MB: Well one of the things that we probably should be looking at is seeing what the policy is in the party itself and whether the party itself has passed resolutions on this. If it has, it gives us more strength because then there can be lobbying within the party to try to get this to be one of the items considered under labour law when we return to office. So I think that would be a very important route.

BP: Frances Lankin had wondered whether it would still be good to lobby each party of the government. I'm very hesitant to raise anything with the conservatives because it seems as though the more it's forgotten by them, the better. I'm afraid that even the regulatory changes which we appreciated as one good step could be destroyed.

MB: They have made it clear that they intend to do a complete review of the Labour Standards Act and ESA. And I think that's something to be very fearful of. I don't think there's any question that they're out to erode any protections that are there in the act. So yes, absolutely. I think that is a genuine area of fear. Any information OFL or any of the groups around employment standards are getting about any plans that they have would be very helpful to you.

BP: Do you have any suggestions about lobbying for our coalition?

MB: As a lobbying effort, you were partly successful with us because you clearly had done, and no pun intended, your own homework. You really had the stuff there and you presented it in a way that was easy to read and understand and that was great. And you were always extremely respectful which I think is very important when you're dealing with governments, even when you're really disappointed that you're not getting the kind of action that you'd like. Quite frankly, there is so much pressure on an agenda of any government that people who stomp all over the people who are most likely to help them are really difficult to get along with. It makes it very hard to sell to a caucus to give priority for this group. So I think you went about that very well.

My guess is that you'd be awfully smart if you have members of our party or members of any of the other parties see if they can't lobby within their party. Because that is extremely important. You may run into what is quite fashionable at the moment, "Well all the parties are the same and there's no reason to get involved in a party," or "This has to be an apolitical movement." Well the reality is that apolitical movements don't get legislation passed. So you're either going to play the game or not get legislation.

BP: And what of work with the bureaucrats?

MB: I think it's difficult to get access to them. They're running so scared right now. The person you develop a relationship with may be gone tomorrow. Nineteen thousand public service jobs are gone already. Maintain any contacts you did make with people who are still there.... I think that's important and certainly ask for a meeting to talk with the minister and the bureaucrats.

BP: What amount can we press for? My bias is to keep pressing for the full gamut of what we need, rather than saying we'll go for voluntary compliance.

MB: Your job is to push for the whole thing. Those who want voluntary compliance will be doing their pushing. With any luck, you might at least get that basically. I don't know that the big firms would think they even need to lobby this government.

BP: What of having letters, from church leaders, unions?

MB: Yes and petitions. It helps. Petitions get read out in the legislature. It helps the public to understand this is an issue. Try to put them in the proper format so that you get a response. That does help. Rather than having large numbers sign one petition, have more petitions, with just twenty or twenty-five names on each. Because then we can have them every day. There's an appropriate format for it, available here. Otherwise, they'll just keep sending them back to us.

BP: In addition to working on legislation, we're focusing on company image because that is the crack in the wall.

MB: Oh, I think so. Little starts are significant. People are feeling pretty helpless right now. They're looking for something they can do to be active in at least some respect. Education kits would be very helpful.

BP: I want to encourage you in your work in the legislature. It is frustrating for me to see that there is no chance for dialogue and discussion because of the way the system operates. Representatives seem to excel in shouting each other down. It is hard to watch it even on television.

MB: It's a very hostile workplace. It's similar to the courts. Basically it's set up as an adversarial system, when you have a majority government that is not in any way looking for any kind of consensus from anybody on anything. I don't think there is anything you can expect by an adversarial system. It's trying to win the allegiance of sufficient voters to see people as strong and aggressive. It's very counter to the preferred way of making decisions that certainly most women would talk about.

BP: Is there any behind the scenes, even rumbling movement to shift the scene? In this environment, to talk about shifting to a dialogic mode sounds so absurd and yet it's the distortion and bias that make this seem absurd. It indicates the amount of distortion there is in our whole culture....

MB: Well that's true. Sure, there's a lot of talk now about proportional representation which would make a difference, but at both the federal and provincial levels, what is increasing the hostility is that we haven't had a period of minority government in the province since 1987. A lot of the accomplishments of the Davis government and of the Robarts government before it were minority government situations. Minority government is a good way. Otherwise it's bully tactics. They know what they are doing. We can delay them a little bit.

I think, in fairness, from their perspective they saw us doing the same thing. And I can tell you it didn't feel as though we were doing it. But I'm not sure that it didn't feel the same to them as it does to us and that worries me sometimes. It's different. We took consultation seriously. You got to see us a lot. We simply worked that way. We wanted to hear from people. If we weren't going to be able to do what they wanted us to do, we wanted to tell them directly that we're working toward it but we can't do that and take the responsibility for saying that. But they're not out there genuinely trying to reach consensus.

BP: In fact that's what some of the labour groups are saying, that there was too much effort at consensus.

MB: We kept trying to tell the labour groups, "Our focus groups and our polling tell us that there's been a huge swing to the right and that you may think we're bad but you ain't seen nothing yet."

BP: What helps you in the midst of all this?

MB: When feminists have a perspective, we work very hard and there are some setbacks. We never get immediate gratification. What my male colleagues, particularly, want is immediate gratification and it isn't there, whether you're government or whether you're not.

BP: I appreciate your saying that because the work is long term. I need to keep reminding myself of the mighty river that's on the move so that I don't get caught in little eddies.

MB: I feel very grounded in what I do, not because I want to be a politician but because I want to keep working on this kind of issue. I don't know how people do this work if they don't have something that grounds them and something which is not only a goad but a refuge. A little group among our caucus staff is discussing how, within a party that has its roots very clearly within a religious tradition and yet has very strong secular methodology, we can help people who respond to the Tommy Douglas language about why we're doing what we do. How can we be sure that remains strong within our party and within work among ourselves?

After further discussion about fair tax reform, we ended the interview. The dialogue with Marion Boyd speaks for itself in clarifying government perspectives. It offers material for the Labour Behind the Label Coalition to discuss for further clarity. While continuing to lobby for legislative protections, I think that remembering where power lies is crucial.

Popular support remains critical to obtain and enforce even minimal change in view of the well-financed opposition of retailers. Ongoing work will need to focus on consumer response as a key point of entry because it touches a rare vulnerability among those who control the industry.

At issue then is what prevents us as consumers from recognizing and employing our power with corporations and with governments. Fear of conflict within families and among friends blocks many from even looking at the issue seriously. This is complicated by the overwhelming extent of our socio-economic problems, coupled with the personal and group sense of inability to make a difference. Healing the rage that festers because of unemployment, the recession and increasing violence requires linking the causes of our economic collapse with courageous action for change.[43] Fear of conflict can lead people to avoid analyzing and discussing core issues, particularly when they touch issues as basic as "race"-ethnicity, wealth and capital accumulation and gender. Homeworking, maximization of profits and "the place" of women in society touch all of these central issues, as does the scapegoat issue of projection of blame on immigrants for the present unemployment crisis. Groups around the globe, however, show us that perhaps the central obstacle is a sense of powerlessness. Even bitter hardship will not stop people if they believe change is possible. Hope and solidarity cast out fear. And a sense of both humour and vulnerability strengthens resolve as people can laugh and cry together.

Organizing efforts for public response has been steady and intense. It has not, however, been adequate for the exploitation at hand. There simply are not resources of personnel and finances in the union and among partners themselves to do more. While major unions, churches and solidarity networks gave vocal support (mainly in private communications) and sent some letters to government leaders, there was minimal assistance to mount a larger campaign.

Suggestions were made to me that we needed to follow bureaucratic routes of time and paperwork with particular people to lobby our causes. This response points to a real problem when the issue at hand is overwork related to direct involvement in campaigns on justice concerns. A long-term challenge remains as to how churches, large unions, governments and solidarity networks might increase their ability to stand in solidarity with the exploited, to hear their needs and to respond without putting further burdens on their backs. An underlying unsettling question is how such institutions might be *effectively* in solidarity with the exploited by educating their constituencies, through public encouragement of solidarity, and continued (or increased) allocations of personnel and finances. It seems evident that issues of the exploited are not really considered *societal* issues. At least there is mounting outcry for job creation and for alternative budgets. This offers some hope.

A key concern for the Homework Coalition and Homeworkers Association is how to influence decisions about new work processes, social policy and macroeconomic management. What methods may facilitate us to devise new strategies to combat management's drive to expand its powers? Social devaluation of women makes a campaign for transformation a major challenge indeed. Coalition approaches to advocacy have focused on public education and political advocacy to alter current structural relations of ruling. Although fear of reprisal limits homeworkers' participation, some have come to press conferences and consultations. The further problems of access, legal expertise, language, lost revenues and child-care expenses emphasize that privilege and the ability to participate are socially and politically constructed.

The issue is complex. The Homework Coalition is "multiracial" and faces issues of power privilege. Given the social construction of knowledge that is not gender or "race" neutral, the task is obviously lifelong. We discussed among ourselves and asked the homeworkers about their needs and desires regarding advocacy. The HWA encouraged the lobbying. Some homeworkers joined us and are beginning to take the lead. Public profile has deprived some of work. Because of the high stakes for homeworkers, they have asked the Homework Coalition, including their co-ordinator, to represent them. We accept that this approach has temporary validity. Sue Findlay challenges, however, how feminist organizations reproduce privilege by engaging in representation that "might be more of a problem than a solution."[44] The thinking behind this position is that dividing our lived reality into categories that basically separate "race" and class encodes privilege. Such representation appeared to be the only way to have HWA and Homework Coalition interests represented in current policy making by the provincial government. While deciding to proceed, we had to fit our representation into "existing hierarchies of class, gender and race that define our system of governing and maintain the interests of the dominant groups in society."[45] Overcoming this obstacle requires provision of alternative, secure work for those courageous enough to speak publicly.

Focus on legislation as a coalition priority meant that Homework Coalition meetings included many references to labour practice and law, and to bureaucrats and politicians known to some. Those of us who had come with different expertise and ways of working sometimes found the process difficult to follow. Patient explanations helped. Capacity to contribute and to be creative were, nevertheless, limited for some participants during this part of meetings.

The ILGWU staff was extremely committed in working to obtain grants for both HWA and Homework Coalition research, organization and leadership formation, and in co-ordinating research which they linked directly with the HWA in order to mobilize actions. Legal clinics worked with the Workers' Information and Action Center and the ILGWU to process homeworkers' problems that required legal action. Other participants' strengths centred on analysis, popular education and action. Lack of funding to do the extra work posed another limiting factor for the ILGWU and for the coalition partners.[46] The fact that complex, diversified relations strengthened coalition work also meant that remembering to convey decisions made by some to others could be a challenge. My experience was that I needed to remain very alert to follow conversations and plans, and even to know what questions to ask about gaps in my understanding. We have discussed these issues at Homework Coalition meetings.

Since this was my first immersion into union culture, that too was enriching and challenging. I was often deeply encouraged and inspired as we collaborated in this broad-based solidarity. The concerted action and lobbying of the Homeworkers' Association, Homework Coalition and the Ontario Federation of Labour, to launch our Clean Clothes Campaign, for example, was outstanding. In the public forum of four hundred women at an OFL women's conference, I found myself longing for churches to take up women's issues so passionately, thoroughly and publicly. My inner desires for doing justice and my action in solidarity came together in that event. That night I dreamt of huge waves crashing magnificently on the shore and of many white horses bounding out of the sea! I painted this image of integration and I refer to it here because the personal is profoundly political. Public action can also be deeply healing and therapeutic, especially when it offsets structural causes of poverty. Since the latter are the foundation and framework of much exhaustion, depression and despair, only social solidarity and effective societal change can bring transformation.[47]

Representing an ecumenical churches' coalition within a union-dominated culture was quite difficult for the first two years. Mostly I listened. Each culture has its own jargon and inner circles of knowing. In time, we got to know and trust each other with ease. Members have also emphasized their enthusiasm about including churches' ethical concerns about wages and working conditions in discussions with government and business representatives.

My experience as an educator has shown me the amazing value of holistic relations, especially for work requiring solidarity and transformation. As a coalition, we have not included process, song, holistic approaches at meetings, except for the neck and shoulder massages which the homeworkers love! So I focus on what we have in common, learning their approach to bring about significant change.

Another source of complexity and a possibility of strength lie in the fact that legislation protecting homeworkers directly relates to union-ized factory contract negotiations as well as to homeworkers them-selves. Organization is needed among garment factory workers, those recently unemployed and homeworkers.

Campaign initiatives and other events bring the Homework Coali-tion and the Homeworkers' Association to a juncture with new possibil-ities for collaboration. Homework Coalition members are convinced that effective social change depends on commitment and capacity to network in creative, inclusive, non-hierarchical ways. Engaging in social unionism or broad-based solidarity campaigns is in itself a radi-cal step forward within union tradition.

The complexity of privilege in social organization based on educa-tion, experience, "race" and class was being clarified. This critique offered us knowledge of what blocks participation, creativity and greater effectiveness. All of these needed to be taken into account as new plans of action were put forth. It was a source of hope for me that operative capacity to dialogue, to critique courageously and to be imaginative together, strengthened the Homework Coalition for long-term solidarity. Meanwhile, the coalition and individual members' groups consolidated contacts so that we could identify where to focus future campaign efforts.

For the end of 1994 and early 1995, Homework Coalition members were invited to attend meetings of the Homeworkers' Association Advi-sory Group, which was established during the organizing of the HWA Women's Leadership Training Program. It continues to assist the HWA co-ordinator. Other coalition activities were on a temporary hold. Early 1995 was later recognized as a natural end of the Coalition for Fair Wages and Working Conditions for Homeworkers.

Unionized plant closures depleted the ILGWU to the extent that it faced insecurity regarding jobs, priorities of homework organization and coalition building. In the midst of what might signal an end of the road for some, the HWA and workers at the ILGWU sorted out their directions and brought forth alternatives. HWA members determined their own actions, expansion and participation in the Homework Coali-tion. The union was undertaking new projects in direct response to its analysis about global restructuring and local needs.

ILGWU Initiatives and Challenges

Several ILGWU initiatives moved both research and action forward in very significant ways. I now describe aspects of the Garment Workers' Action Project which was supported by the Jobs Ontario Community Action (JOCA). It is also necessary to refer to a major merger that is shaking the ILGWU in the Ontario District and to consider ILGWU recommendations regarding relations with the Homework Coalition.

Garment Workers' Action Project: Jobs Ontario Community Action

The ILGWU embarked on an Action Project with funding from the Jobs Ontario Community Action Fund. A major component of this project was to support Southeast Asian and Chinese outreach in Toronto. Workers developed campaigns and workshops for the union in both unionized and non-unionized workplaces, with homeworkers and with recently unemployed garment workers. The purpose of the gatherings was to build strong leadership capacity among garment workers in the respective communities. The outreach workers also contacted individual workers to provide information on issues like employment rights, social services and immigration.

An educational programs co-ordinator was hired to work mainly in the Hispanic community to design and implement a garment workers' leadership training course and to co-ordinate a conference for garment workers. Not wanting to replicate organization among Hispanics done by the Metro Labour Education Centre, the ILGWU established satellite offices in the greater Toronto area to work with contract and factory workers.[48]

The Southeast Asian homeworking is mainly food preparation and light assembly work. ILGWU outreach within this community was with garment workers in small contracting shops of five to sixteen workers. Some research on the other forms of homeworking is being conducted by the Ontario Federation of Labour.

The ILGWU is researching whether to proceed with an action project to hire a market and business analyst to investigate worker-centred alternative economic strategies for garment workers in the Greater Toronto Area. The researcher would conduct two detailed feasibility studies to analyze possibilities: first, for a production co-op, worker-run, manufacturing company for homeworkers and, second, for channels of distribution for marketing a socially responsible, union-made clothing product line. The studies would evaluate previous sewing co-ops, such as the Portuguese women's Modistas Unidas, and investigate sources of longer-term capital support. Other elements of this research project would involve co-ordinating workshops with the community of interests including homeworkers, factory workers and unemployed workers; consulting consumers and advisory groups to design further outreach and educational components; and helping to co-ordinate a final conference for garment workers and the community partners to evaluate the feasibility study results.[49]

Merger of Unions

Garment workers have traditionally joined either the International Ladies' Garment Workers' Union (ILGWU) or the Amalgamated Clothing and Textile Workers Union (ACTWU). Both have their head offices in New York. The Ontario District ILGWU, central to this study, is part of the larger union. Because of plant closures and widespread unemployment of garment workers, the president of each union negotiated an agreement to merge the two unions. While acknowledging that the garment and textile industries hold much in common, the Ontario District Council passed a resolution on the merger in March. Noting that it had not been consulted, that it had no information about the implications for the district and that its members had no desire to see their union disappear into another organization in Ontario, the Council claimed "the right to determine by secret ballot of its membership whether it wishes to be part of the proposed Merged Union, consistent with the principles of union democracy of the ILGWU and the Canadian Labour Congress."[50] The District Council also resolved that, if it rejected the merged agreement, it was "free to join, amalgamate or merge with another union on terms of its own choosing or become an independent organization."[51] Finally, the council requested full co-operation from the ILGWU to carry out this resolution.

In spite of the initial ILGWU response that the Ontario District Council had no legal right to vote, the president of ACTWU guaranteed the Ontario District Council that their vote to remain separate or to join would be respected. The Ontario District was faced with a critical decision at a very difficult moment. The ILGWU made its final decision at their International Convention in Miami, Florida, in June 1995. Good will has been expressed by union members in either eventuality.[52] In 1995, the ILGWU amalgamated with the Amalgamated Clothing and Textile Workers Union to form the Union of Needletrades,

Industrial and Textile Employees (UNITE). A new coalition, the Labour Behind the Label Coalition, formed in 1996 and embarked on a Wear Fair campaign, focusing on public education, negotiations with retailers regarding codes of conduct, wages and working conditions of homeworkers and legislation. Their "Wear Fair Action Kit" provided background information and suggestions for action for a wide range of educational and activist groups across Canada.[53] I was an active member of this coalition.

By the end of 1999, the Labour Behind the Label Coalition wove a broad-based campaign. They are closely linked to the Maquila Solidarity Network (MSN) whose comprehensive Web site provides campaign updates, action tools, resources and background information. They focus, for example, on college students against sweatshops, both in Canada and the U.S.A., and on the need for effective codes of ethics. The MSN *Stop Sweatshops: An Education and Action Kit* is a particularly useful resource.[54] Their leadership in encouraging thousands to petition for a federal task force on sweatshop abuses was very significant. The Canadian government, after consulting with labour, religious and non-governmental organizations, with retailers, manufacturers and their associations, established a new Canadian Partnership for Ethical Trading. This joint industry/civil working group decided to develop a Canadian Base Code of Labour Practice for the apparel, footwear and related consumer products industries, to consider mechanisms to guarantee compliance with the code and to decide procedures for workers and third parties to deal with violations.[55]

Technology Adjustment Research Project

The ILGWU, Ontario District, spelled out and assessed options for governmental industrial strategy.[56] The first option they considered was market-led development that requires the lowest labour costs, excludes government intervention and accepts free trade, export-led industrialization and fiercely competitive contracting-out strategies. Most of the federal government's Fashioning the Future campaign recommendations promoted this option. The second option built on technological advancement and flexible specialization. In part, it was promoted in the provincial government's industrial policy framework. Allowing for a more proactive approach for workers than the first option, this direction still isolates competition based on technological modernization alone. The just-in-time, quick-response system is a high-tech, low-wage strategy in which costs for workers are minimized or ignored. Nor does having this system guarantee a manufacturer's survival. The ILGWU points out that from 1988 to 1994, their three largest and most modernized factories closed. This system accepts free trade and trade liberalization, the existing power and control of retailers over garment manufacturers and over distribution and the notion of flexibility defined in management's interests. Both these options base the survival of the industry on extreme exploitation of immigrant workers in sweatshops, in small subcontracting arrangements and in homework. They are unacceptable.

The ILGWU developed what they promote as a viable third option: a worker-centred strategy. Calling for direct intervention by federal, provincial and local governments into the market, the union's goal is reintegration of garment production so that costs of restructuring are not placed on workers. The strategy has five main components. Within a macroeconomic context of promoting lower interest rates and fair exchange-rate policies, the union called for a clear and explicit goal of full employment and international fair, managed trade. Without these, communities lack democratic control over production choices. In this option, the government sets clear targets for Canadian garment production and distribution, curtails offshore imports and assesses alternative production techniques. The government also legislates Canadian content regulations for retailers and super-label manufacturers, ties imports to workers and social rights clauses and expands the consumer affairs number information system to facilitate tracking garments from the point of sale back to production. Placing self-sufficiency and fair, managed trade at the centre of sectoral strategy requires consumer education and new policies.

The ILGWU asks long-term questions about key needs of Canadian consumers, about the production of socially useful clothing, such as occupational clothing and women's wear, and about linking clothing design and production with social and cultural needs and uses. Such questions evidence concern for resource use, and for filling people's needs. Import and export policies must respect these values and meet International Labour Organization workers' rights and social rights specifications. In this approach, the government monitors production chains and facilitates decision making through accurate, effective registration, including homeworking.

A new sectoral strategy reintegrates production by focusing on ways for an entire sector rather than individual firms to become more productive. All technological innovations must be evaluated in terms of their impact on workers. Clusters of contracting shops are unionized and/or agree to a comprehensive employment standards review. In this worker-centred strategy, the liaison committee for the city of Toronto oversees a sectoral strategy with several components or points of leverage. Contractors are included in this approach. Development of partnerships between retailers and contractors may establish stable production systems with a high value-added, quality strategy based on workers' rights and well-being. Clustering a subsector offers the possibility of providing access for contractors to electronic data inventory (EDI) capabilities and to both technological and work-in-progress development. If production networks are established, schedules of production runs can be used and technology can be shared, with the overall possibility of producing some economies of scale and of reaching larger markets. More secure connections can offset aspects of competition based only on low wages and prices. Homeworkers may thereby have prior knowledge of their schedules and labour costs will not be the key component of competition.

This new sectoral strategy calls for reregulation of the labour market. Retailers and manufacturers control wages and working conditions, but do it indirectly through contractors who hire cutters and sewers. At the top of the production pyramid, retailers are being challenged to be responsible for their labels. Accountability for wages and working conditions of homeworkers can be legislated through joint liability provisions in the Employment Standards Act. Enforcement involves government action, negotiating and implementing fair international agreements and monitoring by groups whom workers trust. Popular demand for fair production and fair trade is perhaps the most effective tool. It could also provide adequate pressure to obtain registries for public access to information about domestic and international sourcing, including contractors and subcontractors.

The ILGWU set several directions. It recommended ongoing links with community groups to expand the Clean Clothes Campaign and to obtain increased enforcement of labour standards. The union wanted new government initiatives tied to improving wages and working conditions for homeworkers and support to firms linked with monitored employment standards. Since existing labour laws are a barrier to effective organizing in the restructured industry, the union proposes an alternative model of collective bargaining. Through sectoral or broader-based bargaining, workers in a sector may negotiate basic standards together for the entire sector. Examples of positions that are being negotiated include narrowing the wage gap between women sewing operators and male cutters; technological change language such as advance notice, wage protection, job security, seniority, training and arbitration; securing access to unionized contractors; and labour-management committees. The union promotes coherent planning for adjustment programs to incorporate needs of immigrant women such as language, schedules, location, meetings and provision of child care.

The challenge the ILGWU sets forth is creative even as it requires immense dedication and energy. On a daily basis, it means a "factory by factory approach" as they encourage manufacturers to develop new productive capacities by reorganizing inefficient lines, to create new work designs and to increase training opportunities. In the long term, the union is involved in a process between labour and community groups even as it negotiates with industry and seeks government intervention. Union workers are eager to engage in whatever dialogue and struggle are necessary to forge an industrial worker-centred strategy. In order to build the voice of workers, they are focusing on organizing, educating and bringing together workers in unionized factories, in small contracting shops and in homes. They are looking for an actual, community-based drive with the understanding that this is a long-term strategy of developing worker and community solidarity.

As indicated earlier, the ILGWU established contacts between workers and researchers in Mexico, Central America and Europe. With limited resources, the union continues research on the global assembly line and modernization strategies. A hope for the future is to bring workers together to forge an international worker-centred strategy.

In summary, the ILGWU offers an alternative worker-centred strategy with a clear focus for a productive industry. It requires active intervention by both federal and provincial governments as well as collaboration of unionized, non-unionized and recently unemployed workers. The union wants to ensure that workers and their communities have democratic control over production, consumption and investment choices. The worker-centred modernization strategy involves macroeconomic changes; regulating retailers; reintegrating production; regulating labour legislation; a factory-by-factory approach; community organizing and educating to build workers' voices; collective bargaining; worker training and adjustment; child care; expanding the Clean Clothes Campaign to involve consumers and to investigate alternative production and distribution channels; and, finally, international, fair and managed trade.[57]

Webs of Solidarity Worldwide

Homeworkers *themselves* are starting to make global links. Sheila Rowbotham emphasizes the tremendous significance of this: "It indicates the possibilities of a new kind of labour movement which challenges hierarchies of race, ethnicity, gender and class."[58] In 1992, an international meeting of homeworkers at the St. Augustine Centre in Bradford, England, brought together about a hundred women, with a significant proportion from Asia. Some were very young. This gathering was a further development of British organizing in West Yorkshire, Yorkshire and Humberside. Jane Tate moves internationally from her West Yorkshire base to connect with homeworkers and to establish links around the globe: in Asia, the Americas, Africa, Europe, Australia and New Zealand.

Sheila Rowbotham based her book, *Homeworkers Worldwide*, on materials gathered by Jane Tate, including those gleaned from her visits to the ILGWU in Toronto. Rowbotham describes a wide range of homeworkers' networks. Less visible ones in Italy, Indonesia and Tanzania organize around women's groups, savings societies and family members. The more known Self Employed Workers Association (SEWA) in India has about 40,000 members. SEWA works at all levels from grassroots, the municipality and the state to the international community. It presses the International Confederation of Free Trade Unions and the International Labour Organization (ILO) to recognize homework as work and to initiate legislative changes globally. Homeworking was the main theme of the ILO in Geneva in 1995.[59] Self-representation by homeworkers and involvement of those in direct solidarity with them, such as members of the ILGWU and of the Homework Coalition, are crucial for conferences of this nature. It is extremely difficult, if not impossible, to gain this representation.

Several initiatives indicate the extent of international organization.[60] Many Portuguese groups, like The Portuguese Knitting Cooperative, have chosen to create their own companies. Based on a large rural women's association in the Philippines, PATAMBA became the National Network of Homeworkers in 1989. Members want home-based workers recognized as a sector of the labour force. Well-established associations in Japan led to a general confederation of all Japan's homeworkers' unions as early as 1960, with an annual symposium since 1972. The Chiang Mai Home Net in Thailand integrates technical and marketing training to develop microentrepreneurial skills among homeworkers. Palestinian women living in poverty participate in embroidery training programs offered by the United Nations Refugees Welfare Association. In all of these countries, marketing is a major problem.

The Association of Women Workers in Hong Kong has had difficulty with their attempts to work with trade unions. The Clothing and Allied Trade Union in Australia, however, led a campaign in 1986 within the union and nationally to inform people about homeworking. Within a year, 6,000 outworkers contacted the union and many joined. The Women's Union in Holland links women left out of other trade unions. Rowbotham finds that reassessment of labour organizing within the trade union movement is particularly advanced in Canada where the Ontario District of the ILGWU, as already described, is actively engaged in creating new forms of solidarity and unionism among factory, home and recently unemployed garment workers.[61]

A network of maquila workers and of organizers along the Mexico-U.S. border has held regional workshops in Tijuana, Torreon and Ciudad Juarez.[62] Another venture in Mexico brought together over sixty representatives of unions and popular organizations from South, Central and North America in Oaxtepec. After discussing the impact of economic integration and restructuring, and common strategies to confront them, they formed a unanimous agreement.[63] Their commitment to joint action included redefining integration processes as an opportunity to build a Continental Social Network to which they committed their efforts.

The global organization of production has made global solidarity an urgent issue among producers in factories and homes. The range of models just cited for organizing homeworkers makes it clear that homeworkers have gone well beyond any single model of organizing. Most integrate the economic and social. Some try co-operative production. Both international women's networks and international church networks have spread awareness and forged direct links among homeworkers. Some homeworkers gather to read Hebrew, Christian or Muslim scriptures. Some find their greatest help was their early education in Catholic workers' movements. A homeworker from England spoke at a European church conference in Naples in a general discussion about global economic disparity. Ecumenical groups in Toronto have sponsored workshops on homeworking.

Relations of Solidarity

Following an entire chapter about a campaign of solidarity, I underline the central importance of attentiveness and solidarity with those who work in sweatshops and homes, those who make visible the effects of present federal and provincial policies. As Anne Patrick clarifies, responsible action requires that all ask, "What are you going through?" and then *listen* with openness to whatever they say, with recognition of the systemic injustice that causes suffering. By hearing anguish into speech and into the public realm, "the question of action will be addressed much more adequately than if we limit our attention to traditional rules of conduct" or simply to what has been legislated.[64] A second step toward a praxis of solidarity is to internalize the voices of injustice, standing with them, allowing the realities to inform our personal and social consciences so that we may in fact hear the voices of those adversely affected by the systems we live by. Since living and acting in solidarity is so demanding, Anne Patrick adds a third step, one set in a faith context, that we "allow the challenging protests and demands to play over a ground alto of God's healing and empowering and justice-making love for us all."[65] Action for change involves walking a road requiring steady generosity, openness, gentle listening, disciplined dialogue, deep appreciation for the gifts of each person and humour that keeps foibles in perspective.

Conclusion

The ILGWU and the Coalition for Fair Wages and Working Conditions for Homeworkers launched historically significant initiatives in several areas:
1. persevering broad-based solidarity, locally, nationally and internationally;
2. the formation and support of the Homeworkers' Association which is linked with the union as a local associate;
3. remaining closely allied with those who suffer the effects of corporate, bank and government decision making;
4. initiating dialogue with retailers and designers and, because of the ineffectiveness of these efforts, broadcasting the issue in the public imagination in a wide range of creative educational projects and actions;
5. orchestrating well-researched proposals for legislative protection on the provincial level and lobbying to inform and urge all parties to act; and

6. researching with extremely limited resources to pinpoint abuses and
   alternatives for the direction of the industry itself.

A myriad of questions arises from reflection on the first four chapters. Some of the core issues include: (1) the relationship between
recently unemployed, factory and homeworkers in garment production, (2) the challenge of creating new forms of social organization
inclusive of gender and "racial"-ethnic specificities and (3) the nature
of a process broad enough to foster transformation of social values
which would become manifest in legislation, organization and education, as well as in issues of privileged power.[66] The task is to search
out, foreground, analyze and counteract factors in our society that support exploitation of the working poor, while promoting initiatives that
foster solidarity and societal transformation. We are challenged to discern and judge the extent to which we engage in authentic and
exploitative webs of relationships, and then to act with integrity.

Transition to Part II

The task at hand is not just to implement and enforce legislative change. This is a work looking toward the transformation of communities and culture in which economic disparity and violence are
increasing dramatically.

How is it that people who profess good will across sectors cannot
dialogue? How is it that only the rich and powerful voices dominate?
Disturbing differences of perspective shape experience, interpretation of
events and data and judgements about relations. Engagement in this
campaign reinforces the relevance of horizon, bias, difference, the pub-
lic/private split and social organization. The issue of individual and
group horizon is foundational in order to shift from debate based on
control gained through capital, wealth and privilege and move to dialogue, with full transparency and participation. The very integrity of our
culture and democratic base is at stake. Critiquing and creating cultural
vision, value systems, definitions of what is meaningful, of what we
allow as legitimate information and means of communicating and of
how we express our societal relations all come under scrutiny. These are
minimum requirements if we are to scratch below the surface of the
crises evident in the exploitation of women's work but extending far
beyond it. Closely related are the obstacles or biases that limit and distort our vision and our ability to comprehend differences in horizon.

At the heart of the conflicting relations are power differentials based
on differences themselves, and on division between the public and the

private. These factors point to the need to do economics, business and governing ethically. Norms which extend beyond those of recent capitalist economic history should be examined in the search for social and economic justice. What principles, attitudes and methods will effect social-institutional change in ways that empower us to assume responsibility for the social, economic and ethical systems we create and/or allow?

Unless we embark on this extensive challenge to critique and shape domestic and global contexts of homeworking responsibly, those who seek transformation will forever be frustrated by dealing only with symptoms and bandages. In the next part, therefore, I engage in ethical reflection that is far more than a list of principles. It involves the individual and communal critical appropriation of both tradition and the situation, and calls for both long- and short-term transformations. I explore the relevance of diversity, radical pluralism, collaborative responses and hopeful, authentic paths in this postmodern era. Readers focusing on ecological, social and economic justice issues other than homeworking may also find this of significant assistance.

Notes

1 Borowy, Gordon and Lebans, "Are These Clothes Clean?" 305.
2 Ecumenical Coalition for Economic Justice, Toronto, ON, 15 January 1990, unpublished minutes of an administrative council meeting. Note that this explanation in no way limits dialogue, future elaboration, correction and/ or expansion of this work in progress.
3 We also supported Lorraine Michael's work as co-director of The Future of Women's Work Committee and later as co-chair of the social policy campaign within her ECEJ work. Both are committees of the National Action Committee of the Status of Women (NAC). We see this collaboration as mutually beneficial, effective means to establish solidarity, to expand research capability and to implement economic justice. The position was subsequently held by Kathryn Robertson and then terminated in 1999, with lack of funding given as the reason.
4 Janet Silman, "A Women's View from Within: Indian Women as Moral Agents of Change in Canada" (Ph.D. diss., Emmanuel College, Toronto, 1990), 151, 193-94, 203, 250.
5 Borowy, Gordon and Lebans, "Are These Clothes Clean?" 314: Homeworkers' employment remains so precarious that joining the Association is an act of bravery. But diverse motivations coalesce into a common purpose to work together to change the situation.
6 Subsequent co-ordinators: Rose Cho (1995-96) and Angela Choi (1997).
7 Parkdale Legal Clinic has taken the lead in providing this information. There has been other support for projects such as obtaining funding to cover start-up costs to produce a documentary film addressing issues arising from the development and proliferation of homework.

8 Refer to "The Homeworkers' Association," in Borowy, Gordon and Lebans, "Are These Clothes Clean?" 310-11. Although other ethnic/linguistic communities talked with coalition members about the probability of homeworking in their constituencies and suggested contact possibilities, lack of resources delayed early expansion and follow-up beyond the South Asian focus.

9 Ibid., 309. The Associate ILGWU Members' locals range "from retirees to factory workers who hadn't (yet) been successful in organizing, to flower vendors in New York City. The ILGWU Ontario District reasoned that creating a new Associate Members' local would be an appropriate way to provide an organizational structure for homeworkers.... The International Office accepted the drive despite its position of banning homework, recognizing that Ontario labour relations law is quite different than in the U.S. The International Office even provided resources to assist in hiring an organizer. The support from New York was significant. They had allocated a special grant on only one previous occasion."

10 Ibid., 309, 316.

11 ECEJ, "Not by Choice," 3. Current vulnerability of these working poor, often without the mainstream language, has meant that they will not pursue individual grievances to ensure their rights. The ILGWU now includes homeworking in their present collective bargaining process. Hoping to obtain official contracts, public registers and associate membership in the union, the intent is to set standards for wage rates, employee benefits and health and safety regulations, as well as bargain for more effective governmental enforcement through company audits. Resistance to protection of the homeworkers' rights is strong because use of homeworking keeps wages lower through competition for subsistence levels, minimizes pressure for publicly supported child-care services and full assumption of parenting responsibilities by the partner (if there is one).

12 Borowy, Gordon and Lebans, "Are These Clothes Clean?" 310: "Bargaining committees were pushed to accept wage concessions, lengthened work weeks and work speed-ups at the negotiating table because employers were obliging union members to compete with the less-than-minimum wage that homeworkers could be forced to accept. The ILGWU Ontario District attempted to introduce new collective agreement language so that homeworkers would be considered part of the bargaining unit with a particular employer. This strategy has not yet been successful."

13 For a more complete history of American ILGWU attempts to prevent deregulation of industrial homework up to the 1984 permanent lifting of the forty-two-year ban on homeworking, refer to Virginia duRivage and David Jacobs, "Home-Based Work: Labor's Choices," in *Homework: Historical and Contemporary Perspectives on Paid Labor at Home*, ed. Eileen Boris and Cynthia Daniels (Chicago: University of Illinois Press, 1989), 258-71. See also Borowy, Gordon and Lebans, "Are These Clothes Clean?" 316.

14 The homeworker who told about some of her experiences to October 1992 OFL conference participants and lobbies of Liberal, Conservative and New Democratic MPPs has been cut off from her supply of work by her employer, in spite of coalition and media precautions. Kitty is an active

member of the Homeworkers' Association (Borowy, Gordon and Lebans, "Are These Clothes Clean?" 327, n. 24). Fear of employer retaliation is increasing to the extent that homeworkers generally give only anonymous interviews.

15 "Homeworkers' Association" (promotional flyer), Toronto, 1992.

16 Coalition for Fair Wages and Working Conditions for Homeworkers, "Homeworkers Win Thousands of Dollars in Back Wages," *Newsletter* (June 1993): 2.

17 Borowy, Gordon and Lebans, "Are These Clothes Clean?" 313. Homeworkers now have an organized way to stand together for their rights. One homeworker described her relationship with employers: "These people are like monsters, and I am just an ant. They can step on me easily" (ibid., 17).

18 As quoted in Borowy and Yuen, *International Ladies' Garment Workers' Union 1993 Homeworkers' Study*, 10.

19 Employment Standards Act, in *Revised Statutes of Ontario 1990*, chapter E14, article 16.

20 Intercede and ILGWU, *Meeting the Needs of Vulnerable Workers*, 25.

21 Borowy, Gordon and Lebans, "Are These Clothes Clean?" 323. Estimates of the number of homeworkers unreported by their employers in Toronto ranged from 60 to 90 per cent of the homework labour force. (This is a low estimate since only seventy-five were registered in 1991 and there are at least 2,000 garment homeworkers in Metro Toronto alone.) Even a year later, there was no effective response to the coalition and ILGWU submission to the Employment Practices Branch of fourteen employers not using permits in early 1992 (Johnson and Johnson, *The Seam Allowance*, 102-103).

22 See Employment Standards Working Group, *Bad Boss Stories: Workers Whose Bosses Break the Law* (Toronto, 1996).

23 Dagg and Fudge, "Sewing Pains," 24-25.

24 Ibid., 25.

25 Swasti Mitter, "On Organizing Women in Casualized Work: A Global Overview," in *Dignity and Daily Bread: New Forms of Economic Organizing among Poor Women in the Third World and the First*, ed. Sheila Rowbotham and Swasti Mitter (New York: Routledge, 1994), 20-21.

26 Employment Standards Act, in *Revised Statutes of Ontario 1990*, Regulation 325, "General," 4f, 6e and 7d. The cabinet could delete these exemptions by issuing an order in cabinet.

27 Handout at the OFL Convention, November 1991. For a more detailed explanation of section 12, see the Coalition for Fair Wages and Working Conditions for Homeworkers, *Fair Wages and Working Conditions for Homeworkers: A Brief*, 7. A problem lies in the interpretation of common law that property owners are free to organize their businesses the best way they see fit. This tends to provide an inhibition to effective application of the provision. The brief also explains subcontracting and the enforcement of labour standards, the current framework for regulating homework, legal solutions, suggestions for the effective enforcement of the Employment Standards Act and other reforms. Refer to 6-17.

28 They urge labour law reform, rather than regulatory changes alone, in order to address "the structural basis for profound inequality in bargaining

power" (Ontario Federation of Labour booklet on the lobby agenda, Toronto, 1 October 1992, 9-10).

29 "In 1985, nearly 84 per cent of all of Ontario's registered businesses employed fewer than ten workers" (Intercede and ILGWU, *Meeting the Needs of Vulnerable Workers*, 25, referring to Urban Dimensions Group, Inc., *Growth of the Contingent Workforce in Ontario: Structural Trends, Statistical Dimensions and Policy Implications*, a report prepared for Ontario Women's Directorate, February 1989.

30 Intercede and ILGWU, *Meeting the Needs of Vulnerable Workers*, 59. Proposals for effective sectoral regulation are outlined on 60-71 and province-wide mandatory broader-based bargaining on 71-76.

31 News conference, 16 December 1993, Toronto, Ontario, "Notes for Remarks by the Honourable Bob Mackenzie, Minister of Labour for Ontario." See also "Homeworkers Receive Aid," *The Globe and Mail*, 17 December 1993, A6; Leslie Papp, "Home-Based Garment Workers Get Raise," *The Toronto Star*, 16 December 1993, A2; Steve Payne, "Garment Workers Will Get Pay Hike," *The Toronto Star*, 17 December 1993, A14. Public demonstrations such as on 23 November 1993 by both organizations had kept the concern in public view. Regular lobbying continued, such as with Ministry of Labour personnel, 13 August 1993; Attorney General Marion Boyd and Labour Minister Honourable Bob Mackenzie, 1 January 1993; Frances Lankin, minister of Trade and Economic Development, 10 November 1993; and Steven Mahony, opposition Labour critic, 16 November 1993.

32 In response to trade union pressure, the government initiated research to reform the Ontario Labour Relations Act. This promoted members of Intercede and of the Homework Coalition to question how this could benefit homeworkers and to lobby for sectoral collective bargaining. Refer to Intercede and ILGWU, *Meeting the Needs of Vulnerable Workers*.

33 Refer to William Walker, "NDP Puts Election Over New Policies," *The Toronto Star*, 30 March 1994, A1, 23.

34 James Rusk, "Garment Trade Conditions Protested," *The Globe and Mail*, 15 February 1994, A16; Tony Van Alphen, "Help Urged for Garment Workers," *The Toronto Star*, 15 February 1994, A7; and Rashida Phooma, "Still Fighting," *The Toronto Sun*, 21 February 1994, S6.

35 Refer to *Our Times*, an independent Canadian labour magazine, and *Practice of Ministry in Canada*, an ecumenical journal. We made presentations at conferences such as Labour Notes in Detroit, 1993; the Toronto School of Theology Women's Day, 26 March 1993; and Our Local Economy, Toronto, 8-13 May 1993.

36 Lisa Wright, "Protesters Swamp Eaton Centre: 1,000 Marchers Seek Justice for Workers on Strike," *The Toronto Star*, 7 March 1993, A7; Judy Steed, "And the Revolution Goes On ... 90s Women Focus on a 'Fairer Share' of Power, Money," *The Toronto Star*, 8 March 1993, A1; and Martin Powell, "Marchers Call Firms Exploitative: Protest Precedes Women's Day," *The Toronto Star*, 8 March 1993, A10. ETAC Sales Ltd., which controlled Alfred Sung, Brettons, Ports International and Tabi International, went into receivership because of mismanagement by Alfred Chan. See Maureen

Murray, "Business Handled Poorly, Alfred Sung Complains," *The Toronto Star*, 21 February 1994, B1; Maureen Murray, "Banks to Topple Retail Empire," *The Toronto Star*, 29 March 1994, B1, 16; and Maureen Murray, "500 Out of Work as Judge Rules ETAC Bankrupt," *The Toronto Star*, 30 March 1994, C1.

37 Mark Zwolinski, "Women Mark Historic Year: Annual Event Organized by Women of Colour," *The Toronto Star*, 6 March 1994, A3.

38 The Public Service Alliance of Canada (PSAC), Ontario region, co-sponsored the conference along with the ILGWU, the Centre for Research on Work and Society (York University) and the Coalition for Fair Wages and Working Conditions for Homeworkers. Funding came from groups such as the Ontario Women's Directorate, Social Sciences and Humanities Research Council of Canada, School Sisters of Notre Dame and the Technology Adjustment Research Project. Regis College donated the use of their entire classroom building for the weekend and the Toronto Dominican Friars provided equipment for interpretation.

39 Refer to Jan Borowy, Shelly Gordon, Belinda Leach, Barbara Paleczny and Lynda Yanz, *From the Double Day to the Endless Day: Proceedings from the Conference on Homeworking, November 1992* (Ottawa: Canadian Centre for Policy Alternatives, 1994). Conference organizers decided that formation of policy statements or a charter on homeworking, which would have been a new step for us though not new historically, were too ambitious at this time. Policy statements from Europe provide evidence both of the scope of the problem and of concerted attempts to bring about more just labour practices. They include three from Britain: 1907 statement by the National Anti-Sweating League, a 1984 Homeworkers' Charter and 1985 Trade Union Policy Proposals on Homeworking and The Council of Europe's Study Group's Proposals on Homeworking 1989. Initiatives to protect homeworkers have been undertaken by the Home Work Support Centre of the Netherlands, the Self-Employed Women's Association (SEWA) of India and The Clothing and Allied Trades Union of Australia. Refer to West Yorkshire Homeworking Group, *A Penny a Bag: Campaigning on Homework* (Batley: Yorkshire and Humberside Low Pay Unit, 1990), Appendix 1 and 2, 111-27.

40 ILGWU office, 29 September 1993.

41 Frances Lankin, MPP, telephone interview, Toronto, 4 December 1996. Lankin was minister during the New Democrat government when the Homework Coalition lobbying was strong.

42 Interview with Marion Boyd, MPP, Ontario Legislature, Queen's Park, Toronto, ON, 20 January 1997.

43 Refer to Dalton Camp, "Politicians Blame Recession on Its Victims," *The Toronto Star*, 23 March 1994, A23.

44 Sue Findlay, "Problematizing Privilege: Another Look at Representation," in *And Still We Rise: Feminist Political Mobilizing in Contemporary Canada*, ed. Linda Carty (Toronto: Women's Press, 1993), 217.

45 Ibid.

46 By the end of 1996, cancellation of several provincial funding grants and the loss of many union-dues-paying members resulted in loss of union staff:

one union representative, one researcher/educator, three outreach workers, one organizer and one adjustment worker. In March 1997, another four staff who work with the unemployed were cut.

47 In another work in progress, I explain some of the biblical ties.

48 Interview with Janet Borowy, ILGWU researcher, 27 March 1995, Toronto.

49 International Ladies' Garment Workers' Union, "Challenging Employment Opportunity," job description, Toronto, 1994.

50 International Ladies' Garment Workers' Union, "Special Edition on Union Merger," *Fabric* (24 March 1995): 1. See also Alexandra Dagg, "Information on the Proposed Merger of Our Union," *Fabric* 10, 2 (March 1995): 1.

51 ILGWU, "Special Edition on Union Merger," 1.

52 Refer to Alexandra Dagg, "Manager's Report," *Fabric* 9, 4 (May 1995): 1.

53 Labour Behind the Label Coalition, "Wear Fair Action Kit" (Toronto: Labour Behind the Label Coalition, 1998), http://www.maquilasolidarity.org.

54 Bob Jeffcott, Musonda Kidd, Sonia Singh, Kevin Thomas, Ian Thomson and Lynda Yanz, *Stop Sweatshops: An Education and Action Kit* (Toronto: Maquila Solidarity Network, 2000), http://www.maquilasolidarity.org.

55 Maquila Solidarity Network, "Codes of Conduct." 9 September 1999, http://www.maquilasolidarity.org. The meeting on 11 November 1999 included representatives of the Canadian Council for International Cooperation, the Canadian Labour Congress, the Labour Behind the Label Coalition, the Social Affairs Commision of the Canadian Conference of Catholic Bishops, the Steelworkers Humanity Fund, the Union of Needletrades, Industrial and Textile Employees, the Hudson's Bay Company, Sears Canada, Arrow Shirts, the Grand National Apparel Company, the Apparel Manufacturers Association, the Retail Council, the Shoe Manufacturers Association and the Alliance of Manufacturers and Exporters.

56 ILGWU, *Designing the Future for Garment Workers*, 50-69, as the reference for this section. Initiated by Alexandra Dagg, the third phase of the ILGWU TARP project builds on phase one in 1990-91, the evaluation of existing training and adjustment programs, which led to the Apparel and Textile Action Centre, and on phase two from 1991-93, the homeworkers' study, and the initial plans for the homeworkers' conference. Phases one and two were co-ordinated by Barbara Cameron. Teresa Mak and Deena Ladd were research assistants. Jan Borowy developed and co-ordinated the research for phase three, including the industry analysis, policy overview, manufacturers' linkages survey, case studies and focus groups and the special conference for the union.

57 ILGWU, *Designing the Future for Garment Workers*, 70-76.

58 Rowbotham, *Homeworkers Worldwide*, 3.

59 International Labour Organization, *Homework: International Labour Organization Conference, 82nd Session, 1995*, Report 5 (1) (Geneva, 1995, approved in 1996). Responses of member states to the ILO's questionnaire indicated deep divisions over the feasibility and means of regulating homework. Reluctance stemmed from the alleged difficulties of enforcing legislation, of protecting vulnerable non-unionized workers from reprisal and of understanding weakened governmental capabilities in the midst of apparent international taxpayer revolt. Although this occurred after the period of

focus in this book, I note the importance of critical identity and socio-economic analysis of each of these reasons. Political will and solidarity offer alternative solutions.

60 Rowbotham, *Homeworkers Worldwide*, 56-66.

61 Ibid., 78.

62 Yanz, "Women's Maquila Network," 4. Refer to the Nicaraguan Centre for Labour Studies and Analysis (CEAL), *Union Organizing in the Maquilas*, LAWG Letter #46 (Toronto, September 1994), for a country-by-country analysis of maquila factories in Central America and union organizing.

63 "Declaration, Oaxtepec, Morelos, Mexico, 13 March 1994," reported in "Popular Alternatives and Continental Alliances", *Correspondencia* 16 (May 1994): 20-22. The participating organizations are listed according to countries.

64 Anne E. Patrick, *Liberating Conscience: Feminist Explorations in Catholic Moral Theology* (New York: Continuum Publishing, 1997), 196.

65 Ibid., 198.

66 That the Homework Coalition needed to mount a broadly based campaign to obtain minimum employment standards and recognition of responsibility for these indicates problems in our culture. That over two years of persistent, public efforts and political advocacy have left us without protective legislation is evidence of the extent of injustice and the depth of the need for conversion. See Wildung Harrison, *Making the Connections*, xiv-xx.

Part II

Constructing Feminist
Socio-economic Ethics as
Transformative Theology

5

Horizon, Bias and Specificity/
Difference Analysis Related
to Homeworking

Quiet wisdom
Working, resting
Weaving wondering watching

The first step of identifying underlying core issues involves an exploration of horizon, bias and operative application of attitudes about specificity and difference. These make visible the connections among prevailing attitudes, myths and customs in a society which tolerates exploitation. First, I examine the dominant horizon to uncover presuppositions that comprise the views of reality within which economic decisions are made. Second, I attend to unacknowledged biases that distort the capacity to imagine and to decide, and even the will to recognize and respect differences. Third, I explore some of the sources and justification of the devaluation of women which include attitudes about gender, "race" and wealth/empire and their instrumentalization as means of exploitation. In this section I ask, "What difference does difference make?"

Notes to chapter 5 are on pp. 161-66.

Horizon and Feminist Analysis

What is the meaning of horizon in this context and what is its relevance both for feminist consciousness and for economic theory?

Meaning of Horizon

The ability to hear and understand the perspective of home-workers is contingent upon the extent of one's horizon or worldview. Since descriptions and explanations of what is happening historically regarding women's work vary significantly and also determine preferred solutions, the meaning of horizon becomes important. In the long term, considerable changes may emerge, not on the basis of the dominant, contemporary socio-economic horizon, but rather by envisaging a quite different and perhaps, at first sight, incomprehensible alternative. In oppressive situations such alternate envisioning is essential. It requires conversion and transformation.

Societal and individual horizons underlie generally accepted myths that sustain social and economic relations.[1] This relates to what Thomas S. Kuhn calls a paradigm: "an entire constellation of beliefs, values, techniques, and so on shared by the members of a given community."[2] Horizon denotes the extent of an individual or group field of vision and is different according to one's standpoint.[3] Differing standpoints give rise to different selective processes and different accounts of events that may in fact be incomplete and approximate portrayals of an enormously complex range of meanings and values.[4]

By engaging in critical reflection to see what is going forward in its particular history, a group may reflect on its standpoints and fields of vision. Group process may enable participants to prefer data to surmises as a basis for inquiry. As members move beyond original assumptions and perspectives, the investigation gradually offers understanding of the issue to reveal further significant data for inquiry. They can improve their ability to prioritize what is most relevant and urgent, to connect inquiries and to discover ways to collaborate, dialogue and modify views. These skills open them to experience insight, to reject obstacles to understanding and to reconsider the importance of previously unconsidered relevant data.[5] Their interaction may, in fact, extend their horizon.

Limits of horizon leave some objects beyond one's vision. In this analogous use of horizon, what lies outside one's horizon is simply outside the range of one's comprehension, interest and concern. One's standpoint determines the greatness or smallness of topics of interest and knowledge within one's horizon. Differences in horizon may be (1) complementary with respect and recognition of the need for others with different interests and specialties; (2) related within successive stages of development in different stages of growth; and (3) dialectically opposed. What for one is intelligible, true or good, for another is unintelligible. One may tend to attribute the other's horizon to wishful thinking, to an acceptance of myth, to ignorance or error, to blindness or illusion, to immaturity or, in religious terms, to a refusal of divine invitation and gifts.

Since learning happens organically by building on previous learning, so intentions, statements and deeds arise within, and are shaped by, contexts. Appeals to these contexts are used to explain goals, qualify statements and give rationale for deeds. What does not fit within a horizon will either be ignored or deemed irrelevant or unimportant. "Horizons then are the sweep of our interests and of our knowledge, ... but they also are the boundaries that limit our capacities for assimilating more than we already have attained."[6] Issues of home management and its relationship to both standard and non-standard work, for example, may well be outside the horizons of both government policy setters and corporate officers.

Our experiences tend to be very patterned. Our way of seeing or imagining functions in accordance with our own expectations, interests or artistic, intellectual and practical preferences. These are partially self-determined. At the same time, socio-economic realities shape contexts and frameworks of thinking. As Robert Doran, and Paulo Freire before him, point out, patterns can be functions of psychological, social, economic, political and linguistic conditioning, and of social and psychological determinisms. These, in fact, may be conveyed as if there are no other alternatives, no options in how to consider problems and no latitude in imagining solutions. In other words, the categories of thinking are presented as unchangeable. But critical reflection and reasonable judgement create liberating power to break open closed horizons:

> The primary and indispensable feature of Freire's pedagogy entails helping people recognize that they can reach an understanding of their experience that is outside the conditioned pattern and that launches a possibility of a new interpretation and a new pattern by setting one on a process of further questions. Freire brings people to this insight into insight by raising questions that would shake them out of the conditioned patterns.... He brings them to ... appropriate the fact that latent within them is a power of raising questions that can break the patterns of their experience, that can lead to

insight.... The very power of understanding, when owned, is a source of liberation from patterns of oppressed consciousness.[7]

Discovery of capacity to think critically and to feel deeply can be revolutionary, especially when shared in solidarity. These abilities have
been critically skewed for us as whole peoples in the West.

Feminist Consciousness and Horizon

A steady process of open inquiry to determine questions relevant to issues such as wages, relations of ruling, societal myths, profit
accumulation and working conditions becomes a significant way of
expanding consciousness and setting conditions conducive to the creation of alternative solutions. The process of inquiry and of broadening
horizons lies at the heart of the feminist consciousness which defines
homeworking as a public issue. Doing feminist ethical theory requires a
horizon with a complex alteration of consciousness from that of supporting the status quo. Rozena Maart, for example, makes this point in
relation to racism in feminist theory when she says, "the *false assumptions* inherent in the belief that knowledge and the ability to generate
knowledge has a position of privilege—that being an agent of racism
and classism entitles one to generate and create knowledge."[8] The
clear challenge is "to dismantle the relations of white domination
through its many levels of thought, word and action."[9]

Cynthia Crysdale examines trends of how women know and the
significance of moving beyond deprivation-reinforced silence. Not only
can we receive knowledge, we can discover or construct knowledge.
Such learning has power to change lives:

> Many contemporary women, if they are not totally "silent," can only con-
> ceive of themselves as receivers of knowledge. Even those who move
> beyond this to some confidence in their own "inner voice" find assertion of
> their role as "discoverers" of knowledge to be radical, revolutionary, and
> requiring courageous changes in their communities of meaning. Thus, self-
> appropriation for women, even in its descriptive, untechnical form, seems to
> engage them in powerful existential struggles, not only with the operations
> they use in knowing, but with their roles as agents of their own discoveries
> rather than as mere receivers of others' knowledge.[10]

Sheila Mullett sees several steps in such feminist horizon change. A
first step is one of sensitivity, contrasted with the lack of consciousness
of women's suffering and the lack of white consciousness of others'
"racial"-ethnic suffering, which makes people inadvertently perpetuate
suffering in ordinary social patterns and institutions. Sensitivity to vari-

ous forms of violence against all women broadens the horizon and reveals social arrangements which contribute to suffering.[11] Though sensitivity forms a necessary first moment in doing feminist ethics, it takes more than awareness of women's suffering to constitute feminist consciousness.

A second step is the recognition of the social construction of relationships and of questions of agency and social responsibility. Feminist consciousness or horizon includes awareness that social situations are not merely natural, inevitable or inescapable.[12] It involves a double perspective of seeing situations in their present social contexts while imagining possibilities for transformation. It is a way of perceiving and imagining differently. Such consciousness may cause ontological shock "because it opens up whole new areas of ambiguity and uncertainty and requires continuous attempts to formulate new possibilities for action. In short it puts everything into question."[13] Both thought and feeling are called into play as we sort out the apparent from what is really happening, as we experience how intolerable the suffering is and how confusing it is to have access to only partial knowledge. This confusion is compounded by shock as familiar categories of interpretation shift, even though possibilities of social transformation are hardly conceived.[14] Such contradictions in society foster either the emergence or the suffocation of this consciousness.[15] So do concrete circumstances which make a significant alteration in the status of women feasible.

A third step of feminist horizon is discovered in collective awareness. Thinking itself is transformed when a collective is concerned with transformative possibilities within a given social context. For white women, the call for transformation requires us to shift and expand horizons sufficiently to gain collective awareness and to understand implications for how we listen, dialogue, produce knowledge, collaborate, process, advocate and critique.[16] Embedded in this approach to praxis is "the idea that our perception of reality emerges in our efforts to transform it."[17] Transformative perceptions arise out of collective integration of thought and action and out of subsequent discernments as groups dare to imagine alternate constructions of reality.

There are differing horizons among those who are aware of violence against women. Some people privatize both causes of problems and solutions. Others take account of social connections and solidarity. Taken in isolation of the social, privatization shackles healing of root causes. Adherence to a horizon inadequate to the scope of the problem drains energy from building social movements.

Sharing in a collective process offers possibilities for thinking, imagining and constructing socio-economic relations anew. Through engagement, both individual and social consciousness also become progressively more interior and nuanced. Willing to sort out values collaboratively, people with feminist consciousness are facilitated in incorporating new perspectives that transcend previously rigid moral normativity.

Our ways of being in relationship both within ourselves and with each other, and our ways of theorizing challenge how we know and how we act. Ethical imperatives emerge. They are so essential that they may be regarded as a transformed approach to natural law, one that recognizes our full potential as human beings. As Bernard Lonergan describes them, they are "the demands of the human spirit: be attentive, be intelligent, be reasonable, be responsible and be in love."[18] I adapt and expand his explanation of these. Being attentive involves attending to the data of the conscious and unconscious in a personal, social, differentiated and earth-centred horizon. Being intelligent involves use of a balance of both right- and left-brain activity. Being reasonable requires gathering sufficient information to make informed judgements and not deferring decision making when such information is available. Being responsible implies action to implement just relations. Being in love heals, makes fulfillment of the other demands possible and opens those who love to the Spirit or power of love. Doing these dynamic operations becomes a condition of cultural advance, enabling us to turn from and overcome destruction and allowing us to imagine alternatives and healing. They are transcendental in that each is the condition of finding meaning, truth and value.

Praxis that flows from and causes expanding consciousness is constitutive of the self and of the world we decide to build together.[19] In spite of the importance of this expanded horizon, people tend to drift into a horizon without adverting to it or attempting to discern its adequacy.[20] Feminist goals include broadening horizons and choosing ways of relating. Both involve deliberate decision. Different horizons may result in different notions of history itself, incompatible standpoints and irreconcilable histories.

An example demonstrates the importance of horizon for this study. Beverly Wildung Harrison clarifies reference to horizon by applying it directly to gender relations.

There is, I submit, a clear connection between our psychic tolerance for subjugation at the interpersonal level and the social, economic and political

forms we tolerate or approve at the socio-economic level.... This basic perception of power-in-relationship affects in turn both our feeling for what
sort of world is possible and our sense of what ought to be, what is desirable. In sum, our sense of reality foundational to our moral development,
what we may call our overall horizon of moral expectation, is shaped by
gender patterns and our experience of gender relation.[21]

Such a correlation suggests that our very categories of thinking, questioning and imagining alternative relations depend directly on our
awareness of outer-directed, other-determined subjugation. Experience
tends to set the boundaries for what is possible and even desirable; in
other words, our sense of reality is foundational to our overall horizon
of moral expectation. Similarly, androcentric patterns of home and
work may limit ability to comprehend issues opened by feminist consciousness. Horizon filters the data accepted as relevant information
and shapes how we judge facts.

Economics and Horizon

Contemporary economic theory is a major constituent of
social consciousness, shaping what we as a people think is possible and
what we believe we must simply accept in difficult times. In practice,
looking for solutions to the conceptual frameworks only within an economic discipline limits creative imagination. Experience is bypassed as
a source of concern, information and insight into the socio-economic
world and as a basis for alternative approaches to the present crisis.[22]
Individual consciousness is organized largely by its own actual position
in society and by the existent methods of doing economics. Dorothy
Smith explicitly applies this to conceptual, theoretical relations: "We do
not recognize the degree to which our knowledge of the world is
already located at a conceptual level prior to the development of a theoretical apparatus."[23]

As we become more and more deeply ingrained in accepted ways
of thinking about economics, we hardly notice that the established discourse organizes our social relations and our possibilities. Such a
method eliminates recognition of our own and others' subjectivity. We
become objects and commodities unto ourselves. For this reason, I
extend Dorothy Smith's sociological critique more broadly to the disciplines of economics and social ethics which are organized mainly by
specialists who control working conditions, levels of employment, cost
of living and wages. Theory that is detached from the actual situations
and effects loses its grounding and validity.

Historically in Canada, the economic agenda has been embodied in the working world and relations, mainly of men whose experience and interests rule society. These men, and more rarely some women, own large corporations, control the media, set prices and profit levels, have formal access to government strategizing and not only evade tax payment most skillfully but also receive the lion's share of tax grants.[24]

In view of this horizon in which economic analysis and priorities are proclaimed without participation of those most affected, the concern is not just to include women in the neutered, genderless public face of the economy. Coming from outside the traditional frame, from a different horizon, solidarity with homeworkers and factory garment workers challenges not only the method of setting economic policies but their content as well: the relevancies, the conceptual apparatus, themes and conclusions.

Homeworkers and all the working poor make visible the implications of "free" market control of the economy that is dispersed among powerful players who communicate their common interests to the bureaucratic regulators. As those long subservient to this control shatter their traditional silence and uncritical acceptance of the status quo, they employ agency or autonomy on a social level. They expand the vision, the horizon out of which more comprehensive decisions may be made.

At the same time, division is deepened between those, on the one hand, who cling to familiar boundaries, standpoints and horizons to maintain power and capital/wealth and those, on the other hand, who challenge existing relations. In view of the global crisis of the economy, horizon must in fact be worldwide with an eye and heart open both to the international connections and to local well-being within an earth economy. No smaller horizon is adequate to the task at hand.

Forms of Bias and the Obstruction of Transformation

In this section, I focus on attitudes that paralyze us as peoples, with the results that we accept, however bitterly, imprisonment under exploitation and even think there is no alternative. By analyzing the fault line of how such a basis solidly blocks efforts for societal transformation, we can glimpse possibilities for action. Flowers grow in the cracks!

Our emerging experience, understanding, judgement, decision making and acting are shaped by our horizon, previous experience and understanding, as well as by the limits of societal realities. These processes are intrinsically linked, separated only temporarily for further clarity. But the extent to which we are authentic or inauthentic in our search for horizon and transformation is affected by bias. Our grappling with it determines, in part, whether we are engaging in a virtuous or vicious circle of inquiry.

To a great extent, we determine the breadth or narrowness of our horizon and thus of our ability to understand by our conscious and unconscious acceptance of bias and distortion. Four aspects of bias, described by Bernard Lonergan, are critical to my analysis. I add examples of each as clarification. The first, *dramatic bias*, is caused by psychological conditioning, often beyond the individual's control, caused for example by early childhood abuse. It usually requires professional assistance for healing.[25] For a wide range of reasons, dramatic bias may be at work in some people as psychic numbness about the crisis of women's suffering. It blocks feelings associated with certain images because they are too painful or unacceptable.[26] Fear of rejection, mockery or physical violence can lead women both to censor their own critical thinking and to stifle their courage to speak and act in ways deemed unacceptable within the abusive context.

A second form, *individual* or *egoistic bias*, interferes with intelligence, reasonableness, responsibility and intersubjective spontaneity. Such bias ignores the question of social good in practical living. Criteria for intelligent action may be quite different for oneself and for others. Although unaware of self-deception, the individual habitually stifles the "dynamic criterion of the further question immanent in intelligence itself."[27] Further understanding is excluded. This bias is also manifest in an assumption that power and ability to achieve some goal, like possession of great wealth or other weapons, make it acceptable and worthwhile. Capability is mistakenly equated with legitimacy.

Individual bias is compounded by the third form, *group bias*, by which groups reinforce and promote only their own practical insights for their own interests. We saw that tension underlies intersubjective relations when individual bias is operative. Under group bias, however, people find support in relating to others who maintain a similar position.[28] Group bias is operative, for instance, in economic stratification with its gendered, "racist" subtexts. Income groups have become separated with rewards for capital accumulation. Powerful hierarchies have emerged on this basis. Those who control capital may in fact find that their interests are not served by agreeing to codes of behaviour and laws that limit profit accumulation. They may disregard practical insights which contribute to the common good as a criterion of social construction because they meet no resistance or because they are powerful enough to overcome that resistance. Groups with competing interests may divert energy by implementing offensive and defensive mechanisms, with those in favoured circumstances gaining power exponentially so that society becomes stratified by success.

Socio-economic stratification marks societal decline.[29] It is expressed in domination by a corporate elite and in the deep frustration and resentment of the subjugated. The realized social order becomes a distorted reality, not corresponding to any coherently developed, practical common good. Laws and structures are practical to protect interests of the few who dominate. Refusing to regulate homework, for example, perpetuates control by those at the top of the chain of production.[30] Such refusal ignores the need for legislative protection of the Canadian garment industry itself. Group bias bends to retailers' threats and fills their desires instead of implementing regulation to protect homeworkers.

Group bias is also operative in patriarchal decision making. Patriarchal control is evident as people in hierarchical positions consult others when, if and to the extent they choose, and then incorporate suggestions according to their own exclusive prerogative and insights. It might be more truthfully named dictatorship, even if it is benevolent and sincerely done for others' well-being.

Another example of group bias is active child neglect by many fathers. Overcoming this requires broad-based attitudinal change as well as practical, structural and organizational work adjustments. Homeworkers repeatedly speak of the stress of adding waged employment when they already have sole responsibility for parenting and household work.

Group bias has been deeply internalized in our culture. Matthew Lamb writes, for instance, of bias and sexism that are now deeply embedded in the human psyche on a societal level:

> The blind rage of sexism ... runs like a morally biased fault throughout human history. If the bias runs deep in the caverns of the human psyche, the social distortions and alienations of male-female relationships are all too plain for those with eyes to see.... Here, as in other forms of bias, ... one is staggered by the overwhelming evidence of anguished human suffering resulting from bias in our historical world. Millions upon millions of women have been battered, dominated, raped, tortured, and destroyed simply because they were women.[31]

An example of this is the controversy over recognizing gender persecution as grounds to obtain refugee status in Canada.[32]

Group bias is supported by use of structures of signification to conceal domination. This is evident, first, in the entrenchment of a symbol system. "*Any* symbol-system or idea-system may become ideological, including science and technology," inasmuch as such symbol structures are mobilized to legitimate particular interests to conceal domination.[33] Male-based research of history and current events, for example, may be presented and accepted as if it were universal. Second, contradictions in dominant theory and methods are denied or camouflaged. An obvious example of this is the reasonable claim that the best applicants, regardless of gender or "race," ought to be given jobs. Practice reveals that white males dominate those who receive paid work and promotions disproportionate to their population and personal capacity. A third way to conceal domination is to reify changing, historical conditions to make them appear embedded in nature. The myth that a woman's place is in the home is a standard example of this bias in which a partial truth is made total and absolute. It omits critique of the results of this imaging for society, the family and the individual. It is silent about the partial truth that men's place is also in the home. Furthermore, when ideological reifications are allowed to absorb or ground structures and paradigms and then are identified with rational agency itself, refutation of such abstractions can be equated with refuting reason itself. Questioning everyday myths may then be deemed grounds to discount thinkers themselves as unreasonable.

Group bias has been reinforced by a fourth form of bias, *general bias*, which sets the ground for long-term destruction: common sense or practical intelligence is extolled so exclusively that society as a whole becomes entrenched against theoretical inquiries, long-range consequences, further relevant questions, more complete integrations and ultimate concerns.[34] There are several complex historical processes that are involved here, and they are all the more dangerous because they are largely unrecognized and uncritiqued. The problems are multiple and they relate to the visible result of exploitation and exclusion of even masses of people. I will separate the issues to show their profound significance in creating a society that allows a few to be a capital-accumulating sector with the rest serving it.

Capital formation, technology, economy and politics are all practical dimensions that arise from using common-sense thinking. So are artistic and other practical dimensions of living in community, such as household and environmental protection. These are creative functions and healthy use of them is essential for communities. A problem is created if exclusivity is given to common sense and if a bias is formed against expression of another kind of thinking, critical consciousness. The danger is that questions of interiority, meaning and the effects of decisions are considered impractical and irrelevant.

By going further and asking how it happens that the general public rejects critical consciousness and calls for common sense, I can name societal strangleholds more clearly. I think the crux of the matter is that abilities both to think and to feel have been skewed throughout Western society at least. Decision making, language and texts are distant from ordinary living. As corporations and states usurped control over capital, technology, economics and politics, their texts became the sites of action. Priorities such as having a successful, happy, glamorous, rich image dominate the media. Privatization, competition and accumulation become entrenched to limit categories of thinking quite generally in society. Common-sense functions of capital formation and technology, economics and politics are no longer "common," that is, they are controlled by a minority. Practical in the short term for the elite, they are impractical and exclusionary for the majority. Capital formation, technology, economics and politics themselves have been split so that decision making and profits are usurped within public macrolevels, controlled mainly by men. These unconnected abstractions are given the status of theory and, for example in economics, considered the inevitable "law of the market." The actual, "hands-on" or concretely practical services to maintain and expand such capital formation, technology, economics and politics are relegated as private, and built into a myth that this work is proper to women. Theoretical economics is supposedly for a few and eking out a living for the vast majority.

The problem becomes two-edged in that critical consciousness is disconnected from ordinary living situations such as in the divisions between middle class, working poor and unemployed. Ideas and even the capacity to think are themselves considered irrelevant in favour of practicality. I often hear that "ordinary folk" want practical, local participation and material improvements such as employment opportunities and fair trade. Establishing and implementing these require *both* common sense *and* critical consciousness. In my assessment, we as a people are generally denied public recognition and encouragement to use either common-sense thinking or critical consciousness. The former is usurped by elites for their own control of capital formation and the latter taken over as economic pseudo-theory, again according to the interests of the few. Through gender/"race"/difference analysis, that is, through valuing specificity, I conclude that group bias is a major cause of general bias which in turn entrenches long-term societal decline. Masses of people internalize attitudes that perpetuate oppression. These attitudes are also structural causes of poverty.

Figure 3

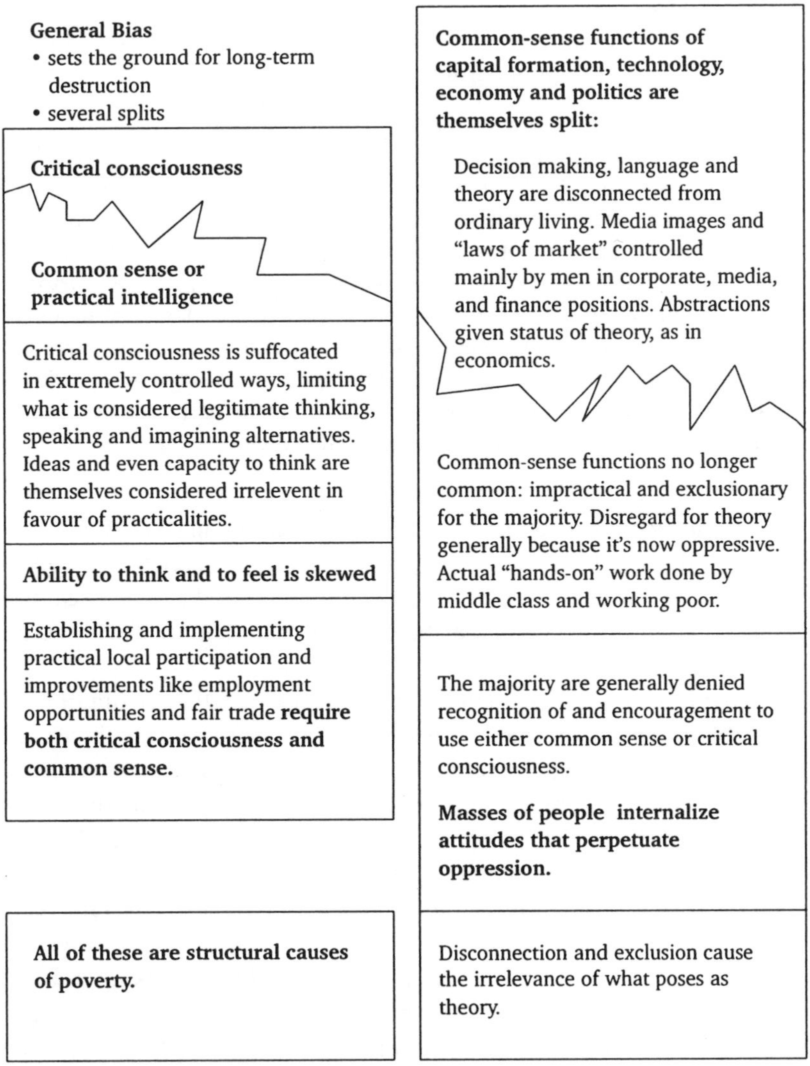

General Bias
- sets the ground for long-term destruction
- several splits

Critical consciousness

Common sense or practical intelligence

Critical consciousness is suffocated in extremely controlled ways, limiting what is considered legitimate thinking, speaking and imagining alternatives. Ideas and even capacity to think are themselves considered irrelevent in favour of practicalities.

Ability to think and to feel is skewed

Establishing and implementing practical local participation and improvements like employment opportunities and fair trade **require both critical consciousness and common sense.**

All of these are structural causes of poverty.

Common-sense functions of capital formation, technology, economy and politics are themselves split:

Decision making, language and theory are disconnected from ordinary living. Media images and "laws of market" controlled mainly by men in corporate, media, and finance positions. Abstractions given status of theory, as in economics.

Common-sense functions no longer common: impractical and exclusionary for the majority. Disregard for theory generally because it's now oppressive. Actual "hands-on" work done by middle class and working poor.

The majority are generally denied recognition of and encouragement to use either common sense or critical consciousness.

Masses of people internalize attitudes that perpetuate oppression.

Disconnection and exclusion cause the irrelevance of what poses as theory.

Bernard Lonergan suggests that general bias arises out of reliance on the accumulated insights of common sense, that is, of practicality, technology, economics and politics, to the point of excluding a spirit of inquiry and reflection. I maintain that if we consistently connect good common-sense thinking to actual local needs of women and children, we will also think openly in ways that foster critical consciousness. It is disconnection and exclusion that cause the irrelevance of what poses as theory. The latter is better regarded as pseudo-theory. It needs to be unmasked. (See fig. 3.)

The following analysis of work in Ontario suggests further understanding of the cause of general bias:

> The search for the flexible worker has also been called the casualization of work. Labour is purchased only when and as needed. Benefits such as holiday pay, overtime, Canada Pension Plan, severance pay and the employee health tax are thereby avoided by employers. While a firm gains total flexibility in its use of labour, it is gained at a significant cost to the worker. Surrounding the core workers are the "periphery"—the fragmented sector, of predominantly women workers, who are part-time, temporary or casual workers, who have few benefits and are not entitled to basic protection under employment law.... Work in the peripheral sector, which has previously been viewed as atypical employment, precarious or non-standard employment is now one of the most rapidly expanding sectors of the economy.[35]

Women, and increasing numbers of men, tend to work long hours without fair wages. Economists speak of inevitable market trends, the irreversibility of global restructuring. This kind of economic theory is promulgated out of truncated practice and is rejected by the excluded. We are wise to do so! Particular theories must be critiqued with actual connections in mind.

A habit of developing theory out of malpractice, that is, out of decision making and texts that are disconnected from ordinary living and considerations of common good, and of extolling common sense exclusively for ruling interests, steadily led to the disregard of theorizing itself. The crisis mounts as specialization and bureaucratic complexity are used to protect vested-interest, "out-of-touch" theorizing, or pseudo-theory. This has brought us to the present crisis because our abilities to think critically and to feel deeply have been seriously skewed, generally for us as peoples, at least in Western societies. Speaking publicly and even in small private groups about what we think and see is prevented by force. Consider an example. Twelve of us from the Labour Behind the Label Coalition went for a peaceful shopping trip in

Toronto's Eaton Centre. We stopped in front of stores like Disney World and Nike where one person explained the company's oppressive labour practices. At the GAP store, the favourable action of the GAP's agreeing to independent monitoring of its clothing production at the Mandarin plant in San Salvador was emphasized. Security officers quickly ended our gatherings. Around the globe, the military is used more and more frequently to protect the accumulated power and wealth of those who depend on it.

Startling evidence exposes both a lack of critical thinking in establishing labour relations and a need for a new system of collective bargaining:

> In Metro Toronto alone, part-time employment grew by 99 per cent between 1983 and 1989. Statistics Canada reported 129,000 full-time jobs were lost while 100,000 part-time jobs were created. In 1989 over 70 per cent of part-time workers in Canada are women.[36]

New ways of organizing and bargaining are urgently needed. So is government regulation to protect workers.

The present employment situation signals long-term societal decline characterized by disconnection from basic needs of workers and of the unemployed. It is also marked by neglect and stifling of critical consciousness by both the elites and society as a whole, although some hopeful awakenings are happening in Ontario due to the government's severe cutbacks to the majority while servicing large corporate interests.

The nature and implications of this decline become more evident upon further consideration. Economic practice is basically a function of common-sense thinking and it must be guided if we are to direct history responsibly with conscious grasp and deliberate choice. Repeated exclusion of real-life costs, of effects and of fruitful ideas leads to a cumulative departure from coherence so that both reflection on societal processes of gathering data, making judgements and decisions and creative thinking are considered irrelevant. The quality of being true to what one can intelligently grasp and reasonably affirm is devalued and any proposals that would axe the root of social problems are considered idealistic. Culture, religion and philosophy are limited in meaning to become exclusively personal, inward or impractical affairs; or reduced to being festivals to display various foods. A consequence is the surrender of well-developed intelligence itself, except for an occasional escape into these cultural or religious events, though the latter are privatized and separated from the everyday business of life.

I propose that practical, common-sense functions themselves have been severely distorted within the abuse of common-sense applications and in their separation from community relations. Community relations and practicalities are the two basic parts of community by which we hold essential aspects of living in creative tension.[37] Unless a serious obstacle has destroyed capacity for relationality, intersubjectivity is a quality inherent in being members of the earth community. So too, in order to provide for our basic necessities and social organization, practicalities are intrinsic. These need to be held together in creative tension to form a healthy community. Use of practical intelligence, on the one hand, and intersubjectivity on the other have been split both *from each other* and, I add, *within* their own realms by the construction of public and private applications. I have focused on the need to connect the practical aspects of economics, politics, technology and capital formation with community relationships, and on linking critical evaluation to the actual living situations of the poorest. I simply note here, first, the split in community relations and, second, in international relations, particularly regarding peace negotiations, warfare, arms trade and other finance and commerce. The latter areas are controlled by men and split from the so-called private relations of family, home and local communities, the very locations where the effects are suffered. Women are praised for their skills in interpersonal and community relations and in peace making as long as we confine ourselves to microrealities. (See fig. 4.)

Lonergan predicted that what can emerge from such a state is a radically uncritical, empirical, scientific, pseudo-realistic culture which takes its stand on things as they are, without distinguishing between what is meaningful or what is detrimental. Cumulative deterioration of the socio-economic reality parallels continued disregard for intelligence and for integration and connectedness. Society declines because it is imprisoned in ever less comprehensive viewpoints.

The discontent and increasing hopelessness among the general population are data for assessing the adequacy of societal functioning. Such unrest presents an opportunity for people to weigh the evidence, analyze causes and results, make informed judgements and decide effective strategies for the common good. When the discontent is complicated by a sense of powerlessness such as that engendered in Canada's colonial mentality, the unrest settles as cynicism. Potential for critique was lost as we became entrenched in an incredulous paralysis which dominates even thought processes.

Figure 4
Community Relations

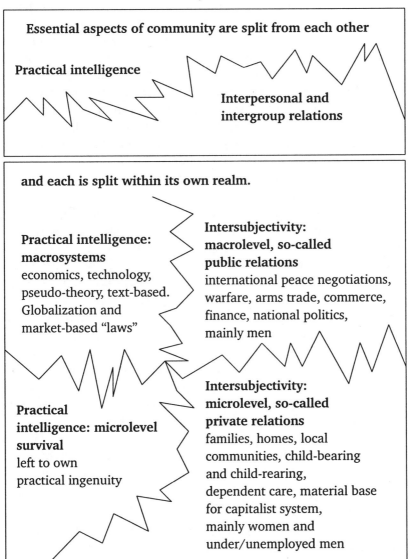

Essential aspects of community are split from each other

Practical intelligence

Interpersonal and
intergroup relations

and each is split within its own realm.

Practical intelligence:
macrosystems
economics, technology,
pseudo-theory, text-based.
Globalization and
market-based "laws"

Intersubjectivity:
macrolevel, so-called
public relations
international peace negotiations,
warfare, arms trade, commerce,
finance, national politics,
mainly men

Practical
intelligence: microlevel
survival
left to own
practical ingenuity

Intersubjectivity:
microlevel, so-called
private relations
families, homes, local
communities, child-bearing
and child-rearing,
dependent care, material base
for capitalist system,
mainly women and
under/unemployed men

The decline can be offset by understanding and imaging the kind of society we as peoples want to create for ourselves, and by fostering the ability to critique, to think, to evaluate, to grasp the whole picture and discern long-term priorities for decision making and action in solidarity. Concern for historical process and recognition of collaborative possibilities may break the vicious circle of illusion and witness the creation of alternatives. Determination is needed, as Lonergan points out, "to prevent dominant groups from deluding humanity by the rationalization of their sins" and then contributing to the longer cycle of decline by extending these sins as universal principles.[38] What is needed is healing, critical consciousness and transformative decision making and action. Because our very abilities to do these have been distorted, we also need courage to risk making mistakes. What seems extreme in our distorted state may in fact be only a hint of what is required. A practical exercise may be to have fun imagining "what if" statements aloud in a group. For example, "What if it is unethical for one person to be annually remunerated or compensated over a million dollars while others have no paid work?"

Critiques of history such as I have presented, particularly regarding the rationalization of abuses and the creation of myths which are used to exploit, are essential as we lay groundwork that may help us to direct and shape history toward just relations. Awareness of the story of the universe and of our belonging to a greater horizon sets the context for this withdrawal "from practicality to save practicality." Using both practical intelligence and critical consciousness serves the well-being of the earth community in all its forms. Ignoring practical intelligence and critical consciousness leaves incremental destruction of peoples and death of a planet for our children and grandchildren.

I have been considering how group and general bias affect community in its ability to relate practicalities and intersubjectivity. They deeply instrumentalize persons, economy, politics and our culture itself.[39] From this epistemological groundwork on horizon and on societal decline through bias, I now focus on the critical issue of difference and specificity. It is foundational to socio-economic relationships.

Specificity and Difference

Every aspect of our planet is characterized by difference and uniqueness or specificity. This is certainly a healthy quality of people as well. I turn to the theme of difference and specificity for many reasons, all of which are significant in shaping socio-economic ethics. The most glaring reason for taking up this issue is its link with bias because of the blatant privilege gained by exploiting differences of gender, "race" and wealth. This is certainly evident in garment homeworking in Toronto.

Second, difference is the basis of the global division of labour. Third, a perspective other than the dominant one demonstrates how our economics, politics and culture actually function. By taking the traditionally marginalized as the standpoint for interpretation, those of us who are white middle class may come to some understanding both of their experience and of how our system actually works.[40] Fourth, understanding diversity offers a fresh viewpoint regarding duality and dualism, a confusion underlying historical separations of men and women.[41]

Fifth, appreciation of difference and specificity is an integral heuristic or anticipation of being, evident in differentiated creation, differentiated consciousness and social consciousness.[42] Sensitivity to difference and specificity anticipates recognition of, and capacity to express, beauty, intelligibility, truth, goodness and love in particular ways. It grounds the search for direction in the movement of life. Elizabeth Johnson, for instance, lays the foundation upon which we can come to know the God of difference and specificity, the all-holy who, according to ancient tradition, sides with the powerless:

> In fact, sensitivity to difference is an intellectual virtue being positively celebrated by feminist thought in resistance to centuries of univocal definition of "woman's nature." The diversity, cultural, interracial, and ecumenical, is consciously prized as a condition for connectedness, for women have the insight born in pain that a monolithic position inevitably works to the disadvantage of somebody, usually the most powerless.[43]

Finally, and very central to this work, awareness of subjectivity, differentiation and communion, as fundamental principles of the universe, grounds solidarity.[44]

Critique of Racism Essential for Solidarity

As I have explained in Part I, the explosion of homeworking in the form of unprotected employment is a low-wage strategy, particularly for immigrant women, but including all whose employment status is vulnerable. The widespread expansion of this exploitation calls for extensive solidarity first of all interracially among women and second with men. Solidarity requires recognition of difference and specificity and analysis of racism. As Rosemary Brown emphasizes,

> The miscarriage of justice because of race is as systemic to this nation as is the violence done to women, simply because they are female. Sexism and racism both are, as Stephen Lewis so eloquently put it, a "deep infection of

the soul of our society." If I were to write a book about Canada and its people, the title would be "Let's Pretend. Let's Deny." The first line would read, "Canadians are a tolerant and compassionate people, ... at least that's what they tell me."[45]

Rosemary Brown backs this up with many examples of discrimination based on sex, "race," disability, age, sexual orientation, religion, culture and class. Critique by black women and women of colour is transforming a white, middle-class, feminist movement in Toronto, not without conflict but certainly with greater vision, understanding and enrichment for those open to the richness of diversity shared and the strength this offers. The acclamation of Sunera Thobani as president of the National Action Council on the Status of Women has been considered "important symbolic progress" in interracial collaboration within the movement, in spite of formal parliamentary protest by Conservative MP John MacDougall.[46]

Susan Brooks Thistlethwaite focuses on difference as a central theoretical issue within white feminist theology. Just as it has been "the genius of patriarchy to deal with difference by obliterating it, by projecting a white male face onto the definition of humanity,"[47] so also white feminists must shift methods to avoid similar suppression of differences. Audre Lorde challenges us to make our differences our strengths, asking "Can we be different but not alienated?"[48]

Defining racism as "the uncritical appropriation of what is normative to only one "race," the one deemed dominant,"[49] Brooks Thistlethwaite points to epistemological roots of domination in the power of definition and control in which oppressed peoples are objectified and perceived as things. Bias and decline lie in the fundamental deception resulting when destructive, false ways of being and thinking reify persons and preclude any differentiation of consciousness that respects real differences among people. Obliterating differences leads to separation. A worldview or horizon based on the insights and decisions of only one "race," or, worse, of one "race," sex and class, is obviously inadequate, and amounts to false consciousness. What impulse from within arises to change a system from which one is benefiting? An exclusively white analysis is at best incomplete and inadequate.

Brooks Thistlethwaite's insights are helpful in unmasking socio-economic and political causes of deeply rooted white racism. Socialized in a racist culture, it is difficult to own one's racism, particularly because such consciousness leads to deliberation and decision about many factors of the culture and about ways of relating to both the dominating and the oppressed within it.[50] Marlee Kline discusses the same issue:

> The problems resulting from ignoring or submerging the different experiences of oppression of women of Colour are, however, not merely the result of ethnocentrism. They are, rather, a reflection of the structures of racism in Western society, from which white feminists, with our assertions of the common bonds between women, have not been able to escape.[51]

Awareness of racism can either paralyze us or, hopefully, help us understand and analyze how systemic forces impact on our way of being, thinking and choosing.

Liberatory Potential

Focus on difference and specificity raises issues of foundational anthropological views, of separation and solidarity and of patriarchal dualism and separatism. I now clarify these in order to discover liberatory potential in recognition of difference and specificity.

A fundamental debate within consideration of difference is whether women and men share a single anthropology or human reality and unitary consciousness, or whether we embody a dual anthropology. The latter may be expressed in separatism with belief in the inherent superiority of either sex, or in complementarism with espousal to equality. It should be noted that complementarism is particularly susceptible to operative subjection under the guise of respecting and promoting difference.[52] An *essentialist* femininity entails "belief in an essence, an inherent, eternal female nature that manifests itself in such characteristics as gentleness, goodness, nurturance and sensitivity."[53] A key problem is that such attributions are used normatively, that is, believed to be describing how women *are*. Such usage perpetuates women's inferior social status, ignores diversity within and among "races," excludes socio-cultural influences and serves to keep women in "their place." Sandra Schneiders further nuances this discussion by making two points. First, we need to eschew both unisex denials of women's uniqueness and complementarity as a model for male-female relations. Second, we need to embrace individual rights and relational responsibility for both men and women on the basis of self-definition and self-determination of both, and not the self-determination of men and the male definition of women.[54]

The ethical issue is the degree of moral relevance given to biologically based gender differences. Biologically based gender differences are not sufficient moral reason for unequal participation in society and inequitable access to wealth.[55] Struggling to effect a praxis of full human power, participation and justice, I reject the notion that there is any *fundamental* dimorphism in human nature/being. There are not two natures, one male and the other female. Elizabeth Johnson clears a path beyond the impasse of single or dual nature anthropology by emphasizing a diversity of human expression, "one human nature celebrated in an interdependence of multiple differences.... Human existence has a multidimensional character."[56] This implies that "age, race, period in history, bodily handicap, social location, and other essential aspects of concrete historical existence are at least as important in determining one's identity as sex."[57] To unmask the roots of women's invisibility in society, one must look further than nature and identity.

Specificity and difference are not in themselves the source of oppression. In fact, recognition of diversity offers strength for justice making. Duality is actually a fundamental dynamic of personal development. The me/not-me experience is critical to the entire process of self-differentiation, including cognitive and ego development. Problems arise when shifts are made from *duality* to *dualism* and dichotomies, and from *difference* to *subordination* and *subjection*. Problems deepen when these dualisms and subordinations are actively interstructured with systems of racist control and economic exploitation, including cultural and political imperialism, to shape and distort social relations. Lorraine Code distinguishes

> thinking in terms of *differences* rather than dichotomies. Differences need not be construed as bipolar opposites, nor as pairs of terms pulling against each other, on a quasi-conflictual model, as is almost inevitable in dichotomous thinking. Rather, one might recognize a plethora of differences, shading into one another and reciprocally influencing each other.[58]

Evaluation of ethical assumptions requires examination of how our language sustains the power of dualisms to entrench domination.

Foregrounding difference/specificity may raise concern whether such an emphasis promotes separation instead of the goal of solidarity. Some groups may function best autonomously in order to establish their own identity and agency. This can serve to strengthen mutual exchange and collaboration by clarifying and removing long-term barriers. Some women, for example, name themselves feminists, womanists or mujeristas. These depictions suggest more than a perspective, a way of seeing or even of knowing. They indicate a way of being in the world. Liz Stanley clarifies that such a choice does not automatically indicate separation since "there is nothing about the acknowledgment of 'difference' that precludes discussion, debate and a mutual learning process."[59] With Sue Wise, she points to the liberatory potential of such a position:

> Many people have noted that being "Other" brings with it the possession of knowledge concerning "rulers" and their ways, but also the different and subversive knowledge that accrues to the "ruled," as a consequence of seeing the "underside" of oppression and oppressors both. Black feminists are more readily aware than white that the ontological experience of "women" is multiply characterized by difference, by different and overlapping contextually grounded material experiences of oppression. For these black feminists, "theory … speaks to contextually grounded experience and recognizes difference and complexity."[60]

Differing emancipatory positions provide knowledge *for* commitment to liberation and praxis, which unites theory and research in a symbiotic relationship.[61] Regard for difference, specificity and "a feminist standpoint epistemology" is *not* to favour female or "racial" separatism:

> It is rather to propose *to remove an existing methodological separatism*, one which understands and researches the social world through an assimilationist and textually mediated alienated knowledge which proceeds by measuring social life against pre-existent theoretically (that is, ideologically) derived categories.[62]

Such malestream methodology, adhered to by both men and women, ignores and silences feminist/"racial" standpoints which lie beyond its horizon. For many men, it bears a similar alienating and colonizing relationship.

I return to the question of shaping a more nuanced view of anthropology as a way forward. A transformative model focuses on humanity's shared single nature with specificity to acknowledge, affirm and rejoice in differences.[63] Upholding a single anthropology while valuing differences and specificity offers a position to transform the bias that makes one sex, "race" and/or class normative. Such respect offers grounds for solidarity.

Paradoxically, both assertion of difference and specificity and historical exclusion now offer the possibility of looking at everything in a new way. To want this difference and specificity is a revolutionary desire, for it is in direct contradiction to the approach of the patriarchal, racist and classist thought, which functions according to the economy of sameness. To discover common bonds is not to obliterate differences. This bonding does not, like the patriarchal economy of sameness, become a force of domination and conformity. So, for example, struggles, laughter, theory, history, love, ecstasy and tenderness can be put together. Reinsertion of love, tenderness and critical consciousness into our struggles shakes up the status quo.[64] It is difficult to express the indefinable, to imagine the unimaginable. In justice we require structures that ensure equitable access to society's resources and advantages rather than identical opportunity. As our consciousness is raised, we often realize, first, that negative experiences are due to oppression rather than to personal failure and, second, that the oppression is structural, based on sex and "race," rather than being incidental. Appreciation of difference/specificity provides a direct position to offset the general bias in which all must be the same, unthinking and unfeeling servants of the system which serves the interests of the capital-accumulating sector.

Division of Labour

Bias regarding difference constitutes a major theoretical issue used economically to gain and maintain supremacy. This phenomena prevails throughout the world, as blatant abuses in the division of labour and the distribution of wealth give ample evidence. It is essentially patriarchal. Without engaging in a dialogue about the merits of various definitions of patriarchy, I rely here on a description offered by Alicja Muszynski for whom patriarchy is a

> form of consciousness that defines material reality through dichotomizing people, their relations to nature and to each other. Patriarchy shapes and transmits the idea-systems and the culture that underlies the capitalist mode of production. It also shapes the idea of labour: what it entails, the relations to which it gives rise, and the division of labour.... The specific class relations that emerge with capitalism are economic relations of exploitation built upon relations of oppression related to both patriarchal forms of domination and previous relations of class exploitation. For it was the same mentality that created woman as other that could be further pushed to create racial dichotomization.[65]

This definition of patriarchy addresses various aspects of the relations of ruling described in chapter 2.

Consciousness and concrete circumstances are profoundly related. Feminist/"racial" consciousness is more than a mere reflection of external material conditions, for the transforming and negating perspective which it incorporates first allows these conditions to be revealed *as* the conditions they are. But the apprehension of some state of affairs as intolerable, as to-be-transformed, does not, in and of itself, transform it.[66]

It follows that consideration of difference and specificity leads to the question of community organization and division of labour within it. The problem lies in ordering some tasks as superior to others and in denigrating some people as inferior to others. How garment manufacturers use subcontracting arrangements to exploit a "racially" and sexually divided labour market to ensure that wages and working conditions are depressed is a fundamental social question in Ontario.

Exploitation of this nature relies on a myth that Canada is a white country. The myth is insidiously ingrained in the national consciousness but it lacks foundation.

> Racism ... afflicts an entire society; it is ingrained and reinforced in all the major and minor institutions of society. Even in the most seemingly "objective" of undertakings, such as the writing of our national history, racism has operated to exclude minority groups from the historical landscape, thus rendering their accomplishments invisible, and therefore insignificant.
>
> Second, racism is not something which simply affects its victims in various adverse ways. It also benefits all those against whom it is not directed, by affording certain privileges.... Many well-intentioned white Canadians fail to recognize that their life-style and position in society is based on a system of class and race privilege.... [They] should examine the problem from the standpoint of their own situations of privilege.[67]

An example clarifies the issue. The Ontario Labour Relations Board uses gender-biased criteria to determine appropriate bargaining units. In the garment industry, the nature of work, skills required and conditions of employment differ for male cutters and supervisors in contrast to female machine operators and homeworkers.[68] This becomes part of the bargaining structure:

> Thus it is not surprising that standard occupational units reflect and reinforce the gendered occupational structure of the labour market.... Since women are often employed in female-dominated establishments, the policy of defining the appropriate bargaining unit in terms of a single location and a single-employer ... reinforces the perception that male-dominated and female-male dominated units have different communities of interest. Thus, the result of the Board's standard unit policy has been a bargaining structure which is deeply fragmented along gender lines.[69]

Analysis of this situation shows that group and general bias have merged domestically and in the global division of labour in the instrumentalization of persons. Use of functional relationships becomes reified and separated from the actual relations to such an extent that people are instrumentalized. Racism underlies this destruction of both practicality and community relations. When racism is compounded by extensive unemployment as it is now, a frequent question arises about the scarcity of work and the right of any to complain about poor working conditions and low wages. Effective, common analysis is usurped by division that pits one group against another.

Broadening the Horizon

We need a broad horizon for appreciation of difference and specificity and for a foundational worldview for just relations. Such a horizon grounds my analysis of the function of differentiation. It has been described, in part, by Thomas Berry and Brian Swimme, whose thesis is that the very existence of the universe depends on the preservation of subjectivity, differentiation and communion, each in relation to the others. These themes "refer to the nature of the universe in its reality and in its value. These three features are themselves features of each other."[70] Differentiation, for instance, also refers to the quality of relations taking place in the universe. It includes a full spectrum of modes of knowing and represents particular relationships we establish in the world. In the universe, "to be is to be different. To be is to be a unique manifestation of existence."[71] Subjectivity refers to identity and points to the dynamic, interior dimension of things which emerges with an inner capacity for self-manifestation.[72] Furthermore, the universe is organized by interdependence. As Swimme and Berry present it,

> To be is to be related, for relationship is the essence of existence.... Alienation for a particle is a theoretical impossibility.... Nothing is itself without everything else. But in addition to this, the universe advances into community—into a differentiated web of relationships among sentient centers of creativity.... Relationships are discovered even more than they are forged.... The loss of relationship, with its consequent alienation, is a kind of supreme evil in the universe.[73]

Interdependence of all living and inanimate forms within the earth community, therefore, is the material-psychic-spiritual context in which all aspects of life unfold. Being in touch with the story of the universe provides the horizon to discern better what is going forward in history and what contributes to long-term decline. Operative appreciation of subjectivity, differentiation and interdependence provides the standpoint.

I turn to Robert Doran for assistance in showing the significance of a cosmological worldview for my study. Doran explains that cosmological meaning roots our human constitution in biological and affective interdependence with all creation. At the same time, and equally important, we are grounded anthropologically to reflect, deliberate and decide, in a word, to be responsible for the histories we create.[74] Both cosmological and anthropological constitutive meanings give rise to modes of symbolization which carry meaning for the direction we give to life. These two aspects form an integral unity and need to be held in creative tension.[75] Both our differences and our capacity for decision making are directly significant for the kind of society we establish.

This interpretation of essential aspects of the universe within which human beings gather information, weigh evidence, decide, are responsible and loving is solid ground on which to build an ethical system. The goodness of all creation is upheld. So is our innate ability *to know*. We know when we do not have enough information and we know when an answer or solution fits. We have capacity to reflect on experience, understanding, judgements, decisions and actions. A major task for our time is to learn to trust and to use this natural capacity in concrete situations. More of this later.

I shall return to ethical considerations in the last chapter to suggest further implications for meanings and values as criteria for socio-economic ethics. How we describe the above horizon can be strengthened and celebrated by communities of faith, hope and love. By incorporating appreciation for the spiritual, by co-creating our world in union with the divine creator, we expand what I just described, not negate it. Use of scripture and traditional moral norms can assist in the process. Caution is needed. I emphasize that proceeding on this path requires enough love for the faith communities to use critical consciousness. Overcoming bias and distortion mean that we need to discern what in scriptures and tradition reveals sexism, racism, bias and distortion, even if we assume intentions were good. If we are to be true to the living God, we must in fact have courage to name what is blessing and what is distorted and/or sinful in our past. Intentions alone are not adequate historical criteria. Effects need to be made visible.

Conclusion

In this chapter I have drawn out the meaning of horizon, bias and difference and specificity to establish a basis for the construction of socio-economic ethics. The extent of one's horizon determines one's ability to accept and to understand perspectives of homeworkers, particularly regarding child and elder care, stresses between employer and family expectations and the isolation and low wages. Issues of home management and its relation to both family and garment homeworking may be outside the horizons of the majority of decision makers in corporations, banks and governments and some church groups, and, therefore, outside the range of their interests and concern. This situation is distorted further by group bias to perpetuate the social devaluation of women.

By working with feminist thought regarding some operative implications of difference, I showed how critical reflection challenges existing racism, hierarchies and division of labour. This engagement leads me to the following conclusion which will be incorporated into my work. Analysis of exploitation based on gender, "race" and wealth/ empire confirms the importance of uncovering bias against women generally. Bias is increased against women according to "racial"-ethnic differences and is directed against many men as well. This analysis also foregrounds the urgency of overcoming racism and all oppression based on difference if we are to work in solidarity.

Expanding horizons through feminist, "racial" consciousness enables collaboration through increased awareness of causes of exploitation, through recognition of the social construction of relations and through development of collective perceptions. Collaboration for transformation actually facilitates emergence of greater capacity to understand, to appreciate, to risk and to imagine alternatives. Such communal consciousness and solidarity serve to create horizons adequate to the scope of the problem. Appreciation of difference and specificity is a key to the way forward.

Part of my concern is how biases distort our capacity to imagine and to decide alternatives. This distortion becomes evident in community relations and causes both general bias and societal decline. I claim that there is a split not only between common-sense practicality and intersubjectivity, but also that each of these is split within itself. These splits are structured socially according to gender, "race" and wealth/ empire. People are instrumentalized according to difference for the purposes of sustaining the privilege of those in dominant positions. General disregard for critical thinking and for theory itself result from the control of the production of knowledge and of practical policy setting in ways largely disconnected from relations of family/kin/ friendships.

I claim that theory arising from distortion is in fact pseudo-theory, and that the general populace is wise to reject what is not connected with the well-being of the earth community. Lonergan's analysis of horizon, bias and heuristics provides a framework of support for feminist, "racial" theory only when and if the latter also functions critically, using such categories. Lonergan's warning of the danger of rejecting critical consciousness itself, however, is most relevant and urgent. In fact, it calls for a position to counteract domination, inviting in-depth analysis and proactive, confident strategizing.

Deconstructing out-of-touch abstractions is directly related to homeworkers' situations since it impacts how we shape economic praxis. What becomes imperative is engagement in "in-touch" critical consciousness, creation of alternatives and reflection on the entire process of experience, understanding, judgement and decision making in order to assume responsible collaborative directions. This requires some analysis of the traditional, operative division between the public and private spheres.

Notes

1 Lonergan uses myth in a technical sense "to mean the symbolic expression of the known unknown produced by the psyche of either an inauthentic or a less developed and less differentiated subject. "Myth" is thus equivalent to the symbolic expressions of intellectual and existential counterpositions" (Doran, *Theology and the Dialectics of History*, 124). Refer also to Bernard Lonergan, *Insight* (New York: Harper & Row, 1978), 531-49. "We know of an unknown through our unanswered questions" (ibid., 532).

2 Thomas S. Kuhn, *The Structure of Scientific Revolution* (Chicago: University of Chicago Press, 1962; 2nd ed., enlarged, 1970), 175, as cited in *Paradigm Change in Theology: A Symposium for the Future*, ed. Hans Küng and David Tracy (New York: Crossroad, 1989), 7.

3 Lonergan, *Method in Theology*, 237-39. Refer also to Nancy Hartsock, "The Feminist Standpoint: Developing the Ground for a Specifically Feminist Historical Materialism," in *Feminism and Methodology*, ed. Sandra Harding (Indianapolis: Indiana University Press, 1987), 159-60, regarding epistemological and political claims implied in the position that the real relations of humans with each other and with the natural world are not visible in some perspectives, regardless of good intentions.

4 Lonergan, *Method in Theology*, 218-19.

5 Ibid., 187-88.

6 Ibid., 237.

7 Doran, *Theology and the Dialectics of History*, 39-40. Awareness of intentionally and psychically differentiated consciousness are radically foundational; who we are determines how we analyze the situation.

8 Rozena Maart, "Consciousness, Knowledge and Morality: The Absence of the Knowledge of White Consciousness in Contemporary Feminist Theory," in *A Reader in Feminist Ethics*, ed. Debra Shogan (Toronto: Canadian Scholars Press, 1993), 132.

9 Ibid., 154.

10 Cynthia Crysdale, "Women and the Social Construction of Self-Appropriation," in *Lonergan and Feminism*, ed. Cynthia Crysdale (Toronto: University of Toronto Press, 1994), 99.

11 Sheila Mullett, "Shifting Perspectives: A New Approach to Ethics," in *Feminist Perspectives: Philosophical Essays on Method and Morals*, ed. Lorraine Code, Sheila Mullett and Christine Overall (Toronto: University of Toronto Press, 1988), 115.

12 This characteristic is a major emphasis of present third-wave feminism. Womanists and mujeristas share this tenet. I develop other aspects of feminist consciousness, especially regarding the interconnections of "race," gender and class oppression, later.

13 Ibid., 115. Refer also to Sandra Lee Bartky, "Toward a Phenomenology of Feminist Consciousness," in *Feminism and Philosophy*, ed. Mary Vetterling Braggin, Frederick A. Elliston and Jane English (Totowa, NJ: Littlefield Adams, 1977), 253-54.

14 Mullett, "Shifting Perspectives," 115.

15 Sandra Lee Bartky, *Femininity and Domination: Studies in the Phenomenology of Oppression* (New York: Routledge, 1990), 12. Refer to 12-21 for a fuller analysis of feminist consciousness raising, possible concurrent awareness of its social implications and of "*double ontological shock*: first, the realization that what is really happening is quite different from what appears to be happening, and second, the frequent inability to tell what is really happening at all" (ibid., 18).

16 Maart, "Consciousness, Knowledge and Morality," 155-56.

17 Mullett, "Shifting Perspectives," 116.

18 Lonergan, *Method in Theology*, 13, 268, and Doran, *Theology and the Dialectics of History*, 529.

19 Decision and action, therefore, embody our intentionality in incarnate meanings. In later writings, Lonergan stresses that this healing vector is released by love. Even as I emphasize the importance of breaking open the walls that imprison our vision of what is possible, I stand cautious of voluntarism, knowing the weight of socio-economic factors that limit our freedom to respond.

20 Lonergan, *Method in Theology*, 269.

21 Wildung Harrison, *Making the Connections*, 27. This very challenging position raises issues of co-dependency. Refer to Vicki Obedkoff, "Crossing Over: A Feminist Theological Exploration of Co-dependency, the Recovery Movement and the Church" (Ph.D. diss., Emmanuel College, Toronto, 1994).

22 Smith, *The Everyday World as Problematic*, 72-73.

23 Ibid., 63.

24 The Citizens for Public Justice and the Interfaith Social Assistance Review Coalition have been lobbying the Ontario government since 1986 to be recognized as participants in government consultations on economic policies, similar to that already in place with the businesses through the Business Council on National Interests. See also Linda McQuaig, *Behind Closed Doors: How the Rich Won Control of Canada's Tax System ... And Ended Up*

Richer (Markham: Penguin Books, 1988), 112-13, 242-330. The Ecumenical Coalition for Economic Justice relies on a Statistics Canada study of actual causes of the federal government's debt to reveal that half of the deficits occurring from 1975 to 1991 were the result of tax breaks mainly to corporations and wealthy individuals. High interest rates set by the Bank of Canada caused another 44 per cent of the deficits. Refer to ECEJ, *Reweaving Canada's Social Programs*, 35.

25 Lonergan, *Insight*, 191-203.

26 Susan Brooks Thistlethwaite and Mary Potter Engel, eds., *Lift Every Voice: Constructing Christian Theologies from the Underside* (New York: Harper & Row, 1990), 98, citing Robert Jay Lifton, *Indefensible Weapons* (New York: Basic Books, 1982), 104.

27 Lonergan, *Insight*, 220-21.

28 Ibid., 222-25.

29 By societal decline, I mean the steadily decreasing ability to think, gather information, make informed decisions and engage social agency in ways conducive to transformation. It is marked by serious lack of social consciousness and social conscience, by ever less comprehensive viewpoints and by constantly diminishing ability to seek, recognize and incorporate truth into societal priorities and ways of being.

30 Intercede and ILGWU, *Meeting the Needs of Vulnerable Workers*, 19.

31 Matthew Lamb, *Solidarity with Victims: Toward a Theology of Social Transformation* (New York: Crossroad, 1982), 6-7.

32 Alan Thompson, "Persecuted Women May Be Accepted as Refugees," *The Toronto Star*, 30 January 1993, A1. See also Michele Landsberg, "Unfair Media Biases Scrutinized by Women," *The Toronto Star*, 16 January 1993, J1; Michele Landsberg, "To Valcourt, Raped, Beaten Women Aren't Refugees," *The Toronto Star*, 19 January 1993, C1; Alan Thompson, "Canada First in Recognizing Abused Women as Refugees," *The Toronto Star*, 10 March 1993, A2.

33 Matthew Lamb, "The Dialectics of Theory and Praxis within Paradigm Analysis," in *Paradigm Change in Theology: A Symposium for the Future*, ed. Hans Küng and David Tracy (New York: Crossroad, 1989), 83. Lamb relies on the work of Anthony Giddens, *Central Problems in Social Theory* (Berkeley, CA: University of California Press, 1983), 184-97.

34 Lonergan, *Insight*, 225.

35 Intercede and ILGWU, *Meeting the Needs of Vulnerable Workers*, 4. The Economic Council of Canada documents this trend in *Good Jobs, Bad Jobs: Employment in the Service Economy* (Ottawa: Ministry of Supply and Services, 1991), chap. 5.

36 Borowy, Gordon and Lebans, "Are These Clothes Clean?" 304, referring to the Economic Council of Canada, which documents this trend in *Good Jobs, Bad Jobs*, and to Armine Yalnizyan in "Full Employment—Still a Viable Goal," in *Getting on Track: Social Democratic Strategies for Ontario* ed. Daniel Drache (Montreal: McGill-Queen's University Press, 1992).

37 Lonergan, *Insight*, 217-18, and Doran, *Theology and the Dialectics of History*, 34-35, 75-76, 88-89, 95, 101-103, 145-47, 149, 359, 364-86, 390. They refer to these two essential aspects as the dialectic of community.

38 Lonergan, *Insight*, 239. Lonergan names the attitude of critical consciousness described on 238-42 "cosmopolis." I call it "healing, critical consciousness."
39 They constitute major personal, group and societal obstacles preventing
   respect for differences.
40 Rosemary Radford Ruether, "Eschatology and Feminism," in *Lift Every Voice:
   Constructing Christian Theologies from the Underside*, ed. Susan Brooks
   Thistlethwaite and Mary Engel Potter (New York: Harper & Row, 1990),
   111.
41 Ibid., 110.
42 Lonergan, *Method in Theology*, 22.
43 Elizabeth Johnson, *She Who Is: The Mystery of God in Feminist Theological
   Discourse* (New York: Crossroad, 1993), 10.
44 Thomas Berry, *The Dream of the Earth* (San Francisco: Sierra Club Books,
   1988), 106.
45 Rosemary Brown, "Overcoming Sexism and Racism—How?" in *Racism in
   Canada*, ed. Ormond McKague (Saskatoon: Fifth House Publishers, 1991),
   168. Refer also to Arun Mukherjee, "A House Divided: Black Women and
   American Feminist Theory" (unpublished paper, York University, Toronto);
   Michèle Barrett and Mary McIntosh, "Ethnocentrism and Socialist-Feminist
   Theory," *Feminist Review* 20 (June 1985): 23-47; Caroline Ramazanoglu,
   "Ethnocentrism and Socialist-Feminist Theory: A Response to Barrett and
   McIntosh," *Feminist Review* 22 (February 1986): 83-86; Hamida Kazi, "The
   Beginning of a Debate Long Due: Some Observations on Ethnocentrism and
   Socialist-Feminist Theory," *Feminist Review* 22 (February 1986): 87-91;
   Heidi Safia Mirza, "The Dilemma of Socialist Feminism: A Case for Black
   Feminism," *Feminist Review* 22 (February 1986): 103-105; and Chandra
   Mohanty, "Under Western Eyes: Feminist Scholarship and Colonial Dis-
   courses," *Feminist Review* 30 (Autumn 1988): 61-88.
46 Barbara Aarsteinsen, "'Racist, Sexist' Slam Hits Heir to NAC Job," *The
   Toronto Star*, 24 April 1993, A6, and Michele Landsberg, "Anti-Immigrant
   Bigotry Sparks Attack on New Women's Leader," *The Toronto Star*, 29 April
   1993, F1. See also Ruth Roach Pierson, "The Mainstream Women's Movement and the Politics of Difference," in *Canadian Women's Issues* vol. 1, by
   Ruth Roach Pierson, Marjorie Griffin Cohen, Paula Bourne and Philinda
   Masters (Toronto: James Lorimer, 1993), 207. In 1995, Sunera Thobani
   was acclaimed president of NAC for a second term. In 1996, Joan Grant-
   Cummings, a black woman, was elected by a vast majority.
47 Susan Brooks Thistlethwaite, *Sex, Race, and God: Christian Feminism in
   Black and White* (New York: Crossroad, 1989), 2.
48 Ibid., 2, referring to Katie Cannon, Carter Heyward et al., *God's Fierce
   Whimsy: Christian Feminism and Theological Education* (New York: Pilgrim
   Press, 1985), 36.
49 Brooks Thistlethwaite, *Sex, Race, and God*, 16.
50 To continue uprooting unconscious aspects of racism in myself, I took a
   double-semester course, "Gender, Race, Class," given by Arun Mukherjee at
   York University. Weekly, my perceptions were stretched and I treasure the
   friendships that endure from this experience. Five of us, including Arun

Mukherjee, drove to Boston in 1989 for a conference, Troubling the Waters: Gender, Race, Class, offered by the Women's Theological Center. For a month that summer, I also lived with Ana Vilma and Ramonde Quintanilla and their children Cessia and Moises, Salvadoran refugees who did garment homeworking in Montreal. Their combined wages were less than poverty-line income. Daily, I joined women from thirteen Latin American countries at a women's centre downtown.

51 Marlee Kline, "Critique of the 'Feminist Standpoint,'" in *Race, Class, Gender: Bonds and Barriers*, ed. Jesse Vorst et al. (Toronto: Between the Lines, 1989), 48.

52 Sandra Schneiders, public lecture given at a Women Church Conference, Cincinnati, OH, 1988.

53 Lorraine Code, *What Can She Know? Feminist Theory and the Construction of Knowledge* (Ithaca: Cornell University Press, 1991), 17.

54 Sandra Schneiders, *Beyond Patching: Faith and Feminism in the Catholic Church* (New York: Paulist Press, 1991), 12. See also Beverly Wildung Harrison, Review of *Feminism and Process Thought, Signs* (Spring 1982): 709.

55 Wildung Harrison, *Making the Connections*, xvi-xvii.

56 Johnson, *She Who Is*, 155.

57 Ibid., 155.

58 Lorraine Code, "Credibility: A Double Standard," in *Feminist Perspectives: Philosophical Essays on Method and Morals*, ed. Lorraine Code, Sheila Mullett and Christine Overall (Toronto: University of Toronto Press, 1988), 81-82.

59 Liz Stanley, ed., *Feminist Praxis: Research, Theory, and Epistemology in Feminist Sociology* (New York: Routledge, 1990), 14-15.

60 Liz Stanley and Sue Wise, "Method, Methodology, and Epistemology in Feminist Research Processes," in *Feminist Praxis: Research, Theory, and Epistemology in Feminist Sociology*, ed. Liz Stanley (New York: Routledge, 1990), 30-31.

61 Stanley, ed., *Feminist Praxis*, 15.

62 Stanley and Wise, "Method, Methodology, and Epistemology in Feminist Research Processes," 39.

63 Lorraine Code, "Feminist Theory," in *Changing Patterns: Women in Canada*, ed. Sandra Burt, Lorraine Code and Lindsay Dorney (Toronto: McClelland and Stewart, 1988), 42-44, 49.

64 Wendy Johnston, "Introduction" to Madelaine Gagnon, "My Body in Writing," in *Feminism: From Pressure to Politics*, ed. Angela Miles and Geraldine Finn (Montreal: Black Rose Books, 1989), 366-67.

65 Alicya Muszynski, "What Is Patriarchy?" in *Race, Class, Gender: Bonds and Barriers*, edited by Jesse Vorst et al. (Toronto: Between the Lines, 1989), 76-77. Brooks Thistlethwaite and Engel Potter suggest that liberation theologians are beginning to recognize that the many "isms," racism, sexism, classism, heterosexism and homophobia, sexual and domestic abuse, "form an interlocking chain of oppression, which collectively may be called patriarchy" (*Lift Every Voice*, 4). Rosemary Brown says that "Patriarchy, by definition, is about the inherent right and power of men to control and dictate the exercise of all four structures" of production, reproduction, sexuality

and socialization of children which Juliet Mitchell has described as combining to produce the complex unity of woman's position ("Overcoming Sexism and Racism—How?" 173; also refer to Juliet Mitchell, *Woman's Estate* [New York: Random House, 1977], 101). Brown ("Overcoming Sexism and Racism—How?" 174) emphasizes another of Mitchell's insights that modification in any one of these leads to reenforcement of another (*Woman's Estate*, 121). Adrienne Rich's definition is comprehensive, "Patriarchy is the power of the fathers; a familial-social, ideological, political system in which men—by force, direct pressure, or through ritual, tradition, law and language, customs, etiquette, education and the division of labor—determine what part women shall or shall not play, and in which the female is everywhere subsumed under the male" (Adrienne Rich, *Of Woman Born, Motherhood as Experience and Institution* [New York: Norton, 1976], 56, as quoted in Brooks Thistlethwaite and Engel Potter, *Lift Every Voice*, 7).

66 See Lee Bartky, *Femininity and Domination*, 15.

67 Shadd, "Institutionalized Racism and Canadian History," 4.

68 Examples of this are not limited to the garment industry. Throughout the history of British Columbia fisheries, large numbers of Indian women have been paid wages inferior to those of Chinese labourers, to Indian men and to white women. Although wages were not determined according to "racial" or gender identity, employers created new job classifications that they later filled using "racial" and gender criteria. The job came to be linked with the group hired (Muszynski, "What Is Patriarchy?" 79).

69 Intercede and ILGWU, *Meeting the Needs of Vulnerable Workers*, 29.

70 Brian Swimme and Thomas Berry, *The Universe Story* (San Francisco: Harper, 1992), 73.

71 Ibid., 74.

72 Ibid., 75-76.

73 Ibid., 77-78.

74 Doran, *Theology and the Dialectics of History*, 510.

75 Ibid., 295. Doran identifies them as the dialectic of culture.

6

Home Outside the Public Eye

Sun fed webs
Soft silk,
Strong, sturdy webs sticky silk
Webbed wisdom woven wisdom
                    Sun fed threads

his chapter focuses on attitudes that have been ingrained
widely enough to become structural causes of poverty for
women and youth, especially regarding all work in
homes and domestic labour beyond homes. I probe the meaning of
Beverly Wildung Harrison's critique that the public/private split legitimizes "both a capitalist mode of political-economic organization and
female subjugation in personal and domestic life."[1] Experience of
boundaries between public and private varies among rural/urban,
native and other racial groups throughout Canadian society.[2] Because
of my focus on a Toronto context throughout this study, I am particularly concerned about the urban experience of this split as it affects
homeworkers and those in solidarity with them, and how it functions
to provide a rationale for maintaining a system that devaluates women.

Heeding Gail Cuthbert Brandt's caution regarding use of the separate spheres, public and private, as a conceptual framework, I point out
that it is limited, particularly as an artificial construct of what is
claimed to be self-contained and isolated. Many women and men did

---

Notes to chapter 6 are on pp. 203-208.

not conform either to the separate spheres of public and private or to the ideology underlying it.[3] My attention centres on critique of social attitudes that promote the separation and embody the split as a means of control, as well as on both paid and unpaid work in the home which both defy and suffer under this artificial socio-political category.

Wherever the split is a dominant part of thought patterns, the subsequent organization tends to embody and legitimate subjugation according to differences in individual, familial and societal relations. The family is central in importance. I identify and respect as family all those who choose to so name themselves and who may be defined by the following, according to the Ontario Ministry of Education's use in a secondary school family studies course:

> a social unit of interacting persons who make commitments, assume responsibilities, nurture each other, become socialized, transmit cultural and religious values, and share resources over time. This definition emphasizes the social, psychological, and economic aspects of the family unit, taking into consideration both physical and emotional relationships.[4]

or as defined by the Social Sciences and Humanities Research Council and Health and Welfare Canada in a joint program against family violence and against violence against women: "a grouping of individuals who are related by affection, kinship, dependency or trust."[5] I quite generally speak of family/kin/friendships to recognize a range of preferences. Later in this chapter, I foreground family/kin/friendships as a lifelong, foundational, constituent element of society. As Statistics Canada points out, "A generally accepted notion of the family is that it is a fundamental building block of society."[6]

The intertwined roots of the problem prompt me to rely on a spiral approach. I correlate social organization with the shift from preindustrial family which was organized around agricultural production to the child-centred home; with entrenchment of "women's place" ideology; with the idea of a "good woman"; and with the material base of the public/private split. I refer to domestic divisions in terms of interrelated gender roles, economic dependency, social ownership and organization, and note their impact as structural causes of both social instability and of the rise of women's movements. By foregrounding gender analysis throughout the chapter and linking it with social organization, I lay the groundwork to suggest key elements of a societal framework in which we may overcome multifaceted splits. These elements can be used as an evaluation grid of organizational priorities and budget allocations.

I develop my analysis in five sections: (1) The Myth of Women's Place and Market Strategies; (2) Social Construction of Gender Relations; (3) Implications for Socio-Political Organization; (4) Foundational Elements of a Framework for Socio-economic Ethics; and (5) Construction of an Integrative Framework.

The Myth of Women's Place and Market Strategies

Correlation of capitalist development in Ontario with the myths that support it reveals what shapes and limits contemporary provincial horizons regarding women's *place*. It does the same regarding men's *place*. Although the socio-economic system did not produce the myth of women's special nature, according to which women are born to domesticity and to nurture children, what the rising white capitalist class did was

> to lock the myth into Western consciousness so deeply that the conceptions of women's experience as unchanging, as totally child-centered and domiciled became axiomatic. Most people actually believe that the single family unit has been a central social institution throughout history—a seriously erroneous notion.[7]

Though the roots may go back to the Protestant Reformation in Europe, it was only in the shift away from preindustrial, agricultural production, in which women and men were both producers, that

> the social ideal of the child-centered home became even the normative social aspiration, not to mention a general reality. Only then did a social stigma come to be attached to poor women, either in rural areas or in cities, for "violating" that ideal.... Poor women, even those who followed the protocols of legal marriage, lived on the edge of survival and did what they had to do—whether behind a plow or in the marketplace—to survive or help provide wherewithal for young children. Only when the child-centered family was widely established did such women come to internalize the social disapproval that made any extra-domestic activities less than "feminine" and therefore a source of social stigma.[8]

In addition to family maintenance, poor women endured long hours of work, low pay and social disgrace.

The rise of market capitalism effected a great transformation in society by changing the motive of action from one of subsistence to one of gain. This resulted not from a natural process but from particular choices made by those who control the market. It becomes increasingly important since time is allocated between market and non-market activities. When it is assumed that the allocation of time within the household or between household and market must be based on maximum total utility for monetary gain, then we see that the division of labour by sex within a household is the result of a rational economic calculation. Social implications are significant: if behaviour is based on some economic law, then a split would be rational, a powerful argument for justifying the status quo.[9]

The dominant ideology of women's special place sharpened class distinctions and widened the gap between the social ideal of women's lives and the actual condition of most women's lives. The cult of true womanhood with its emphasis on domestic arts and gentility was in reality a cult of a white leisure class. It imprisoned aristocratic women in social powerlessness as decorative displays of the family's economic success.[10] The first strong wave of feminism in England and in the United States arose against such destruction of women's personhood.

Depicting women's nature universally in this way had introduced and entrenched a social ideal of "unprecedented differentiation and separation from any productive economic function."[11] Women's former economic role had eroded and their social power weakened as the ideology expanded to shape an ideal of what women should be. Increasingly, this idealism was also used to justify the moralization of class specificity and to measure both goodness and failure according to economic and domestic gentility. Along with the trend of extolling freedom according to classical liberalism, economic success became the indicator of personal moral rectitude. When production was moved out of the household in the process of industrialization, home and paid work were separated and the economic role of family/kin/friendship relations shifted to becoming a centre for consumption.[12] Rising affluence and the ideal of the good woman made class and "race" differences more marked, with deeper stigma for the very persons who were experiencing increased pressure for direct participation in wage labour just for survival.

I note several relevant ramifications of this situation.[13] First, the simultaneous need for poor women to contribute wages or provide them solely, the fear of failure in the arts of true womanhood and the pressure to perform as a good mother and respectable homemaker providing a restful haven for her partner and children tended to become measures of self-worth and possible sources of envy of richer women. Second, many working-class men and women aspired to middle-class sex role division as a gauge of self-worth and/or a more humane way of shedding the double bind of women's roles. Third, such social expectations of women reveal that the ideology of public and private is an artificially constructed mechanism of control. Few allegedly private activities are allowed to remain a woman's private concern. Fourth, holding a family together became women's work.[14]

The horizons of Canadians on foreign battlefields and of those responsible for both public and private realms here in Ontario expanded considerably in wartime. Women were temporarily needed in industrial production. In varying ways men and women learned the horrors of war. The stage was set to recognize public responsibility to insure peacekeeping alternatives, to achieve full employment and to provide child care. After so much bloodshed, men may have found healing relationships and grounding through care of the home and parenting (if they were well enough emotionally, of course). What might have been a complementary merging of women and men's horizons did not emerge in public debate.[15] Postwar times were moments ripe for creative change to share parenting, household tasks and waged labour. Tragically, the opportunity was lost in an entrenchment of the women's place ideology, as a war-weary population reverted to private concerns of home and family life.[16] Prevailing horizons limited the social reconstruction of gender roles. Men were to be given priority by right in the public sphere while women provided their castle at home. Imagination seems to have been paralyzed by warfare, to the extent that men could not allow themselves space in the private sphere to grieve and to parent. Children could hardly be educated into genetically related, integrated development of the so-called public/private. Instead of emphasizing both public and private, men and women were generally limited to focus on either the public or the private domain. The gains made for equal access to jobs were short term.[17]

The clear line dividing public and private also separated the economy and the family. Gender roles received new impetus. For some, there was increasing affluence with greater freedom in dress, movement and personal expression, but, in fact, this affluence camouflaged the erosion of the social and economic base of women's power. The dissatisfactions that gave rise to the first wave (and later waves as well) of women's movements are rooted in broad-based structural reasons.[18]

Belinda Leach suggests that ideologies and cultural practices regarding family and work interact to support and reinforce the social relations of homework:

> Ideas about "family" influence work patterns in ways people are frequently
> unaware of, while ideas about "work" constrain the way families operate to

survive. Through the medium of the family, labour is mobilized in different ways, depending on gender, age, relationship and life cycle stages.[19]

Leach refers to family and work as two categories of meaning since they operate together to shape peoples' lives even as they create familiar opposition within capitalist culture. This division is evident as some speak of family and work as competing demands on their time, as requiring sacrifice one for the other or as suffering on account of the other. By deconstructing both terms—family and work—Leach uncovers historical and cultural developments which sustain an ideology of division.

From interviews with homeworkers, however, she observes that

> what the homeworkers call family and work are not simple oppositional categories at all. They are complex, interrelated terms, which in practice are enmeshed, and because of their complexity and interrelatedness produce in the lives of the homeworkers more contradiction than stability, more fragmentation than cohesion.[20]

For homeworkers, work includes paid and unpaid work whether it is done in the home, factory, on their living accommodations and/or land, for the family or for an employer. Structural relations for each, and value accorded to each, vary. Family is used to refer mainly to a household unit. I note that it is the fragmentation in societal practice that causes the contradiction. Their integration is a strength in itself but problematic in societies built on oppositions.

Leach shows that literature about the family in sociology, anthropology and history emphasizes a deeply embedded model of the nuclear family and clear sexual division of labour in terms of tasks and location in spite of cultural variations. What is most relevant here is the degree to which the ideology of the nuclear family is accepted as a crucial component of society, prescribing which people should live together, and affecting social legislation, especially financial transfer payments on the basis of family relationships. This code sets limits regarding exchanges of affection and loyalty: "The idea of a blood or marriage bond is then used to include people in a privileged category, the family. In short, it provides for people a frame of meaning around which to organize their lives."[21] Ideologies surrounding the family are compelling in affecting people's relationships to the labour market and to different activities.

Women's vital role of reproducing the work force and of servicing or recuperating other adult workers is an "indispensable base of the entire economic system, although its value remains invisible and unaccounted for in the GNP."[22] Women are to be kept largely invisible and isolated, dependent and privatized, in order to maintain the present capitalist direction of power and privilege.[23] Furthermore, unless the injustices arising from this dual role for women are addressed systemically, our political and economic powerlessness will remain a growing source of social instability.

In short, the understanding of women's place is a social construction. It is operative in shaping expectations of what constitutes a good woman, in placing responsibility for children and home on women, in isolating women and in marginalizing women in socio-economic organization. Clarification of the impact of this construct reveals the importance of societal organization. It also provides background regarding the intense debate surrounding efforts to integrate women in the public sphere.

Social Construction of Gender and "Race" Relations

Not satisfied with marginal accounts, feminists see the importance of regarding the relation of the sexes and "races" as integral to the social order and any study of it. This includes considering the impact of changes in the social order on family patterns and psychosexual development. As distinctive social groups, feminists now see clearly that our public invisibility cannot be ascribed to female nature. Rather, the relations between the sexes and "races" are socially constructed. Sex and "race," then, also become categories of social thought.[24]

In patriarchal social order, women function as the property of men in the maintenance and production or socialization of new members of the social order and this is worked out in kinship organization. Thus, organization of the productive forces of society reveals the rationale of the domestic order to which women have been primarily attached.[25] As a complement of social production, this organization of the family has been the alleged reason for underpaying women. Women's wages were regarded as supplemental to the real income which is that of the men to whom they were to be attached. This means that economic control on the public, macroeconomic, theoretical and decision-making level is patriarchally controlled and split from vital, microeconomic, practical sustenance, the so-called private needs of families. In this context, public problems such as lack of employment and food are often left to private ingenuity for solution.

Another relevant issue is the amount of control that those who work in the family/kinship/friendship relations have over the "products" of their labour. Often family/kin/friendship is a locus of struggle over inequities in the division of labour, although it has the potential for interdependence and unity. Heidi Hartmann suggests that the prevailing concept of family/kin/friendship relations as an active agent with unified interests is false. Family/kin/friendship relations are rather a place of struggle, where production and redistribution take place.[26] Production conflicts within the household raise questions of who does housework and child care, according to whose standards and whether women should work for wages outside the home and/or possibly for men from inside the home. In the public domain, questions of employment availability, trade negotiations, tax reform, interest rates, use of fast foods or home-cooked meals and about parent co-operative child care or state-regulated child care centres arise.

The family/kin/friendship relations are a locus of internal formation, where we learn about gender and experience the class and "race" systems in personal ways. As Jane Flax puts it, the family is "one of the central mediating structures between all other structures of oppression."[27] Along with understanding the power differential between men and women, and the importance of providing a foundation for action, feminist theory includes understanding of family/kin/friendship relations as one of its crucial goals. Whether nuclear or extended, heterosexual or homosexual, private family/kinship/friendship relations have been ignored in the politics of social interchange. A male head of a family represents its interests in the public sphere and, with his increasing political importance, legitimizes the ideology of individualism, of control at home and of male public power. Those without such representation are totally invisible. Control of women's work allows men to benefit from women's provision of personal and household services, including relief from child care, cooking and any tasks considered unpleasant.

Analysis takes us beyond individual advantage to the systemic; as Heidi Hartmann says, "Patriarchy's material base is men's control of women's labour; both in the household and in the labour market, the division of labour by gender tends to benefit men."[28] It benefits men at different income levels in both public and private realms. Rosemary Radford Ruether explains how deeply ingrained and extensive this ideology is:

> The home is designated as a realm of compensatory status and ownership for males who are denied ownership and control over the means of production on the job. Protest against or even awareness of lack of ownership of

the work world is suppressed by directing each worker to think of his home as the sphere of his pride in ownership and personal possessions. His wife and children are themselves seen as a part of this ownership. His ability to decorate his home with conspicuous objects of consumption is the measure of his status in a capitalist society.[29]

Lack of a home and/or job complicates the already burdened expectation that women and home will decorate and service male work and provide outlets for frustration. The point is that

no matter how many women actually work and must work, no matter how few members of the society actually live in the nuclear, heterosexual monogamous family with sufficiently paid husband and unpaid wife, this still remains the ideological norm, rendering any other role of women or any other type of family non-normative and questionable. This domestic ideology continues to socialize men and women to think that men should rule and women should serve, not only at home, but on the job as well.[30]

This ideology of female subordination thereby strengthens basic capitalist structures.

Mary O'Brien pinpoints the actual process of reproductive labour as the material ground of both species continuity and the separation of public and private life. But contrary to the prevailing idea, she claims that the split results not from biological function but from social relations. In this regard, it is of import to note that contraceptive technology is making a major impact on the social relations of reproduction. In fact, since it is actually transforming the process of reproduction, it is rightly judged as a world historical event.[31] Yolande Cohen explains that by controlling our bodies, our sexuality, women disturb the traditionally established controls. Breaking barriers between the social body and the human body in our fertility, "by mixing sexuality, work and reproduction (of both children and surplus value), women are exploding the carefully erected "natural order" of our society.... Because we are not limited to politics, we can overturn politics."[32]

Feminist projects seek a new, daily tranquillity where conflicts are not resolved by domination of one sex/"race" over others and where the confinement of one is necessary for the survival of the other. This requires understanding of difference/specificity, what Audre Lorde calls the "creative spark" and what Susan Brooks Thistlethwaite names disorder because "order is often a code word that for oppressed peoples signifies maintenance of the status quo. When applied to class, the ordering function becomes classism; when applied to "race," it becomes racism, the suppression of conflict and change."[33]

Consideration of the social construction of gender/"race" relations reveals how social organization is shaped by gender and racial dualisms and by male/white supremacy. The split between public and private embodies these social constructions. It is my view that justice for women, the realization of our full personhood in worth and work, entails a reordering of society that overcomes this split. An analysis of the social constructs and gender and "race" relations is an important part of such reordering.

Implications for Socio-political Organization

The social construction of gender relations has implications for socio-political organization. The public/private ideology has become institutionalized in ideas and practices which lead to under-development, to the domestication of women, to systemic crises and to the feminization of poverty. Repression of difference and specificity analysis is a means to control the production and dissemination of knowledge, which in turn usually entails excluding women from public decision making. As well, women's social and moral aspirations and perspectives either do not surface at all or are trivialized. Lack of gender/"race"/specificity analysis in social organization leads to "a mystification of the gender-power relations that constitute the subtext of the modern economy and state."[34] The association of women's experience almost excessively with the private has been used to keep women's issues off the public agenda and to delegitimize them.[35] But Angela Miles, rooting feminism's progressive power in its affirmation of both women's specificity and equality, proclaims the need to integrate the public and private:

> Women's entry into politics, *as women* is in fact, the emergence of the long subordinate, devalued and marginalized sphere of private life and reproduction into the public and political world. It is, potentially, the transformation of politics, and is an event of world historical significance.[36]

A dynamic, critical and creative perspective is needed to reclaim and affirm the traditionally devalued aspects of women's life and work in order to move toward a realistic and truly liberatory ethic.

Redefinition of the concept of what it is to be free and human in an inclusive way is necessary to offset the domination that is institutionalized in the fragmentation of human life. Challenging both the exclusively male and white definitions of women as well as of humanity is needed to provide concrete values and goals, such as integrating the psychological and social, the individual and collective, the personal and political. In this redefinition effort, we must recognize specificity. In fact, "to shirk the question of woman's specificity is to avoid the central ground of struggle altogether."[37]

I proceed now to show how the public/private division fosters a triple split in consciousness, gender roles and social organization. Rosemary Radford Ruether's historical overview of the rise and effects of dualisms across Western cultures deals with the same concerns of child-rearing and family life as those upholding the traditional "women's place" idea, but from another perspective, and with different conclusions.[38] It is clear that Radford Ruether values child-rearing, and she is also concerned about origins of male resentment and violence and male strategies of exploitative subversion of women's power. Her study of cultures and the roots of violence lead her to call for

a new pattern of mutual parenting [to] balance maternal primacy in reproduction. We need to structure new forms of gender parity. This must begin by changing a pattern that goes back to the beginnings of hominid development and even earlier; that is, the social construction of the primacy of maternal gestation into the primacy of early childhood nurture and domestic labor by women. Men and women must share fully the parenting of children from birth and the domestic work associated with daily life. A genuine change in the pattern of parenting must be understood, not as a slight adjustment toward males "helping" females with child care, but a fundamental reconstruction of the primary roots of culture, transforming the gender imaging of child-parent relations and the movement into adulthood for both males and females. *This implies a reconstruction of the relation of the domestic core of society to the larger society.* One must look at all the hierarchies of exploitation and control that emanate out of the family pattern of female mothering and domestic labor.... Simply seen in isolation, such changes can do little and may be used to psychologize and privatize complex structural problems. *We must work on new understandings of culture and power relations in all dimensions of society.*[39]

By clearly affirming these traditional values *and* by recognizing specificity and equality, we can critique the system. Many men are left impoverished by split consciousness because of their separation from the material base of relationships such as child care. This factor reveals a connection between private and public dominance, that is, between domestic patriarchal control and its translation in the socio-economic sphere as gender, "race" and class oppression. Separation of the public and private leads to formulation of theory cut off from its base, to dualism and to exclusion of women in labour and in the production of both knowledge and categories of consciousness. Such alienation leads not only to oppression of women but also to the destruction of men as well. Ignoring this separation as operative in socio-economic-political organization leaves us with the status quo, a situation clearly not working since poverty and unemployment are increasing.

After surveying major elements in social structure and culture that both shaped and reflected the systems of patriarchal domination in the West, Rosemary Radford Ruether is unflinchingly clear about the tragedy:

> But there are also elements of sin in the sense of culpable evil in this story. The roots of this evil lie ... in patterns of domination, whereby male elites in power deny their interdependency with women, exploiting human labor and the biotic community around them. They seek to exalt their own power infinitely, by draining the lives of these other humans and nonhuman sources of life on which they depend. They create cultures of deceit, which justify this exploitation by negating the value of those they use, while denying their own dependence on them.[40]

Exponential growth in productive and destructive power globally has coincided with the distancing between people and the biotic chain.[41] It is no accident that nature is exploited. It happens even as the rich amass more wealth and the poor sink into destitution and exclusion. The decline is systemic.

The split of both the practical and intersubjective aspects of the dialectic of community *from each other* into public and private realms and the split *within* each of these aspects into public and private maintain this domination. On the public level, the combined effect of this amounts to male domination of theory and decision making for capital formation, technology, economics and politics. Public international relations fall into this domain, not just for trade but for all negotiations and connections. All these public areas have been so split within themselves that the practical, material base becomes the nearly exclusive private concern of women. The myth that a woman's place is in the home and/or in supportive roles reinforces this. A bias against women extols female common sense for child/elder/health care and household microeconomic responsibilities, but implies female ineptitude for critical thinking, international relations and practical, macroeconomic responsibility.

Within this apparently genderless impersonal realm of the economy, we generally learn to reflect upon ourselves in impersonal terms.[42] We experience the split between our own experience, knowledge and autonomy, on the one hand, and what is regarded as valid and authoritative in society on the other. When ideas of what is acceptable for the economy originate beyond our experience and are not compatible with it, they become, as Dorothy Smith says, "a forced set of categories into which we must stuff the awkward and resistant actualities of our worlds" if accepted uncritically.[43] These false constructs constitute the bases of common perspectives, a set of imposed positions in the structures that rule.

Though not necessarily intentionally manipulative or deceptive, those who rule (control, manage, organize, administrate) relate almost exclusively within their formally and informally organized circles of discourse.[44] They form

> the basis of an active process of organization, producing ideologies that serve to organize the class itself and its work of ruling, as well as to order and legitimate its domination.... We are talking about control over the means of producing and disseminating ideas and images—that is, control over the educational process, over the media. The silence of those outside the apparatus is a silence in part materially organized by the preemption, indeed virtual monopoly, of communications media.[45]

In confusion, women and men without power surrender control, withdrawing from the complexity of the public and of formal economics to a seemingly more relevant and manageable private sphere. A multi-billion-dollar advertising strategy reinforces this privatized, consumer mentality. In a consumer mentality people fear ignorance, inadequacy and powerlessness or being thought of as personally ignorant, inadequate and impotent. Internalizing the corporate message that a person "is not good enough unless" leads to paralysis and apathy without confidence either to initiate or to participate in systemic critique or change. Little concern is given to the deception inherent in internalizing such fears individually or as groups. Our sense of agency and ability to act, or even to think of alternative possibilities, are destroyed.

Myths and confusion surround the private sphere. One of these myths is that women simply want to abandon reproductive concerns to move solely to production and public life. Some women may. So may some men. But referring uncritically to an adult female population as though it were divided between housewives and "working women" mystifies the fact that both housework and motherhood are *work* and that the "working woman" also does housework and may have children. This phraseology thus creates artificial barriers among women by ignoring common ground. Global facts shatter this myth by exposing the key role of unpaid labour and dependent reproductive labour in defining women's reality. According to a United Nations survey, women worldwide do between 66 per cent to 75 per cent of the work of the world, earn 10 per cent of the income and own 1 per cent of the property. Beginning from a recognition of women's actual wide range of work and values means affirming and transforming how we (women) name our values and identify ourselves.

The public/private split surfaces even in the separation of work and leisure arising as it does from male experience of paid employment outside the home and lack of (or minimal) parenting and household responsibilities. The social organization of the roles of wife, housewife, mother, homeworker and/or employee outside the home do not conform to the divisions of being at work and not being at work.[46] In fact, what prevails is "a 1980s pattern of work outside the home with a 1950s division of labour at home."[47] In this case, functionalist theory attempts to assimilate rationally a social phenomenon of women's roles that cannot be assimilated in practice. It does so largely by ignoring women's realities or trivializing them. Wage scales and the connection between gender, "race" and conditions of work reflect this bias.[48] To limit women's wage earning as mere supplements for family survival, rather than being essential to it, is to neglect the many for whom it is primary.[49]

The dominant societal image of home is particularly significant in that it "evokes an emotional response which is at odds with seeing it as a place of employment. Homes are considered private places into which the law ought not to intrude. It is precisely these kinds of notions which have left domestic work virtually unregulated until recently."[50] The fact that domestic workers do tasks which many women perform without pay leaves the impression that their work is not productively active real work and that they are not employees with legal rights. Devaluation is translated into low pay for frequently long hours. Although garment homeworkers do the same work as done by women in factories, their location diminishes its value. An impression prevails that they control their own schedules and easily combine child care, domestic chores and paid work. That the skills of both domestics and homeworkers are undervalued is evident in the low priority given toward regulation of their work by legislators.

A contemporary functionalist procedure capsulizes women's work and social relations in the household and family as concepts to be analyzed in terms of their relation to capitalist economic processes. At least this approach exposes how women's unpaid work supports the system. Previously, such relations were disregarded in economic theory as irrelevant. Women's unpaid work life simply does not fit into traditional, bureaucratic, professional or administrative categories of public organization and theory.

Taking household and parental responsibilities seriously challenges more than the distribution of goods, services and roles between men and women. Integrating the public/private service of women calls for transformation of the vocabulary, method, forms of thought and aims of the socio-economic agenda. It shifts the location of the discourse from the ruling apparatus to participation by all, specifically incorporating the horizons, concerns and solutions of those most excluded— namely, women generally, but especially Native and black women and women of colour and youth. State participation in this agenda has slowly broadened since the development of the welfare state brought discussion of equal opportunity for women into the public sphere. Efforts for equal opportunity in the public world largely co-existed with patriarchal relations in the private world until the late 1960s. Sandra Burt points out, however, that since then women's groups have demanded radical transformations in the structuring and distribution of roles in both public and private spheres. Governments have responded cautiously.[51] Only strong commitment to participate in breaking down gender/racial roles will change the ability to define horizons for action.

Another prevalent social myth is that "ours has been the greatest social experiment in human history and that here the possibilities for human fulfillment have come to fruition as never before."[52] With code words like "opportunity," "success" and "freedom," some imagine that everyone who really works at improvement will achieve it. At a feeling level it serves as a measure of worth and self-esteem. This may lead homeworkers, other working poor and the unemployed to hold themselves fully responsible for supposed failure. This myth fills in the gap between the actual social relations and the way we have been socialized to think about possibilities. More seriously, attention is diverted from the need to analyze our social structure and its effects on our lives. Vested interests on the part of the wealthy maintain this illusive invisibility of relations of ruling. Governments, churches and educational systems in Ontario seem quite generally reluctant to admit publicly and confront the astonishing inequalities of wealth and privilege in our midst with clear analysis of their systemic causes.

The split between public and private includes differential valuation and remuneration. It is a source of economic inequality between the sexes generally and a root cause of sexual subjugation. Economic inequality makes women more vulnerable to dependence on males and/or to poverty. Those who are full-time homemakers, children/ elder caregivers and/or homeworkers need secure, financial recognition of their contribution. It should also be noted that economic equality is not simply a matter of receiving "equal pay for equal work." It is blatantly clear in the present stage of financial capitalism that men themselves are not considered equal.[53]

In contrast to the myths that homeworking and global market forces are inevitable and that corporations will always protect the home and family values, the reality is that increasing numbers of women are trapped in competitive poverty. Homeworking is not a realm separate from formal employment; it is unprotected labour. It is increasingly part of the restructuring process and promoted as a way for industries to remain competitive. But what is really being promoted is

> the notion that the family's role in reproduction can be extended into areas previously located in the market sphere.... They will be able to provide alternatives to the income and identity formerly associated with waged employment.... The family is also being asked to provide alternatives to services provided by the state as well as those produced for or purchased by the market.... Cuts in social services and welfare benefits, reinforced by the ideology of community care, assume that families will care for the sick, handicapped and elderly, and will support young people who, through unemployment or low wages and state regulations, are unable to live separately and maintain themselves.[54]

This perspective serves to isolate families in a privatized cycle of production and reproduction. Links between households, the commercial and state economy are destroyed, except to exploit households as consumers. Diminishing place (or none at all) is given in federal, provincial or local budgets for essential production and reproduction issues.

In this context, what is crucial is that homeworking does not remain invisible, that implications for the workers themselves be of primary importance in all restructuring processes, that casualized employment be recognized as a symptom of economic recession, not a solution. The impact of homeworking on the workers, according to Sheila Allen and Carol Wolowitz, is

> a particularly important example in showing how assumptions about gender are, on the one hand, used by firms and others to explain and justify low

pay and employment insecurity and, on the other, conveniently ignored when claims about the benefits of home-based work are made.[55]

The issues of quality, affordable child and elder care, of the public/private split, of sexism, racism and wealthism merge as women confront the pyramidal structure inherent to the particular relations of ruling in the clothing and textile industries.

Subjugation conditions women's ability to speak up about needs and positions in the home and in public. It leaves women psychically and socially vulnerable. For some, reputed "conservatism" is a way to prevent further beatings/abuse in the home, or at least the disrepute and multiple forms of exclusion that result from taking even a mildly radical stance in social/public settings. As a press representative at the U.S. National Women's Conference in Texas in 1977, Andrea Dworkin interviewed women who were against the Equal Rights Amendment. As a result, she urges feminists to face the conundrum of women's voluntary acceptance of policies and practices which restrict us to inferior status as a central issue. While qualifying her generalizations, I think her assessment is significant in raising possible key factors:

> Right-wing women ... see that work subjects them to more danger from more men; it increases the risk of sexual exploitation. They see that creativity and originality in their kind are ridiculed; they see women thrown out of the circle of male civilization for having ideas, plans, visions, ambitions.... They see no way to make their bodies authentically their own and to survive in the world of men. They know too that the Left has nothing better to offer: leftist men also want wives and whores; leftist men value whores too much and wives too little. Right-wing women are not wrong. They fear the Left, in stressing impersonal sex and promiscuity as values, will make them more vulnerable to male sexual aggression, and that they will be despised for not liking it. They are not wrong.... They know they are valued for their sex ... and so they try to up their value: through co-operation, manipulation, conformity; through displays of affection or attempts at friendship; through submission and obedience; and especially through the use of euphemism: "femininity," ... "maternal instinct," "motherly love." Their desperation is quiet; they hide their bruises of body and heart; they dress carefully and have good manners; they suffer, they love God, they follow the rules. They see that intelligence displayed in a woman is a flaw.... They do what they have to [in order] to survive.[56]

At times, oppression is so deep that we are not aware of our lack of freedom and/or choice in adapting a position.

Sandra Lee Bartky contrasts women's knowledge of men's general power with the experience of a woman who sees the real hurts and fears of the concrete man before her in a heterosexual relationship. She must set aside her own needs

> in order better to attend to his. She does this not because she is "chauvinized" or has "false consciousness," but because *this is what the work requires.* Indeed, she may even excuse the man's abuse of her, having glimpsed the great reservoir of pain and rage from which it issues. Here is a further gloss on the ethical disempowerment attendant upon women's caregiving: In such a situation, a woman may be tempted to collude in her own ill-treatment.[57]

The majority of women, however, now need paid income. The fact that women continue to *need* men's economic support indicates the extent of undervaluation of women's waged work. Exploitation is quadrupled as women are expected to provide a disproportionate share of domestic work, child care, health care and emotional care.[58]

An additional complication to women's economic dependency is the resentment and sense of control-as-a-right that this may raise in men. Decreasing availability of jobs and increasing numbers of women who need them set the conditions for hostility and abuse of women and children. Toronto homeworkers speak of the problem of men's consistent expectations for service and contribution to family economic resources coupled with resentment about the time given in the evenings and on weekends for waged labour. Many women face endless days of low-waged labour and home care. If they are in a position of needing to end a marriage, however, the destitution which they and their children face keeps too many in bondage.[59] In severe poverty, even with overtime homework.

This fuller picture regarding the implications of exclusive emphasis on family, home and nurturing, linked with a triple split in consciousness, in gender roles and in social organization, points out the depth and complexity of a dichotomous either/or approach. Protection of values and social transformation require a significant increase in women's participation and power in politics, production and medical control of reproduction. These call for a corresponding evaluation of organization of the domestic sphere. Counteraction of the privatization of domestic labour, its invisible and unremunerated nature and the reality that it is mainly women's work entails challenging the division between public and private, leisure and work, reproduction and production.

Some Foundational Elements of a Framework to Restructure Society

There is considerable consensus that the public/private dichotomy is detrimental to women as a principle of social organization. But Seyla Benhabib and Drucilla Cornell raise an important question: "Beyond this consensus ... what kind of a restructuring of the public/private realms is possible and desirable in our societies such as would further women's emancipation as well as create a more humane society for all?"[60] Taking up this question with garment workers in mind, I have found key constructive concepts in the works of Linda Nicholson, Nancy Fraser and Nancy Folbre.

First, *gender relations such as production and reproduction reflect the emergence, dominance and decline of institutions.* Translated into homeworking concerns, this means that factory work, piecework in the home and child-care practice are affected by new forms of capitalism, particularly in its present, brutal stage of financial or speculative capitalism. Social and environmental responsibilities are outside the realm of competitive greed. Whereas kinship fundamentally structured differential power relations in early societies, the analysis of power relations today centres on financial gain and privatization of all other concerns. Capitalist social relations, "race" and gender are deeply related.

Second, in contrast to economism (the assumption that economic gains for those who control wealth are primary), *healthy relations allow the economy to be neither primary nor autonomous in society.*[61] The economy is to be only a subsystem within social relations, not the driving force. Biased profit motivation has exploded the importance of food, clothing and other object production in capitalist organization beyond necessity for those with purchasing power. As Linda Nicholson suggests, "The ability of such activities to generate a profit gives to them a priority that can be mistakenly associated with their function in satisfying such needs."[62] Similarly, exclusion of child care and human relations from corporate "economic" gains robs them of priority in policy setting. At the same time, basic needs for these by the impoverished and excluded are not even registered in economic calculations and policy setting.

Third, *family/kin/friendship, child-rearing and elder care are components of the economy and must be recognized in economic theory and policies.* Elimination of conflicts over socially necessary activities, such as child-bearing and child-rearing, and their organization, from public, economic and theoretical consideration devalues women. They are considered significant only in the opportunities they present for profitable market consumption. When civic and family organization and reproductive issues are considered as secondary to economic development of production, commerce and consumption, a clear ideological link becomes visible. Child-rearing belongs within historical categories as both labour and socialization. Socialization, solidarity and cultural transmission happen in both family and paid workplace. In fact, families are economic systems, involving labour, exchange, calculation, distribution and, unfortunately, exploitation.[63]

Families and kinship are economic systems requiring unpaid labour and they interlock with broader economic systems involving paid work. A socio-economic framework to end women's subordination needs to address both normative-domestic-patriarchal power and bureaucratic-patriarchal-racist power.[64] Separation of the official economic sphere from the domestic sphere enclaves child-rearing from the rest of social labour, thereby entrenching women's subordination.

Fourth, *the value of family, kinship and friendships must be claimed in organizing the production and distribution of goods as well as in gender relations.* As the principle of exchange and of investment historically replaced the principle of kinship, access to control over these activities diminished. The subservience of both state and family to economic forces further excludes these from policy making.

Fifth, *gender/"race"/difference analysis involves women and men of all "races" who must be incorporated in mainstream politics, economics and education.*[65] Social power is complex and multidimensional. Gender, "race," age, sexual preference, nation and class are significant bases of identity and of interests.[66] Classifying women, visible minorities, poor and disabled as special interest groups and using this category to trivialize or ignore their claims betrays the fact that male, white and corporate are identity groups with vested interests.

In every group, identity and interests are linked within asset distributions, political rules, cultural norms and personal preference. These four categories shape potential for co-operation and conflict. They may be referred to as structures of constraint to convey their influence in delimiting people's desires and methods of obtaining what they want. They are significant factors in fostering group identity and interests, in strategizing and in encouraging patterns of behaviour based on socially constructed differences. In short, these factors affect overall productivity, distribution of public expenditures and investments, accounting for/or disregarding social and environmental costs and the designing of property rights.

Sixth, *the official economic and state system is intrinsically related to family life as a complementary environment for money-labour exchange.* It is likewise related to political participation through power-service exchange. There are gender subtexts in these relations. For example, Fraser's assessment is that "there is a very deep sense in which masculine identity in these societies is bound up with the breadwinner role."[67] Conversely, the role of consumer links the economy and family/kin/friendship relations through a subtext assigning women the unpaid, unrecognized work of purchasing and preparing goods and services for domestic consumption. Thus, money and power exchanges are not gender neutral.

Child-rearing links all of these roles. Lack of mention of it in the construction of social organization leaves gender identity unnoticed. It confirms the gender subtext of citizen roles. Dissonance increases between traditional female roles and capacities central to citizenship.

Constructing a just society involves uncovering: an idealized image of the workplace linked to the modern, restricted, male-headed, nuclear family; the fact that money and power exchanges are not gender neutral; and, finally, the link between traditionally female child-rearer roles and public/private institutions. Gender identity, according to Fraser, is

> a basic element of the social glue that binds them to one another. Moreover, a gender-sensitive reading of these connections has some important theoretical and conceptual implications. It reveals that male dominance is intrinsic rather than accidental to classical capitalism. For the institutional structure of this social formation is actualized by means of gendered roles.... They are ... premised on the separation of waged labour and the state from female childrearing and the household. It also follows that a critical social theory of capitalist societies needs gender-sensitive categories. The foregoing analysis shows that, contrary to the usual androcentric understanding, the relevant concepts of worker, consumer and wage are not, in fact, strictly economic concepts. Rather, they have an implicit gender subtext and thus are "gender-economic" concepts. Likewise, the relevant concept of citizenship is not strictly a political concept; it has an implicit gender subtext and so, rather, is a "gender-political" concept.[68]

Similarly, these roles have a racial subtext to be brought forward. Male dominance and both inter- and intraracial privilege used to amass wealth are intrinsic to the system. I quoted Nancy Fraser at length to underscore the importance of recognizing gender in the political economy, the need for a framework which integrates gender, politics and the political economy internally and the link between emancipatory transformation of male-dominated capitalist societies and gendered roles.

Seventh, *social movements need to interpret and communicate transformed gender/racial roles as the base of contemporary social organization*. This involves transformation of the content, character, boundaries and relations of the spheres of worker, child rearer, citizen and client vis-à-vis one another. The struggles lead Fraser to ask, for example, if child-rearing might replace soldiering as participatory citizenship and why soldiering would be paid and child-rearing unpaid. It is important to critique the patriarchal, norm-dominated, capitalist, economic systems; the systemic, money and power-mediated character of male dominance in the domestic sphere; and the multidirectional channels of influence among institutions. We must challenge how both the state-regulated economy of paid work and social assistance, along with the male public sphere, are separated from privatized female responsibility for child-rearing.

In summary, crucial requirements of a feminist, social framework are many. First, there is the need to align family, kin and friendship relations and a state-regulated official economy. If they are left separated, a gender-racial subtext serves to enforce our subordination, appropriate our labour and limit our participation in the interpretation of our needs. Second, the framework must allow for diversity and multifaceted, societal and environmental factors in shaping structures to protect and foster well-being and health. Third, it must "not be such as to posit the evil of welfare capitalism exclusively or primarily as the evil of reification. It must, rather, be capable of foregrounding the evil of dominance and subordination."[69] These requirements are foundational for the construction of a socio-economic framework in which women are recognized fully in our personhood and work.

Further Construction of an Integrative Framework

Our task is one of integration. I use framework here not in any sense of a final, specific description of how every or even any society or community is to organize itself. A framework names only essential components. Specific communities can implement these aspects in creatively diverse, extremely practical ways. Concrete evidence that these values are held in creative tension can be assessed in the recognition given each in budget priorities, participatory representation, accountability and responsibility, transparent decision making, real dialogue, inclusive process, projects, committees and especially their effects. These are criteria by which we judge the authentic implementation of foundational elements just described in the last chapter and those I now put forth.

Since liberal changes made to legislation do not address the roots of the problem, my present focus is to describe a broad societal framework for transformation that includes the horizon within which women's issues and values can be made visible and receive appropriate attention. Taking seriously the issues already raised requires much more than applying bandages like raising subsistence wages to minimum ones. It calls us to transform every aspect of our present structures and of our appreciation for persons, for family, kin and friendships, for community and for human capabilities within an interdependent cosmos. Since I believe that my study already offers compelling evidence of the need to change societal patterns of thinking, I turn at this point to the basic structure of society.

I propose a grid of essential aspects to be given place in community priorities, in governmental structures and in public budgets. Structures will vary according to cultures, ecology and regional creativity. So will budgets and accounting systems.

All of what follows is a both/and approach, *not* either/or. The breadth of concerns I have identified leads me to value a dialectical method so that different aspects can be given *full* attention even as they are held *in relation to others*. I separate aspects to foreground their importance. In fact, full integration of all the aspects which I am about to describe is essential for transformation. From both the disjuncture and solidarity I have described in chapters 1 to 5, I think elements for an alternative view become evident.

In order to facilitate understanding of the whole scheme, I begin with a grid of four key dialectics, in which all the aspects need to be held in creative tension or healthy relation with all the others. The dialectic of culture, broadly interpreted to involve cosmological interdependence and anthropological responsibility, embraces and informs all the others.[70] (See table 1.)

I focus on basic dialectics within the person or subject, family/kin/ friendships, community and culture.[71] All are differentiations of one complex movement of life in which we are challenged to hold aspects of each dialectic in creative tension with its counterpart.[72] Every aspect is important through entire life cycles of individuals, families and society, and must accordingly be protected in customs, laws and budgets. I explain each dialectic because I think they are all essential if we are to do ethics in a comprehensive, transformative way. Taken as a whole, the following section grounds a turn to authentic persons-in-dialogue as a basis for ethical decision making!

Table 1

Dialectics	Holding aspects of each dialectic in creative tension with the other(s)	
1. The person or subject	Body-Psyche-Spirit: soul, intentionality or mind	
2. Family, kin, friendships	Agency: individuation	Mutuality: social consciousness
3. Community	Intersubjectivity: relationships	Practicality: economics, politics
4. Culture	Cosmology: evolutionary horizon based on subjectivity differentiation, and interdependence	Anthropology: attentive, intelligent, reasonable, responsible, loving, decision making and action

The Person or Subject

My purpose in focusing on the person is to set forth an alternative to the extreme individualism evident in the relations of ruling which I described in chapter 2. I emphasize the person here for five reasons: (1) to recognize the value of all persons. Millions of unemployed are now excluded even from this minimum respect and value. As "disposables," their needs are omitted from all economic calculations. Such children are regularly "cleaned off the streets" (killed) in Rio, while homeless "disposables" in Bogota are used in practising methods of torture.[73] (2) to focus on the importance of an authentic turn to women and men as agents of ethical decision making and as creators of just societies; (3) to highlight the capacity of persons to be attentive, intelligent, reasonable, responsible and loving; (4) to foreground the importance of data of the body, psyche and spirit as they give rise to symbolization which both reflects and shapes the values and meanings of societies; and (5) to root our knowledge in body-psyche-intelligence dynamics. These reasons are foundational as we foster creative imagination to discover ways for transformation and as we strive to make informed judgements and courageous decisions to achieve it.

As persons, we are a unity of body-psyche-spirit. The latter may also be described as intentionality or intelligence. Societies are challenged to foster bodily health and the habitual collaboration of intelligence with imagination and the psyche. The latter controls this balance by selecting what it will allow to consciousness.[74] The relevance of this censorship function is directly related to the shaping of one's horizon and the overcoming of all forms of bias, themes of the previous chapter.

The body-psyche-intelligence is to be affirmed as a unity. Doran explains the profound relevance of Lonergan's detailed process:

> What, then, am I asked to affirm about myself: I am asked to affirm that I am a knower, where this means that I am a conscious unity, identity, whole, whose consciousness unfolds on three levels: first, an empirical level of presentations through sense and imagination; second, an intelligent level that consists of inquiry, insight into these presentations in which I grasp an intelligibility immanent and emergent in the data, and conceptualization and formulation of my understanding; and third, a reflective and rational level on which I seek to verify my understanding, and on which I grasp that the conditions for positing and affirming the conceptual synthesis in which I have formulated my understanding either are or are not fulfilled. If I grasp that the conditions are fulfilled, I cannot withhold affirmation without being unreasonable; if I grasp that they are not fulfilled, I cannot reasonably proceed to affirmation.... The fulfillment of the conditions for the particular judgement that Lonergan invites the reader to make ... is given in consciousness itself. The judgement, again, is "I am a knower," where knowing entails operations on the three levels of experience, understanding and judgement, where the levels are united by the desire to understand correctly, leading us to raise ever further relevant questions and where the pivotal moments are the events, first, of direct insight into data and, second, of a reflective grasp of the fulfillment of conditions for a prospective judgement.[75]

This means that individuals reach self-affirmation not by experience alone, nor even by experience, understanding and judging. The process involves reflection on all of these in relationship and bringing decisions to fruitful action. The unified structure of empirical, intelligent and critical consciousness is the basis of self-presence which involves far more than perceiving or looking inward. The cognitional process of experience, understanding and judgement operate on the data of sense and the data of consciousness.[76] Individual interests, concerns and objectives will cause different patterning of sensitive experience, including unconscious neural demands: as biological, aesthetic, intellectual, practical, mystical and dramatic patterns of experience. The latter involves our relationships and how we create our world.[77]

Persons are shaped within heredity and social-environmental factors as our bodies both register and express what is needed for conscious integration and image/symbol formation. These interact intimately with intentionality or intelligence, and with imagination so that we are capable of designing, choosing and shaping specifics regarding our inner identities, clear expression, communication and modes of relating. They also help us image the kind of world we will create.[78] Robert Doran focuses attention on fundamental processes in relation to what I consider is a critical issue for my study: the movement of life and one's capacity for change as one seeks direction in life. "The movement of life is experienced in the sensitive psyche; the search for direction is experienced in the questions and answers of intentional consciousness."[79] Consciousness of this enables us to know our deepest desires as they originate in a dialectic between the conscious and the unconscious. Both are rooted physically.[80] Our bodies know. They communicate clear messages regarding, for example, what we can or cannot stomach or stand up to. Even a physical restlessness may signal some significant information for us if we take both our body-psyche-spirit unity and our ability *to know* seriously. Our psyches convey symbols and dreams as gifts for interpretation. Our emotions provide information to indicate how we are touched by or involved in relationships and events. Using conscious intentionality or intelligence, we can gather relevant information, weigh it, discern, judge, decide and act. All of this in tune with the Spirit of God within us!

The materiality of our interdependent ecosphere influences, and to a great extent shapes, what is possible in terms of both limitation and transcendence. The interrelated web of life contains and explodes our current ability to imagine and create. Wisdom nurtures limitation to live within the limits of the earth, and our own "earth" (physical limitations). Openness to ever fuller being fosters transcendence, to go beyond present awareness, understanding, intuition, faith, hope and love. I do not mean separate or disconnected when I say transcendent. On the contrary, my deepest ecstasy in transcendence is consistently rooted in the senses and intuition. Transcendence is rooted and known in immanence. Likewise, knowing the all-holy God flows from doing justice.

Ability to ask relevant questions grounds both limitation and transcendence.[81] These capabilities flow from levels of consciousness which range from dreams, experience, understanding, judgement, to decision making, to being in love.[82] These functions are operative in decision making, in existential, interpersonal and historical agency, in responsible direction of well-being and the movement of life and in praxis.[83] Accordingly, they inform ethical and theological deliberations and offer the possibility of considerably expanding both data and method in much contemporary decision making.

Family, Kin and Friendships

I repeatedly indicate the relevance of family, kin and friendship relations within themselves and in relation to societal structures. Relations of family, kin and friendships are perhaps the most essential influence in developing persons-in-relation.[84] Overlapping the other dialectics, family, kin and friendships are the locus for integration of both the process of individuation and the formation of both social consciousness and social conscience. If this tension is allowed its rhythm, relationships will foster both autonomy and mutuality. Family, kin and friendships provide opportunities for learning and testing out meanings and values, self-worth, dynamics of interaction and what is pragmatic, just and the basis of wisdom. They can foster the ability to feel, to think critically, to be interdependent and to appreciate one's own and others' contributions. The process includes the tensions and joys of family life. Over a lifetime, wisdom can integrate individuation, social consciousness and social conscience.

Blatant and subtle forms of violence, abuse and dysfunction, however, destroy both autonomy and mutuality. All forms of bias can make and/or break people in troubled relations. The historical reality of family, kin and friendships is in crisis in terms of internal relations and in a vicious circle perpetuated by social factors such as unemployment and societal devaluation of women.

Valuing individuation and social consciousness implies that both boys and girls mature not by total separation from parents or guardians, but through healthy tension or a dialectic of identification and differentiation, with two parents or with a single parent/guardian, either female or male. Jessica Benjamin shows that a child may learn boundaries by relating to one or more significant adults. Benjamin emphasizes that parental/guardian response of either collapse or attack seriously harms a child's interactive and independent learning.[85] The self, then, is formed in ever-expanding relationship with others, as Elizabeth Johnson says, in "a model of relational independence, freedom in relation ... by an intrinsic connectedness."[86] The process of maturation in autonomy and mutuality is lifelong, with an ebb and flow of rhythms to foreground each and then be integrated with the other.

Relationships encompass identity formation and ability both to love and to accept love. They can encourage healthy independence and interdependence, and facilitate appropriation of oneself, of the local and global context and of tradition. Personal autonomy in no way involves a solitary or disengaged self. Rather, it stresses the social foundation of optimal self-directing action.[87] Maria Mies interprets the concept of autonomy as the "innermost subjectivity and area of freedom" essential to human essence and dignity.[88] Since focus on atomized individuals in marketing strategies has largely perverted understanding of autonomy, however, the resulting individualism presents a formidable obstacle for feminist solidarity and societal transformation.

Many women's organizations choose a healthy autonomy to preserve their specific identity and independent base. Early women's movements lost their identity and were dissolved when they joined male-dominated organizations (parties, trade unions and, I add, church-affiliated groups).[89] By exercising autonomy, feminist groups are claiming their capacity for responsible agency in personal and socio-economic, political and religious organization.

The distinction between responsible agency and individualism is significant. The former is intrinsically connected to social consciousness, to mature personhood, to individuation, agency and autonomy. The latter is isolated, selfish and self-centred. The extreme of individualism has erupted globally. It is evident in economic stratification in which the marginalized eke out an existence with hopes of entering the market-consumer world. "Corporations roam the globe looking for the poorest who are willing to work for the lowest wages," says Charles Kernaghan.[90] He also notes that a Haitian worker receives twenty-eight cents an hour to sew a "101 Dalmatians" children's outfit for Disney Co. in contrast to the $10,000 per hour wage of its chief executive officer in 1995. Millions of children work in branch plant garment, shoe, electronics, carpet and textile factories in conditions amounting to slavery.

The more both responsible agency and mutuality function in a healthy way, however, the more each promotes the other. I think this dialectic parallels that of the person in shaping responsible agents capable of collaborative transformation. Its aim is to nurture subjects-in-relation, thereby both strengthening the individuation process and enabling individuals and groups to claim their specificity and agency in socially conscious ways. Each aspect of this dialectic has been severely skewed in our time. To think, feel, speak, choose and act as a responsible agent and to maintain critical, social/historical consciousness are deeply transformative actions. In a predominantly unjust culture, these functions may be considered threatening, countercultural, suspect and/ or irrelevant.

In the context both of a rejection of extreme individualism and of support for collective action, questions arise as to how people define and pursue their desires, and how we make purposeful choices. Some needs are separate and autonomous while others are interdependent. Here I emphasize that realization and expression of commitments to others are part of a process of individuation. As Folbre notes, "Collective action helps individuals constitute their own identity."[91] Personal choices and opportunities are limited or supported by actual situations and by public policies. My later focus on values expands the importance of context in the formation of mature persons with social consciousness and social conscience. At this point, I highlight the importance of taking connections seriously among collective identity, action, personal agency and social consciousness, as well as social constructions of individual preferences and of cultural norms.

Living in relationships also provides homes for child-rearing, elder care, production, reproduction, paid and/or unpaid work, leisure, distribution of goods, conflict resolution, dialogue, responsibility, decision making and action, celebration, socialization, solidarity and cultural transmission. These possibilities lead me to repeat the concern I expressed earlier in this chapter, about privatization of functions such as child-rearing, health care and waged production. Current increased promotion of this trend is foreboding in terms of the invisibility of people and policies which it supports.

Omission of explicit concern for family, kin and friendships from societal structures makes space for further exploitation. Neglect of it means that a person's earliest, most intimate and lasting opportunities for ongoing formation in social consciousness and social conscience are bypassed in accepted discourse and in policy setting. Silence regarding relevance of home management has in fact kept women and our concerns out of sight in significant public decision making and in policy setting that affects issues like child/elder care.

Community

In chapter 4, I analyzed distortions that result from splitting the practical aspects and the interpersonal relations of community from each other and within themselves and claimed that these splits cause general bias. Now I focus again on the necessity of holding both interpersonal relations and practicalities like economics, fiscal policy, technology and politics in creative tension. This balance refocuses the place of economics as a subsystem within broader relations and recentres both economics and politics in their purpose of serving interpersonal and ecological well-being.

Taken as human togetherness, as interpersonal relations and as spontaneity, community constitutes society.[92] Interpersonal and group relations must be held in creative tension with ability to deal with practical issues.[93] The test of the success of practical endeavours in turn is the health and well-being of the environment and of the community at the relational level. Technological, economic and political systems are products of our decision making at a very practical level even as they reflect the vision, meanings and values we hold within a particular culture.

Figure 5

Destruction of interpersonal and intergroup relations
and of practical skills results from three basic splits.

Practical realms of everyday experience

split from

socio-economic decision making

Social relations

So-called public, mainly men

split from

so-called private, mainly women

Relations and practical undertakings,
including economics

split from

consideration of meanings and values,
causes of poverty
and effects of corporate decision making

By integrating both practicalities and interpersonal/group aspects in community, we create possibilities for a society "conducive to the intelligent and free participation of dramatic subjects in the forging of world and self as works of art."[94] To the extent a community is able to maintain this creative tension of holding interpersonal and group relations in balance with practicalities, it assists individuals and groups with their seeking and finding direction in the movement of life, which in turn supports community. This artistry lies in expanding the realm of conscious grasp and deliberate choice regarding social, cultural and personal progress and decline, grasping the prevailing relations among these values and choice of a new alignment more in harmony with an agreed-upon understanding and differentiation of values. (See fig. 5.)

Destruction of interpersonal and intergroup relations and of practical skills results, however, from three basic splits: (1) splitting the practical realms of everyday experience from socio-economic decision making; (2) splitting social relations into public and private gendered worlds; and (3) dividing both our relations and practical undertakings from consideration of meanings and of values. Practicalities and personal/group relations necessarily meet in the dynamics of families, kin and friendships. Racist and sexist separation of public jurisdiction from the relational at these levels and in broader community formation perpetuates control based on power and capital accumulation.

Since economic and political control is transnational, construction of just societies today is a universal project. Imperialistic domination of worldwide structures means that any effort to transform a regional cultural matrix and particular economic and political realities must take corporate influence and relations of ruling into account. Community relations and practical issues have become a global concern. Doran points out the consequent responsibility for cosmopolitan "collaboration that would generate cultural values capable of promoting an integral dialectic of community on a global scale."[95] Such a commitment to understand and implement community requires long-term responsibility for historical process. Individual cultures must both preserve their own identities and collaborate to know planetary implications of decisions made within the practical realms of family, economics, technology and politics.[96] Since global problems require global solutions, cross-cultural collaboration in strategizing, prioritizing and effecting remedies is an essential partner to local and regional creativity and initiative.

Culture

To remain true to my purposes, first, of uncovering causes of the social devaluation of women which allows us to perpetuate exploitation and abuse and, second, of contributing toward societal transformation, I need to give prominence to the centrality of culture. Culture may be defined as "the set of operative meanings and values informing a given way of life."[97] It functions at the everyday level of family, kin and friendships, of ritual, of music and of art. Our deepest meaning and values may be both discovered and expressed, as Lonergan says, in "delight and suffering, laughter and tears, joy and sorrow, aspiration and frustration, achievement and failure, wit and humour." These indicate what practical issues really mean to us and invite us to assess individual and communal choices.[98] People can pause to ask what life itself is about. Culture provides the occasion to ask, reflect and reach answers that at once satisfy our intelligence and speak to our hearts. How everyday culture functions will inspire or distort both interpersonal/group relations and provision of practical services in community.[99] Culture also operates on the reflexive level arising from our familial, scientific, philosophic, religious and scholarly pursuits.[100]

Culture can be interpreted in a far-reaching, comprehensive sense to include all of creation as it pulses with life, and our capacity as peoples to constitute just, macroeconomic relations in our world. I introduced aspects of culture in chapter 4 in order to root appreciation for differentiation and specificity in its rightful context of actually being a fundamental principle of creation. Now I loop the spiral in a larger circle. A cosmological horizon embraces all aspects of creation, including culture and anthropological perspectives.[101] As a basis of my cosmological emphasis, I select Thomas Berry and Brian Swimme's focus on an evolutionary horizon of subjectivity, differentiation and interdependence. For my position on the anthropological, I focus on Doran's attention to self and world-constitutive decision making based on Lonergan's criteria that it be attentive, intelligent, reasonable, responsible and loving.

Focus on the anthropological aspect draws attention to the importance of action that is within reach of all in daily living: decision making, celebrating everyday culture and discernment of meaning and of values. Another facet is that anthropological emphasis establishes a basis for linking deliberations to "divine reality's attracting force within the minds and hearts of individuals" and of communities.[102] This can offer a source of strength and of wisdom as people collaborate in the task of transformation. Integration of both the cosmological and the anthropological facilitates consciousness of the divine-human relationship and partnership in the context of interdependence with all of creation. Both consciousness and context in turn offer sources for symbolizations to ground meaning and values adequate to counteract the decline I have been describing.[103] This realization brings us forward in a meaningful way as we create symbols that are rooted sufficiently to grip our collective imagination and to shape cultural meanings and values.

A critical significance of attending to this dialectic is that awareness of intentionality and of the sensitive psyche on a cultural level, especially when expanded by relationship and partnership with divine mystery in world-constitutive praxis, makes possible the emergence of an axial shift in consciousness.[104] Such a position grounds communal hope and shifts the discussion far beyond maxims and rules in ethics. This position invites conversion that transforms our horizons and ability to imagine alternatives capable of solving the dilemma of the public/ private split. And far more! Increasingly habitual and spontaneous capacity to integrate can improve relations qualitatively. Only if holistic discernment is given a central place in daily life can attentive reflection, judgement, deliberation and decision in relation to the sensitive process become habits conducive to epochal change.[105] I note that respect for difference and specificity is a non-negotiable condition for consciousness that is capable of recognizing and distinguishing directions of affectivity and meaning.

As peoples, we have to a serious extent devalued use of intelligence and psyche on a cultural level. We have also tended to disregard personal and communal partnership with divine mystery. This denigration and vacuum lead us even quite generally to abandon explicit search for meaning. Desire for power and subjection of the individual to society then take hold. An illusion of order suffocates and gags us. It also signals surrender of concern and of responsibility for well-being.[106] Though people are angry and resentful about societal and environmental destruction, we are so locked into our attitudinal prisons of paralysis or powerlessness that suggestions of alternatives are often mocked. Without a hearing. The vacuum distorts all of the essentials for personal, relational, practical, cultural and ecological well-being.

I have outlined basics of person; of family, kin and friendships; of community and of culture in order to suggest a societal structure on which to base my approach to socio-economic ethics. What shape these take necessarily varies in concrete situations.

Understanding these aspects is incredibly meaningful with practical implications for society and for the earth as a whole, and also for the garment industry and homeworkers within it. Transformation requires that we dare to imagine, to think out and to choose to create in concrete terms the kind of world we *know* is just, loving, inclusive and creative in all aspects. This holds for both long- and short-term goals.

The profound relation of each area to the others (person, family/ kin/friendships, community, culture), all within recreating ecological health, individuals and groups can start on *any*, holding the other aspects and other priorities in respectful support knowing that they are all interconnected and mutually essential. Transforming the context in which we live, work, play, raise our children and tend our gardens *requires* that we always stay involved and connected with the actual living situations, no matter which area of focus we are tending. Second, it requires that we reach both within ourselves and beyond ourselves in time and space.

In terms of the garment industry campaigns, this means that we trust our ability to *know* what is needed and what is just. Knowing that change is possible, we can continue to speak the truth we know, casting aside fear because we are willing to support each other concretely in doing this. In broad-based solidarity, as peoples we will act together for practical change. I list six examples. We can require, first, independent monitoring of garment production and of trade policies with corporate and other community funds to do this. Second, we can require retailers to assume responsibility for fair production. Their image will automatically be on public trial over significant injustice.

Third, we can establish ethically sound garment manufacturing here and abroad. Fourth, we can call an immediate halt to present focus on economic growth, increased exports and expanded, subsidized presence of transnational corporations as the basis for job creation. Since our earth cannot sustain it, industrial expansion for increased consumerism is at best utter folly. We will produce garments needed here for work and all kinds of weather, and support similar garment production abroad. Only an encrusted layer of biases dismisses these as utopian dreams. These are minimum requirements unless we want to leave our children and grandchildren only a legacy of waiting for the government to act. Fifth, we can require health, safety and environmental protection at all stages of production and of trade. Sixth, we can also make immediate shifts in budgets to include child and elder care, to institute fair tax reform and to assure full participation and open dialogue in public decision making. Present shouted-out debate in our so-called "parliamentary process" resembles an image of children at war. It makes a mockery of government. Only with substantial listening, clarification and dialogue can we move forward in democratic process. Such change is non-negotiable so that women and people of all "races" will even *want* to participate.

Because of the breadth and depth of the transformation that is urgently required, we need to stay connected with each other, with victims and with the earth itself at every step. These are so interrelated that it does not matter where one begins. Of course, my work only hints at all that is needed *and possible*. This overview is deceptively simple and obvious in each aspect and as a whole. It is overwhelmingly neglected in practice. In a world crushed by multiple crises, we live as if no crises exist. Long-term, achievable goals that call for immediate attention include deepening our social and environmental consciousness so that we as peoples will eventually live with social and environmental conscience. Individualism, destruction and greed are on trial, not care for the earth and for each other. The latter are the givens.

Conclusion

The method of beginning with wages and working conditions of homeworkers followed by a steady process of asking further relevant questions throughout this study led me to focus on micro and macroeconomics related to the garment industry, to consideration of feminist analysis of horizon, of bias and of difference and specificity, and in this chapter to focus on the public/private split and its consequences for women as garment homeworkers. I have concentrated on elucidating contemporary norms, values, attitudes and behaviour patterns about women and women's place in societal life. As a basic consensus of how our society has viewed women, these attitudes and values express the dominant way in which relationships with women have been shaped. Whether generally acknowledged or not, these relations also function to justify existing structures, which, in fact, perpetuate injustice for women.[107]

To expand understanding of this dominant social consensus regarding women, I turned to some basic features of social organization. In the midst of historical attempts to establish new values and forms of co-existence, women's perspectives and concerns have been kept invisible. Our present socio-economic system expresses acceptance of inequality of persons on the basis of difference/specificity, whether it be due to "race," sex or family origins, an inequality which is embodied in institutions. Economic and political systems are used as means to control participation, decision making, the production of knowledge and communication systems which justify domination and exploitation. As a result, the majority in society tend to share the morality expressed in the vested interests of a societal minority. This established injustice is largely unchosen in that it is passed on and augmented uncritically through generations.

Thus while I formulated what has been going forward in the history of homeworking and the clothing industry in concrete narrative in chapters 1 to 3, I reflected critically on that story in chapters 4 and 5 to discover changing patterns of experience and the accumulations of insights. Raising unconscious social determinisms to consciousness reveals the critical need and importance of creating a new inclusive and just societal scheme. My focus on dialectics of the person or subject, of family, kin and friendships, of community and of culture is a way to highlight the wide range of public/private concerns which have been kept off the public agenda and to provide a framework in which we may throw each of these aspects into relief for the sake of more authentic integration.

The complexity of contemporary crises invites application of the four dialectics as a grid for analysis, policy setting and action. The entire grid is one way to take into account multiple aspects of experience and relationships. This organization provides: (1) an appropriate visibility or significance to traditionally ignored essential aspects for well-being of the earth itself, for persons and communities-in-relationships; (2) a tool in which participants in a dialogue can be assured that their values are being explicitly recognized; (3) a means of assessing neglected aspects and indicating policy directions; (4) an overview of the whole system in which subsystems like economics can be evaluated more effectively; and (5) a method of clarifying values and meaning.

Of course, these basics for societal organization will have to be fleshed out in widely divergent ways, according to the needs and creativity of particular communities. Public budgets, goals, policies, allotment of personnel and time all need to reflect the importance of all aspects of at least the four dialectics. These essentials may serve as a starting point for comprehensive communal assessment, first of all, of our communal understanding of the importance of each for earth and societal well-being. It can provide a basis on which to fill out the practical aspects for differing cultures while ensuring inclusion of essential aspects. Use of this grid, however, needs to be complemented by careful attention to values and meanings which I do in the next chapter.

Notes

1 Wildung Harrison, *Making the Connections*, 28.
2 Sandra Burt, Lorraine Code and Lindsay Dorney, eds., *Changing Patterns: Women in Canada* (Toronto: McClelland and Stewart, 1988), 10-11.
3 Gail Cuthbert Brandt, "Postmodern Patchwork: Some Recent Trends in the Writing of Women's History in Canada," *Canadian Historical Review* 72, 4 (December 1991): 445.
4 Janet Che-Alford, Catherine Allan and George Butlin, *Families in Canada*, Statistics Canada Catalogue No. 96-307E (1994): 9.
5 Ibid., 10. This Statistics Canada reference also explains two official definitions found in the *1991 Census Dictionary*: the census family and the economic family.
6 Ibid., 5.
7 Wildung Harrison, *Making the Connections*, 45.
8 Ibid., 46.
9 Marjorie Griffin Cohen, "The Problem of Studying 'Economic Man,'" in *Feminism: From Pressure to Politics*, ed. Angela Miles and Geraldine Finn (Montreal: Black Rose Books, 1989), 153.
10 Jeanne Boydston, Mary Kelley and Anne Margolis, *The Limits of Sisterhood: The Beecher Sisters on Women's Rights and Woman's Sphere* (Chapel Hill: University of North Carolina Press, 1988); Janet Wilson James, ed., *Women in American Religion* (Philadelphia: University of Pennsylvania Press, 1980); and Rosemary Radford Ruether and Rosemary Skinner Keller, eds., *Women and Religion in America*, vol. 1: *The Nineteenth Century* (New York: Harper & Row, 1981).
11 Wildung Harrison, *Making the Connections*, 47.
12 Marilyn Legge, *The Grace of Difference: A Canadian Feminist Theological Ethic* (Atlanta, GA: Scholars Press, 1992), 78.
13 See Burt, Code and Dorney, eds., *Changing Patterns*, 12.
14 A study on immigrant housewives conducted in Toronto showed that, compared with living in their countries of origin, "housework seemed more difficult; life seemed more hectic; there were more worries, from the husband's paid employment to the kinds of troubles that children could get into. The same study discovered that they become totally immersed in a money economy" (Roxana Ng, "Immigrant Women and Institutionalized Racism," in *Changing Patterns: Women in Canada*, ed. Sandra Burt, Lorraine Code and Lindsay Dorney [Toronto: McClelland and Stewart, 1988], 195). The study was conducted by Roxana Ng and Judith Ramirez for Immigrant Housewives in Canada (Immigrant Women's Centre, Toronto, 1981).
15 Hilary Rose, "Hand, Brain, and Heart: A Feminist Epistemology for the Natural Sciences," in *Sex and Scientific Inquiry*, ed. Sandra Harding and Jean O'Barr (1975; Chicago: University of Chicago Press, 1987), 277.
16 Rosemary Radford Ruether, "Spirit and Matter, Public and Private: The Challenge of Feminism to Traditional Dualisms," in *Embodied Love: Sensual-*

ity and Relationship as Feminist Values, ed. Paula Cooey, Sharon Farmer and Mary Ellen Ross (San Francisco: Harper & Row, 1987), 70-71.

17 See Ruth Roach Pierson, *"They're Still Women After All": The Second World War and Canadian Womanhood* (Toronto: University of Toronto Press, 1986).

18 Naomi Black, "The Canadian Women's Movement: The Second Wave," in *Changing Patterns: Women in Canada*, ed. Sandra Burt, Lorraine Code and Lindsay Dorney (Toronto: McClelland and Stewart, 1988), 80-102. Shirley Jane Endicott describes some of the development in Toronto in the story of her personal journey, *Facing the Tiger* (Winfield, BC: Wood Lake Books, 1988). See also Wildung Harrison, *Making the Connections*, 44.

19 Belinda Leach, "Ideas about Work and Family: Outwork in Contemporary Ontario" (thesis, University of Toronto, Toronto, 1992), 77. Refer to 77-85 as well.

20 Ibid., 79.

21 Ibid., 82.

22 Radford Ruether, "Spirit and Matter, Public and Private," 70.

23 Refer to Mies, *Patriarchy and Accumulation on a World Scale*, 38.

24 Joan Kelly Gadol, "The Social Relation of the Sexes," in *Feminism and Methodology*, ed. Sandra Harding (Indianapolis: Indiana University Press, 1987), 18-21.

25 See ibid., 24: "Patriarchy, in short, is at home at home. The private family is its proper domain. Where domestic and public realms pulled apart, sexual inequalities became pronounced as did the simultaneous demand for female chastity and prostitution." Refer also to Nancy McGlen and Karen O'Connor, *Women's Rights: The Struggle for Equality in the 19th and 20th Centuries* (New York: Praeger Special Studies, 1983), 324-43.

26 Heidi Hartmann, "The Family as the Locus of Gender, Class and Political Struggle: The Example of Housework," in *Feminism and Methodology*, ed. Sandra Harding (Indianapolis: Indiana University Press, 1987), 111. Addition of kin/friendship is mine.

27 Jane Flax, "Women Do Theory," in *Women and Values: Readings in Recent Feminist Philosophy*, ed. Marilyn Pearsall (Belmont, CA: Wadsworth Publishing, 1986), 4.

28 Hartmann, "The Family as the Locus of Gender, Class and Political Struggle," 114.

29 Radford Ruether, "Spirit and Matter, Public and Private" 72.

30 Ibid., 73. Radford Ruether adds that the Christian churches reproduce "the dominance of males over females in the symbolism and hierarchy of the church," making it "clear that their version of the idealization of service sacralizes the hierarchy of dominance and servitude, rather than subverting it. Women are "highest" Christians by acquiescing to be the "lowest." Rather than fostering liberation, the gospel is used to sacralize servitude" (ibid.).

31 Mary O'Brien, "Feminist Praxis," in *Feminism: From Pressure to Politics*, ed. Angela Miles and Geraldine Finn (Montreal: Black Rose Books, 1989), 333. See 328-44 for a fuller explanation of this. Refer also to Code, "Feminist Theory," 40-42.

32 Yolande Cohen, "Thoughts on Women and Power," in *Feminism: From Pressure to Politics*, edited by Angela Miles and Geraldine Finn (Montreal: Black

Rose Books, 1989), 368. Analysis of reproductive rights requires that "race" and class be problematized. Refer to Carty, *And Still We Rise*, 8.

33 Brooks Thistlethwaite, *Sex, Race and God*, 50.

34 Seyla Benhabib and Drucilla Cornell, *Feminism as Critique: On the Politics of Gender* (Minneapolis: University of Minnesota Press, 1987), 9.

35 Linda Christiansen-Ruffman, "Inherited Biases within Feminism: The 'Patricentric Syndrome' and the 'Either/Or Syndrome' in Sociology," in *Feminism: From Pressure to Politics*, ed. Angela Miles and Geraldine Finn (Montreal: Black Rose Books, 1989), 127.

36 Angela Miles, "Ideological Hegemony in Political Discourse: Women's Specificity and Equality," in *Feminism: From Pressure to Politics*, ed. Angela Miles and Geraldine Finn (Montreal: Black Rose Books, 1989), 275.

37 Ibid., 277.

38 Rosemary Radford Ruether, *Gaia and God: An Ecofeminist Theology of Earth Healing* (San Francisco: Harper, 1992). The entire book traces the sacralization of patriarchal hierarchies in Western tradition.

39 Ibid., 171-72. Emphasis added. I note, however, that in this excerpt her view of parenting is limited to two heterosexual parents.

40 Ibid., 200.

41 Ibid., 201. "It becomes increasingly difficult for élites in modern cities even to recognize these links or to imagine the ripple effects of destruction unleashed by the operations of their daily lives."

42 Smith, *The Everyday World as Problematic*, 52.

43 Ibid., 55.

44 Ibid., 56.

45 Ibid., 57.

46 Ibid., 68.

47 Susan McDaniel, "The Changing Canadian Family: Women's Roles and the Impact of Feminism," in *Changing Patterns: Women in Canada*, edited by Sandra Burt, Lorraine Code and Lindsay Dorney (Toronto: McClelland and Stewart, 1988), 110.

48 Legge, *The Grace of Difference*, 83.

49 Veronica Strong-Boag, "Working Women and the State: The Case of Canada: 1889-1945," *Atlantis* 6 (Spring 1981): 8.

50 Intercede and ILGWU, *Meeting the Needs of Vulnerable Workers*, 22.

51 Sandra Burt, "Legislators, Women and Public Policy," in *Changing Patterns: Women in Canada*, ed. Sandra Burt, Lorraine Code and Lindsay Dorney (Toronto: McClelland and Stewart, 1988), 154.

52 Wildung Harrison, *Making the Connections*, 155.

53 See Code, "Feminist Theory," 46-49.

54 Allen and Wolowitz, *Homeworking*, 175-76, 180. They explain that this approach has been analyzed as a kind of "neo-familialism," referring to Francis Godard, "How Do Ways of Life Change?" in *Beyond Employment*, ed. Nanneka Redclift and Enzo Minigone (London: Macmillan, 1985).

55 Allen and Wolowitz, *Homeworking*, 181.

56 Andrea Dworkin, "The Politics of Intelligence," in *Ethics: A Feminist Reader*, ed. Elizabeth Frazer, Jennifer Hornsby and Sabina Lovibond (Oxford: Blackwell, 1992), 127. See also Wildung Harrison, *Making the Connections*,

95. Naomi Black notes that Canadian resistance to second-wave feminism of the 1960s has been slow to emerge; only in the late 1980s is it becoming significant in a misinformed defense of a traditional family that no longer exists" (Naomi Black, "The Canadian Women's Movement," 84).

57 Lee Bartky, "Toward a Phenomenology of Feminist Consciousness," 114.

58 See Ng, "Immigrant Women and Institutionalized Racism," 196-97. Ng emphasizes these factors for immigrant women's work in Toronto.

59 Fifty-seven per cent of single-parent families headed by women live below the poverty line. Half of all unattached women over seventy-five years of age live in poverty. From 1971 to 1986, the number of women living in poverty in Canada grew by 110.3 per cent. The number of men in poverty increased by 23.8 per cent during the same period. Refer to Canadian Advisory Council of the Status of Women, *Expanding Our Horizons: The Work of the Canadian Advisory Council on the Status of Women and Its Context, 1973-1993* (Ottawa: CACSW/CCCSF, 1993), 75-76, using data from the National Council on Welfare, *Women and Poverty Revisited* (Ottawa, 1990), 2, 99: n. 19.

60 Benhabib and Cornell, *Feminism as Critique*, 9.

61 Folbre, *Who Pays for the Kids?* 66.

62 Linda Nicholson, "Feminism and Marx," in *Feminism as Critique: On the Politics of Gender*, ed. Seyla Benhabib and Drucilla Cornell (Minneapolis: University of Minnesota Press, 1987), 20.

63 Nancy Fraser, "What's Critical about Critical Theory? The Case of Habermas and Gender," in *Feminism as Critique: On the Politics of Gender*, ed. Seyla Benhabib and Drucilla Cornell (Minneapolis: University of Minnesota Press, 1987), 37.

64 Ibid., 39.

65 Ibid., 28, referring to Iris Young, "Beyond the Unhappy Marriage: A Critique of Dual Systems Theory," in *Women and Revolution*, ed. Lydia Sargent (Boston: South End Press, 1981), 49.

66 Folbre, *Who Pays for the Kids?* 54.

67 Fraser, "What's Critical about Critical Theory?" 42.

68 Ibid., 45-46.

69 Ibid., 56.

70 I have been deeply influenced by the works of Bernard Lonergan and Robert Doran, and what follows is my own appropriation of their contribution as I expand and relate it directly to my work.

71 Lonergan focused on dialectics of the subject and community. Doran's contributions include focus on the psyche and on the dialectic of culture. I supplement these three dialectics with the dialectic of family/kin/friendships.

72 Lonergan, *Insight*, 244.

73 Juan Pablo Ordoñez, "No Human Being Is Disposable," Report (Washington: Project Dignity for Human Rights, 1995).

74 Doran, *Theology and the Dialectics of History*, 180. "Our censorship may be constructive or repressive depending on whether its orientation is toward or away from insight, reasonable judgement, responsible decision, and love" (ibid., 181). It operates prior to reflection and deliberation and within one's established orientation to select projected courses of action. By

our very existence as intelligent beings and through socialization, we generally hold immanent norms equipped with sanctions which we do not have to invent or impose. See ibid., 185-98, and Lonergan, *Insight*, 234.

75 Doran, *Theology and the Dialectics of History*, 21.

76 Lonergan, *Insight*, 274.

77 Ibid., 187-89, and Doran, *Theology and the Dialectics of History*, 72.

78 Doran, *Theology and the Dialectics of History*, 72.

79 Ibid., 510.

80 Ibid., 70.

81 Lonergan, *Insight*, 472. I expand Lonergan's reference by applying both limitation and transcendence to materiality, the psyche and intentionality.

82 Ibid., 14-15, 290.

83 Refer to Doran, *Theology and the Dialectics of History*, chap. 1, 19-41.

84 I intend this use of "relations" to be inclusive of relationships within ourselves, with each other, with all of the earth community and with divine mystery.

85 Refer to Jessica Benjamin, *The Bonds of Love: Psychoanalysis, Feminism, and the Problem of Domination.* (New York: Pantheon Books, 1988), 183-218. Adaptation is mine.

86 Johnson, *She Who Is*, 68.

87 Wildung Harrison, *Making the Connections*, xiv-xx.

88 Mies, *Patriarchy and Accumulation on a World Scale*, 40.

89 Ibid., 41.

90 Charles Kernaghan, National Labor Committee, forum sponsored by the Labour Behind the Label Coalition, Toronto, 11 December 1996. Refer to the National Labor Committee's video, *Mickey Mouse Goes to Haiti* (1996).

91 Folbre, *Who Pays for the Kids?* 28.

92 Lonergan, *Insight*, 212.

93 Doran, *Theology and the Dialectics of History*, 360-61.

94 Ibid., 364.

95 Ibid., 366.

96 Lonergan, *Insight*, 238-39. Lonergan calls this attitude of commitment "cosmopolis."

97 Doran, *Theology and the Dialectics of History*, 368.

98 Lonergan, *Insight*, 236.

99 Together the dialectic of community and everyday culture constitute the infrastructure of society.

100 This constitutes the guiding structure of society, more often named as a superstructure. In order to avoid the impression that this structuring of society is an addition, something imposed beyond the rest and optional, I refer to it as the guiding structure, one that arises from within and is essential to its direction. It demonstrates in concrete fashion the meanings and values established by reflexive familial relations and friendships, by intersubjective relations at the community and cross-cultural levels and by collaborative, sustained, critical inquiry. The dialectic of family and friendships grounds both the infrastructure and the guiding structure of society.

101 Doran, *Theology and the Dialectics of History*, 510. Refer to Doran for another analysis.

102 Ibid., 541. Since transcendent, theoretic, scholarly and interior differentiation flow from anthropological symbolization, research focusing on these
could offer insight regarding their possibilities as avenues for conversion.

103 Ibid., 508.

104 Ibid., 541-44.

105 By sensitive process, Doran includes the flow and expression of energy in
the universe as seen, for example, in the emergence of energy from the
unconscious, through various forms of consciousness: (1) dreaming: integrating at the psychic or experiential level underlying neural manifolds;
(2) empirical: attentive to data of outer sense and of inner consciousness;
(3) intelligent: intending intelligibility; (4) rational: intending truth and
being; and (5) existential: intending moral and religious self-transcendence
(ibid., 669).

106 Ibid., 511, 507, 542.

107 Leonardo Boff, *Liberating Grace* (1979; Maryknoll, NY: Orbis, 1987), 38-39.

7

Discerning Elements for Socio-economic Ethics

Encasing, consuming fire
Sun solidarity
Sun spiders solidarity
    World webs
    World watch
    Soft strong silky sun
    Woven carefully

U nmasking injustice in the corporate relations of the garment industry is part of a process of establishing justice not only through protective legislation and enforcement but also in our very ways of being and relating as whole societies. The very nature of the issues at hand involves making judgements and decisions at every turn. It is a work of ethics. Grounded in a transformed approach to natural law, doing ethics involves a turn to authentic persons/groups-in-relation within our intrinsic ecological interdependence. From a faith perspective, I add that all of this is God's own work of creation, a work of love, integrity and justice in which we are co-creators.

As such it is of profound theological concern for faith communities. By making the implications for faith explicit, we can tap the transfor-

---

Notes to chapter 7 are on pp. 263-73.

mative possibilities of theology to strengthen and celebrate the work at hand. Leaving underlying theologies unexamined could mean that the operative assumptions, attitudes and beliefs that support capitalist exploitation are untouched or even reinforced. I will first summarize some of the pertinent aspects of my theological stance as I move into this chapter.

Theology is an intellectual ministry to faith communities and to society.[1] Theological endeavour is related in every aspect to God whose mystery intimately shapes, nourishes and shares personal, social and cosmic reality. My operative understanding is that God is intrinsically related with creation and social relations. Reversing major decline as it is evident in the social and economic devaluation of women, therefore, impacts theology even as theology can contribute significantly to a process of societal transformation. In this context, truth making encompasses the action of establishing just relations, of implementing relations of solidarity in concrete situations, locally and globally. It is foundational to discovery of God as love.

Divine-human relations are simultaneously moral relations involving societal organization. The site of action for theological endeavour involves the whole range of personal and societal experience, understanding, judgement, decision and implementation, none of which may be omitted for adequate production of theological knowledge. Its context involves the well-being of the ecosphere.

Through critique and construction, my present theological endeavour is praxis to establish integrity and justice, wisdom and love within the context of the homeworking webs. This chapter includes my appropriation of aspects of Christian faith tradition as I highlight values, with particular reference to integrity, justice, wisdom, genuineness and love. These values need to be actualized to be known. This insight is a key to understanding theology as transformative praxis. It is also essential for a healthy spirituality in an age of corporate rule and of financial capitalism. Doing theology and living a spirituality of justice making are imperatives for faith communities. The following outline suggests key aspects of what these involve:

Doing theology and shaping a spirituality of justice-making

Start anywhere. Engage in a deepening, progressive spiral of God's love and power and of ecolgical interdependence:

1. Be attentive to experience: personal, familial, social, ecclesial, religious, ecological, corporate:

a) Person: body-psyche-spirit or body-mind-soul
b) Family-kin-friendships: personal and social agency and social consciousness as the framework for development of conscience
c) Social and ecclesial organization and celebration in communities: practical issues (economics, technology, policy setting) and local/global relationships
d) Culture: interplay of decision making, action within the laughter and tears of life and within earth's realities and limits.

2. Gather data, information
   • Remember scriptures, tradition, faith, whatever of history and the gifts left by our ancestors to shed light on the present reality being considered.
   • Interpret data of feelings, values, dreams, hopes, fears...
   • Raise relevant questions, issues.

3. Weigh information, possibilities, alternatives, implications of action/non-action and make judgements
   • What do we know?
   • What do we believe?

4. Make decisions and initiate appropriate action
   • Integrity calls us to live out what we know in our heart, what we know in our body, mind and soul.

5. Live in love
   • God's will is that we care for the human community and the earth, strengthened and enriched by God's love and power, loving and accepting love at the heart of our being.

6. Act! Celebrate! Continue the evolving, deepening spiral!
   • Know that the all-holy God reveals the God-self in justice and integrity. (Based on Isaiah 5:16.) "Act justly, love tenderly and walk humbly with your God." (Micah 6:8)

Clearly, long-term commitment and solidarity are foundational requisites if we are to establish effectively just relations. As noted previously, praxis is a reflective-active process in which participants appreciate inherent limitations and cherish grounds for transcendence. By the power of God's action and our action as co-creators, conversion to view theology as praxis moves us beyond words alone to become engaged in a process of transformation. Recognizing and celebrating this dynamic offers strength, hope and joy for the action.

My concern is that protection for vulnerable workers and for the unemployed not be limited to liberal, minimalist reform. Socio-economic ethics goes far beyond rules and principles to the ground, roots and food supply of the crisis. The depth of current devaluation of women calls for ways to heal distorted intentionality and psyche on individual and collective levels. The self and communal appropriation of tradition and of the situation that praxis requires is a constitutive element of transformative theology. Doing theological ethics today is radically transformative praxis.[2] In other words, the new situation of globalization requires that we grapple with the faith content of scriptures and tradition and with current injustices to formulate what we really believe and what will be most significant, meaningful, inspiring and challenging in doing the mission before us. Such appropriation facilitates unambiguous mediation of faith and culture in contemporary crises.

Creating just relations is intimately connected with values and meaning, particularly as these arise and are expressed among people of differing cultures, "races," orientations and perspectives. Shaping socio-economic ethics requires collaboration of peoples locally, nationally and globally. This new era challenges us both to think globally and locally and to act globally and locally. This involves naming values and priorities, envisioning the kinds of relations we want to create and choosing societal structures to protect and promote these goals. The possibility of formulating socio-economic ethics is, nevertheless, a controversial issue in the context of operative belief in a global value-free market economy.

I begin this chapter, therefore, by describing the radical, global task at hand. My second step is to examine a range of value clusters or categories whose importance has been implicit throughout my study. I relate these values to the societal framework described in chapter 6. I proceed to consider how we both generate and express values and meaning in the context of cross-cultural relations. This lays the basis for collaboration to make judgements of facts and judgements of value regarding priorities and the global economy.

The analysis also reveals the significance of different expressions of meaning and symbols in discovering sources of energy and direction for the work of constructing just relations. I pick up earlier analysis of consciousness from chapter 5, this time in relation to trusting our ability *to know*, and I consider the import of both in concretely shaping truth and the good in society.[3] I presume that what is good is always concrete, revealing directions, vision and understandings to support transformation.[4] Thirdly, I foreground other essential threads woven throughout this study: some implications surfaced by recognition of difference/specificity, by making women's social and economic realities explicitly visible, by integrating the public/private split and by fostering reflection on how we know and on what we think. I also draw on these implications to foster reorientation of economics.

A Radical, Global Task

First, the challenge to create socio-economic ethics that is deeply rooted in daily living is radical. A growing consensus uncovers the nature of the issue. Michael Zweig, for example, points to the extreme individualism underlying mainstream economics, to the social marginalization resulting from current economic organization and to the myth that the market is value-free. These are grounds to conclude that mainstream economics confuses and blocks genuine ethics when exploitative relations persist unhindered: "the idea of humane economic ethics is an oxymoron."[5] Mainstream global economic practice limits itself to the operations of economic actors within self-serving structures and sets rationality according to pleasure/profit rules which are then embraced as constitutive of human nature. This system is based on extreme individualism that obliterates community values. Social and environmental realities are ignored or hidden, even as relatives may be suffering from terminal pollution-related diseases.

The vacuum becomes clear: a horizon of individualism provides no foundation for social and ecological values. Nor for doing justice. When individual interests alone are regarded as the starting point and end of economics, internal points of reference within a privatized consciousness become normative to guide choices and other people are disregarded.[6] A double distortion results with only autonomy or individuation emphasized within family/kin/friendships. Unfortunately, even the healthy sense of individuation or agency is twisted to emerge as individualism. Basic openness to the process of inquiry, and therefore authentic subjectivity or respect for persons, is destroyed. Individualism becomes structured into societal horizon and rationalized as an acceptable basis for economics. Individualism is a major cause of long-term societal decline as it generates steadily less comprehensive viewpoints.

The fact that economics is prided as a "science free from value judgements" with amorality as a basic principle leaves economists to draw only on personal values.[7] I certainly do not minimize the importance of personal values. In fact I base my stance on a turn to persons and communities-in-relation within an ecologically interdependent world.[8] This position clarifies my analysis of how the public/private split within economics masks values inherent in market function, of how injustice is structural in character and of the fact that overcoming socio-economic injustice is not simply an individual concern or an application of microeconomic principles.[9]

Second, the challenge to create socio-economic ethics is a global task. Examples of abuse in the garment industry like the following abound:

> Over 600 Honduran women, fed up of being beaten and forced to remain childless, have occupied the factory whose owners impose these conditions on them. The women, employees of a firm called El Paraiso (Paradise), are protesting the firing of 8 of their workmates who tried to organize a union.... Fifteen soldiers and 10 policemen went to the factory and arrested 103 of the demonstrators.... Nineteen are still in jail.... 25,000 Honduran women work in maquiladora factories.[10]

The Ecumenical Coalition for Economic Justice reports that around the globe,

> clothing is expected to be made with as little worker cost as possible reaping untold profits for manufacturers and retailers. El Paso, Toronto, Dhaka, Hong Kong, Montreal, Ciudad Juarez, Jakarta, Manila, London. These cities around the world have at least one thing in common—a garment industry that is based on the cheap labour of women and children ... in sweatshops, factories and homes.[11]

The global nature of the market economy and of exclusion on the basis of differences is coupled with an amassing of unaccountable economic power and wealth that calls for counteraction in local, national and global contexts. Each of these factors becomes the particular challenge of socio-economic justice making and ethics.

In contrast to the undifferentiated universalism of the global economy, however, networking of groups and of communities needs to be based on an operative respect for difference/specificity, for the values surfaced by peoples in their own way of searching for meaning, values and ways of being in relation. At the same time, the context of the earth as a living system of interdependent species requires a value system with radically expanded spatial and time horizons.[12]

Global, interdependent networks of particular communities would allow the oppressed to claim their right to participate in policy setting. Fostering such networks needs the creativity and expertise of the world community on a scale effective enough to offset the unprecedented crises at hand. Since what has been produced by many has been taken by a few, effective resistance requires more than withdrawal from the dominant system.

An example of international networking in the clothing industry is the Clean Clothes Campaign in Europe, undertaken in 1990 to link people focusing on the garment industry and on consumer interests, and groups conducting research on transnational corporations. The aims of their newsletter, *Clean Clothes*, are to keep in touch with established contacts in different regions, to forge new connections, to provide a link between a wide variety of organizations concerned with labour organization in the clothing industry and to keep readers informed of developments and activities in the entire subcontracting chain, from homeworkers to consumers, in all regions of the world.[13] The *Newsletter* reported, for example:

> Solidarity action in the U.S. has helped force a garment manufacturer in Guatemala to reinstate dismissed workers and pay them some of their back wages. Major North American chains, including Sears, JC Penney and Wal-Mart, were made to take action in this case under pressure from the lobbying group U.S./Guatemala Labour Education Project. As a result, 30 workers were reinstated, after being fired in 1991 for trying to form a union. They returned to work on August 3, [1993] with partial back pay.[14]

The Ontario division of the ILGWU is constructing links particularly in Latin America. The Maquila Solidarity Network and the Latin American Working Group are also engaged in this research and in facilitating contacts for solidarity.

Values as the Foundation for Alternate Choices

My analysis of homeworking, of relations of ruling, of societal myths and of biases provides ample grounds to focus on social transformation in which women, child-rearing, home, work and relations may be valued in themselves and in public policy. I have accentuated aspects of long-term social decline and its devastating effects for all. This section is particularly significant for analysis of long-term possibilities for transformation.

We can now delve deeper by focusing on meaning and values. Long-term exclusion on the basis of gender and "race" has blocked understanding both of the central importance of meaning and values and of the differing ways they may be expressed. Inter- and intracultural communication is essential to shape just societies, social solidarity and trade relations in which difference/specificity is an operative value.

Attending to various sources and expressions of meaning among us also opens up possibilities of discovering how we may touch sources of energy and discover direction to effect societal change. This is a difficult process largely, I think, because of our undeveloped sense both of difference and specificity, and because of our lack of appreciation of symbols, images and realities to which specificity gives rise. This section on values and meaning is not only foundational for responsible decision making but also for collaborative problem solving and creativity in expanding how we think. Choice of values shapes horizons and sets the foundation in turn for personal and societal choices. It can be a virtuous or a vicious circle of cause and effect. I begin by situating values in relation, first, to economics; second, to the essentials of societal structure as described in the four dialectics in chapter 6; and, third, to the formulation of socio-economic ethics.

Situating Economic Systems

Rejecting the prevailing unchangeable "law of the market" mentality, Hazel Henderson situates economic systems:

> From a general systems theory perspective, all economic systems are sets of *rules*, devised to fit the specific culture, values and goals of each society. Thus, even so-called free market or *laissez-faire* economics are designed by humans and *legislated* into existence, while prices and wages reflect the values of each society and its state of knowledge of its real situation in the physical world. In fact, the notion of "objectively set," "free market" prices is revealed as a myth (albeit a politically useful one) since all markets are, in one way or another, created by *human*, rather than any "invisible" hand. Resource allocation methods, whether planning, prices, regulation, rationing, barter or reciprocity, are only as good as the state of human knowledge.[15]

Reexamining cultural notions of value becomes a priority! As Henderson repeatedly emphasizes, "In fact, we must now acknowledge the difficult truth: that values, far from being peripheral, are the dominant, driving variables in all technological and economic systems," and "values are the primary forces in all human societies.... Values drive all the different economic systems."[16] Distortion and bias legitimate false conflicts between economics and well-being. Assessment includes, for example, evaluation of overreward of competitive activities, like sports, in contrast to undervaluation of co-operative activities which hold the society together, like child nurturing.

Examination of values also means questioning the normative nature of economics and exposing how subconscious value assumptions weight its analyses. The free trade agreements (FTA and NAFTA), for example, determine trading rules that impinge dramatically on social, cultural and health issues. They dramatically undermine national sovereignty. The Ecumenical Coalition for Economic Justice emphatically urges a complete reversal of these relations of ruling: *"It cannot be overemphasized that we must decide on trade policies in light of our other goals, rather than treat trade as the central motor of the economy."*[17] This approach would make an enormous difference. National trade policy would protect the labour-intensive garment industry by restoring tariffs on clothing imports, by focusing on production of necessary apparel such as workwear and winterwear, by managing trade with commitment to workers' well-being nationally and globally and by giving priority to ecological revivification when determining resource use.

In government structures, such grounding of economics requires regular official consultation with those most affected by particular negotiations. In contrast to the ready accessibility to government personnel by the Business Council on National Interests, interfaith coalitions and other citizens' groups lack accessibility. The latter must be recognized as significant consultants. The Ecumenical Coalition for Economic Justice also calls for the institution of both a Canadian and an international Fair Trade Act.[18]

Widespread cultural confusion over our changing values and goals, ethics and regulations is evident in recent disillusionment of the political and economic process, and in the fact that these issues are reaching higher thresholds of public awareness and debate.[19] Yet clarification of the complexity of issues requires forms beyond voting. Alternative research and mobilization of the general public in multifaceted campaigns are urgently needed.

Significant movements with these goals have been initiated. Much ethical framework in the form of agreements and of protocols is already in place through transcultural collaborative efforts. Key examples of this are evident in reports and treaties by the Women's World Congress for a Healthy Planet and by the Global Forum during the United Nations Conference on Environment and Development.[20] Nationally, the Action Canada Network is a broad-based network of unions, community groups, professional associations and churches to facilitate research and solidarity regarding issues like free trade agreements and social policy.[21]

Application of this type of process is of immediate concern to the garment industry: "Only when this ethical girder work is in place, can ethically aware, responsible companies live up to their moral codes without fear of unfair competition by others willing to cut corners and exploit people and the environment for short-term gain."[22]

Basis for Structuring Society

We structure society according to our operative values. The often unacknowledged values by which we shape our lives for good or for ill are the sources of our attitudes and our organizational models. As long as underlying values such as the right to accumulate unlimited capital and legality and profitability as sole criteria of assessment remain unexamined, ethical inquiry about structural causes of poverty is severely hampered. I cluster values in categories in this section not to impose limitations, but to foster breadth in how we think about social relations.[23] A wide range of values reveals foundational elements for a just society. Key values which I have integrated throughout the book may be clustered as vital, familial, social, ecological, cultural, personal and religious or spiritual values.[24] These values are all intrinsically and causally related to each other in a web of just relations. They enable us to be authentic agents of genuine collaboration, expressing "love in the world mediated by meaning and motivated by values."[25] The point here is that what is visibly before us now in an economic, political or legal system is not an adequate scope for human endeavour. We must at least add information about the effects of decisions in these realms, about causes of poverty, about responsibility, compassion, biases and meaning in life.

A healthy society involves implementing vital and social values in all the practical necessities and in interpersonal and group relations: for health, social policy, economics, technology, politics and law. Everyday living of culture is expressed in familial, religious and ecological values as well as through ritual, music and art. These values and cultural expressions inform social process and actually constitute the infrastructure of society. In a sense they make a culture's values visible. The reflexive component of culture, as it emerges in families, kin and friendships, in personal and religious values, becomes an often unexamined, yet powerfully influential guide. It motivates or stifles the elaboration, expansion, evaluation, and justification or rejection of particulars and of the overall direction of a way of life. These reflexive values therefore are at the heart of a guiding structure for a way of life. Since the long-term process of shaping values and expressing them as part of cultural identity happens in the context of the infrastructure, all values are mutually conditioning. Since their meaning extends beyond particular cultures, dialogue about them offers an opportunity for solidarity.

This analysis clarifies the importance of the integrity or inauthenticity of the guiding structure of familial, kin and friendship values, of personal and religious values in shaping the infrastructure and social process. I have described the breakdown of the everyday level of culture by focusing on injustice to homeworkers.

Societal breakdown is also expressed in the abuse of resources evident in frivolous overproduction and accumulation of apparel for some people. It is certainly obvious in the greed and ostentation which shift the drive for clothing production from filling genuine human needs to accumulation of profit and to a very limited view of fashion as a world of competitive vanity.

This decline needs to be reversed at its roots in our very identity and desires. It directly challenges advertising and global production. Reversal calls us to reinterpret all aspects of our priorities, to broaden our horizons quite radically especially in terms of reflexive components of culture, of familial, kinship and friendship values and of personal and religious and/or spiritual values. Integrity of persons-in-relation within themselves, with the earth community and with the divine is essential for healthy interaction in a just society and for the emergence of this wide range of values.[26] Integrity of groups or communities-in-relation is equally significant.

To maintain multidirectionality in structuring social reality, I emphasize the rhythm that accentuates different values as appropriate, while holding the others with care. Disdain, neglect or exclusive emphasis of any of them undermines all of the others. How all of these are interpreted, lived out, evaluated, celebrated or destroyed varies considerably among groups. In all its direct simplicity and possibilities for depth, it is the cumulative process of human inquiry that is the major tool for us to discover how we apprehend values, the preferences we assign to them and their interrelationship in terms of naming basic needs, conditions of healing and resolution of problems.[27] Learning to ask relevant questions and to engage in open dialogue about possibilities, implications, alternatives and skills can lead to radical difference. The key is that we become a thinking, feeling, responsible and loving people.

Religious values of genuineness and wisdom are critical to the process of counteracting societal decline and of fostering transformation.

Genuineness and wisdom arise by relying on both limitation and transcendence as operative dimensions of our consciousness. So enabled to
consider issues, implications and consequences, with confidence,
courage and creativity, we can be strengthened to live within personal
capabilities, respecting the limits of others and of the earth itself.[28] In
so doing, we are then also able to make a major shift in our understanding of transcendence. Instead of linking transcendence with dis-
embodiment and separation, we can make the essential connection
between transcendence and bodily, psychic and spiritual energy as well
as with the energy of cosmic evolution. The latter intrinsically involves
intentional capacities and spiritual meaning and values. Divine mystery, the human and all the rest of creation meet in myriad forms of
energy. These relationships are destroyed as the various forms of
energy are destroyed.

The work or art of integration (of all the splits I have described)
needs an active, playful imagination in order to understand how
deeply our social and personal body-psyche-spirit/mind interact.
Together they root us in the interdependent earth community (all creation); are the source of images, symbols and attitudes; nourish vibrant
thinking and feeling; and expand our capacity to know divine energy.
To the extent we value limitation as a gift of the universe, we can be
free to taste the ecstasy of creative imagination, of respect for all differentiation in creation and of the healing, life-giving friendship of divine
mystery. These are intimately linked to our ability to envision alternate
possibilities. Anything less may provide liberal bandages but hardly
grapple with the roots of social decline. Attending both to limitation
and transcendence and to the multiple sources of energy offers possibilities to expand horizons for such creativity.

Wisdom, genuineness, courage and creative imagination may be
fostered by attending to the significance of both limitation and transcendence in implementing the wide range of what we consider to be
valuable. Being caught in either limitation alone or transcendence
alone skews the balance needed to foster wisdom and courage. Homeworkers, for example, are trapped if they see only limitation. By contrast, retailers may be imprisoned by a drive to transcend past records
of profit maximization.

Nurturing a sense of limitation in living provides occasion to integrate, to discover wisdom, to deepen appreciation and to rest sufficiently to practice discernment.[29] Awareness of limitation offers information about capabilities and grounds every aspect of the dialectics.

Limitation serves to connect each aspect of persons, family/kin and friendships, communities, human possibility and cosmic interdependence to consciousness.

This consciousness is discovered in relation to the world of immediacy and the world mediated by meaning. This means that we learn to be conscious as we activate our senses to see, feel, hear, touch and taste *and* as we learn to wonder about and reflect on the meaning and values of all our interactions, experiences and relationships. Our culture stifles development of consciousness, meaning and values. In fact, it stifles even alert use of the senses in the immediate world of sense. With the foundation destroyed, the very capacity to discover meaning and values is distorted. In the midst of such a vacuum, people grasp for connection and power in sexual abuse, violence and greed. Or retreat in fear.

The home and source of consciousness is the psyche, in the neural demand functions that are expressed in images and feelings. Body conversion opens the person to respect and value use of the senses, to be aware of physical signs of unrest and of meaning and to cherish the profoundly blessed, intricate nature of blood, bones and flesh. And how these are intrinsically linked to how we *know*.

Psychic conversion opens the person to appropriate limitation. Respect for limitations on a societal and on a global scale is one of the most essential keys for survival. I find that the regular challenge of living within the limits of my little bit of earth (myself!) is one of the concrete ways I can contribute to the healing of our exhausted earth community. When we go beyond our limits with extensive overtime, for example, we jeopardize not only our health and relationships but also the well-being of society. As a society, we have shifted to extremes: fairly paid earners must often work overtime to keep their positions; the working poor must hold several part-time, low-waged jobs to survive; and the unemployed exhaust their energies trying to cover basic needs and looking for paid work. We are so overworked that we lack time, energy and wisdom to provide meaningful work and adequate financial security for all. We are also too exhausted to foster gratitude, a sense of beauty—a spiritual life. Issues like the four-day work week and simple, meaningful lifestyles challenge us as whole peoples.

Openness to transcendence fosters discovery and implementation of the next step in a call to conversion; creative engagement in alternate thinking, play and networking; expansion of horizons; and encouragement of inquiry, imagination and dialogue. Transcendence operates to suggest new meaning, perspective and possibility through ever fuller inquiry. Its source is intentionality that is intelligent, reasonable and moral. Intellectual conversion opens persons and communities to ask further relevant questions. Transcendence does not mean being disconnected. In fact, we need to be grounded and in touch to ask the next relevant question. It can be fostered by full use of our capacities in what are often termed right-brain functions like art, music, design, cooking, sewing and gardening.

Synthesis of limitation and transcendence occurs through the dynamism of being in love. Loving and being loved helps us to find meaning, happiness and overflowing generosity to be aware of and respond to needs of others. Loving and being loved also heal compulsions to compete and to accumulate, on the one hand, or to remain silent in the face of exploitation and injustice, on the other. Love places us in front of our own and others' limitations and allows us to enter into transcendence by both lovingly accepting ourselves and doing the same for others, nurturing and giving life as we are able. By accepting the reality of human limitations, we foster healing of the distorted psyche itself, awaken our senses and develop our capacity to go beyond past hurts. We foster reflection and the ability to risk and dare.

The sins of racism and sexism do the opposite. We exploit what others offer to serve our own purposes. There is no openness to relate to others as persons or be touched and converted by them in the transcendence they carry. Relations lack humanization because there is no mutuality or relationality. Interdependence is an intrinsic, essential aspect of the universe. It is part of natural law. Crushing it is sinful.

Self- and communal-appropriation of limitation and transcendence sets conditions to foster optimum quality of living in the particular circumstances of individuals and/or communities. The psyche, through its constructive censoring function, will provide information for discernment that prompts acceptance of real capabilities and connections and/or encouragement to move beyond present plateaus.[30] These two are intimately linked. As an area of limitation is accepted, an unexpected experience of transcendence may arise. A virtuous circle is introduced and wisdom is fostered.

As principles of subjectivity, differentiation and interdependence shift from being strange thoughts to familiar ways of being, we are better equipped to value all aspects of our personal-social-ecological life and its organization. We recognize how they inform an ethics of integration and differentiation, an ethics of well-being, rooted and fruitful.

Celebrating life as subjects-in-relation and as communities-in-relation is revolutionary action offsetting isolation and despair which perpetuate the status quo of unjust power relations—in-relation always within oneself, with each other and with the earth.

The construction of an integrative framework based on creative dialectics and values uncovers fundamental criteria and challenges which are directly related to women in society and to the international web of production in the garment industry. First, as already recognized, global technological, economic and political interdependence establishes the need for cross-cultural collaboration capable of generating cross-cultural values equal to the task of global transformation. Setting about this task in particular regions is absolutely essential but not adequate. Nor will reform of economic practice alone result in massive transformation of concrete infrastructural institutions.[31] Transformation calls for global networking. Since both the clothing industry and devaluation based on difference are global, constituting just relations for all in the homeworker-to-consumer web requires global networking.

Second, only change in the operative meanings and values informing a society's way of life can transform social infrastructure.[32] Change is part of an interdependent web of influence and of conversion as persons, families, friends, communities and cultures relate. Doran summarizes the issue well:

> If the problem is to be met as it presents itself to us, the human sciences must differentiate practically realizable technological, economic, and political structures that can meet the demands of a global humanity for the recurrent satisfaction of the most vital human needs. Such structures, demanding as they will the creative tension of limitation and transcendence that informs all authentic development, and so respecting the autonomy of local cultures while at the same time mindful of the globally interdependent community, will be practically realizable only by means of a transformation of cultural values, and in this case by the crosscultural generation of cultural values adequate to the exigencies of a global social order.[33]

This transformation of operative meanings and values is at the heart of theological praxis in solidarity with all those excluded from power and wealth/capital on the basis of difference from prevailing norms.

Third, cultural values promoted intentionally by dominant forces pressure peoples internationally to homogenize culture through the marketplace. The uniformity, appearances of success, wealth and total happiness portrayed by the market may be more honestly called dysfunctional antivalues or "mcvalues." Because of the unprecedented nature of commercial competition to dominate cultural values, it is critical that faith communities and others of good will uphold essential guiding values: familial/kinship/friendship, cultural, personal and religious. Conversion and world-transformative praxis can be integrated by relating and implementing values in concrete circumstances until they yield cross-cultural praxis to establish integrity. This challenge is praxis or contemplative action, deep enough to heal our distorted personal and collective psyches and to be visible in how we transform society.

Fourth, decision to live out of cross-culturally generated meanings and values requires understanding of the crucial links between how we guide and live out all aspects of culture itself. It also involves linking our cultural values as a whole with our choices of social organization. This is a minimum requirement to protect relationships and practical services.[34] Integration happens as people realize that the necessary integrity for all the functions lies within them as subjects-in-relationship and as communities-in-relation. We achieve integration by making decisions and acting upon this potential.

The process of the development or maldevelopment of persons and the progress or decline of social reality have to be understood as reciprocal.[35] Both depend on being in touch with total actual realities and increasing "the realm of conscious grasp and deliberate choice."[36] In every society, people's consciousness of meaning and values is diverse and affected in interaction, collaboration and conflict. The nature of the prevailing consciousness is obviously significant, even to allow reflection on meaning and values and to incorporate policy setting according to this expanded horizon. The challenge is to transform intelligence collaboratively with a commitment to meet social decline at its roots. Theoretical recognition of the fullness of the range of the infrastructure brings one closer to the integration of theory with practice, of contemplation with action and of concept with performance. Similarly, reorientation of the guiding structure, of theory, of reflective discernment and/or contemplation is an indispensable requirement for the realignment of the infrastructure itself.[37] Both come together in personal and social interiorly differentiated consciousness (discussed later) and in the implementation of social justice.

Fifth, how we shape our culture provides the link between conversion and social transformation.[38] Without concern for what is just, integrated, inclusive, beautiful, intelligible, true and good in our concrete situations and globally, we skew all aspects of community and culture in the direction of instrumentalization for the sake of short-term expediency. As Lonergan insists, good and evil are specific and concrete, not abstractions.[39] Whether practicalities flow from interpersonal relations or are split, for example, from women's concerns is intrinsically linked to a society's operative value system. Priorities are evident in budgets and democratic participation across identity issues like "race" and sex. Concrete choices make our values visible. Some values are operative in our midst. Others are given only lip service.

Sixth, world-constitution and self-constitution emerge from both cognitive and existential praxis.[40] This means that we shape ourselves and our world, who and what kind of society and world we want according to our actual praxis (integrating reflective-discernment and practice, theory and performance, contemplation and action). This involves all of our potential for knowing and for living with integrity. This project is actually a work of art, a new creation. It follows that any instrumentalization of intelligence must be critiqued as radically inadequate. Doran carries the import of this further:

> Intelligence is artistic precisely in proportion to ... its fidelity to its own inherent dynamism, which heads toward correct understanding, and its fidelity to the implementation of such understanding in existential, world-historical praxis. The criteria that ultimately govern in a normative fashion the history-constituting exercise of both speculative and practical intelligence are artistic.[41]

Knowledge is brought to fruition and tested in action for justice, which in turn expands a basis for analysis. Collaboration that expands the effectiveness of this process can serve to unite people in creating a just world. It makes visible both God's action in our midst and our co-partnership in that action.

Grounds to unite reflective-discernment and practice to form praxis can be found in these criteria and challenges. Cultural values, for example, unite both spontaneous intersubjectivity and practical intelligence as principles of social change. What becomes clear is that undistorted and unbiased intellectual comprehension of, and existential engagement in, social realities must be empirical to make critical judgements between good and evil. Such comprehension and engagement must also be ready to advance the range of concerns of persons, family/kin/friendships, of communities, of culture and of the environment. It must also be courageous to reverse or stand against any bias which may exclude or diminish the importance of any aspect. In so doing, they become normative, making meaning, values and intelligibility visibly operative in the situation. Concern for values and the structure we give to society are major components of the context within which a contemporary ethics and Christian theology are to be constructed.

Meaning as the Heart of Socio-economic Ethics

Goals, purposes and values are intrinsic to social organization. Ethical reflection weighs the appropriateness of the goals and values in particular situations and evaluates movement toward or away from them. Foundational issues for socio-economic ethics include deciding, first, who and what are valuable enough to be accorded visibility and full participation in debate, decision making and policy setting and, second, both what to produce and for whom it will be.[42] Ethics also concerns what gets produced, who benefits or suffers, how production happens and what impact it has on the ecosystem. My process of inquiry leads me to delve deeper to uncover the soil, roots and food supply needed to construct ethics that lead to the establishment of just relations. I find some indications of ways to move out of the crisis toward justice by focusing on sources, expressions and interpretations of meaning related to the shaping of cultural value systems.

Collaborative Praxis

Concern for meaning or value is present in a latent state from the start in all healthy human knowing and deciding. It follows that attention to meaning in oneself and as communicated by others is foundational. The process does not stop there. Explicit consideration of what is valued opens the possibility of comprehending alternative insights, interpretations and judgements. Collaborative engagement in inquiry regarding unanswered questions and possibilities indicates for us how we anticipate that truth, value and concrete good can be realized concretely.[43] The inquiry is the seed itself. Sorting out and deciding issues regarding what is true, valuable and concretely good are at the heart of doing socio-economic ethics.

The globalization of the economy and of particular cities or clusters of cities, like Toronto, means that ethical reflection must be collaborative. Since dialogue requires authenticity, it constitutes a call to conversion. Our challenge is to learn to respect and to recognize fully the agency and autonomy of all peoples in practice. It also signals an imperative that privileged white men and women confront the ramifications of domination by exposing attitudes, expression, customs and value systems that maintain control. Personal good will is not enough to overcome sexism and racism. Transformation of our psyche and of systemic exclusion need to be addressed. These attitudes are implicit in the following quotation from Doran but the urgency of the crisis and the extent of racism and sexism in our midst require that distortions also be foregrounded explicitly:

> The mediation of religion and culture today demands the generation of new cultural values capable of informing the way of life of a global network of communities whose operative scale of values is a true alternative to that informing the competing and escalating imperialistic systems now vying for domination of the human world. Since it is theology's task to mediate religion and culture, theology in direct discourse must assume responsibility for the constitutive meaning of world-cultural values. The constitutive meaning of the imperialistic systems reflects a distortion and derailment of ... intentionality from the psyche. The distortion is a function of a rift within interiority between intentional consciousness and the symbol-producing psyche.[44]

Analysis of the split between intentional consciousness and symbol-producing psyche in interiority leads to the awareness that the split is a central cause of domination. Integration of images, symbols and awarenesses arising from the body, psyche and spirit is foundational to transformation. A critical task for theology, therefore, is to promote this integration on a social level. It is an essential work requiring collaborative effort to shape a world constituted by meaning and values adequate to a vision of just relations.

Sources of Meaning

On a global scale, meaning refers to viewpoints or values shared by inter- and intracultural networks of communities committed to authentic persons-in-mutuality.[45] Inter- and intracultural values are inclusive, not by stripping people of specificity, but by mutual engagement in the midst of particular necessities and differences. Sources of meaning lie in experience, insights and critical reflection, the dialectical unfolding of human intelligence on an individual and collective level.[46] Sources of meaning are all conscious acts and all intended contents, whether in the dream state or on any level of waking consciousness. These sources encompass the very dynamism of intentional consciousness, a capacity that consciously and increasingly both heads for and recognizes data, intelligibility, truth, reality and value, all of which ground questioning. Sources of meaning also include determinations reached through experiencing, understanding, judging, deciding and acting.

Thinking, considering, defining, supposing, formulating, judging fact, judging value, deciding and acting are essential to ethical process. These operations are also acts of meaning. The difference these acts of meaning make for ethical praxis is that they both clarify and lead to decisions and action regarding how we shape or constitute social institutions, policies, the economy and human cultures. Religions, art-forms, the family/kin/friendships, the state, the law and the economy are not fixed and immutable entities. They adapt to changing circumstances. They can be reconceived in the light of new ideas. But all such change involves change of meaning, a change of idea or concept, a change of judgement or evaluation.[47]

Expressions of Meaning

One of the most essential ethical tasks is to learn to understand each other's meanings and interpretations. Appreciating the breadth and depth of meanings held by different people is complex in that expression of what is meaningful can be communicated in a wide variety of ways: artistically, symbolically, linguistically and non-verbally in the myriad forms of body communication. Expressions of meaning include realistic common sense, theory, modern science, art, scholarship, interiority, transcendence, ecological participation in nature and faith experience.[48] These different expressions of meaning are significant for ethical reflection in community because, as Doran explains,

> Through each of these specializations, human consciousness has gained a familiarity with various ways in which the objective of the search for direction can be incrementally realized, whether through the experience of beauty, the grasp of intelligibility, the affirmation of the real in true judgements, the existential praxis of furthering the human good through deliberate world-constitution and self-constitution, the orientation in ultimate concern to the world-transcendent measure, or the discovery of God's healing and saving gift of redemptive love and the invitation to live in accord with the pattern of that embodied love.[49]

The task of constituting our world according to preferred values calls for sustained sensitivity to differing expressions of meaning. Understanding the scope of expressions of meaning offers a position to counteract elitist control over criteria and interpretation of meanings in cultures.

To be comprehensive and compelling, collaboration to shape ethical values must appreciate all expressions of meaning in their different modes. The import of this understanding, as Emilie Townes points out, is that expression of meaning can be extensive and profound among oral, literate and electronic/aural cultures.[50] If transformation is a global endeavour, which it must be to offset global exploitation, then it is critical that all expressions of meaning be privileged, not just white theory and/or theory promoted by the wealthy. Interpretation and judgements may also be expressed in a wide range of forms. We need to learn to appreciate and comprehend such communication.

Emilie Townes has presented, I think, a way to go forward in solidarity. For white, literate cultures, her thought implies a foundational call to conversion, to broaden horizons, to appreciate differences and specificity and to surrender exclusive control over meaning and values. Pursuing the implications which Townes suggests stands as an invitation to the collaboration, openness, vulnerability and creativity that are central to the conversions needed for cross-cultural communication and healing. I hear Townes' critique as a challenge to let go of distorted power, to feel the blessing of our need for others' wisdom and to taste the ecstasy of expanded horizon, vision and interdependence. Ethical reflection and decision making require such action.

Fidelity to basic integration of attitudes, values and action in divergent cultural expressions facilitates the discovery of meaningful direction in life, which can be incrementally realized under any conditions whatever of compactness or differentiation of consciousness. The process can also be articulated in precepts, as Lonergan does: "Be attentive, Be intelligent, Be reasonable, Be responsible, Be in love."[51] Praxis of this type anticipates or makes possible discovery of the beautiful, the intelligible, the true, the good and the world-transcendent partner. In the course of history, interpretations of meaning and events become increasingly differentiated through the various expressions of meaning, including images, stories and inquiry. How those committed to justice-praxis name and celebrate their source of hope, integration and meaning, for example, makes a difference whether the same praxis is valued as a spiritual and religious event or not. Some name their sense of faith, hope and love as religious values, sustaining them in a community of solidarity.

Determining and Choosing Concrete Good

One of the most basic questions to be answered is what subjects-in-relation value as true and good in particular relations and situations. To the extent values are unbiased and undistorted, existence itself and values are naturally directed toward concrete good.[52] This translates directly into a concern for world-constitutive and self/group-constitutive praxis. We surmise the authenticity of what is of value for the community-in-relation in cultural expression, in dialogue and in decision making directed on local, national and/or global levels. As we have seen, we face a critical problem. The challenge remains to make implementation of the range of values and concern for persons, for family, kin and friendships, for the earth, for communities and for cultures the operative directing energy for action and integration.

The need to offset exploitative relations of ruling described in this study raises a profound challenge for the community to author its own history, for example, by turning right side up the professed amorality of economics. Our task is not to justify respect for difference and specificity and the inclusion of social consciousness, of community responsibilities, of fully participatory decision making and of access to information as if exclusion, irresponsibility and control of information in order to dominate were normative. Although the latter may be standard practice, they are unethical. Group and general bias distort our perception so thoroughly that we miss the obvious: individualism, distorted dialectics and splits in the entire fabric of our society and world are on trial, not the good of the earth community. As Beverly Wildung Harrison concludes,

> The social world that our antisocial corporate actions have constructed and sustained over time is now characterized by injustice, so now our interests often are set in deep opposition. But my well-being and yours are not inherently at odds.... Justice is a praxis that realizes conditions that make my fulfillment and yours possible simultaneously, that literally creates a common good. All moral goods are *inter*-related possibilities. They seem irreconcilable to us because the world our freedom has constructed and construed is distorted by the heavy hand of privilege and domination.[53]

The power that wealth conveys is often maintained through the anonymity of abstract individualism by sustaining the myth of value-free, immutable market forces. The split between private morality and public responsibility is so complete that accountability for social and ecological irresponsibility is neglected. In this milieu, intelligent inquiry regarding structural causes of poverty and practical solutions is suspect.

Relating the dialectics and the range of values already outlined offers direction for setting moral criteria. Moral principles and deeply religious values of justice, participation and equality depend on mutuality and social consciousness, which are integral elements of the dialectic of family, kin and friendships. Only lifelong nurturing of autonomy and mutuality in creative tension by both women and men is adequate to ground socio-economic relations. This calls for "a radically relational understanding of justice as rightly ordered relationships" with mutuality, reciprocity and interdependence explicitly held as criteria for "equal dignity-in-relation and in-power."[54] Wildung Harrison points out that development and implementation of just relations are intrinsically connected with the critical evaluation of norms as

> human constructs that state our presumptions about what constitutes the general direction acts should take to qualify as "moral." Since norms are conceptual formulations of envisioned values, they may be expressed as principles of action.[55]

Such a historical, socially conscious perspective calls for a deep transformation of moral norms themselves.

In contrast to definitions of individuality, which leave the moral subject separate from social and historical relations and abstractly without limits to apply rational principles simply by making the will primary, focus on autonomy and mutuality in relation shifts the focus. As Ruth Smith shows, when the community or group is accorded its place as a major "unit of consciousness raising, of hearing and speaking a new self-relation and relation to others into being," social criticism and envisioning alternative social relations are fostered since social goals are deeply related to self-redefinition.[56] Awareness of how we are social in specific, historical ways leads us to struggle with our rationality and our moral freedom within the social structure of relations and within the relations of our identity as moral subjects. In this context, we recognize conflict as well as harmony in social relations. We also assert that we are creatures with limits, that human rationality and objectivity are social and historical and that we are embodied participants in life, not detached spectators.

Becoming an authentic subject and an authentic community are central moral tasks. As subjects of our actions, we no longer collude in our own oppression. On the contrary, we attempt to transform conditions of alienation and negation into conditions of affirmation and fulfillment. Recognizing our historical incompleteness, we remake ourselves, our relations and our society through collaborative moral activity, particularly through fostering one's own authentic group/racial identity and interracial, intercultural and interclass praxis.

For both personal and communal morality, conditions for acts of correct understanding include genuineness, openness and willingness.

Good will is concretized, however, only in judgements of what can be intelligently grasped and reasonably affirmed.[57] Judgement requires sufficient data, full disclosure of information (transparency) and readiness to make judgements when there is sufficient information. Procrastination in the midst of adequate information, even when legitimized by legalities, denies justice. What this would involve, for example, in the homeworking-to-consumer chain of the clothing industry is disclosure of subcontractors, costs, taxes actually paid, tax deductions and profits by retailers. It also points out the need for corporate officers to listen and take seriously those most affected by their business practice. For the government, it means acknowledging sufficiency of information and refusal to be dominated by elite lobbying.

Desire to know what is best, to determine criteria honestly and to choose wisely indicate desire for well-being, goodness and value. This historical consciousness forms a basis on which to judge whether what is corresponds to what ought to be; to clarify the basis for objectivity, for setting criteria and for making true judgements by locating them in authentic subjectivity-in-relation; and to encompass inquiring, existential, critical process that remains open to ask further relevant questions. All of these capacities are within us and among us. Trusting our ability to know in these ways and daring to shape a society accordingly are means that offer profound transformation and they are within our grasp.

Lonergan locates the source of criteria to determine what is good in human consciousness, in the desire to know, which he characterizes as

> the dynamic orientation manifested in questions for intelligence and for reflection.... It is the prior and enveloping drive that carries cognitional process from sense and imagination to understanding, from understanding to judgement, from judgement to the complete context of correct judgements that is named knowledge. The desire to know, then, is simply the inquiring and critical spirit.[58]

Determination of criteria regarding what is deemed good and true is dependent upon full respect for differing, authentic subjects-in-relation and communities-in-relation.

The search for correct understanding relies on a self and communal correcting process of learning which results from critical reflection on the broad range of experience included in all aspects of the dialectics I have presented. The quest requires that we verify perceptions and causes, raise further relevant questions and acknowledge when data and answers satisfy or do not satisfy bodily needs, mind and heart. This inquiring, critical spirit, on an individual and communal level, is then the source not only of answers but also of their criteria, not only of questions but also of the grounds on which they are screened. Intelligent inquiry and critical reflection yield both relevant questions and satisfactory answers. Essentially, the reality to be considered is all that can be intelligently grasped and reasonably affirmed, according to whatever is appropriate in a particular instance. Reality includes the world mediated by meaning as well as the "already out there now." Authenticity involves intelligent and reasonable affirmation on both subjective and communal levels of one's own and the society/group's process of inquiry.

A vision of what is necessary and possible clarifies praxis as transformative theology. Such a vision specifies concrete good and finds its direction related to actual situations, like the international chain of production in the garment industry. To avoid being idealistic, the process draws upon a wide range of facts, like the accumulation of capital and consolidation of power by major retailers and bankers. Such attention to causes lays the basis for ethical decision making based on critical realism.

Radical Foundation of Socio-economic Ethics: Interiorly Differentiated Consciousness

I have focused mainly on sociological and economic categories with reference to their ethical applications. But none of these alone provides adequate conditions to understand the structured relations that constitute a cultural matrix. I concur with Doran's assertion that

> advertence to the data of interiority is a yet more radical condition for understanding the sets of meanings and values within which these variables function.... The interaction of classes and indeed even their very economic relation to productive forces are more radically to be understood as a function of the integrity or disintegration of the dialectic of community.[59]

And the dialectic of community depends on the authentic or inauthentic function of operative values arising from family/kin/friendships, subjectivity, ecology, authentic religion and culture. How these values are lived determines the social and economic orders. Socio-economic categories are consequent upon, rather than foundational for, cultural evaluation and critique even as they become part of a virtuous or vicious circle in praxis. The ultimate foundation lies in interiority analysis, that is, in meanings and values.

The emergence of interiorly differentiated consciousness is a radical source of learning the foundation, method, content and meaning of ethics for today. First of all, what is interiorly differentiated consciousness? The depth of its significance prompts me to introduce this carefully. Understanding it involves a process like bread making: mixing ingredients, kneading the dough, letting it rise, punching it down, letting it rise and baking it in a hot oven!

Interiorly differentiated consciousness: Both exterior and interior worlds are crucial as we shape meanings and values. Knowledge of the exterior "already, out-there, visible" tangible, audible, sensory world is accessible for all with the appropriate physical capabilities. Communications technology makes world realities part of everyday living. The first challenge for institutions that shape political and economic policies, and even technological innovations, is to take this real world seriously and responsibly by seeing the poverty and violence for what it is among peoples and for the earth itself. Even making these connections would be a major step forward.

The next step is to ask about the meaning of the global crisis, about the values and lack of values implied, about causes and effects and about the kind of world we want. This step involves the mind and heart, putting our hands and feet to work as well.

The interior work involves individual and group reflection and interpretation. It is a multifaceted task involving reflection on the sensory world of relationships and our choices of political, economic, social, technological and fiscal systems; reflection on how we know systems are adequate or not; reflection on how we decide the adequacy and effectiveness of our work; and reflection on the overall genuine unfolding of societal good or the accelerating social decline. And interpretation of these.

Interiorly *differentiated* consciousness: If we are not willing to tolerate visible differences in the exterior world, as in racial differences, styles of eating and fashion, we press for conformity even in externals. The dangers are clear: supremacy of one external over another, domination of one group over another on the basis of difference.

The cosmos and every facet of the earth, however, are marked by uniqueness, difference and interdependence. Appreciation for uniqueness, difference and specificity and communion opens hearts and minds to be able to accept others in their own right, to communicate, to dialogue and to collaborate. It also opens people to surprises of awe, wonder, gratitude and ecstasy. It follows that values must be far broader than profit making for a few. We are concerned with a whole range of values: vital, ecological, social, cultural, personal, familial and authentically religious values. And with images and symbols related to feelings and values that surface from widely divergent experiences.

Interiorly differentiated *consciousness*: The link between consciousness and knowledge reveals a foundation for ethical praxis in appropriation, agency and integration. What is at stake here is that the full process of experience, understanding, judgement, decision and action constitute knowing. Objectivity is a consequence of intelligent inquiry and critical reflection, emerging only through thorough familiarity with an issue or situation. Objectivity is the fruit of authentic personal and communal subjectivity. It is made visible as people willingly engage in reflecting upon and critiquing experience, understanding, judging, deciding and acting.[60]

Expanded consciousness is directly related to feminist consciousness, described earlier. Consciousness surfaces an urgency for consistency, for action consonant with new awareness in order to transform the structures which perpetuate our culture of injustice. Such adequate self/communal knowledge is to be appropriated not only cognitively, but also existentially and sensitively, because, as Doran explains,

> our reasonableness demands consistency between what we know and what we do; and so there is a volitional appropriation of truth that consists in our willingness to live up to it, and a sensitive appropriation of truth that consists in an adaptation of our sensibility to the requirements of our knowledge and our decisions.[61]

Consciousness has a threefold nature of intentionality or spirit, of psyche and of body, all needing to be integrated and held in the context of the different aspects of family/kin/friendships, community and culture. Since "consciousness is merely the presence of the subject to himself or herself in all the operations and states of which he or she is the subject," it includes consciousness of body, psyche and spirit as well as social and ecological reality.[62]

Knowledge, however, is a function of experience, understanding and judging. Consciousness is a prerequisite for knowledge, not a sufficient condition.[63] Knowledge results from understanding personal and communal experience, gathering sufficient data for judgements of both fact and value about experience, and making decisions to establish personal and communal consistency with judgements of what is deemed true and good. It is in *deciding and acting* that we know concrete expressions of being, truth, goodness and justice. Attitudes preliminary to willing or desiring them only indicate what this knowing may mean. Such knowledge is accessible to all in varying degrees to the extent that we act together in justice. It is an anticipation of fuller goodness, truth and justice, of being.

Let us return to the basic knowledge that arises from both the world of immediacy and the world mediated by meaning. This position on knowledge facilitates existential praxis, including and surpassing the capability of theory because the expanded basis of knowledge offers potential for reflecting on meaning and values and on the processes of how we know, judge, decide and act.[64] Accordingly, the importance of meaning grounds ethical horizons beyond establishing maxims. It shifts ethics to an imperative for conversion from bias, to comprehensive integration of a range of vital, ecological, social, cultural, personal, familial/kin/friendship and authentically religious values. Ethical action requires inclusion of all peoples in diversity, integrating all realities of persons, family/kin/friendships, community, culture and ecology.

Praxis is existential, interpersonal and historically world-constitutive when deliberating subjects-in-relation constitute or create the self, family/kin/friendships, community, culture and a healthy ecosystem. We shape society and world. We value ecological interdependence. Praxis presumes deliberation, evaluation, discernment, decision and action. Praxis also requires reflective discernment on use of all of these functions in terms of a particular engagement or project.

These connections offer, I think, significant ways to ground intercultural solidarity and to give hope. When we value differences and specificity and when we make connections among all the different aspects of how we shape our personal and social organization, we are more free interiorly to assess what is meaningful and valuable. We can be aware of the wide range of feelings and emotions as communicated in diverse ways by different peoples. Then we can discover together what these indicate for us. And more. Feelings are intimately related simultaneously both to the images and symbols that are meaningful to us and to the values we hold. Feelings, images, symbols and values: a treasure or a time bomb depending on the meaning or futility of our overall personal and social life or decline.

The images and symbols that dominate in our cultures and the interpretation we give them are intrinsically bound up with how we shape our personal, interpersonal, societal and ecological worlds. They are crucial to the political, economic, technological and fiscal systems we create. And profoundly linked to our religious expression. The prevailing media images of success, wealth, total happiness, women as sex objects, the lure of bloodshed and gore and gambling obsessions profoundly shape the context of valuing or exploiting women's work, for example.

Existential, interpersonal and world-constitution, therefore, is intrinsically bound up with elemental symbols and their interpretation. These can now be incorporated into analysis of human intentionality. Decision making adequate to an emerging axial shift in consciousness must therefore include data arising from the threefold basis of human consciousness: body, intentionality and psyche.[65] This includes feelings and images and symbols arising from all three. Since psychic spontaneity can either aid or obstruct the intention of insight, judgement and responsible decision, psychic conversion becomes foundational for cultural transformation.[66]

Heightened consciousness through appropriation facilitates the use of symbolic categories in theological endeavour itself. On the personal and communal levels, it provides categories for theological discourse across cultures.[67] This is profoundly relevant to societal transformation. Some of the most popular approaches within feminist, black, lesbian/gay and Native circles include image-based expressions of stories, dreams, rituals, art forms and dramatization. These set conditions to communicate all three forms of consciousness. In addition to being laden with affective power, images inform or give rise to insight which facilitates truth making through knowledge and judgements both *of fact* and *of value* for world-constitutive and self-constitutive dramatic praxis.[68] Imaginal expressions condition the possibility of psychic conversion and transformation of cultures and religious traditions. They may also lead whole groups to critical reflection and judgement, to responsible deliberation and decision as people are concerned with authentic and inauthentic relations on personal, interpersonal, familial, social, corporate and religious/spiritual grounds. The bonds established within these groups foster courage to face flights from understanding both personally and regarding evidence of it in others.[69]

The change in the control of meaning from theory to interiorly differentiated consciousness constitutes this breakthrough as axial. It is far beyond a paradigm shift. The new consciousness seems to be arising out of the earth itself as Native peoples, blacks, people of colour, gays and lesbians, women of all "races," the marginalized and excluded shape our identities and recognize our capacities as agents of

transformation. I think it is an axial shift in consciousness comparable
to the shift that gave rise historically to the major world religions. The
present shift involves reflection on how we know, judge, choose, act,
reflect and celebrate. It is holistic, involving persons, cultures, all forms
of social organization and care for the earth, all within the power and
love of the Spirit of God in whatever way this divine energy is recognized and named. It takes meaning, values, uniqueness, specificity, differentiation and interdependence very seriously. This is the horizon in
which we do ethics, the context in which we value women and youth,
all the excluded and work. This is the context in which establishing just
relations requires an expanded vision of faith adequate to counteract
global injustice and to sustain peoples in the long process of transformation.

Such transformation depends on differentiation and integration
rather than on splits in human consciousness. Explanatory self and
communal appropriation of human interiority on a holistic basis intro-
duces a genuinely postmodern differentiation of consciousness. What is
emerging is a profoundly significant option. On the one hand, we can
surrender meaning, disregard persons and abdicate historical responsibility. Or we can opt for authentic persons and groups-in-relation, in a
new era that protects the earth, meaning and values as significant
constitutive factors in living.[70] I emphasize once again the importance
of the different expressions of meaning and values among different
peoples and the necessity of conversion to learn from each other. Praxis
is for the long-term victory of integrity for all peoples according to
their own varied expressions of meaning in all aspects of living, named
for example at least in the four dialectics or more broadly.

As large numbers of women and "races" as a whole take subjectivity and moral agency seriously, people dare to think, gather adequate
information and make informed judgements. These awarenesses are
also shared and made public to expose what was formerly overlooked
by the patriarchy and by the white "race" generally in exclusionary
supremacy.[71] The axial shift in consciousness is happening not because
a few leaders suggest conceptual shifts in paradigms. It is broadly
based and arises from a conjuncture of factors: the contradictions of
the global dis-economy, racism, the dis-ease of the planet itself, questioning what is meaningful, searching out what heals and what brings
life and the emergent appropriation of personal and communal agency,
consciousness and conscience. Groups of oppressed are grasping the
authenticity of their own perceptions and abilities and the possibilities

of assuming responsibility for decision making on a social scale. Personal and collective consciousness is being awakened and shaped interdependently with the entire ecosystem. These new, deep signs of life emerge in stark contrast to the extreme violence and exploitation of this age.[72]

This data is also significant for information for theological foundations, to assist interpretive and evaluative appropriation of the situation and tradition. Such appropriation requires critique, reversal of inauthenticities, clarification of confusions and inconsistencies and promotion of its transformative potentialities. This applies particularly to issues raised by radical questioning of intellectual, moral and religious/spiritual authenticity.[73]

For Doran, the import is clear:

> At this point of generativity and creativity, theology not merely illuminates, but becomes, praxis. For a change in constitutive meaning is a change in the world, and the labour involved in changing constitutive meaning is itself historical, world-constitutive praxis.[74]

Generative power to mediate the emergence of these constitutive meanings is available for theological discourse in recognizing the significance of the body and psyche as well as intentionality for foundations of symbolic categories in affirmations of belief, in systematics and in communications. Symbolic and imaginal expressions of meaning are central data for transformation. They are also central to ethical reflection and decision making. The more we connect all earth and lived realities, the more authentic relations are possible. Those who trust their dreams, art and stories as significant data for interpretation hold a key to local and global conversion. These activities also offer a key to conversion for those who resist such integration. Change, then, is a personal and communal cumulative process resulting in somatic awareness, psychic integration and conscious representation, on the one hand, and dramatically patterned intelligence and existential responsibility for world constitution and self-constitution, on the other hand. I reemphasize here the importance of psychic, social and body conversion as well as affective, intellectual, moral and religious conversions. These conversions constitute dimensions of theological foundations for justice making, inclusive communities, effective regard for specificity and valuation of both home and child-rearing.[75]

Collaborative generation of inter- and intracultural constitutive meaning is profoundly significant for theological/ethical praxis in constituting an alternative interdependent world. Such networking will not happen without widespread participation and recognition of divergent contributions. Nor will it be comprehensive without integration of psychic, spiritual and somatic data as entire peoples express and interpret meaning profoundly in diverse ways. Integration of the psyche by individuals and by small groups, I suggest, is also a profoundly social act. As we grapple with our experience, understand its meaning, gather information and make informed judgements, the truth we see and share is publicly significant. Such action lays the groundwork for people to assume full participation and responsibility in shaping societal policies. We have yet to do this extensively in cross-cultural, intergenerational dialogue.

The Implications for Theological Ethical Reflection

Systemic devaluation of women, of women's work and of the earth itself is evidence of ongoing profound social decline. It challenges theologians to use all their capabilities for research, contemplation and action to expose deception in present unjust cultures and to contribute to the creation of transformed attitudes, values and meaning. These must be linked to prevailing images and symbols, feelings and actual realities. In other words, the clear call to theologians today is to discover the powerful Spirit of God in such a way that we can shape all aspects of theology to guide transformation. This necessarily involves critique and collaboration in interdisciplinary work.

Our natural, historical, cultural and economic interdependence constitutes much of our very existence on this globe. Theology and socio-economic ethics must be grounded in reality, which is a concrete, interactive, cosmic-world-historical process.[76] Exposing the dynamics that enslave people and prevent life-giving relationship in human communities is proper to systematic theology. This process calls for integrated, interdisciplinary studies "in cognitive and existential praxis addressed to a prevailing situation in such a way as to evoke an alternative situation."[77] Obviously, this requires integration, transformation and an asceticism of doing theology in ways that deeply grapple with the content and communication of faith in tandem with current global realities.

Such praxis sets multiple challenges. The long-term task of shaping global vision to offset current, profound societal decline requires full use of empirical, intelligent, rational, responsible and loving intentionality, integration, decision and action.[78] Normativity rests, as Lonergan suggests, "in the quite open structure of the human spirit—in the ever immanent and operative though unexpressed transcendental precepts: Be attentive, Be intelligent, Be reasonable, Be responsible"[79] and "Be in love."[80] Norms are locate "in nature itself, not as abstractly conceived, but as concretely operating" in holistic ways.[81] This approach counteracts any interpretation of natural law that promotes racism, sexism or biological determinism. It respects the work of the Spirit of God within peoples and allows for the possibility of Native, black, women's and men's theologies all standing together to be assessed according to their capacity to evoke transformation of persons, faith communities, social organization and cultures.

Attentive praxis also requires: (1) integration of all aspects of persons, families/kin/friendships, communities and cultures within the horizon of ecological interdependence; (2) assuming responsibility to direct social relations according to principles that respect subjectivity, differentiation and interdependence; (3) thorough transformation in understandings of the value and possibilities of families, kin and friendships, of social movements and of the academy, university and religious institutions in their creation of the reflexive, guiding values of culture; (4) promotion of integrity in a global recognition of intersubjectivity and practical organization in community through respect for cross-cultural values; and (5) basing clarification in interiorly differentiated consciousness, grounded on the understanding that "Genuine objectivity is the fruit of authentic subjectivity."[82] Finally, evidence of truth making is tested in implementation of vital values among all those presently excluded, especially women and children.

As a world-community of subjects/groups-in-relation, we are responsible for all aspects of the dialectics and their relationship to values—in short, for the total well-being of the earth community. The synthesis of intersubjectivity and practicality, for example, depends on subjects and communities'

> answer to the question of what the drama of human life is all about, an answer that satisfies our intelligence and speaks to our hearts. And it is the function of culture to provide this answer. Thus it is that cosmopolitan intellectual collaboration assumes the integrity of culture as its primary responsibility. At the superstructural level of culture, that responsibility entails the construction of a human science that is at once empirical, critical, dialectical and normative. And a theology that would mediate between a prevailing cultural matrix and the significance and role of Christian faith within that matrix will "take a professional interest in the human sciences and make a positive contribution to their methodology.[83]

Cultural integrity is the ongoing context that makes the integral dialectic of community possible. By contrast, lack of cultural integration of the infrastructure and the guiding values is a radical source of poverty.

Creation of a culture of justice requires unqualified reciprocity of neighbour love with, as Henderson advises, "conscious effort to expand and exercise our capacities for loving and altruistic, cooperative behaviour."[84] This involves a repatterning of the exploding information age and calls for profound wisdom to make sound judgements and implement only what we deem helpful. Light, darkness, interdependence and webs of relationships become significant images for the present and guides for the future. To value only light, for example, is a half-truth. Darkness itself is a symbol of creativity, love sharing and life giving. When darkness is devalued, black skin is related in the cultural imagination to feelings and values connected with evil and fear, on at least a subconscious level.[85] Cultural images and symbols are also deeply heuristic, which means that they indicate and anticipate the source and direction of energy, wisdom, meaning and life itself. I conclude that a fuller discovery of divine mystery may arise from within the very necessities of our age if theological reflection focuses anew on its twofold task of a comprehensive disclosure of reality and of commitment to engage in transformative praxis.[86]

Difference and Specificity as a Gift of God

Women's socio-economic vulnerability reveals the urgency of valuing difference and specificity.[87] Making women's social and economic reality visible brings to light factors disregarded or marginalized in traditional economy and theology.[88] Separation of relations of family/kin/friendship from the public realm in which women generally lack adequate participation means that central aspects of life are privatized and unsubsidized. Racism and misogyny become rationales for unequal access to the common good, explaining why the majority of women do not have control over resources, not even our own bodies. Racism and sexism set distorted boundaries to explain why some people deserve what they have and other people deserve not having it. In the face of this hidden world of meaning, we discover that women's situations turn out to be different and thus judged to be not relevant to the justice arena.[89]

The task touches personal attitudes, interpersonal relations *and* systemic change. Of course interpersonal relations are vital and their importance deeply significant. This is as it should be in any graced encounters. To miss the profound importance of the systemic, however, runs the risk of limiting solutions to privatized options, without touching systems. Within the stance of wanting to support women, some men of good will are offended when women clearly want more than personal respect and kindness. Such men do not consider the focus and rationale of women's critique. This position is deceptive under a guise of good because it prevents *systemic analysis* and uncovering the relations of ruling, relations that appear gender neutral but exclude and exploit according to difference. In effect, such men will engage in otherwise healthy relationships with women, but leave a culture and systems that exploit in place. They, and women who support this approach, block facing and removing the *causes* of exploitation and violence that continue to afflict women and girls globally and here in Canada.

The scope of difference is global and it must be addressed intentionally and systematically because of the differential participation and the differential impact caused by abuse of it. Since the economy is built on global exploitation of difference, both the material and ideological bases of subordination and their interrelation must be taken into account. As Pamela Brubaker explains, "It is inadequate to treat women's oppression simply as cultural. Ideological and cultural dynamics must be recognized and proposals for cultural change addressed."[90] This theme constitutes a non-negotiable foundation for socio-economic ethics as transformative theology. On principle, it means that the social dynamics of "race," sex and class must be simultaneously valued in concrete historical circumstances.

Within these dynamics, the home is particularly significant. Skills, attitudes and meaning gleaned in the traditionally private sphere are extremely valuable in their own right and are acutely needed in what has been labeled public. The activities and practices involved in child-bearing and child-rearing, in identity formation and interpersonal relations and in ecologically protective home management depend on moral agency and creative initiative. Home-learned values are significant for public political economy. In fact they are capable of subverting market priorities, as they provide evidence that alternatives have been tried and need to be applied in the public realm. "Working-class and poor women in particular have much to offer to such a change in practice, because their work has been especially critical to their families' survival."[91]

Appreciation for difference and specificity does not lock people into gendered roles. In fact, it is already freeing men to discover the blessings and responsibilities of child-rearing. It does involve shattering many myths. Desacralizing the home involves understanding what in fact is happening in homes. It also requires decision making both to value the good there and to challenge oppressive attitudes and practices. At the same time, valuing specificity, agency and mutuality in the inherent lifelong creative tension of the dialectic of families/kin/friendships offers insight and expertise for the larger project of transforming structural domination for the good of women and men of all "races."

The importance of difference and specificity as essential cultural values goes much deeper. It touches the production and control of cultural images. It also relates to our ability to imagine alternatives. Disregard for difference, of whatever nature, destroys the veracity and adequacy of societal images and principles. Because of different life experiences, whether based on gender, "race," empire classification or any other category denoting difference, different images are meaningful. It follows that more adequate principles will emerge for the whole fabric of society when the wide range of difference is fully included. Such a realization leads me to highlight again that ethical process must incorporate differences that emerge from physical constitution, intentionality and the symbol-producing psyche.

In order to heal the biases that distort collective psyches, we need to expose images and symbols that destroy and to foster images that set a context of integrity. Two examples: The first centres on an image that promotes feelings and meaning linked to racism. As already mentioned, making darkness a symbol of evil has been promoted in the name of religion. The second example: Historical symbolic references to female blood as unclean may also be directly related to devaluation, exploitation and violence against women. The image of blood in collective unconscious or shadow side leads to repulsion of blood, on the one hand, or attraction to blood and violence, on the other. The question stands whether or how we can love women and respect child-bearing, or even our very selves, if we have an aversion for blood at the very heart of who we are. Traditions in faith communities of exalting male blood as a pure sacrificial offering and shunning female blood as unclean and needing purification are being uncovered. Although awareness of the roots is largely lost to the majority, the feelings remain. Surely blood is a sign of life and love, giving oxygen and nutrition to every fibre of our being, created in our very bones, creating a child, carrying passion and healing wounds.[92]

Racial and sexual differences are gifts of God to create a vibrant, caring community with provision for all. The profoundly sinful, prevailing distortions of racism, sexism and wealthism stand as indictment and invitation to all faith communities. I ask forgiveness for ways I have contributed to these. I recognize that all of us are part of patriarchal oppression. That awareness is not enough. The Catholic Church, for example, has a wonderfully blessed history and an extensive sin history and is beginning to ask forgiveness corporately for exclusion, exploitation and persecution of the past. Feminist, womanist, mujerista and other liberationist theologies assess how some aspects of theology promoted racism and the devaluation of women.

As faith communities, conversion away from racism, sexism and wealthism is made visible in imagery and symbols, in language, in the ability to be inclusive-in-deeds and practice and in confrontation of structures (attitudes, customs, laws, corporations) that cause poverty. Without respect for differences and specificity, celebrations of eucharist, which are to be meals of inclusive communities, lack integrity. So do claims to love God who creates differences. A faith community proclaiming that love casts out fear can be expected to act courageously to offset sexism, racism and wealthism, in particular circumstances as well as in general attitudes and statements.

Difference and specificity also form a basic heuristic category in doing ethics and theology ethically. This means that differentiation in the cosmos and among peoples is an indication of what concretely good ethical praxis involves. In particular ways, differentiation reveals and anticipates what ought to be. It becomes a criterion to judge what is. Reflecting on lived appreciation for difference and specificity shapes theology and can be a spiritual path to come to know God. Images of the divine expand. Valuing inclusion and mutuality and specificity open up an adventure of discovery and a lifelong project of doing justice.

Co-existence in difference requires structure to facilitate it, in churches and in society. Giving this priority in words necessarily requires concrete expression in providing resources of personnel and finances to implement it. Such a project of structural transformation can emerge only through collaboration as people are attentive, intelligent, reasonable, responsible and in love.

An Ethics of Integrity and Truth

I now weave the strands of meaning and judgements from the perspective of integrity and truth making. A minimal requirement for integrity and an ethics of truth in the clothing industry is disclosure of corporate practices, such as complete global sourcing of garment production, including names of manufacturers, subcontractors and homeworkers, profits, wages and prices. This information is part of the data required to make judgements of fact. It also leads the way for cultures and cross-cultural networks to make judgements of value, setting priorities in socio-economic policies and in employment practices.

Current opposition by elites, however, is well funded and well entrenched, controlling even discourse for defining the issues and articulating alternatives.[93] Homeworkers' speaking publicly about their less-than-minimum wages costs them their jobs. With debates closed and voices excluded through distortion and/or silencing, the power of the market is so triumphant that it becomes unfashionable even to speak of fundamental options.

Although technology is now popularly available for information to be an abundant resource rather than a scarce commodity, tight control of significant data obstructs justice making.[94] Integrity calls for open disclosure and honest dialogue regarding surplus profits and communal rights to surplus for basic needs of the whole of society.[95] Technological opportunities demand new co-operative codes of ethics from local to global levels. Information alone does not enlighten. Clarifying what is significant information, *mis*-information, *dis*-information or propaganda in the midst of an overload of fragmented raw data becomes a critical task. It is part of a search for meaningful new patterns of knowledge and wisdom basic to ethical reflection and decision making. Evaluation requires dialogue.

Intercultural, interracial dialogue presumes, as Thomas Kopfensteiner suggests, "a willingness to take seriously the validity claims of the other," which "leads to the transformation of perspectives, the discovery of new possibilities, and a growth in knowledge."[96] Genuine dialogue fosters expression of truth and meanings by people from different perspectives. It sets conditions for mutual transformation. Integrity requires discernment, whether assigned meanings, values, interpretations and policies really fit lived realities of those exploited on the basis of difference. In other words, what is the truth of the meanings? One goal of personal and communal life projects is to do what is meaningful for groups and individuals. Meaning conditions freedom—"the ability to achieve the good"—and it "provides legitimate boundaries of freedom."[97] This freedom involves unifying moral goodness and rightness in specific expressions. The importance, therefore, of formulating legitimate expectations collaboratively is clear. They may be shaped in reflection, judgement and decision about communal moral praxis in dialogue from different perspectives.

Praxis reveals meaning and effective history. It shows what people actually value and put into practice. The changing contexts of praxis ground both insight and freedom. Within a culture of dialogue-seeking-truth that refuses to dominate others, criteria and standards of decision making can be "criticized, destabilized and revised in order to set into motion a new history of moral insight."[98] A task for moral reasoning is to expand the mutually conditioning relationships between freedom and praxis, between experience and insight. Introducing different perspectives expands horizons and makes possible deeper realization of particular truths, good and rightness. As historical accomplishment, judgements about what is true may be critiqued, changed and improved according to contextual requirements.

Creating an ethics of integrity and truth that respects diversity of gender and "race" is a work of dialogue and it requires context-dependent analysis. The context for ethical decisions about the garment industry, for example, is global and local. It is interracial and gender specific. Evaluative history of women's work in this trade reveals the historicity of societal, ethical perspectives and choices in praxis, whether by design or omission. Analyzing the international web of production from the perspective of homeworkers challenges how social relations are evaluated. Recognition of the immanent historicity of ethical knowledge in this way invites transformation of moral norms for business, government and families—in all aspects of the relations of ruling. It evokes capacity for mutual learning, dialogue, decision and effective action in order to constitute just relations.

An ethics of truth reaches deeply and extensively. I quote Lonergan at length here because he moves analysis forward by showing the all-encompassing nature of the task at hand:

> If we are not simply to flounder, we have to take our stand on authenticity: on the authenticity with which intelligence takes us beyond the experimental infrastructure to enrich it, extend it, organize it, but never to slight it and much less to violate its primordial role; on the authenticity with which rational reflection goes beyond the constructions of intelligence ... on the authenticity with which moral deliberation takes us beyond cognitional process into the realm of freedom and responsibility, evaluation and decision, not in any way to annul or slight experience or understanding or factual judgement, but to add the further and distinct truth of value judgements and the consequent decisions demanded by a situation in which authenticity cannot be taken for granted....
>
> [Praxis] starts from the assumption that authenticity cannot be taken for granted. Its understanding, accordingly, will follow a hermeneutic of

suspicion as well as a hermeneutic of recovery. Its judgement will discern between products of human authenticity and products of human unauthenticity [sic].[99]

Lonergan concludes that this basic discernment between the authentic and the inauthentic calls for a distinct method that relies on both theoretical and practical judgements of value, based on love.

The distinction between the authentic and the inauthentic raises what I consider the most troubling problem within the entire process of seeking just relations for women, particularly homeworkers. How can we achieve transformation in the midst of a culture deeply marked by violence, deceit and power based on wealth?[100] The Homework Coalition reached out to corporate retail executives and designers for dialogue only to meet either total disregard for our request or such differing horizons that the process was frustrated.

What is clear in the clothing industry is that the sides are not equal, that dialogue is skewed and that practice by large corporate retailers is unjust and oppressive to those lower on the pyramid of production. I have indicated the injustice of banking practice in terms of interest rates and causes of the recession and of debt, all directly related to increasing hardship for the working poor and the growing numbers of unemployed. In this conflict, I apply principles cited by Albert Nolan. The injustice is not merely a matter of misunderstanding. Apparent neutrality by consumers serves to maintain the system as it hides the nature of the conflict. Tension, social disruption and conflict to achieve justice may be essential to expose exploitation. As Nolan makes clear:

> The commonly held view that Christians should always seek harmony and a "middle way" in every dispute assumes that tension and conflict are worse evils than injustice and oppression. This again is a false supposition based upon a lack of compassion for those who suffer under oppression. Those who are afraid of conflict or confrontation, even when it is non-violent, are usually those who are not convinced of the need for change. Their caution hides an un-Christian pessimism about the future, a lack of hope. Or they use the Christian concern for reconciliation to justify a form of escapism from the realities of injustice and conflict.[101]

Conflicting interests make the promotion of truth and justice costly. Although taking unequivocal stands for justice may appear to create conflict and dissension, they actually reveal structured injustice and counteract false peace in favour of peace that arises from truth, justice and love. Such truth making does not focus on personal condemnations, although bringing discrepancies to light may reveal the need for conversion. The clothing chain of production involves structural injustice. This brings us face to face with the dilemma of finding methods of transformation that in fact shift power and capital/wealth from those who control them to their own advantage. The crisis brings into relief the realization that we have come to a time for decision making and social solidarity across lines of difference.

Relating Ethical Imperatives and Economic Possibilities
A Matter of Community Choice and Solidarity

Any acceptable imperative must be rooted in possibility. The question of whether the "ought" of social justice implies the "can" of economic policy is obviously complex.[102] I concur with Samuel Bowles and Herbert Gintis who call for increased accountability and social participation as reasonable criteria for economic justice. They claim that traditional economic theory "vastly understates possibilities for progressive change."[103] They ground notions of dignity, freedom and community in an ability to learn and to choose who and how we want to be as peoples. This inquiry and decision making involves concerted action to shape societal relations according to preferred values. It challenges whole societies not to withdraw because lack of involvement and of resistance leaves the status quo dominant. The time is ripe to take up proactive leadership for transformation. The paths to such far-reaching change are as simple as confident, kitchen-table talk, as revolutionary to a rigid system as celebration and as demanding of creative initiative and perseverance as the most intricate art work or child-rearing.

At the same time, the process of change is as complex as the problem is deep. As previously noted, a key area exhibiting lack of social process is the division of labour with its extreme fragmentation of tasks, split between thinking and working, hierarchical control of labourers' work and exploitation on the basis of difference or of economic disadvantage. As Bowles and Gintis claim, these practices

> concentrate information, information processing and decision-making at the narrow pinnacle of a pyramidal structure.... The structure of capitalist production promotes a sense of political ineffectiveness and assigns to racial, sexual, and other differences a set of hierarchical meanings that are as inconsistent with tolerance and respect as they are hostile to the forms of solidarity and cooperation necessary for effective political intervention.[104]

Such hierarchical ranking according to difference in order to promote vested interests is a major symptom of societal decline.

A judgement of fact in this case is that labour is not a commodity. Employment is a relationship with social understandings and commitments. It requires the same balancing of autonomy and mutuality as the basic dialectic of families, kin and friendships. Fragmented work that makes people dispensable destroys the person (body-psyche-spirit) and community (practicalities and interpersonal/group relations). Both community relations and practicalities are distorted through unjust power relations. Workers are pitted against each other. Prestige, power and property become lodged in social attitudes as immutable rights to further privilege of every kind. Popular anger and resentment are imprisoned by the prevailing myth that the general public has no power. It deceives and paralyzes. The extent of ruling power through fiscal, corporate and political liaison means that change is related to the ability of social movements to gather popular support by exposing sources of the pain, anger, distortion and disjuncture. The latter alert us to what ought to be. We *know* that these relations are incredibly unjust.

At every turn, the issue comes home to popular and political will. That the problems appear overwhelming is no accident. The question is whether we, as cultures, have the will to identify the roots of domination and to choose alternatives. It is a matter of claiming personal and collective autonomy that have been destroyed by individualistic greed and competition. We have become so accustomed to focus on individualism that even self/communal appropriation looks radical.

As a community of differing subjects, our question is how mutuality, social consciousness and justice can operate in a predominantly unjust culture. The response we give needs to provide both long- and short-term strategies. In the garment industry, immediate imperatives include provincial legislation establishing joint liability for transgression of employment standards; central registries to provide access to information for vulnerable workers and to the government for enforcement; extension of sectoral bargaining; and affordable, quality child/dependent care.[105] Long-term response includes dialogue about, and change of, trade agreements, choice to maintain a worker-centred garment industry in Toronto, clarification regarding the relation between standard and non-standard work and the broader, critical issues of overcoming group bias, valuing those excluded on the basis of difference, tax reform and integrating the public/private realms. Responsible resource use also demands that priorities be determined between focus on high-fashion or concentration on socially useful, needed garment production.

Values are undermined in all categories: vital, ecological, familial, social, cultural, personal and religious. It follows that socio-economic ethics adequate for today must not be limited to a set of new rules. The situation of injustice cries out for broad vision and commitment to shared meanings and values. This deeply ethical issue of meanings and values entails a profound reorientation of our societal structure to incorporate at least all of the dialectics central to this study. The horizon needed is no less than ecological interdependence, which constitutes an enduring matrix giving form and substance to individual lives, families/kin/friends and cultures, all of which are relational and differentiated by nature.[106] Accountability, participation, respect for difference/specificity, justice, initiative, courage, truth making, limitation, transcendence, balance, judgement and action are values basic to this challenge. Henderson highlights values essential to the transition to full participation:

> foresight as a form of prevention; co-operation, in order to build consensus and balance the market's emphasis on competition and profit; acceptance of diversity as one of the basic principles of "living systems"; and clarification of unifying global concerns and ethics.[107]

The continuing process of personal and social transformation assumes that persons are subjects-in-relation and that all aspects of all the dialectics are to be held in creative balance for justice making.[108]

Discerning Elements to Transform Economics

My concentration has been to unravel factors that allow those with power and wealth/capital to continue exploitation of the working poor and factors that foster solidarity and social transformation. What emerged from that analysis is a clearer understanding of the nature of the values that currently undergird our socio-economic system and why they need to be replaced by a more adequate societal framework in order to obtain just relations. In this section, I specify some implications for economics as a discipline. While being very conscious, as Tamás Szentes says, "that the multidimensional nature of the present crisis is unprecedented," I now suggest some directions which need thorough dialogue, correction and expansion in order to reorient economics itself.[109]

I concur with Marjorie Griffin Cohen's position:

Including women in our analysis of society, then, clearly involves more than extending the field of inquiry, using the same tools of analysis. Rather, including women means something much more radical—it means challenging the very assumptions on which existing theory is based. Women's experience was not part of the original experience and it can't be just tacked on. This is, by now, a fairly familiar feminist refrain, and the chorus, which demands changes in the fundamental tenets of disciplines to reflect a more inclusive analysis, is reaching a crescendo.[110]

I also emphasize economic justice as a baseline criteria of authenticity, as Doran claims:

No religious, personal and cultural values are genuinely beyond illusion and ideology if they support, sustain, or condone the distorted dialectic responsible for injustice in the realm of systemic social reality.... Global maldistribution of vital goods sets the issue for the whole scale of values.[111]

That injustice is being supported on a broad scale is evident in "a historically unprecedented accumulation of unaccountable economic power and an unconscionable degree of inequality of wealth."[112] David Langille exposes the face of corporate rule, the ninety-nine men and one woman, of Canada's hundred largest corporations in Canada. They

reaped record profits while slashing jobs. These are the real special interests—the hundred largest companies in Canada. Collectively, they have made record profits in recent years—over $65 billion in 1965—while 1.5 million Canadians remain without work. The CEOs shown were paid an average of $2,654,116 in 1995, nearly 90 times the average wage of working Canadians at $29,835.[113]

Ken Thomson, media magnate and owner of the Hudson's Bay Company and Zellers, for example, in 1995 received a salary of $1,465,000 and total compensation of $296 million.[114] Refer back to chapter 1 to see the accounts of homeworkers sewing clothes for the Bay.

Social costs of maintaining the status quo are rising exponentially. The price of adjustment is already more than we as peoples can bear. We face the crisis therefore with little option but to stand together in courageous, concerted, active engagement in transformation or to perish. Focus on living out the values and dialectics described here clearly delegitimizes claims to private ownership that concentrate productive property and power in the hands of a few.

Relations set by cultural, personal, familial and authentically religious values guide, and are tested by, the implementation of vital and social values. If, for example, family/kin/friendship values are ignored, the lifelong fostering of the autonomy-mutuality dialectic becomes marginalized and distorted. Distorted autonomy reigns as individualism which assumes the form of divine right of property, as oppressive as the historical divine right of kings.[115] Economic theory is characterized by splits that have been structured into the global economy within public and private domains as well as splits between the practical, common-sense aspects of living and personal relations. Individual and community reliance on critical consciousness provides a key to break open this façade and to reorient the economy.

The integrative structure presented in chapter 6 offers a comprehensive grid on which to base evaluation and policy setting to offset the collapse and long-term social decline evident in today's dis-order and dis-economy. Giving full play to the aspects of each of the person, family/kin/friendship, community, culture and ecological interdependence, and implementing the range of values emphasized in this study, call for profound societal change. Such change must be based on willingness to ask fundamental questions regarding foundational structures and allocation of resources. The task is to subject practice to wider horizons of inclusion and integration.

Valuing family/kin/friendship and community, for example, means holding autonomy and mutuality, as well as the practical and interpersonal, in creative tension. This implies major shifts in several critical areas. Substantial, constructive research is needed to recentre economics, to establish public global regulation of excess capital and to create new measures and indicators of well-being or genuine progress. I indicate areas of concern related to each.

Recentering Economics

Valuing community and culture involve making the well-being of the earth community, not money, the centre of economics.[116] Henderson envisions economy as a subsystem of the larger biological system, that is, human beings in dynamic interaction with the energy and resources around them, conforming to similar cycles of decay and regeneration as do all biological systems.[117] Distorted economic practice destroys biological interdependence. The declining availability of energy and of natural resources is accelerated by exploitative use of it. Evolutionary availability of increasing differentiation of consciousness and wisdom is happening at the same time. These processes and their effects call for evaluation of public investment in industry and job creation, supporting those which create jobs in ecologically safe production of goods and services, such as in the garment industry. And this in the quantity and quality required first of all for domestic needs. International garment trade would fill in gaps left in domestic production and depend on respect for worker and environmental rights by trading partners. As indicated earlier in this chapter, key questions concern whether international trade, both for exports and imports, is the driving force of our economic policy or whether it is *part* of policy.[118]

Establishing Public Global Regulation of Excess Capital

Regular and massive creation of surplus capital by a privileged minority decisively shapes relations domestically and internationally.[119] Transnationalized processes of capital accumulation and relocation of production have remained largely unregulated. While shortage of capital is critical for the majority of the world's population, the abundance of idle capital in the hands of a few is a major cause of global economic instability in general and of control over garment production and retail practice in particular. Abundant capital in the hands of a few is not considered inflationary. Production of capital has become a power game, a social enterprise, based on a tangled web of relationships.[120] The direct challenge is to establish public international research, dialogue and decision making to assess and regulate the production and use of excessive idle capital, the stabilization of exchange rates through regulation of currency markets and of the links between the international flow of money and international trade.[121]

The area is extremely complex and urgently in need of open debate globally since falling rates of profits fuel global competition for high realization of total capital, purchase of raw materials and exploitation of both organized and unorganized labour. Capital has a profit-earning function for some. The Federal Reserve Board of New York found that only about 18 per cent of the one trillion dollars of daily foreign exchange transactions in New York, Tokyo and London support either international trade or investment.[122] The rest is speculation in which enormous volumes are purchased at low rates and sold higher for large overall profit. Since these operations threaten both financial stability and social democracy, limitations need to be set and enforced. Roy Culpeper emphasizes that stabilizing volatile currency markets urgently requires measures to regulate international currency exchanges through retail markets.[123] Security financiers and corporations often bypass banks in their transactions.

In *Turning the Tide: Confronting the Money Traders*, John Dillon and the Ecumenical Coalition for Economic Justice described the new stage of capitalism, financial or speculative capitalism, as well as the means and reasons for the huge transfer of wealth to a small financial elite.[124] The coalition urged international collaboration to institute a tax between 0.1 and 0.25 per cent on international transactions in order to discourage short-term investments. Initially proposed by Nobel prize recipient James Tobin, it is known as "the Tobin tax." The ECEJ explained three key areas for regulating speculative capital and redirecting it into useful and productive activities: (1) regulation of finance capital: a new United Nations conference on money and finance, the Tobin tax, a domestic financial transaction tax (FTT), international cooperation to lower interest rates, debt relief for less-developed countries, renegotiation of NAFTA; (2) national policies to regulate finance: changes to Bank of Canada policy, quantitative controls on capital flows, minimum periods for portfolio investments and regulation of derivatives; and (3) restoration of local control over investment capital: establishing pools of social capital, making banks' charters contingent on social responsibility and creating local currencies. With dialogue and solidarity, change is possible. These options are viable and the coalition invites other means. The point is that we have enough information to make judgements. Integrity requires that we also decide and act. Justice delayed is justice denied.

For the growing majority, lack of capital means that indebtedness accumulates exponentially. Marjorie Griffin Cohen highlights this as "the true significance of the subsistence sector in the whole process of capital accumulation" and applies it to productive relations in families wherever women's work is unrecognized in fiscal policy.[125] Canada's economic and social structures are becoming more divided in two principal socio-economic sectors, each embodying a different mode of production, and one dominating the other. The growth of the capital accumulation sector and the expansion of the infrastructural and institutional network serving it have increasingly diverted resources away from both the local population's basic needs and the infrastructure necessary to meet these needs. This same dualism causes and maintains the global division of labour and feeds on exploitation of difference. The inequalities in productivity and in the structures themselves expose the complexity and depth of the current crisis.

The well-being of the impoverished also depends on reform of international financial institutions. Although the International Monetary Fund (IMF) and World Bank (WB) control only 5 per cent of the international flow of currencies, their structural adjustment conditionalities for repayments and for new loans involve severe deprivation for nations as a whole and particularly for the poor within them.[126] In addition, they exert an inordinate power over nations' social and educational policies.[127] Both the IMF and the WB need to be vigorously reformed, including, as Stephen Lewis encourages, the establishment of an Economic Security Council of the United Nations if it would be established with full participation for member countries and not controlled by the G7.[128]

My concern is not to endorse any particular method. It is to highlight the desperate need of thorough, effective reform of international currency flows and of socio-economic decision making on both global and national scales. These are underlying structural causes of poverty and key components of the permanent recession in which Canada and other countries are held hostage by large corporations and financiers.[129] Elimination of exploitation of homeworkers globally requires public demand for social and economic policies designed with the well-being of people and the ecosystem at heart.

Codes of ethics and of conduct for corporations, financial institutions and government-related mechanisms must establish principles for just relations—principles connected with those most adversely affected by their transactions, and principles requiring transparency in accountability before international and national communities.[130] Implementation of these in turn must be monitored independently by groups whom workers trust.

The issue of control is extremely sensitive. We only need to remember that major garment retailers in Toronto, for example, lobbied the Ontario government not to introduce legislative changes for which the Homework Coalition was campaigning. The question of joint liability moved inquiry into examination of strategies and possibilities for legal support in provincial and in international law. Legalities are minimum standards and enforcement is still a problem. Legal does not necessarily mean ethical. Exploitation that escapes prosecution is still profoundly unethical.

After a two-year highly visible campaign by the Homework Coalition, retailers' advice was that the government should trust voluntary compliance. They said this even in the midst of continued abuse. This legislation was one small, practical example of the opportunity a government held to introduce democratic control over a structural cause of poverty, on the one hand, and large capital, on the other.

The reality was based on the might of the retailers, not on just principles. In this case, what could be achieved by a government in the midst of severe injustice took precedence over what ought to be done. The choice was expedient, given the power of those who dominate. A corporate assumption seemed to be that capital's claims were immutable while labour's rights were both on trial and open to negotiation. The Homework Coalition has been advised to continue a high-profile campaign because of strong, well-financed opposition.

Numerous relevant issues have been raised for public debate, such as the vast disparity in incomes/wealth of retailers, bankers and home-workers; control of capital that belongs to the community for job creation; and public allotment of subsidies and grants to transnationals.[131]

Creating New Measures and Indicators of Well-being or Genuine Progress

A major shift in perception of what is valuable, of the goals to be pursued and of the ways to measure collective progress toward these goals indicates an expanding horizon in the worldview of many around the globe.[132] National and global measures of progress are presently based on market activity, with exchange of money for goods, services and investments between households and businesses. Henderson explains:

> Until quite recently, few decision-makers worried about *fundamental* issues such as whether the entire economic process of pursuing industrial growth (as measured by increases in per capita Gross National Product and Gross Domestic Product) might be leading to *systematic* marginalization of the weak or whether nature could continue tolerating increasing human numbers and industrial activities.[133]

This accounting serves to enforce the status quo and prevailing assumptions in favour of macroeconomic industrial mindsets. David Crosby lists problems with current Gross Domestic Product systems. GDP, for example, is a war planners' tool to link defence production to the whole economy. It does not measure economic welfare. More diversity in measurement is urgently needed. Costs, benefits and investments are undifferentiated. Non-market costs, benefits and investments are underestimated and ignored. The cost side of damaging activities is recognized only as a market benefit. The question of the meaning and value of economic growth needs to be central.[134]

These measures are being evaluated in order to make the household, the environment and all undervalued work more visible in economic policy. The methods, extent and goals of data gathering are all being challenged. Serious critique of traditional indicators of wealth is leading to development of creative alternatives according to more comprehensive, evaluative indicators of well-being and of genuine progress.

New criteria distinguish economic factors which are actually deficits to the earth community as opposed to those which contribute to health and integration of the range of values. A system of implementing a Genuine Progress Indicator (GPI), for example, makes adjustment for depletion of natural resources, income distribution, household work and child care, changes in leisure time, level of underemployment, dependence on foreign assets and environmental damage.[135] Statistics Canada is researching behind closed doors the implications of using GPI. In Maurice Strong's assessment, "The Genuine Progress Indicator (GPI) which you are proposing would substantially enhance the economic climate for radical changes in the policies and expenditure priorities of government, and [would] facilitate society's shift to sustainable modes of development."[136]

Debate in economics now concerns inclusion of overlooked factors, locally and sectorally, adding gauges in order to direct feedback to decision makers quickly and accurately. Inappropriately collected raw data are creating statistical illusions and must now be repatterned.[137] In the reconceptualization of knowledge and values in the context of our interdependent biosphere, it becomes evident that one of the most critical errors of economic theory has been the omission of social and environmental costs, as well as of the informal, unpaid sectors from its models. This gap contrasts the inclusion of making money from money as an indicator of progress. Henderson calls for recognition of a reality principle: "the extent to which economic growth and profits, as we reach boundary conditions, are any more than anthropocentric figments of the imagination."[138]

Deciding what facts are relevant to analysis and to policy setting will continue to be central in re-envisioned economic theory. To do this with integrity, presently bypassed members of the community need to be significant participants. Basically, "we must shift our attention from modeling *content* (that is, the daily quantification of events and data) to modeling the wider *context* of these events and the overall *processes* involved."[139] As basic assumptions and conditions underlying contemporary crises are critiqued, knowledge is being restructured

into new trans-disciplinary policy tools, for example: from macroeconomics to "post-economic" policy studies including technology assessment, environmental impact statements, future studies, scenario building, cross-impact analyses, risk assessments, social impact studies and systems research—all with global, rather than national frameworks. As these new maps clarify the new terrain, new criteria for success and new indicators and measures of performance and development are emerging.[140]

This challenge of creating new conceptual tools makes amateurs of us all.

What is most urgent is that informed economists who are committed to economic justice focus their research and creativity on underlying, structural causes of poverty and offer steps leading to the implementation of alternatives. It is also time to expose publicly the deception that citizens cannot do anything about the situation. As Henderson points out, millions share these seemingly private perceptions of the dissonance in both rationale and choices within our culture.[141]

Such a reorientation to economic participation and responsibility within our culture of injustice meets with powerful resistance in view of the fact that "economists, particularly in the West, often equate democracy and human rights with the freedom of the marketplace, rugged individualism and the frontier."[142] The task at hand is to face "the politics of denial" with reconceptualization and major value shifts. The nature of the transition requires innovative interdisciplinary policy models that are multidimensional, non-linear and interactive in domestic and global interlinkages. Henderson explains that these policies and networks are "governed by positive feedback loops, which push many parts of the system over thresholds simultaneously."[143] New models must, therefore, be open to new, steadily evolving unanticipated structures.

Conclusion: Ethics, Sin and Grace

For *any* theological ethics to be authentically global, it needs to be fully inclusive of meanings, values and principles gleaned through dialogue among women of different classes, "racial"/ethnic groups, and nationalities.[144] This ethics will remain open, but a non-negotiable foundation is the social valuation of women. Feminist/womanist/mujerista socio-economic critiques are an essential service to explain what is missing and what is needed in mainstream values and policies. Marginalization of difference analysis invalidates any theory or practice in theological ethics that claims to be social.

For *any* economy to be ethical, it needs to be regarded as a subsystem serving the well-being of the earth and the poorest, as well as meanings, values and principles gleaned through dialogue among

women and others excluded by current systems. Feminist/"racial"/
difference categories reveal deep conflicts which have been masked
over. Implications are deep-seated for business interests; for example,
comparable pay for comparable work would significantly upset the
current sex/"race"/difference segregation of the labour force and
undermine the present approach to the economy. Justice for women
and personal/group moral autonomy challenge current social-eco-
nomic organization. Key issues revolve around the questions:

> 1. What is valuable under new conditions? and 2. *Who, what, when, why,
> where and how* to regulate or deregulate? This is because all economies are,
> in essence, sets of rules derived from various cultural value systems, which
> determine, in diverse ways, what goals are important and what activities
> and jobs are valuable in attaining these goals.[145]

Economies also both reflect and create priorities as to who is considered of value: "Indicators only *reflect* our innermost core values and
goals, measuring the development of our own understanding."[146] The
task at hand is to create policies based on the knowledge that all our
individual and group interests are intrinsically linked with the well-
being of the whole earth community. Internationally, we are now challenged to function cybernetically, incorporating at every decision level
the necessary feedback loops from those people and resource systems
affected by the original decisions.[147]

Relying on the importance of persons, families/kin/friendships,
communities, culture and ecological interdependence, and on the
range of values to inform ethical process, reveals the context in which
we determine the subsystems of economics and policy setting. If taken
in isolation, the latter are inadequate to resolve the depth of the cultural problems undermining the economic situations of homeworkers.
Causes of poverty for women are connected with ongoing resolution of
all the dialectics in concrete situations.

The ethical shift necessary for just socio-economic relations depends
on the quality of communities of differing persons-in-relation.[148]
Autonomy and mutuality both need to be given full interplay so that
subjects are in fact grounded individuals/groups-in-relation able to
assess, decide and act to effect justice. Cross-culturally generated cultural values depend on the differentiation, appropriation and integration of cross-cultural, intentional and psychic, personal and communal
integrity. Only then will the breadth of the differentiation of personal
and collective integrity match the proportions needed for the development of the inter- and intracultural values on a global scale.

It is certainly evident that overall, present global realities and what we deem as good do not coincide. The depth and long-standing complexity of the crises call for commitment to break the vicious circle of distortions prevalent within the living out of all values: vital, social, ecological, family/kin/friendship, personal, cultural and religious/spiritual. A major ethical task is to clarify our relationships within the context of an interdependent biosphere, to "decide who we would like to become, and then fashion an economy that will foster rather than impede individual and group projects of becoming."[149] The inquiry centres on what we want to go forward in history, in the movements of the direction in life.[150] Always, its base lies in actual realities.

The integrity that makes this possible is a deeply religious value. Integrity is intrinsically connected with the freeing of intentionality and psyche from bias and distortion in order to raise and answer related questions. It leads both to assessment of personal and social integration of the range of values and of non-negotiable key areas of persons, families/kin/friendships, communities, cultures and ecology, and to judgement, decision and action. The consequent justice is also a deeply religious value.

Without naming sin in religious language, I have elaborated aspects of sin as they are evident in decline. Sin is by omission and commission. Preserving the status quo of bias and distortion is sinful, first, by destroying the guiding attitudes, values and structure and cultural values and, second, by supporting theological and economic, political systems that perpetuate exploitation. Individuals and groups may not be aware of the implications of their actions and lifestyle. Since media, lobby groups and alternative sources of information offer ample evidence of the global and local situations, however, ignorance can certainly be culpable. As whole peoples and certainly as churches, we are challenged to foster social consciousness as a basis for personal and group conscience. The wealthy could choose to provide access, both to resources and to means of changing injustice in trade, finance and political decision making.

Doran situates sin and grace in terms of this discussion:

> Sin, then, is basically a refusal on the part of human intentionality itself to fulfill its radically personal, but also cultural and social responsibility to search for and find the direction in the movement of life. Grace awakens intentionality from that refusal. But sin has the consequence of introducing disorder also into the psyche, and distortions into the dialectics of culture and community ... [which are] mutually reinforcing. This mutual reinforcement

establishes ever more rigid schemes of recurrence in history limiting the
potential of the human spirit to raise and answer the right questions, and
binding its powers of effecting the changes that are required to set things
right at the [four] levels of personal, [familial], cultural and social value.[151]

Doran explains that grace is the source of intentionality's ability to
break the vicious circles of disorder and distortion that objectify sin in
human existence. Grace simultaneously promotes the mentality capable of providing a genuine alternative to present possibilities.[152] This
influences how we conduct all relations and all work. Theology's direct
discourse, for example, depends on the relative presence or absence of
conversion in the discoursing theologian(s). Theology is meant to be a
response to God's invitation to co-operate in effecting a solution to the
mystery of evil plaguing human communities. Being aware of God as
the very truth and term of relationship carries the possibility of an
expanding consciousness that we are constituted in a dynamic state of
being loved unconditionally and of being invited to love.[153]

From this perspective, God is working in us to awaken the very disclosure of just relations, to ground cross-culturally generated cultural
integrity and values, to inform a social dialectic of community and to
create genuine alternatives to the prevailing distortions. In addition to
awakening the normative order of inquiry to its spontaneous functioning, God invites retrieval of the very constitution of that normative
order of inquiry through self-appropriation. Attempts to articulate interiorly differentiated consciousness, and to promote it in oneself and in
others, proceed in collaborative partnership with God. They express
what God is doing in history within the range of human experience
that is structured in various degrees of compactness and differentiation
in different cultural epochs.

Call to conversion also concerns overcoming flight from understanding, especially in the flight evident in sexism, racism, wealthism
and all other forms of "supremacy." If this gift and invitation to conversion is available always and everywhere, it is specific and related to
what God bestows on us by nature, for women and men at every time
and place. According to this position, we are graced within creation
and the Spirit of God's profound being-in-relation-with-us is at the
heart of our existence. This intimate presence always calls us to the
God self. A constitutive part of this call is from bias and distortion to
just, inclusive, collaborative relations.[154] Recognition, identification
and celebration of just relations varies profoundly among individuals
and groups. The religious realm of meaning names the ultimate

concern in which we reach out for divine mystery. It explicitly acknowledges that the Spirit of God consistently reaches out for us. This mutuality establishes co-partnership in ongoing creation and healing in all relations, and is clearly more than cognitive illumination. Body-mind-spirit, individually and communally, is graced in the distinct gift of God's faithful, original and ongoing creation. Being-in-relationship with the divine is the source of transformative power. This knowledge strengthens and directs participation in a virtuous circle. Good theological discourse promotes the well-being of meaning itself, in this case of the meaning of grace, as the outer word of God in history. As such, it is praxis.[155]

It follows that all exclusion of and violence against any persons considered different from the prevailing norm of power is distortion and bias that hardens the heart and mind. The sins of sexism, racism and wealthism have introduced deep disorder into the collective consciousness. The consequent mutual reinforcement of disorder limits potential even to imagine broad-based solidarity as a theological imperative. It binds the powers needed to effect changes. Uncritical assimilation of cultural norms, values and patterns, for example, is more dangerous because it is lived unintentionally. Failure to understand the impact of the social transmission of moral codes hinders freedom to evaluate and create values.[156]

Interdependence of subjects and groups in diversity is a basis of social grace, solidarity and strength. Human beings develop one conscience, not a personal one and a separate social conscience added to it. This shapes all aspects of persons, families/kin/friendships, communities' social structure and relationships, cultures and ecology. Interiority and exteriority in touch with manifold strands of the cosmos meet in persons and groups in community. It follows that reflection on grace and the world cannot be separated, though we may distinguish specific aspects for clarity.[157]

Notes

1 Doran, *Theology and the Dialectics of History*, 355-56. I affirm basic principles to assist theological reflection about women's economic reality as they are set forth by Legge (*The Grace of Difference*, 105-106). I also concur with the basepoints and criteria to protect women's economic vulnerability and shape public policy as presented by Beverly Wildung Harrison, *Making the Connections*, xiv-xx, and Carol Robb, "A Framework for Feminist Ethics," in *Women's Consciousness, Women's Conscience*, ed. Barbara Hilkert Andolsen, Christine Gudorf and Mary Pellauer (San Francisco: Harper & Row, 1985), 213.

2 This transformation may be described as affective, intellectual, moral, psychic and religious conversion in personal and collective experience. Refer to extensive, indexed references throughout Lonergan, *Method in Theology*, and Doran, *Theology and the Dialectics of History*. I add bodily and social conversion, as does Doran.

3 Heuristic function: "Every inquiry aims at transforming some unknown into a known. Inquiry itself, then, is something between ignorance and knowledge. Heuristic devices consist in designating and naming the intended unknown, in setting down at once all that can be affirmed about it, and in using this explicit knowledge as a guide, a criterion, and/or a premise in the effort to arrive at a fuller knowledge" (Lonergan, *Method in Theology*, 22).

4 Bernard Lonergan, *Topics in Education*, vol. 10 of *The Collected Works of Bernard Lonergan*, ed. Robert Doran and Frederick Crowe (Toronto: University of Toronto Press for the Lonergan Research Institute, 1993), 28-29.

5 Michael Zweig, ed., *Religion and Economic Justice* (Philadelphia: Temple University Press, 1991), 27. Refer also to viii and 25-26.

6 Ibid., 21-27. Zweig refers to Nobel Prize in Economics winner Ken Arrow as well as Amartya Sen, who find no way to make sense out of social and economic policy by limiting one's view to the interests of those who hold power and wealth. See Kenneth Arrow, *Social Choice and Individual Values*, 2nd ed. (New Haven, CT: Yale University Press, 1963), 60, and Amartya K. Sen, *Collective Choice and Social Welfare* (San Francisco: Holden-Day and Oliver & Boyd, 1970), 36. They conclude that such practice is so restrictive that "they rule out not some *but every possible* social welfare function" (ibid., 36; emphasis in the original).

7 Zweig, *Religion and Economic Justice*, 43-44.

8 Of course I welcome further clarification and foregrounding of values and concerns. The four dialectics represent areas which I think must be brought forward into any alternative even if the method is quite different.

9 To those familiar with Marxist, socialist and ecclesial social justice analysis, the similarities and differences will be clear. While clearly valuing and relying on their historical contributions, it is not my purpose to focus on any of them mainly because I cannot include a critique of their shortcomings in the light of feminist concerns. Such studies are being done with thoroughness. See, for example, Sheila Kappler, "Women and Justice in the Teachings of the Canadian Catholic Bishops: Challenging the Categories" (Ph.D. diss., University of St. Michael's College, 1990); Patricia Jagentowicz Mills, *Woman, Nature, and Psyche* (New Haven, CT: Yale University Press, 1987); and O'Brien, "Feminist Praxis," 327-44.

10 *Clean Clothes Newsletter* (Amsterdam, The Netherlands) 1 (November 1993): 6.

11 Ecumenical Coalition for Economic Justice (ECEJ), "The Global Garment Industry: Industrial Model for the Future," *Economic Justice Report* 5, 1 (April 1994): 2. There was an international meeting of Asian home workers in India in January 1995.

12 Hazel Henderson, *Paradigms in Progress: Life Beyond Economics* (Indianapolis: Knowledge Systems, 1991), 72.

13 Refer to "Clean Clothes Campaign" (Amsterdam, The Netherlands, April 1993), and *Clean Clothes Newsletter* 1 (November 1993). For another extensive example of international networking, see Hans Küng, *Global Responsibility: In Search of a New World Ethic* (New York: Crossroad, 1991), 55-88. Küng addresses multiple problems to be confronted as world religions collaborate in search of a world ethic.

14 *Clean Clothes Newsletter* 1 (November 1993): 6. Wal-Mart's fiercely competitive approach alerted executives of the Hudson's Bay Company, who launched "an aggressive counter-attack strategy" to maintain the dominance which Zellers and the Hudson's Bay Company held. In the first quarter of 1994, sales of women's apparel was up 26 per cent over the same period last year and profit increased to $3.3 million. See Maureen Murray, "Hudson's Bay to Do Battle with Wal-Mart," *The Toronto Star*, 26 May 1994, B3. Refer to numerous Clean Clothes Campaigns on the Internet for updates on codes and action.

15 Henderson, *Paradigms in Progress*, 117.

16 Hazel Henderson, *Creating Alternative Futures: The End of Economics* (New York: Berkley Publishing , 1978), 374, and Henderson, *Paradigms in Progress*, 95, respectively. See also Henderson, *Creating Alternative Futures*, 48.

17 Ecumenical Coalition for Economic Justice, "Fifty-one Alternatives to NAFTA," *Economic Justice Report* 4, 1 (April 1993): 7.

18 Ibid., 7-8. See Szentes, *The Transformation of the World Economy*, 98-103, for an analysis of the U.N. New International Economic Order.

19 Henderson, *Paradigms in Progress*, 100-101.

20 See Women's World Congress for a Healthy Planet, Miami, FL, *Action Agenda 21*, 8-12 November 1991 (New York: Women's Environment and Development Organization, 1992), and "The Earth Charter" and numerous citizens' treaties agreed upon by Non-Governmental Organizations' Global Forum, Rio de Janeiro, during the United Nations Conference on Environment and Development (UNCED), 3-14 June 1992.

21 In January of 1993 in Ottawa, assemblies of both the Canadian Labour Congress and the Action Canada Network clarified issues of the Corporate Agenda and the People's Agenda and planned campaigns to continue the process across the nation.

22 Henderson, *Paradigms in Progress*, 106.

23 Doran, *Theology and the Dialectics of History*, 387.

24 Ibid., 387. Chapter 4, "The Integral Scale of Values," 93-107, presents the essential structure. "Vital values are the values conducive to health, strength, grace and vigour. Social values consist of a social order whose schemes of recurrence guarantee vital values to the whole community. Cultural values are the meanings, values, and orientations informing the living and operating of the community. Personal value is the authentic subject as originating value in the community. And religious value is the grace that enables the subject, the culture and the community to be authentic" (ibid., 94). Familial and ecological are my additions: familial values foster the provision of the affectivity, spirit of inquiry and articulation needed to support both individuation and development of social consciousness/conscience; ecological values lead

us to protect the interdependent ecosystem and ground humanity with the divergent forms of energy. I also alter the concept of scaling values because of the historical distortions resulting from dichotomizing some of these values over others in gender-specific ways to cause group and general bias. Robert Doran agreed with the need for creativity in this regard.

25 Ibid., 93.

26 Ibid., 94-97.

27 Ibid., 28-29, based on Bernard Lonergan, *A Third Collection*, ed. Frederick E. Crowe (New York: Paulist Press, 1985), 208: Apprehending values involves (1) emergence of consciousness, (2) awakening of senses and feelings, (3) inquiry, (4) discovery of a truth and (5) successive negotiation of stages of morality and/or identity, leading to decision to assume responsibility for our lives and world.

28 Ibid., 82-84, and Lonergan, *Insight*, 477-78.

29 Doran, *Theology and the Dialectics of History*, 442-44, adapted. In this brief concentration on limitation and transcendence, I adapt and expand Doran's work even as I rely on it as a foundation.

30 Ibid., 59-60. Censorship is repressive, however, when it blocks significant, unwanted data.

31 Ibid., 477.

32 Ibid., 495.

33 Ibid., 496. See also 480.

34 Ibid., 474.

35 Ibid., 362.

36 Lonergan, *Insight*, 228.

37 Doran, *Theology and the Dialectics of History*, 396.

38 Ibid., 475: "The neglect of culture precisely as link leads in the one case to an excessively spiritualistic or idealistic, and ultimately socially conservative, emphasis on the higher levels of the scale to the exclusion of distributive justice, and in the other case to a materialistic, anti-intellectual, and in the last analysis nihilistic neglect of the higher levels and a pneumopathologically exclusive attention to some vital values and to the instrumental pole of the dialectic of community." This is said within a context of explicit concern that basic vital needs are met.

39 Refer to Lonergan, *Topics in Education*, 28-29, and all of chapter 2.

40 Doran, *Theology and the Dialectics of History*, 401.

41 Ibid., 370.

42 A positive example of a decision to value participation is the Ontario government's hiring of a single mother and former social assistance recipient as an adviser on welfare issues to head the province's new council of consumers. See Kelly Toughill, "A Gleeful Thorn in Their Side," *The Toronto Star*, 4 February 1994, A19.

43 Refer to Lonergan, *Insight*, 564-66, and Doran, *Theology and the Dialectics of History*, 569-71.

44 Doran, *Dialectics*, 650. Refer to 650-80 for a more complete explanation and application of these key insights.

45 The required inter- and intracultural viewpoints and values are historical, concretely specific and significant for transformative praxis, not in abstrac-

tion, but by advancing to the specific, the differentiated, the precise and methodical. See Lonergan, *Insight*, 566-67, and Doran, *Theology and the Dialectics of History*, 572.

46 Lonergan, *Insight*, 582; Lonergan, *Method in Theology*, 57-100 (for a comprehensive analysis of meaning); and Doran, *Theology and the Dialectics of History*, 586.

47 Lonergan, *Method in Theology*, 73-78. See also Lonergan, *Insight*, 357, and Doran, *Theology and the Dialectics of History*, 573, 583.

48 See Doran, *Theology and the Dialectics of History*, 531-36, for a description of these differentiated expressions.

49 Ibid., 535.

50 Emilie Townes, "Critical Book Discussion: Kathryn Tanner, *The Politics of God: Christian Theologies and Social Justice* (Minneapolis: Fortress Press, 1992)," 4-5, presented at the Society of Christian Ethics' Thirty-fifth Annual Meeting, 7-9 January 1994, Chicago, IL.

51 Doran, *Theology and the Dialectics of History*, 529. Refer to the chart given earlier in this chapter for an adaptation and expansion of these transcendental, ethical imperatives.

52 Ibid., 575-76.

53 Wildung Harrison, *Making the Connections*, 39.

54 Ibid., 253.

55 Ibid.

56 Ruth Smith, "Feminism and the Moral Subject," in *Women's Consciousness, Women's Conscience*, ed. Barbara Hilkert Andolsen, Christine Gudorf and Mary Pellauer (San Francisco: Harper & Row, 1985), 242.

57 See Lonergan, *Insight*, chap. 12.

58 Ibid., 348-49.

59 Ibid., 553.

60 See Lonergan, *Insight*, 388.

61 Ibid., 632, based on ibid., 558.

62 Doran, *Theology and the Dialectics of History*, 68. Foregrounding body consciousness in this context is my addition.

63 Ibid.

64 Ibid., 43, referring to chap. 11 of Lonergan, *Insight*, 319-38. This is the basis for fostering emerging interiorly differentiated consciousness.

65 Doran, *Theology and the Dialectics of History*, 626-37. If operations of interiorly differentiated consciousness recur regularly and may continue to recur in our time, a new epoch or axial shift in history is emerging.

66 Doran describes psychic conversion as "conversion to attentiveness in that stream of sensitive consciousness, to internal communication, to responsible activity in regard to neural demands, to an openness to negotiate them persuasively and patiently" (ibid., 85).

67 Ibid., 640, and Lonergan, *Method in Theology*, 292.

68 Doran, *Theology and the Dialectics of History*, 655.

69 Ibid., 646, and Bernard Lonergan, "The Ongoing Genesis of Methods," in *A Third Collection*, 157-58.

70 Doran, *Theology and the Dialectics of History*, 679. See also 660.

71 Refer to Maart, "Consciousness, Knowledge and Morality," 129-70, and Rozena Maart, "Speaking Up, Speaking Out," in *A Reader in Feminist Ethics*, ed. Debra Shogan (Toronto: Canadian Scholars' Press, 1993).

72 Signs of significant social progress are arising to counteract major social decline—a stirring example of emergent probability.

73 Doran, *Theology and the Dialectics of History*, 644.

74 Ibid., 647.

75 Refer to Lonergan, *Insight*, 192; Lonergan, *Method in Theology*, 30-40, 51-52, 240-43, 270-71; and Doran, *Theology and the Dialectics of History*, 35-63, 171-76, 246-53, 548-50, 640-42. Doran adds psychic conversion to Lonergan's affective, intellectual, moral and religious conversions. I add social and bodily conversion.

76 Wildung Harrison makes the point succinctly: "Our agency or action is set within ongoing temporal-historical processes and webs of interrelations. From this perspective, an analysis is theological if, and only if, it unveils or envisions our lives as a concrete part of the interconnected web of all our social relations, including our relations to God" (*Making the Connections*, 245).

77 Doran, *Theology and the Dialectics of History*, 381.

78 Ibid., 159.

79 Lonergan, *Method in Theology*, 302.

80 Doran, *Theology and the Dialectics of History*, 529. Lonergan also stresses the "charged field of love and meaning" as the basis for affective conversion, and being-in-love as rooting the history of salvation (*Method in Theology*, 290-91).

81 Bernard Lonergan, "Natural Right and Historical Mindedness," in *A Third Collection*, 172.

82 Lonergan, *Method in Theology*, 292.

83 Doran, *Theology and the Dialectics of History*, 380-81, quoting Lonergan, *Insight*, 743. I emphasize that my acceptance of normative is based on Lonergan's own breadth of understanding clarified above.

84 Henderson, *Paradigms in Progress*, 144. See also 261.

85 Refer to Vannoy Adams, *The Multicultural Imagination*, 33-58.

86 The challenge for theology, according to Doran, is, first, "to achieve a disclosure of reality that at its roots is universal, normative, and endowed with cross-cultural validity, yet that respects cultural particularity and cultural relativity, the polycentrism of cultural communities, and the specificity of cultural traditions. The second is an ethical and political challenge to participate in world-transformative praxis" (*Theology and the Dialectics of History*, 460).

87 I extend Pamela Brubaker's criteria for illuminating women's economic vulnerability to include exploitation based on any difference. See Pamela K. Brubaker, "Economic Justice for Whom? Women Enter the Dialogue," in *Religion and Economics*, ed. Michael Zweig (Philadelphia: Temple University Press, 1991), 115.

88 Brubaker, for example, claims that "neither Roman Catholic nor World Council liberation theology and ethics adequately address the economic vulnerability of women. Furthermore, their understandings of human

nature and social organization distort women's moral agency in ways that deny full human liberation to women" (ibid., 99).

89 See Wildung Harrison, *Making the Connections*, 8.

90 Brubaker, "Economic Justice for Whom?" 115.

91 Ibid., 119, referring also to bell hooks, *Feminist Theory: From Margin to Center* (Boston: South End Press, 1984), 103.

92 In another book in progress, I include poetry and a series of paintings on the themes of darkness and of blood.

93 Lee Cormie, "On the Option for the Poor and Oppressed in Doing Social Ethics," *Toronto Journal of Theology* 7, 1 (1991): 27, 31. Refer to Code, *What Can She Know?* 265-313, for an analysis of epistemic privilege and the difficulty welfare recipients have in gaining even small bits of information. Code describes the Poverty Game, designed by six women who receive social assistance in British Columbia.

94 Henderson, *Paradigms in Progress*, 263.

95 Refer to Bernard Lonergan, "An Essay in Circulation Analysis: Revised Manuscript" (Boston College, Spring 1983), 79-86, unpublished manuscripts, The Lonergan Research Institute, Toronto, ON; and to Philip McShane, "An Improbable Christian Vision and the Economic Rhythms of the Second Millennium Years," 14-28, unpublished manuscripts, the Lonergan Research Institute, Toronto, ON.

96 Thomas Kopfensteiner, "Globalization and the Autonomy of Moral Reasoning: An Essay in Fundamental Moral Theology," *Theological Studies* 54, 3 (September 1993): 489.

97 Ibid., 490-91.

98 Ibid., 499-500.

99 Lonergan, "The Ongoing Genesis of Meaning," 160-61.

100 This characterization is evident even in the daily press. See Trish Crawford, "Fed-up Parents Unite to End School Violence," *The Toronto Star*, 23 May 1994, A1, 6. The subtitle on A6 is "Pupils Exposed to 'Culture of Violence.'"

101 Albert Nolan, "Taking Sides," *Scarboro Missions* (June 1985): 17.

102 Samuel Bowles and Herbert Gintis, "The Economy Produces People: An Introduction to Post-Liberal Democracy," in *Religion and Economics*, ed. Michael Zweig (Philadelphia: Temple University Press, 1991), 221.

103 Bowles and Gintis, "The Economy Produces People," 222. They press for democratic culture, "the broadest possible diffusion among the citizens of politically relevant information, skills, and attitudes of political effectiveness, as well as the availability of forms of discourse conducive to the effective functioning of democratic institutions" (ibid., 229).

104 Ibid., 230.

105 Refer to chapter 3 of this study.

106 Frances Moore Lappé and J. Baird Callicott, "Individual and Community in Society and Nature," in *Religion and Economics*, ed. Michael Zweig (Philadelphia: Temple University Press, 1991), 248.

107 Hazel Henderson, "The Electronic Revolt," *The Toronto Star*, 29 November 1992, B1, 7.

108 Bowles and Gintis, "The Economy Produces People," 234. I rely on and develop their logic in this paragraph.

109 Szentes, *The Transformation of the World Economy*, 86.

110 Marjorie Griffin Cohen, "The Razor's Edge Invisible: Feminism's Effect on Economics," presented to the Women's Studies Program, University of Toronto, 25 February 1985, 1. An increasing number of men share broader horizons and call for such a reorientation as well.

111 Doran, *Theology and the Dialectics of History*, 555.

112 Bowles and Gintis, "The Economy Produces People," 232-33. See also Amata Miller: "In an interdependent world the current structures are clearly dysfunctional. Massive flows of capital ordered by invisible investors can dramatically shift the resource and employment base of nations without taking responsibility for effects" ("Global Economic Structures: Their Human Implications," in *Religion and Economics*, ed. Michael Zweig [Philadelphia: Temple University Press, 1991], 168).

113 David Langille, "Exposing the Face of Corporate Rule" (Toronto: Jesuit Centre for Social Faith and Justice, 1996). The poster includes photos of the hundred and charts corporation ownership or control, assets, revenue, profit, real tax rate, number of employees and job layoffs, chief executive officer salary and compensation (Langille, "Exposing the Face of Corporate Rule"). Auxiliary Bishop J.S. Knight sent a letter to all parish priests of the Catholic archdiocese of Toronto, banning the poster because it "targets individuals in ways which may alienate them from their communities and which may place them or their family members at risk." Or does the public information simply speak of their existing alienation from communities through excessive capital accumulation in one year? Refer to Leslie Scrivener, "Church Bans Poster Naming Top Earners" and "Executive Salaries Called Unfair to Workers," *The Toronto Star*, 1 February 1997, A3 and K14.

114 Langille, "Exposing the Face of Corporate Rule."

115 Henderson, *Creating Alternative Futures*, 25. See also 14-16, 22.

116 Michael Barrett Brown, *Fair Trade: Reform and Realities in the International Trading System* (Atlantic Highlands, NJ: Zed Books, 1993), 190.

117 Henderson, *Creating Alternative Futures*, 119.

118 Refer to Marjorie Griffin Cohen, "Exports, Unemployment, and Regional Inequality: Economic Policy and Trade Theory," in *The New Era of Global Competition*, ed. Daniel Drache and Meric Gertler (Montreal and Kingston: McGill-Queen's University Press, 1991), 84.

119 This is a major theme developed by Szentes, *The Transformation of the World Economy*, and by Howard Wachtel, *The Money Mandarins: The Making of a Supranational Economic Order* (New York: Pantheon Books, 1986). See also Joyce Kolko, *Restructuring the World Economy* (New York: Pantheon Books, 1988).

120 See Henderson, *Creating Alternative Futures*, 77. On the morning after the Canadian federal election, the *Globe and Mail* business section featured headlines and a "wake-up call from the international financial community" noting that it is monitoring the re- (or new) appointment of the governor of the Bank of Canada, any economic statement or budget the government might set and a deficit reduction plan: "We'll buy your bonds, all right. But before we decide what price you'll have to pay for it (that's rate of interest,

by the way), we'd like to hear some answers to those questions ... quickly"
(Bruce Little and Alan Freeman, "So, What's the Plan, Mr. Chrétien?" *The Globe and Mail*, 26 October 1993, B1.

121 Wachtel, *The Money Mandarins*, 206-11, 219. Unstable exchange rates are a major cause of high interest rates which reduce economic growth and prevent debt payments. International governments could agree to coordinate implementation of lower average interest rates. Refer to the ECEJ, *Debt Bondage or Self-Reliance*, 8-19, and the Ecumenical Coalition for Economic Justice (ECEJ), *The Halifax Initiative: Beyond 50 Years*, A Kit for Popular Use (Toronto: ECEJ, 1995).

122 As reported by Howard Wachtel, "Taming Global Money," in *Beyond Bretton Woods: Alternatives to the Global Economic Order*, ed. John Cavanagh, Daphne Wysham and Marcos Arruda (Boulder, CO: Pluto Press, with Institute for Policy Studies, Washington and the Transnational Institute, Amsterdam, 1994), 74.

123 Roy Culpeper, "Agenda for Development," response to Stephen Lewis' speech given at the Canadian Conference on United Nations Reform, Montreal, 23-25 March 1995.

124 Dillon and the ECEJ, *Turning the Tide*, 93-118. Refer also to Ecumenical Coalition for Economic Justice, "Ethical Reflections on the MAI," *Economic Justice Report* 9, 1 (March 1998). James Tobin, guest speaker at a Canadian Centre for Policy Alternatives Seminar, National Arts Centre, Ottawa, 29 May 1995, Transcript: 5-6. Tobin both explains the principles and management of the tax and counters objections to it. Making it universal with full participation of the G7 and OECD countries is important. Refer also to David Felix, "The Tobin Tax Proposal: Background, Issues and Prospects," a policy paper commissioned by the United Nations Development Program for the World Summit for Social Development: UNDP Human Development Report Office (New York: United Nations, 1994). John Dillon suggests that US$80 billion annually of the approximately $302 billion revenue from such a financial transaction tax could be applied to eradicate poverty, a goal agreed upon by nations at the United Nations Social Summit in Copenhagen in 1995. Refer to Ecumenical Coalition for Economic Justice, "Jubilee 2000: Time for Debt Remission," *Economic Justice Report* 8, 4 (December 1997): 11.

125 Griffin Cohen, "The Razor's Edge Invisible," 18-19. Women's labour is often subsistence production, considered outside of market economy even as it remains critical to capital accumulation. See also Laurie Monsebraaten, "Poverty Stalking Young Families," *The Toronto Star*, 25 May 1994, A1, 6, for evidence of this process for parents under 35 "in recent good times and in bad."

126 Robert Browne, for example, assesses current conceptual inadequacies and structural and operational deficiencies of the IMF. He looks for alternatives that include a neutral reserve currency, democratic voting not controlled by the G-7 nations, a mechanism to stabilize exchange rates (within ranges) and to provide macroeconomic direction for the global economy, public participation and adequate transparency and long-term solutions. All of this requires extensive, deep sensitivity to the social and political realities

within countries. The present flow of capital from the Third World to G-7 nations needs to be reversed. Refer to Robert Browne, "Alternatives to the International Monetary Fund," in *Beyond Bretton Woods*, ed. John Cavanagh, Daphne Wysham and Marcos Arruda (Boulder, CO: Pluto Press, with Institute for Policy Studies, Washington, and the Transnational Institute, Amsterdam, 1994), 57-73 and all of section three regarding the World Bank.

127 Refer to José Luis Coraggio, "Human Capital: The World Bank's Approach to Education in Latin America," in *Beyond Bretton Woods: Alternatives to the Global Economic Order*, edited by John Cavanagh, Daphne Wysham and Marcos Arruda (Boulder, CO: Pluto Press, with Institute for Policy Studies, Washington, and the Transnational Institute, Amsterdam, 1994), 166-71.

128 Stephen Lewis, "Agenda for Development," speech given at the Canadian Conference on United Nations Reform, Montreal, 23-25 March 1995.

129 Jim Stanford, "Economy Being Kept in Permanent Recession," article adapted from a speech and published by the Canadian Centre for Policy Alternatives in *Monitor* 1, 10 (April 1995): 1. Stanford charts statistics of averages contrasting 1950-80 and 1981-94 for interest rates, unemployment and growth rates, wages and share of capital in the GDP.

130 Government intervention is a crucial part of such reform. Chile, Japan and Germany have controlled incoming flows of investment to their long-term advantage. Chile taxed incoming money with a transaction tax of 1.5 per cent. It is less difficult to monitor flows for entry than for withdrawal. Based on Tobin, Canadian Centre for Policy Alternatives Seminar, 10, and Culpeper, "Agenda for Development."

131 Konrad Yakabuski, "'Big Six' Bank Chiefs Take Home $6 Million," *The Toronto Star*, 10 December 1993, A1, A8, and Konrad Yakabuski, "At $800,000, Is This Man Underpaid?" *The Toronto Star*, 10 December 1993, D1. The subtitle reads, "Yes, Analysts Say. First-rate Scotiabank Chief Makes Far Less than Rivals." Allan Taylor of the Royal Bank pocketed a $950,000 salary in 1992.

132 Henderson, *Paradigms in Progress*, 147.

133 Ibid., 29. See Marilyn Waring, *If Women Counted: A New Feminist Economics* (New York: Harper & Row, 1988). Waring exposes the basis and fault of the present global system of accounting and offers new directions. "GDP measures *domestic* production, that which occurs within the borders of the country, regardless of who owns the units of production. The GNP, on the other hand, measures *national* production, that which provides income to the citizens of the country, regardless of whether that production occurs inside or outside of the country" (David Crosby, "A Genuine Progress Indicator for Canada: An Alternative to Growth as a Measure of Progress," in *Alternative Federal Budget 1997 Papers*, ed. Canadian Centre for Policy Alternatives and Choices: A Coalition for Social Justice [Ottawa: CCPA, 1997], 372.

134 Ibid., 377, 378.

135 Ibid., 387.

136 Maurice Strong at the United Nations' Conference on Environment and Development, Rio de Janeiro, 1992, as quoted in ibid., 391.

137 Henderson, *Creating Alternative Futures*, 139-40.

138 Ibid., 144.

139 Henderson, *Paradigms in Progress*, 23.

140 Ibid., 41. For example, Japan's Net National Welfare, The Overseas Development Council's Physical Quality of Life Index and the Basic Human Needs indicator, developed by the U.N. Environment Programme. Refer to ibid., 147-92.

141 Ibid., 18.

142 Ibid., 7.

143 Ibid., 17. See Plate 1-2: Two Cybernetic Systems.

144 Brubaker, "Economic Justice for Whom?" 117.

145 Henderson, *Creating Alternative Futures*, 89. Marketplace competition, for example, is simply not an adequate foundation to deal with a shift from obsolescence/innovation cycles to durability and overall optimization.

146 Ibid., 189.

147 Henderson, *Paradigms in Progress*, 117.

148 Doran, *Theology and the Dialectics of History*, 467. Additions regarding community and difference are mine, in keeping with the overall intentions of *Theology and the Dialectics of History*.

149 Bowles and Gintis, "The Economy Produces People: An Introduction to Post-Liberal Democracy," 223.

150 See Doran, *Theology and the Dialectics of History*, 521. See also 555. The transposition of the explanation is mine.

151 Ibid., 523. The additions are mine from a feminist, liberationist stance.

152 Ibid., 524-28.

153 See Robert Doran, "Consciousness and Grace," *Method: Journal of Lonergan Studies* 11 (1993): 72-75.

154 Refer to Karl Rahner, *Foundations of Christian Faith* (New York: Crossroad, 1984), 34-35; Boff, *Liberating Grace*, 40-46; Juan Luis Segundo, *Grace and the Human Condition* (Maryknoll, NY: Orbis, 1973), 30-35; Jean-Marc Laporte, *Patience and Power* (New York: Paulist Press, 1987), 232, 241.

155 Doran, *Theology and the Dialectics of History*, 629.

156 Boff, *Liberating Grace*, 38.

157 Ibid., 30.

Conclusion

Conclusion

Carefully linked world watch
Sun fed threads
Sure strong power
Surrounding with silk sun.

I now link several strands from the webs I have analyzed in order to convey some of my conclusions about realities of injustice and about opportunities for solidarity.

Location of Ethical Discourse and Norms of Justice Making

Taking the perspectives of homeworkers and of those in solidarity with them opens up an inquiry of socio-economic relations from outside the ruling apparatus and from outside formally recognized economic theory. My perspective is also that of a consumer demanding justice in the clothing chain of production. I stress the importance of knowledge that assumes we are part of and responsible for the world which we explore and institutionalize. Instead of organizing knowledge based on a body of discourse in which issues have crystallized, and in which concepts assume an independent authority more significant than their speakers or readers, I have sought to open up the experience of women almost invisible within theological, ethical discourse, that is, of homeworkers and consumers in Toronto. I have pursued the

---

Notes to Conclusion are on pp. 288-89.

problematic according to the inquiry this reality raises for me. The socio-
economic ethics I suggest is at home and makes sense in this context. It
can be tested in other contexts. The processes and the questions I raise
about both socio-economic relations and theological praxis apply to
many other enterprises. With Dorothy Smith, who has provided a social
theory helpful for my task, I see the possibility of going beyond one particular group, such as homeworkers, to explore the relations of ruling
and the relations of capital. This process depends on

> discovering from within the expanded relations that contain, organize and
> provide the dynamic interconnections linking our one-sided knowledge of
> our own existence into a larger knowledge of a historical process in which
> we are active and to which we are captive.[1]

This standpoint shifts the location of discourse from vested interests of
transnational corporations and financiers, whose authority is considered
normative in our culture. By unmasking the ideology that keeps
women's concerns invisible and outside the decision-making process, I
press the norms for justice beyond the shape they have taken in our
recent capitalist economic history to those that require socio-institutional
change.

These strategies clearly do not transform in and of themselves.
They offer a way to raise consciousness and hence change even the
way we create and use texts. These texts remain merely academic,
however, if they are not grounded in relations of solidarity to give
voice to homeworkers and to provide understanding of relations which
determine women's lives.[2] Confronting the dis-economy and cultural
dis-ease calls for concerted bold strategizing and action. The very
stones cry out for a tidal wave of just relations.

Difference and Specificity Analysis Intrinsic to Theological Praxis

As horizons expand, it becomes increasingly evident that
assigning hierarchical meanings to difference and specificity and then
using such ranking to maintain public/private roles and the global division of labour are symptoms of major social decline.[3] Power and property have become lodged as immutable rights to further privilege of
every kind. In such a culture of injustice, both personal and collective
agency have been destroyed. Global exploitation is justified by negating
the value of persons while denying dependence on them. By introducing
distortion in all the relations of subjects, of family/kin/friendships, of

community, of culture and of ecological interdependence, domination limits potential to raise and answer significant questions. It paralyzes power for change. The depth of the crisis is revealed in the dual system which has emerged in Canada. It is controlled by a capital-accumulating sector which diverts resources from the infrastructure and institutional network. All the rest form the second sector. Having put forth deep roots in personal and collective psyches, individualism has been structured into societal horizon and rationalized, thereby undermining the very foundations of social ethics and of the range of values needed for transformation.

Reality and what we judge to be just and good do not coincide. A radically expanded value system is needed, one that moves beyond words to be inclusive of actual global and local realities. This requires a shift away from regarding capital's claims as immutable in order to recognize the significance of claims made by the working poor and unemployed. A crucial task is to establish personal and group agency and communal responsibility as operative norms, thereby reversing the status quo. Individualism is on trial. Social consciousness and social conscience are the norm.

A significant conclusion arising from my research is that feminist/ "racial"/specificity analysis is a non-negotiable foundation for ethics. Foregrounding specificity analysis significantly impacts theological socio-economic ethics by revealing gender, "race" and wealth subtexts that operate to advantage the dominant. It has become clear to me that the public/private split prevails in cultural attitudes and social organization, role expectations and division of labour, as well as in theological underpinnings. This split is at the heart of concerns I raise, as are the controlling grips of sexism, racism and empire building to sustain wealthism and "supremacy." Thus, conscious analysis of these is critical to reveal the extent to which texts, policies and theological ethics are gender-"racial"-economic, gender-"racial"-political and gender-"racial"-theological. Such relations function to justify existing structures which in fact perpetuate injustice for women. The present system expresses acceptance of inequalities embodied in institutions. The inequalities are then used to control participation, decision making and communication systems that justify dominance and exploitation. Even the categories of thought and expression are defined so that what is regarded valid and socially acceptable serves the purposes of those who rule. As a result, the majority share morality expressed in the vested interests of a societal minority, and this is passed on uncritically to their own detriment.

Devaluation according to sex, "race" or any other specificity violates the very essence of personal and communal identity. In the context of the undifferentiated universalism of the global economy, an inquiry as to how we want to go forward in history surfaces issues of how we apprehend values and of what preferences we assign to them; issues of networking; and, within and undergirding all of these, profound appreciation of specificity and differences. Authentic socioeconomic relations require transformation of our market-based vision and value systems and of our definitions of what is meaningful. Such transformation calls for profound conversions, including making the relevance of difference and specificity visible in imagery, in the division of labour, in cultural praxis, in public policy setting and in theological endeavour. These shifts impact how we express societal and cosmological relations. In practice, expression and shifts in inner meaning influence each other, hopefully to create virtuous cycles that can replace vicious circles.

Revealing meaning and values as they are embodied in subtexts and in effects is essential to theological analysis. This means that theologians will employ two sets of categories: a first set emerges from the theologian's dialogue with an interpreted tradition according to the religious, moral, intellectual and psychic development of the theologian herself/himself.[4] A second set of categories provided by feminist/womanist social analysis and reoriented economics also informs authentic judging and decision making. Theology integrates both special categories to name God's gifts appropriately to emergent humanity and general categories shared with social theory and economics. Theology's contribution is the fruit of theologians' objectification of religious, moral, intellectual and affective integrity. Social theory, theology and economics each offer distinctive information and formation. Their impact on each other is also foundational to the extent that authenticity in each discipline is directly related to integration of basic, reoriented tenets of the others.

To clarify and strengthen my conclusion that taking the second set of categories seriously in doing theology involves recognition of sexism, racism and wealthism as structures of injustice, I cite three examples. The first is the fact that, although the World Council of Churches recognized the relevance of such analysis in Nairobi in 1975, in Vancouver in 1983 and in Harare in 1998, it is still hesitant to criticize patterns of family organization.[5] Sacralization of family/kin/friendships has prevented our culture from taking these relationships seriously as an area of social justice. In what amounts to a socialized conspiracy of silence, these relationships are too often denied both legal protection and adequate economic support.[6] Revealing injustice is not the source of conflict. In fact, silence in the face of devaluation of women perpetuates deep-seated tensions. It may in fact signal bias and distortion and departure from the God of the oppressed.[7] Disturbing surface waters may simply indicate deeply graced currents. Faith communities' historical mission includes that of an intellectual, theological ministry which evokes conversion to offset this decline.

Another example of silencing is seen in the fact that, although the Ecumenical Decade of the Churches in Solidarity with Women (1988-98) aimed to empower women "to challenge oppressive structures in the global community, their country and their church," the family was not named in its official goals. A Korean Decade project, however, focused on challenging oppressive family structures.

Third, mystification of women's work undermines other ecclesial justice efforts, such as Catholic promotion of a "just wage," with a just wage being a family wage with no assurance of access for women and their dependents (young and old).[8] Traditional definitions that limit family to nuclear relations of a husband, wife and offspring are inadequate economically and socially since they do not recognize the reality of millions. Without explicit concern for socio-economic vulnerability and its link with family structure, injustice is institutionalized. Domestic work, homework and mothering are spiritualized, sacralized or idealized. Women's specific needs and concerns, such as for shared parenting and for access to land, credit and support systems, are systemically ignored. Realities named by special theological categories need to be mediated with the realities named by feminist/"racial" socio-economic categories.[9] Each informs the other.

Theological discourse involves critical interpretation of the real world of tradition and the situation. This interpretive task in turn depends on personal and communal orientation to religious, moral, social, cultural, cognitive and affective integrity.[10] Integrity arises from self and communal appropriation that is rooted in religious, psychic, social, bodily, intellectual and moral conversions. I maintain that the praxis of transformation carries possibilities for the generation and integration of appropriation, of conversions and of ethical, theological discourse. In terms of my study, theologians are challenged to engage in transformative praxis by: (1) fostering conditions for the self and communal appropriation of wisdom/justice-making tradition and of

cultural transformation, particularly regarding sexism, racism and
wealthism; (2) taking leadership in being open to conversion, for
example, by engaging in feminist/"racial"/empire issues; (3) contributing to the cultural transformation of constitutive meaning at the levels
of both the guiding values and the infrastructure in everyday meanings
and values, particularly in reference to exclusion by hierarchical ranking of difference; and (4) assisting in social transformation through
broad-based solidarity involving interaction, dialogue and reflection
beyond traditional communication boundaries.[11] Such praxis effects
change in cultural, social and theological constitutive meaning.

Feminist/"racial"/empire critique of the relations of ruling is an
essential service to explain aspects of what is missing and what is
needed in mainstream values and policies. Marginalization of femi-
nist/"racial"/empire analysis, or of other difference/specificity analysis,
invalidates claims to be social in any praxis. The lack of implementation of justice for women is evidence that our very cultural vision is
flawed. Such is the context in which we do contemporary Christian
theology.

Constructing Domestic Just Relations

The challenge is to discover how mutuality, social consciousness and responsible agency can operate in a predominantly unjust culture, and to incorporate them consistently to effect healing of the injustice at its roots: in our collective psyche, images, values and choices of
priorities. Shaping a new understanding of culture and power relations
in all dimensions of society is a deeply ethical issue involving profound
reorientation of social structures. This involves re-construction of relations of the domestic core of society in national, political, economic
and societal concerns.[12] The current trend to shift market functions
and state responsibilities to privatized solutions bypasses important
relations among households, commercial and state economies. Increasingly, family/kin/friendships are expected to assume responsibility for
cycles both of production and of reproduction. This practice threatens
to isolate and impoverish even further. Adequate, publicly subsidized
care of children, elders, the sick and handicapped belongs on the public agenda. Solutions need to be broad enough to allow choices
between remunerated home care and institutional care. Employment
and housing for young and older adults are public issues requiring
public accountability. Child poverty is as well. Governments, corporations and citizens' groups all have responsibility to ensure transparency

and accountability. All are needed in the formulation, supervision and enforcement of codes of conduct (or codes of ethics).

Almost excessive association of women's experience with the private has been used to keep women's issues off the public agenda and to delegitimize them. At the same time, women's work largely constitutes the material base of patriarchy. The public/private split embodies and perpetuates capitalist organization. This reality leads me to re-emphasize the significance of implementing an integral framework for societal organization in order to foreground various foundational elements in relation to the others: of the person or subject: body, psyche and spirit; of family/kin/friendships: agency and mutuality; of community: intersubjectivity and practicality; and of culture: cosmology and anthropology. Distortion of any aspect of these dialects affects them all. Contribution to the healthy functioning of any one of them in relation to the others strengthens the whole.

Societal structures have neglected family/kin/friendships, for example, with the historical effect of leaving lifelong formation in personal agency/individuation and mutuality/social consciousness largely invisible and unattended, at least as a societal issue. Lack of agency manifests itself in patterns of inferiority, persistent inadequacy and powerlessness, as well as the promotion of invisibility as a social virtue. These distortions support the status quo to maintain present domination. As such, they may also be evidence of a consumer mentality, of a mindset that accepts uncritically the inevitability of present relations as suggested by market forces. Agency and social consciousness on personal and communal levels are intimately linked to each other. Their reversals are critical here. Both insecurity caused by lack of individuation and inability to conceive of collective consciousness directly impact capacity to appreciate difference and specificity. Focus on agency and mutuality while foregrounding difference and specificity analysis expands the basis for social criticism and theological ethics.

In view of the need to transform the context of women's work, I return to the question of legislation for homeworkers' rights in Ontario. Legislation alone will not solve the problem. It is, however, a concrete place to raise the issues and to press for retailer responsibility. At least as significant is the establishment of national, publicly funded, quality child/dependent care as a vital component of social structure. Effecting just relations in these concrete campaigns calls for solidarity of churches, unions, community and anti-poverty groups, of all who seek justice for women by counteracting structural causes of poverty.

Coalition building and social movements, like the Homework Coalition, the Homeworkers' Association, interchurch coalitions, international homeworkers' gatherings, the Metro Network for Social Justice, the Ontario Coalition for Social Justice and the Council of Canadians, are keys to how we can move forward in justice research, education and action. Such solidarity is also significant for theological praxis by expanding its base, horizon, analysis and especially its power to transform community. Since values must be actualized to be fully known, praxis grounds religious values. Relating with people of differing cultural, "racial" and religious perspectives in specific projects also serves to challenge operative biases and distortions.

Genuinely Concerned Corporate Business Personnel and Financiers

What might corporate elites and financiers who are genuinely interested in the well-being of those affected by their decisions and by their amassing of wealth do? Many of good will may in fact be troubled. Trusting that God's Spirit is at work in them in their unrest, I encourage them to seek out groups with whom they can reflect and engage in open, respectful dialogue. Dialogue not just about charitable donations. Dialogue about the system, how it works and what it means. Dialogue about their values. Shaping spirituality and ethics for those in big business and finance is also a work of establishing just relations, whether we rely on a faith context or not.

Global Relations of Solidarity to Counteract Global Relations of Injustice

The call to be justice makers is increasingly urgent with a task at hand far greater than any groups can achieve on their own. The mission of transformation requires collaboration within and beyond traditional ecclesial and political boundaries, and within and beyond both denominational and interfaith unity.[13] The response needed is political, ecclesial and social, within local, national and global contexts.

Divine-human relations are simultaneously the relations of social organization, meaning, values and decision making. In mediating the self-understanding of faith communities, contemporary theologies are challenged to examine discipleship in the present situation and to collaborate in establishing both discourse and contact supporting global networking among communities.[14] Taking meaning and values as constitutive factors of theological endeavour, faith communities would

offer a specific, though not exclusive, contribution in upholding freedom to critique methods and goals relating to concrete problems.[15] The
responses of faith communities beyond traditional boundaries will
determine their integrity as credible partners in shaping meanings,
transformative values and just relations.

Doing theology ethically requires evoking cultural values of inclusion, values that overcome global injustice at the most basic functions
of the infrastructure and foster the fullness of revelation through inclusive communities. Achieving full inclusion and respect for women and
men of all "races" in churches and institutions such as theological col-
leges and governments involves shifts in priority setting and in methods. Inclusion gives rise to new images and new interpretations of traditional symbols. Inclusion certainly affects descriptions of identity,
meaning and values. Inclusion shakes rigidity, supremacy and exclusivity at their roots, regardless what guise of good leads us to defend
them. At the very least, theologians are challenged to live with a gentle, soul-searing question, "What if God herself is really doing this new
deed of calling for full participation, of expanding our knowledge and
our possibilities for justice?" And "What if systemic crises really do
require systemic solutions so that individual kindness and respect,
while good, are simply not enough?" At the least, we would learn with
open minds, within every discipline, what feminists, womanists,
mujeristas and Asian women are saying. All can then be equal partners
in dialogue and in the creation of knowledge, including knowledge of
God and of just relations.

A major component of this involves openness to reorient theology
by giving difference and specificity and the integrity they offer their
rightful place as intrinsic factors in theology. Difference and specificity
are intrinsic to the situation to be addressed by theology and economics, and as such provide a test of genuineness of authentic intellectual life. Inclusion of difference and specificity analysis as a constituent
element of theology grounds theory.

At this historical juncture, social decline is not the only reality.
Increasing differentiation of consciousness, groups' agency, global communications and solidarity and incredible suffering are coming together to cause an axial shift in consciousness. Grounded in interiority, we
transcend traditional fears to inquire about and interpret our personal
and global experience, to relate our perceptions to our faith in God and
to note the discrepancies to which this connection gives rise, to critique
causes, to make appropriate decisions and to act for justice. Conversion

leads to reexamination of traditional explanations, especially those used to perpetuate sin. Discovery of the power of open inquiry and of responsible evaluation, decision making and action contains the power to break through centuries of cumulative distortion. It also frees us to name and to celebrate how we are graced socially.

A grace or gift of God for our time is individually and corporately to trust our abilities to gather information, to weigh evidence, to make judgements when we have adequate information and refrain from doing so when evidence is lacking, to make appropriate decisions and to act with integrity—and to risk doing this clearly in the onslaught of financial capitalism and corporate rule, to cherish full participation of inclusive cross-cultural communities, to speak and act as if we believe in God's power at work in us. This is a sure path to finding meaning, spirituality and joy even in the midst of suffering. Such sowing plants seeds of transformation to spread and bear fruit in due season.

Theology today, then, is challenged to mediate Christian faith with an emergent and potentially more differentiated set of cultural components for a global social order, such as I have put forth in this book. Since a new cultural matrix must be inclusive of self-affirmed concerns of women, mediation must also be through the medium of feminist/ "racial" interiorly differentiated consciousness, which values the good of all while making women's interracial agency visible. Interracial/ cultural agency of women and men is an essential source of global integrity. Praxis involving global networking also offers possibilities for a genuine postmodern differentiation of consciousness through the explanatory self and communal appropriation of human interiority on a holistic basis.

Theology is challenged to collaborate in the task of evoking and promoting effective cross-cultural values. These values need to arise from within and respect the autonomy of particular cultures even as they respond to the breadth of interrelated global crises. Such networking calls for holistic integration of family/kin/friendship, cultural, personal and religious values as a guiding structure for global infrastructure and local justice making. Attentive to all aspects of these dialectics, collaboration will be particularly sensitive to the variety of expressions of meaning, imagery and interpretation of differing peoples.

Integrating Images and Social Factors in Theological Endeavour

In this final section, I indicate what this research and solidarity have meant for me as a white, feminist theologian, engaged in socio-economic, ecological, business and political ethics. I share aspects of my own integration not only as a faith response, but especially to indicate the intrinsic relationship of public solidarity, imagery, social factors and theological endeavour. Such data provides information for discernment of religious values and for expansion of one's image and experience of divine mystery. My critical consciousness is being continuously shaped by engaging in solidarity with homeworkers, churches, community groups, unions and the academy. I become steadily more aware of the social, "racial" and wealthist contradictions that underlie both our collective existence and my own life. It is within concrete engagement that I come to understand the meaning of horizon, bias, solidarity, social consciousness, sin and grace.

I reflect on this engagement and research to unmask truth. This process confirms for me, once again, that theological and socio-economic truths must be grounded in actualities. It challenges me to face the implications of my being white, formally educated and publicly linked with churches. It challenges me to refuse complicity in destructive forces and to resist structures that perpetuate life-denying conditions. I have learned that both discovery and expression of meaning for me are closely bound up with various forms of creativity, of solidarity and of serious intellectual endeavour. My commitment is with women and all who suffer domination on the basis of difference. In the context of God's love and power, whether recognized and acknowledged or not, I am encouraged as I see homeworkers engaging in self-education, in organizing locally and in joining global solidarity networks. Our coalitions are linked.

When the Homework Coalition launched our Clean Clothes Campaign at the Ontario Federation of Labour Women's Conference in Toronto, I dreamt for a second time of horses, this time of numerous white horses leaping out of waves which were crashing on a rocky shore. The memory of it energizes me. The dream, which I painted, was one of integration. The social reality of solidarity among and for women fit with my personal convictions. We acted publicly together for justice. With many others, I seek faith and an operative ecclesiology with horizons broad enough to support, challenge and expand our commitment to justice making.

As producers and consumers in the garment industry, together we hold power which can be the nemesis of major retailers' global domination.[16] The network is as local and as global as each home-worker and each consumer. One of my paintings of webs depicts spiders spinning webs on continents, linking regions where garment workers are resisting corporate injustice. According to an Ethiopian proverb, "When spider webs unite, they can tie up a lion." After completing this painting, I read Nancy Cocks' wisdom-image of church as network.[17] The strands are being formed.

As more people of all "races" express their images, symbols, meaning and values, and as we learn to understand each other's communication and interpretations, we discover energizing ways to go forward in solidarity. Intercultural networking carries possibilities of forging a new creation to challenge social decline at its roots. In partnership with divine mystery, we spin webs of just relations. In poetic terms, we discover how and why spiders eat the sun! I painted this image and the one that follows. After rereading and reflecting on themes of this book, I dreamt I saw a brightly coloured pattern. Caught up in the wonder of good energy and of the colour, I received a ptarmigan feather and then realized it was really prairie wheat burning. The flames leapt and danced. The source of life, of colour and of fire burns and dances, nourishing us in the depths of our communal interiority and justice daring.

Notes

1 Smith, *The Everyday World as Problematic*, 223.
2 Ibid., 225.
3 I muse, "Which is different: day or night?" Only imposed normativity allows for stratification of one over another.
4 See Doran, *Theology and the Dialectics of History*, 446-51, for a more complete explanation of the two sets of categories within analysis of theology as praxis.
5 Refer to Brubaker, "Economic Justice for Whom? 102. See also Margot Kässmann, *Overcoming Violence: The Challenge to the Churches in All Places* (Geneva: WCC, 1998), 46-55.
6 Brubaker, "Economic Justice for Whom? 100-102, citing Constance Parvey, "The Community Study: Its Mixed Messages for the Churches," in *Beyond Unity-in-Tension: Unity, Renewal, and the Community of Women and Men*, ed. Thomas Best (Geneva: WCC, 1988), 39.
7 See Doran, *Theology and the Dialectics of History*, 426.
8 Brubaker, "Economic Justice for Whom? 105.
9 Doran, *Theology and the Dialectics of History*, 455, with my additions and adaptations.

10 Ibid., 454. I add social and cultural here. Doran has consistently emphasized these throughout *Theology and the Dialectics of History*.

11 Ibid., 437, adapted.

12 I intend two meanings of domestic in order to integrate home and national concerns.

13 Ibid., 419.

14 Ibid., 418.

15 As Doran says, "We are free to preserve a tension between absolute adherence to God and relative ideologies, where relativity consists in the pertinence of specific systems of goals and means to the overall purpose of the integral liberation of the human community" (ibid., 428-29).

16 Repression of garment workers in many countries also raises the critical issue of arms sales to the regimes, of international arms sales registries and of trade relations with those who abuse human rights.

17 Nancy Cocks, "The Wisdom of Doing Justice," in *Coalitions for Justice: The Story of Canada's Interchurch Coalitions*, ed. Christopher Lind and Joe Mihevc (Ottawa: Novalis, 1994), 348.

Bibliography

Bibliography

Books

Abella, I., and D. Millar, eds. *The Canadian Worker in the Twentieth Century*. Toronto: Oxford University Press, 1978.

Acton, Janice, Penny Goldsmith and Bonnie Shepard, eds. *Women at Work, Ontario, 1850-1930*. Toronto: Canadian Women's Educational Press, 1974.

Allen, Sheila, and Carol Wolowitz. *Homeworking: Myths and Realities*. London: Macmillan Education, 1987.

Anderson, John. *Total Quality Management: Should Unions Buy Into TQM?* Toronto: Ontario Federation of Labour—Technology Adjustment Research Programme, 1993.

Antrobus, Peggy, guest ed. *Alternative Economic Frameworks from a Gender Perspective: Special Issue Prepared for the 4th UN World Conference on Women. Development: Journal of the Society for International Development* (1995): 1.

Armstrong, Pat. *Labour Pains: Women's Work in Crisis*. Toronto: Women's Press, 1984.

Armstrong, Pat, and Hugh Armstrong. *The Double Ghetto: Canadian Women and Their Segregated Work*. Toronto: McClelland and Steward, 1978.

_____. *Theorizing Women's Work*. Toronto: Garamond Press, 1990.

Aronowitz, Stanley. *False Promises*. London: Duke University Press, 1992.

Arrow, Kenneth. *Social Choice and Individual Values*. 2nd ed. New Haven, CT: Yale University Press, 1963.

Assheton-Smith, Marilyn, and Barbara Spronk. *Women and Social Location*. Charlottetown: Gynergy Books, 1993.

Baker, Maureen. *The Family: Changing Trends in Canada*. Toronto: McGraw-Hill Ryerson, 1984.

Bakker, Isa. *The Strategic Silence: Gender and Economic Policy*. London: Zed Books, 1994.

Barlow, Maude, and Bruce Cameron. *Take Back the Nation*. Toronto: Key Porter Books, 1991.

Barrett Brown, Michael. *Fair Trade: Reform and Realities in the International Trading System*. Atlantic Highlands, NJ: Zed Books, 1993.

Baum, Gregory. *Compassion and Solidarity: The Church for Others*. Toronto: CBC Enterprises, 1987.

Baxter, Sheila. *No Way To Live: Poor Women Speak Out*. Vancouver: New Star Books, 1988.

Benería, Lourdes, and Martha Roldán. *The Crossroads of Class and Gender: Industrial Homework, Subcontracting, and Household Dynamics in Mexico City*. Chicago: University of Chicago Press, 1987.

Benhabib, Seyla, and Drucilla Cornell. *Feminism as Critique: On the Politics of Gender*. Minneapolis: University of Minnesota Press, 1987.

Benjamin, Jessica. *The Bonds of Love: Psychoanalysis, Feminism, and the Problem of Domination*. New York: Pantheon Books, 1988.

Berry, Thomas. *The Dream of the Earth*. San Francisco: Sierra Club Books, 1988.

Berry, Thomas, with Thomas Clarke. *Befriending the Earth: A Theology of Reconciliation between Humans and the Earth*. Mystic, CT: Twenty-Third Publications, 1991.

Best, Thomas, ed. *Beyond Unity-in-Tension: Unity, Renewal, and the Community of Women and Men*. Geneva: WCC, 1988.

Bird, Frederick Bruce. *The Muted Conscience: Moral Silence and the Practice of Ethics in Business*. Westport, CT: Greenwood Publishing Group, Quorum Books, 1996.

Bloomfield, Elizabeth. *Canadian Women in Workshops, Mills and Factories: The Evidence of the 1871 Census Manuscripts*. Guelph: Department of Geography, University of Guelph, 1991.

Boff, Leonardo. *Liberating Grace*. Maryknoll, NY: Orbis, 1987. Originally published in 1979.

Bolton, Brian. *The MNCs in the Textile, Garment and Leather Industries*. Brussels: International Textile, Garment and Leather Workers' Federation, 1976.

Boris, Eileen, and Cynthia Daniels. *Homework: Historical and Contemporary Perspectives on Paid Labor at Home.* Chicago: University of Illinois Press, 1989.

Boris, Eileen, and Elisabeth Prügl, eds. *Homeworkers in Global Perspective: Invisible No More.* New York: Routledge, 1996.

Borowy, Jan, Shelly Gordon, Belinda Leach, Barbara Paleczny and Lynda Yanz. *From the Double Day to the Endless Day: Proceedings from the Conference on Homeworking, November 1992.* Ottawa: Canadian Centre for Policy Alternatives, 1994.

Borowy, Jan, and Fanny Yuen. *International Ladies' Garment Workers' Union 1993 Homeworkers' Study: An Investigation into Wages and Working Conditions of Chinese-Speaking Homeworkers in Metropolitan Toronto.* Toronto: ILGWU, 1994.

Bourne, Paula. *Women's Paid and Unpaid Work: Historical and Contemporary Perspectives.* Toronto: New Hogtown Press, 1985.

Boydston, Jeanne, Mary Kelley and Anne Margolis. *The Limits of Sisterhood: The Beecher Sisters on Women's Rights and Woman's Sphere.* Chapel Hill: University of North Carolina Press, 1988.

Brand, Dionne, Lois De Shield and the Immigrant Women's Job Placement Centre. *No Burden to Carry: Narratives of Black Working Women in Ontario 1920s to 1950s.* Toronto: Women's Press, 1991.

Brandt, Barbara. *Whole Life Economics: Revaluing Daily Life.* Gabriola Island, BC: New Society Publishers, 1995.

Brecher, Jeremy, and Tim Costello. *Global Village or Global Pillage: Economic Reconstruction from the Bottom Up.* Boston: South End Press, 1994.

Briskin, Linda, and Lynda Yanz, eds. *Union Sisters: Women in the Labour Movement.* Toronto: Women's Press, 1983.

Brooks Thistlethwaite, Susan. *Sex, Race, and God: Christian Feminism in Black and White.* New York: Crossroad, 1989.

Brooks Thistlethwaite, Susan, and Mary Engel Potter, eds. *Lift Every Voice: Constructing Christian Theologies from the Underside.* New York: Harper & Row, 1990.

Brown, Terry, and Christopher Lind, eds. *Justice as Mission: An Agenda for the Church.* Burlington: Trinity Press, 1985.

Browning Cole, Eve, and Susan Coultrap-McQuin, eds. *Explorations in Feminist Ethics: Theory and Practice.* Indianapolis: Indiana University Press, 1992.

Brydon, Lynne, and Sylvia Chant. *Women in the Third World: Gender Issues in Rural and Urban Areas.* New Brunswick, NJ: Rutgers University Press, 1989.

Buarque, Cristovam. *The End of Economics? Ethics and the Disorder of Progress.* Atlantic Highlands, NJ: Zed Books, 1993.

Burstyn, Varda, and Dorothy Smith. *Women, Class, Family and the State.* Toronto: Garamond Press, 1985.

Burt, Sandra, Lorraine Code and Lindsay Dorney, eds. *Changing Patterns: Women in Canada.* Toronto: McClelland and Stewart, 1988.

Cameron, Barbara, and Teresa Mak. *Chinese-Speaking Homeworkers in Toronto: Summary of Results of a Survey Conducted by the International Ladies' Garment Workers' Union.* Toronto: ILGWU, 1991.

Cameron, Duncan, ed. *The Free Trade Debates.* Toronto: James Lorimer, 1986.

Canada. Textile and Clothing Board. *Report on Textiles and Clothing, 1988.* Ottawa: Ministry of Supply and Services, 1989.

Canadian Advisory Council on the Status of Women. *Expanding Our Horizons: The Work of the Canadian Advisory Council on the Status of Women and Its Context, 1973-1993.* Ottawa: CACSW/CCCSF, 1993.

Canadian Centre for Policy Alternatives and Choices: A Coalition for Social Justice. *Alternative Federal Budget 1995.* Ottawa: CCPA, 1994.

_____. *Alternative Federal Budget 1996.* Ottawa: CCPA, 1995.

_____. *Alternative Federal Budget 1997.* Ottawa: CCPA, 1996.

_____. *Alternative Federal Budget 1998.* Ottawa: CCPA, 1997.

_____. *Alternative Federal Budget 2000.* Ottawa: CCPA, 1999.

Canadian Centre for Policy Alternatives in co-operation with Common Frontiers and the Action Canada Network. *Which Way for the Americas: Analysis of NAFTA Proposals and the Impact on Canada.* Ottawa: CCPA, 1992.

Canadian Centre for Policy Alternatives. *The Tory Record, 1984-1993.* Ottawa: CCPA, 1993.

Canadian Labour Congress. *Canadian Union Women: Toward the Year 2000.* Report from the 7th Biennial CLC Women's Conference. Ottawa: CLC, 1990.

_____. *Organizing for Strength.* Report from the 8th Biennial CLC Women's Conference. Saskatoon: CLC, 1993.

————. *Social Dimensions of North American Economic Integration: Impacts on Working People and Emerging Responses*. Report prepared for the Department of Human Resources Development. Ottawa: CLC, 1996.

Canadian Union of Public Employees, ed. *The Facts of Free Trade: Canada, Don't Trade It Away*. Ottawa, 1988.

Cannon, Katie, Carter Heyward et al. *God's Fierce Whimsy: Christian Feminism and Theological Education*. New York: Pilgrim Press, 1985.

Carty, Linda, ed. *And Still We Rise: Feminist Political Mobilizing in Contemporary Canada*. Toronto: Women's Press, 1993.

Cavanagh, John, Daphne Wysham and Marcos Arruda, eds. *Beyond Bretton Woods: Alternatives to the Global Economic Order*. Boulder, CO: Pluto Press, with Institute for Policy Studies, Washington, and the Transnational Institute, Amsterdam, 1994.

Centre for Research on Latin America and the Caribbean (CERLAC). *North American Integration: Interplay of World Order, State and Production*. Toronto: York University, April 1991.

Chambers English Dictionary. 7th ed. Cambridge: Chambers and Cambridge University Press, 1988.

Chapkis, Wendy, and Cynthia Enloe. *Of Common Cloth: Women in the Global Textile Industry*. Washington: Transnational Institute, 1983.

Che-Alford, Janet, Catherine Allan and George Butlin. *Families in Canada*. Statistics Canada Catalogue No. 96-307E (1994).

Child Poverty Action Group, Citizens for Public Justice and Social Planning Council of Metropolitan Toronto. *Paying for Canada: Perspectives on Public Finance and National Programs*. Toronto, 1994.

Chossudovsky, Michel. *The Globalisation of Poverty: Impacts of IMF and World Bank Reforms*. Atlantic Highlands, NJ: Zed Books, 1997.

Christensen, Kathleen, ed. *The New Era of Home-Based Work: Directions and Policies*. London: Westview Press, 1988.

————. *Women and Home-Based Work: The Unspoken Contract*. New York: Henry Holt, 1988.

Chung Hyun, Kyung. *Struggle to Be the Sun Again: Introducing Asian Women's Theology*. Maryknoll, NY: Orbis Books, 1990.

Clairmonte, Frederick, and John Cavanagh. *The World in Their Web*. London: Zed Press, 1981.

Clarkson, Max, Michael Deck and Richard Leblanc. *Codes of Ethics, Practice and Conduct*. Hamilton, ON: Society of Management Accountants of Canada, 1998.

Cline, William. *The Future of World Trade in Textiles and Apparel*. Washington: Institute for International Economics, 1987.

Coady International Institute. *Creating a Balance: Developing New Relationships between Women And Men*. Antigonish, NS, 1996.

Coalition for Fair Wages and Working Conditions for Homeworkers. *Fair Wages and Working Conditions for Homeworkers: A Brief to the Government of Ontario*. Toronto, December 1991.

———. *Fair Wages and Working Conditions for Homeworkers: A Revised Brief to the Government of Ontario*. Toronto, February 1993.

Cobb, John Jr. *Sustainability: Economics, Ecology and Justice*. Maryknoll, NY: Orbis Books, 1992.

Code, Lorraine. *What Can She Know? Feminist Theory and the Construction of Knowledge*. London: Cornell University Press, 1991.

Code, Lorraine, Maureen Ford, Kathleen Martindale, Susan Sherwin and Debra Shogan. *Is Feminist Ethics Possible?* Ottawa: CRIAW/ICREF, 1991.

Code, Lorraine, Sheila Mullett and Christine Overall. *Feminist Perspectives: Philosophical Essays on Method and Morals*. Toronto: University of Toronto Press, 1988.

Common Frontiers and Latin American Working Group. *Social Charters: Perspectives from the Americas*. LAWG Letter #48. Toronto, c. 1992.

Companies' Creditors Arrangement Act. *Dylex Ltd. and Twelve Other Corporations: Plan of Arrangement of Dylex Ltd., February 24, 1995*. Toronto: Government of Ontario, 1995.

Connelly, Patricia. *Last Hired, First Fired: Women and the Canadian Work Force*. Toronto: Women's Press, 1978.

Cooey, Paula, Sharon Farmer and Mary Ellen Ross, eds. *Embodied Love: Sensuality and Relationship as Feminist Values*. San Francisco: Harper & Row, 1987.

Cornish, Mary, and Lynn Spink. *Organizing Unions*. Toronto: Second Story Press, 1994.

Council of Canadians. *Standing on Guard for Canada's Social Programs: 1995 Federal Budget Analysis*. Ottawa, March 1995, 1-7.

Crawford Cromwell, S. *World Religions and Global Ethics*. New York: Paragon House, 1989.

Crowe, Frederick. *The Lonergan Enterprise*. Cambridge: Cowley, 1980.

———. *Appropriating the Lonergan Idea*. Edited by Michael Vertin. Washington, DC: Catholic University of America Press, 1989.

———. *Lonergan*. Collegeville: Liturgical Press, 1992.

Crysdale, Cynthia, ed. *Lonergan and Feminism*. Toronto: University of Toronto Press, 1994.

Cunningham, Frank, Sue Findlay, Marlene Kadar, Alan Lennon and Ed Silva, eds. *Social Movements/Social Change: The Politics and Practice of Organizing*. Toronto: Between the Lines Press, 1988.

Curran, Charles, ed. *Moral Theology: Challenges for the Future*. New York: Paulist Press, 1990.

Currie, Dawn. *From Margins to Centre: Selected Studies in Women's Studies Research*. Saskatoon: University of Saskatchewan, Women's Studies Research Unit, 1988.

Daly, Herman, and John Cobb, Jr. *For the Common Good: Redirecting the Economy toward Community, the Environment, and a Sustainable Future*. Boston: Beacon Press, 1989.

DAWN. *Development Crisis and Alternative Visions: Third World Women's Perspective*. Bergen: Christian Michelsen Institute, 1985.

Dignard, Louise, and José Havet, eds. *Women in Micro- and Small-Scale Enterprise Development*. Ottawa-Hull: Canadian International Development Agency, 1987.

Dillon, John, and the Ecumenical Coalition for Economic Justice (ECEJ). *Turning the Tide: Confronting the Money Traders*. Ottawa: Canadian Centre for Policy Alternatives, 1997.

Donahue, James, and Theresa Moser, eds. *Religion, Ethics and the Common Good*. Mystic, CT: Twenty-Third Publications, 1996.

Doran, Robert. *Psychic Conversion and Theological Foundations: Toward a Reorientation of the Human Sciences*. Chico, CA: Scholars Press for the American Academy of Religion, 1981.

————. *Theology and the Dialectics of History*. Toronto: University of Toronto Press, 1990.

Drache, Daniel, ed. *Getting on Track: Social Democratic Strategies for Ontario*. Montreal: McGill-Queen's University Press, 1992.

Drache, Daniel, and Meric Gertler. *The New Era of Global Competition: State Policy and Market Power*. Montreal and Kingston: McGill-Queen's University Press, 1991.

Duchrow, Ulrich. *Global Economy: A Confessional Issue for the Churches?* Translated by David Lewis. Geneva: World Council of Churches Publications, 1987.

Dumais, Monique, and Marie-Andrée Roy. *Souffles de femmes: lectures féministes de la religion*. Montréal: Les Éditions Paulines, 1989.

Economic Council of Canada. *From the Bottom Up: The Community Economic Development Approach*. Ottawa: Ministry of Supply and Services, Canada, 1990.

————. *Good Jobs, Bad Jobs: Employment in the Service Economy*. Ottawa: Ministry of Supply and Services, 1991.

Ecumenical Coalition for Economic Justice (ECEJ). *Debt Bondage or Self-Reliance: A Popular Perspective on the Global Debt Crisis*. Toronto: GATT-Fly, 1985.

————. *Recolonization or Liberation: The Bonds of Structural Adjustment and Struggles for Emancipation*. Toronto: ECEJ, 1990.

————. *Reweaving Canada's Social Programs: From Shredded Safety Net to Social Solidarity*. Toronto: ECEJ, 1993.

————. *Social Policy Reform in Canada: Whose Needs Are Being Put First?* An Action Kit for People of Faith. Toronto, ECEJ, 1995.

————. *The Halifax Initiative: Beyond 50 Years*. A Kit for Popular Use. Toronto: ECEJ, 1995.

Ecumenical Taskforce on the Feminine Face of Poverty. *A Woman Named Mary*. Toronto: Women's Interchurch Council of Canada, 1987.

Ellis, Marc, and Otto Maduro. *Expanding the View*. Maryknoll, NY: Orbis Books, 1988.

Employment Standards Policy and Interpretation Manual. Vol. 1, no. 5.2. Factory, Shop and Office Building Amendment Act, 1936, S.O. 1936 c. 21. Toronto.

Employment Standards Working Group. *Bad Boss Stories: Workers Whose Bosses Break the Law*. Toronto, 1996.

Endicott, Shirley Jane. *Facing the Tiger*. Winfield, BC: Wood Lake Books, 1988.

Enloe, Cynthia. *Bananas, Beaches and Bases: Making Sense of International Politics*. Berkeley: University of California Press, 1989.

Evangelical Lutheran Church in Canada. *Sustainable Social Economics: A Proposed Statement*. Winnipeg, 1996.

External Affairs Canada. *The North America Free Trade Agreement* (legal text). Ottawa: External Affairs Canada, 1992.

Family, Women's Rights and Community Responsibilities, The. Journal of the Society for International Development (Rome) 4 (1993).

Fitzgerald, Maureen, Connie Guberman and Margie Wolfe. *Still Ain't Satisfied: Canadian Feminism Today*. Toronto: Women's Press, 1982.

Folbre, Nancy. *Who Pays for the Kids? Gender and the Structures of Constraint*. New York: Routledge, 1994.

Folbre, Nancy, Barbara Bergmann, Bina Agarwal and Maria Floro. *Women's Work in the World Economy*. New York: New York University Press, 1992.

Fonow, Mary Margaret, and Judith Cook, eds. *Beyond Methodology: Feminist Scholarship as Lived Research*. Bloomington: Indiana University Press, 1991.

Frankel, Jeffrey, with Ernesto Stein and Shang-Jin Wei. *Regional Trading Blocs in the World Economic System*. Washington, DC: Institute for International Economics, 1997.

Frazer, Elizabeth, Jennifer Hornsby and Sabina Lovibond, eds. *Ethics: A Feminist Reader*. Oxford: Blackwell, 1992.

Freire, Paulo. *Pedagogy of the Oppressed*. New York: Herder and Herder, 1971.

Fruitman Consulting Group. *An Exploration of the Feasibility of a "Clean Clothes" Programme in Canada: Consumer Research*. Conducted for the Ontario District of UNITE (Union of Needle Trades, Industrial and Textile Employees). Maple, ON, October 1995.

Fudge, Judy. *Labour Law's Little Sister: The Employment Standards Act and the Feminization of Labour*. Ottawa: Canadian Centre for Policy Alternatives, 1991.

Fudge, Judy, and Patricia McDermott, eds. *Just Wages: A Feminist Assessment of Pay Equity*. Toronto: University of Toronto Press, 1991.

Gallagher, John. *Time Past, Time Future: An Historical Study of Catholic Moral Theology*. New York: Paulist Press, 1990.

Gannagé, Charlene. *Double Day, Double Bind: Women Garment Workers*. Toronto: Women's Press, 1986.

Garrett, John, and Angela Travis. *Unfinished Business: The World's Leaders and the Millennium Debt Challenge*. London: Jubilee 2000 Coalition, 1999.

Giddens, Anthony. *Central Problems in Social Theory*. Berkeley, CA: University of California Press, 1983.

Giles, Wenona, and Sedef Arat-Koç, eds. *Maid in the Market: Women's Paid Domestic Labour*. Halifax: Fernwood Publishing, 1994.

Goudzwaard, Robert, and Harold de Lange. *Beyond Poverty and Affluence: Toward a Canadian Economy of Care*. Toronto: University of Toronto Press, 1995.

Griffin Cohen, Marjorie. *The Invisible Hand: Is It Around Our Throats?* Ottawa: Canadian Advisory Council on the Status of Women, 1986.

_____. *Free Trade in Services: An Issue of Concern to Women*. Ottawa: Advisory Council on the Status of Women, 1987.

_____. *Women's Work: Markets and Economic Development in Nineteenth-Century Ontario*. Toronto: University of Toronto Press, 1988.

_____. *Women and Economic Structures: A Feminist Perspective on the Canadian Economy*. Ottawa: Canadian Centre for Policy Alternatives, 1991.

Guinness Book of Answers, The. London: Guinness Publishing, 1991.

Gula, Richard. *Reason Informed by Faith: Foundations of Catholic Morality*. New York: Paulist Press, 1989.

Gunew, Sneja, and Anna Yeatman. *Feminism and the Politics of Difference*. Halifax: Fernwood Publishing, 1993.

Habermas, Jürgen. *The Theory of Communicative Action*. Boston: Beacon Press, 1984.

Hacker, Sally. *Pleasure, Power, and Technology: Some Tales of Gender, Engineering, and the Cooperative Workplace*. Boston: Unwin Hyman, 1989.

_____. *Doing It the Hard Way: Investigations of Gender and Technology*. Edited by Dorothy Smith and Susan Turner. Boston: Unwin Hyman, 1990.

Haight, Roger. *An Alternative Vision: An Interpretation of Liberation Theology*. New York: Paulist Press, 1985.

Hamel, Ronald, and Kenneth Himes. *Introduction to Christian Ethics*. New York: Paulist Press, 1989.

Hanson, Kirk. *Management Accounting Guideline 46: Implementing Ethics Strategies within Organizations*. Hamilton, ON: Society of Management Accountants of Canada, 1998.

Harcourt, Wendy, ed. *Feminist Perspectives on Sustainable Development*. London: Zed Books, in association with The Society for International Development, Rome, 1994.

Hardesty, Nancy. *Women Called to Witness: Evangelical Feminism in the 19th Century*. Nashville: Abingdon Press, 1984.

Harding, Sandra. *The Science Question in Feminism*. Ithaca, NY: Cornell University Press, 1986.

_____. *Feminism and Methodology: Social Science Issues*. Indianapolis: Indiana University Press, 1987.

Harding, Sandra, and Jean O'Barr, eds. *Sex and Scientific Inquiry*. Chicago: University of Chicago Press, 1987. Originally published in 1975.

Harvey, E.B., and J.H. Blakely. *Growth of the Contingent Workforce in Ontario: Structural Trends, Statistical Dimensions and Policy Implications.* Toronto: Ontario Women's Directorate, 1989.

Hayward, Carter. *Touching Our Strength.* New York: Harper & Row, 1989.

Heilbroner, Robert. *Twenty-first Century Capitalism.* Concord, ON: Anansi Press, 1992.

————. *Visions of the Future: The Distant Past, Yesterday, Today, Tomorrow.* New York: Oxford University Press, 1995.

Henderson, Hazel. *Creating Alternative Futures: The End of Economics.* New York: Berkeley Publishing, 1978.

————. *The Politics of the Solar Age: Alternatives to Economics.* Garden City, NY: Anchor Press/Doubleday, 1981.

————. *Paradigms in Progress: Life Beyond Economics.* Indianapolis: Knowledge Systems, 1991.

Hennelly, Alfred. *Theologies in Conflict: The Challenge of Juan Luis Segundo.* Maryknoll, NY: Orbis Books, 1979.

Henriot, Peter, Edward DeBerri and Michael Schultheis. *Catholic Social Teaching: Our Best Kept Secret.* Washington, DC: Center of Concern, 1987.

Hilkert Andolsen, Barbara. *Good Work at the Video Display Terminal: A Feminist Ethical Analysis of Changes in Clerical Work.* Knoxville: University of Tennessee, 1989.

Hilkert Andolsen, Barbara, Christine Gudorf and Mary Pellauer, eds. *Women's Consciousness, Women's Conscience: A Reader in Feminist Ethics.* San Francisco: Harper & Row, 1985.

Ho, Audrey, and Laura Johnson. *Home Sweat Home: Regulation of Industrial Homework in Ontario.* Toronto: Social Planning Council of Metropolitan Toronto, 1982.

Holland, Joe. *Creative Communion: Toward a Spirituality of Work.* New York: Paulist Press, 1989.

Holland, Joe, and Peter Henriot. *Social Analysis: Linking Faith and Justice.* Washington, DC: Center of Concern, 1980.

Hongu, Tatsuya, and Glyn Phillips. *New Fibres.* Toronto: Ellis Horwood, 1990.

hooks, bell. *Feminist Theory: From Margin to Center.* Boston: South End Press, 1984.

hooks, bell, and Cornel West. *Breaking Bread: Insurgent Black Intellectual Life.* Toronto: Between the Lines, 1991.

Hope, Anne, and Sally Timmel. *Training for Transformation: Books One-Three*. Harare, Zimbabwe: Mambo Press, 1984.

Hudson, Peyton, Anne Clapp and Darlene Kness. *Textile Science*. 6th ed. New York: Harcourt Brace College Publishers, 1993.

Human Centered Economics: Environment and Global Sustainability. Development: *Journal of the Society for International Development* 3, 4 (1990).

Human Resources Development Council (HRDC). *Telework Pilot Program in the Public Service*. Ottawa, 1992.

Hurtig, Mel. *The Betrayal of Canada*. Toronto: Stoddart, 1991.

Inter-Mondes. *L'ajustement structurel*. Montréal: L'Association québécoise des organismes de coopération internationale, avril 1990.

Intercede. *Know Your Rights: A Guide for Domestic Workers in Ontario*. Toronto, October 1987.

Intercede and International Ladies' Garment Workers' Union, Ontario District Council. *Meeting the Needs of Vulnerable Workers: Proposals for Improved Employment Legislation and Access to Collective Bargaining for Domestic Workers and Industrial Homeworkers*. Toronto, 1993.

International Labour Organization. *The Impact on Employment and Income of Structural and Technological Change in the Clothing Industry: Third Tripartite Meeting for the Clothing Industry, Report III*. Geneva: International Labour Organization, 1987.

————. *Conditions of Work Digest: Homework* (International Labour Office, Geneva) 8, 2 (1989).

————. *Homework: International Labour Organization Conference, 82nd Session, 1995*. Report 5(1). Geneva, 1995, approved in 1996.

International Ladies' Garment Workers' Union (ILGWU), Ontario District Council. *When One Door Closes ... Another One Opens? A Follow-up Study on the Great Sewing Exchange*. Researcher: Joan Atlin. Toronto: ILGWU, 1994.

————. *Designing the Future for Garment Workers*. Researcher: Janet Borowy. Toronto: Ontario Federation of Labour's Technology Adjustment Research Program, 1995.

Iriarte, P.G. *Estemas para la interpretacion de la realidad*. Ten booklets. La Paz: Ediciones Senpas, 1985.

————. *Deuda externa y etica cristiana*. La Paz, Bolivia: Ediciones Senpas, 1988.

Isasi-Diaz, Ada Maria, and Yolanda Tarango. *Hispanic Women: Prophetic Voice in the Church*. Minneapolis: Fortress Press, 1992.

Jagentowicz Mills, Patricia. *Woman, Nature, and Psyche*. New Haven, CT: Yale University Press, 1987.

Jay, Martin. *The Dialectical Imagination*. Toronto: Little, Brown, 1973.

Jay Lifton, Robert. *Indefensible Weapons*. New York: Basic Books, 1982.

Jeffcott, Bob, Musonda Kidd, Sonia Singh, Kevin Thomas, Ian Thomson and Lynda Yanz. *Stop Sweatshops: An Education and Action Kit*. Toronto: Maqula Solidarity Network, 2000. http://www.web.net/~msn.

Joekes, Susan, with Roxana Moayedi. *Women and Export Manufacturing: A Review of the Issues and Aid Policy*. Washington: International Center for Research on Women, 1987.

Johnson, Elizabeth. *She Who Is: The Mystery of God in Feminist Theological Discourse*. New York: Crossroad, 1993.

Johnson, Laura, and Robert Johnson. *The Seam Allowance: Industrial Home Sewing in Canada*. Toronto: Women's Press, 1982.

Jones, Jaqueline. *Labour of Love, Labour of Sorrow*. New York: Basic Books, 1985.

Jonsen, Albert, and Stephen Toulmin. *The Abuse of Casuistry: A History of Moral Reasoning*. Berkeley: University of California Press, 1988.

Kamel, Rachael. *The Global Factory*. Philadelphia: American Friends Service Committee, 1990.

Kamel, Rachael, and Anya Hoffman. *The Maquiladora Reader: Cross-Border Organizing Since NAFTA*. Philadelphia: American Friends Service Committee, 1999.

Kässmann, Margot. *Overcoming Violence: The Challenge to the Churches in All Places*. Geneva: WCC, 1998.

Kennedy, Margrit. *Interest and Inflation Free Money*. Steyerberg, West Germany: Permkultur Publikationen, 1988.

Kolko, Joyce. *Restructuring the World Economy*. New York: Pantheon Books, 1988.

Kopinak, Kathryn. *Desert Capitalism: Maquilas in North America's Western Industrial Corridor*. Tucson: University of Arizona Press, 1996.

Kroeker, Travis. *Christian Ethics and Political Economy in North America: A Critical Analysis*. Montreal and Kingston: McGill-Queen's University Press, 1995.

Kuhn, Thomas S. *The Structure of Scientific Revolution*. Chicago: University of Chicago Press, 1962. 2nd ed., enlarged, 1970.

Küng, Hans. *Global Responsibility: In Search of a New World Ethic*. New York: Crossroad, 1991.

———, ed. *Yes to a Global Ethic: Voices from Religion and Politics*. New York: Continuum, 1996.

Küng, Hans, and David Tracy, eds. *Paradigm Change in Theology: A Symposium for the Future*. New York: Crossroad, 1989.

Lamb, Matthew. *Solidarity with Victims: Toward a Theology of Social Transformation*. New York: Crossroad, 1982.

Laporte, Jean-Marc. *Patience and Power*. New York: Paulist Press, 1987.

Latin American Working Group. *Open for Business: Canada-Mexico-U.S.* LAWG Letter #45. Toronto, January 1991.

Laxer, Gordon, ed. *Perspectives on Canadian Economic Development: Class, Staples, Gender and Elites*. Toronto: Oxford University Press, 1991.

Lee Bartky, Sandra. *Femininity and Domination: Studies in the Phenomenology of Oppression*. New York: Routledge, 1990.

Legge, Marilyn. *The Grace of Difference: A Canadian Feminist Theological Ethic*. Atlanta, GA: Scholars Press, 1992.

Lerner, Gerda. *The Female Experience*. New York: Oxford University Press, 1977.

Lernoux, Penny. *In Banks We Trust*. New York: Penguin Books, 1984.

Light, Beth, and Joy Parr, eds. *Canadian Women on the Move: 1867-1920*. Toronto: New Hogtown Press and The Ontario Institute for Studies in Education, 1983.

Light, Beth, and Ruth Roach Pierson, eds. *No Easy Road: Women in Canada, 1920s to 1960s*. Toronto: New Hogtown Press, 1990.

Lind, Christopher. *Something's Wrong Somewhere: Globalization, Community and the Moral Economy of the Farm Crisis*. Halifax: Fernwood Publisher, 1995.

Lind, Christopher, and Joe Mihevc. *Coalitions for Justice: The Story of Canada's Interchurch Coalitions*. Ottawa: Novalis, 1994.

Lipsig Mummé, Carla. *Wars of Position: Fragmentation and Realignment in the Quebec Labour Movement*. Kingston: Industrial Relations Centre, Queen's University, 1991.

Loades, Ann, ed. *Feminist Theology: A Reader*. London: SPCK, 1990.

Lonergan, Anne, and Caroline Richards, eds. *Thomas Berry and the New Cosmology*. Mystic, CT: Twenty-Third Publications, 1987.

Lonergan, Bernard. *Method in Theology*. Minneapolis: Seabury Press, 1972.

_____. *A Second Collection*. Edited by William Ryan and Bernard Tyrrell. London: Darton, Longman and Todd, 1974.

_____. *Insight*. New York: Harper & Row, 1978. First published in 1957.

_____. *Understanding and Being.* Edited by Elizabeth Morelli and Mark Morelli. Toronto: Edwin Mellen Press, 1980.

_____. *A Third Collection.* Edited by Frederick E. Crowe. New York: Paulist Press, 1985.

_____. *Topics in Education.* Vol. 10 of *The Collected Works of Bernard Lonergan.* Edited by Robert Doran and Frederick Crowe. Toronto: University of Toronto Press for the Lonergan Research Institute, 1993.

Luxton, Meg, Harriet Rosenberg and Sedef Arat-Koç. *Through the Kitchen Window: The Politics of Home and Family.* Toronto: Garamond Press, 1990.

MacNeill, Jim, Pieter Winsemius and Taizo Yakushiji. *Beyond Interdependence: The Meshing of the World's Economy and the Earth's Ecology.* New York: Oxford University Press, 1991.

Maduro, Otto. *Religion and Social Conflicts.* Translated by Robert Barr. Maryknoll, NY: Orbis Books, 1982.

Mahon, Rianne. *The Politics of Industrial Restructuring: Canadian Textiles.* Toronto: University of Toronto Press, 1984.

Mahoney, John. *The Making of Moral Theology: A Study of the Roman Catholic Tradition.* Oxford: Clarendon Press, 1987.

Maroney, Heather Jon, and Meg Luxton, eds. *Feminism and Political Economy: Women's Work, Women's Struggles.* Toronto: Methuen, 1987.

Mayeski, Marie Anne. *Women: Models of Liberation.* Kansas City: Sheed and Ward, 1988.

McAllister, Pam. *This River of Courage: Generations of Women's Resistance and Action.* Gabriola Island, BC: New Society Publishers, 1991.

McCalla Vickers, Jill. *Taking Sex into Account: The Policy Consequences of Sexist Research.* Ottawa: Carleton University Press, 1984.

McCormack, Thelma. *Politics and the Hidden Injuries of Gender: Feminism and the Making of the Welfare State.* Ottawa: Canadian Research Institute for the Advancement of Women, 1991.

McCullough, Alan B. *The Primary Textile Industry in Canada: History and Heritage.* Ottawa: Environment Canada, 1992.

McDermott, Patricia. *Sectoral Bargaining and the Low-Waged.* Toronto: Ontario Ministry of Labour, 1993.

McGlen, Nancy, and Karen O'Connor. *Women's Rights: The Struggle for Equality in the 19th and 20th Centuries.* New York: Praeger Special Studies, 1983.

McKague, Ormond, ed. *Racism in Canada*. Saskatoon: Fifth House Publishers, 1991.

McMurtry, John. *Unequal Freedoms: The Global Market as an Ethical System*. Toronto: Garamond Press, 1998.

McQuaig, Linda. *Behind Closed Doors: How the Rich Won Control of Canada's Tax System ... And Ended Up Richer*. Markham: Penguin Books, 1988.

————. *The Quick and the Dead: Brian Mulroney, Big Business and the Seduction of Canada*. Toronto: Viking Press, 1991.

————. *The Wealthy Banker's Wife: The Assault on Equality in Canada*. Toronto: Penguin Books, 1993.

————. *Shooting the Hippo: Death by Deficit and Other Canadian Myths*. Toronto: Penguin Books, 1995.

————. *The Cult of Impotence: Selling the Myth of Powerlessness in the Global Economy*. New York: Viking Press, 1998.

Merchant, Carolyn. *The Death of Nature: Women, Ecology and the Scientific Revolution*. New York: Harper & Row, 1980.

Mies, Maria. *Patriarchy and Accumulation on a World Scale: Women in the International Division of Labour*. London: Zed Books, 1986.

Miguez Bonino, José. *Toward a Christian Political Ethics*. Philadelphia: Fortress Press, 1983.

Mihevc, John. *The Market Tells Them So: The World Bank and Economic Fundamentalism in Africa*. Penang and Accra: Third World Network, 1995.

Miles, Angela. *Integrative Feminisms: Building Global Visions 1960s-1990s*. New York: Routledge, 1996.

Miles, Angela, and Geraldine Finn. *Feminism: From Pressure to Politics*. Montreal: Black Rose Books, 1989.

Mitchell, Juliet. *Woman's Estate*. New York: Random House, 1977.

Mitter, Swasti. *Common Fate, Common Bond: Women in the Global Economy*. London: Pluto Press, 1986.

Mowry LaCugna, Catherine, ed. *Freeing Theology: The Essentials of Theology in Feminist Perspective*. San Francisco: Harper, 1993.

National Action Committee on the Status of Women. *Woman's Charter*. Toronto, 1992.

National Labor Committee. *Free Trade's Hidden Secrets*. New York: National Labor Committee, 1993.

————. *Why We Are Losing Our Shirts*. New York: National Labor Committee, 1993.

_____. *Behind Closed Doors: The Workers Who Make Our Clothes.* New York: National Labor Committee, 1998.

_____. *Fired for Crying to the Gringos: The Women in El Salvador Who Sew Liz Claiborne Garments Speak Out Asking for Justice.* New York: National Labor Committee, 1999.

_____. *Help End the Race to the Bottom.* New York: National Labor Committee, 1999.

_____. *Wal-Mart's Shirts of Misery.* New York: National Labor Committee, 1999.

National Council of Women of Canada. *Women of Canada: Their Life and Work.* For distribution at the Paris International Exhibition, 1900. Reprinted by the National Council of Women of Canada, 1975.

National Council on Welfare. *Women and Poverty Revisited.* Ottawa, 1990.

Nett, Emily. *Canadian Families Past and Present.* Toronto: Butterworths, 1988.

Nicaraguan Centre for Labour Studies and Analysis (CEAL). *Union Organizing in the Maquilas.* LAWG Letter #46. Toronto, September 1994.

Niosi, Jorge. *Canadian Multinationals.* Translated by Robert Chodos. Toronto: Between the Lines, 1985.

North-South Institute. *Trade, Protectionism and Industrial Adjustment: Three North American Case Studies.* Ottawa, 1989.

O'Keefe, Mark. *What Are They Saying about Social Sin?* New York: Paulist Press, 1990.

Ontario Provincial Government. *Employment Standards Act.* Amended March 1993 and April 1996.

_____. *Labour Relations Act.* Amended 1986 and 1993.

Ontario Women's Directorate. *The North American Free Trade Agreement: Implications for Women.* Toronto: Ontario Women's Directorate, 1993.

Orme, William A. Jr. *Understanding NAFTA: Mexico, Free Trade, and the New North America.* Austin, TX: University of Texas Free Press, 1996.

Owensby, Walter. *Economics for Prophets.* Grand Rapids, MI: W. Eerdmans Publishing, 1988.

Parr, Joy. *The Gender of Breadwinners: Women, Men, and Change in Two Industrial Towns, 1880-1950.* Toronto: University of Toronto Press, 1990.

————. *Labouring Children: British Immigrant Apprentices to Canada, 1869-1924*. Toronto: University of Toronto Press, 1994.

————, ed. *Childhood and Family in Canadian History*. Toronto: McClelland and Stewart, 1982.

Parry, Robert, ed. *Employment Standards Handbook: A Guide to the Employment Standards Act*. 2nd ed. Aurora, ON: Canada Law Book, 1992.

Patrick, Anne E. *Liberating Conscience: Feminist Explorations in Catholic Moral Theology*. New York: Continuum, 1997.

Pearsall, Marilyn. *Women and Values: Readings in Recent Feminist Philosophy*. Belmont, CA: Wadsworth, 1986.

Pestieau, Caroline. *The Canadian Textile Policy: A Sectoral Trade Adjustment Strategy?* Montreal: The Canadian Economic Policy Committee, C.D. Howe Research Institute, 1976.

Phillips, Paul, and Erin Phillips. *Women and Work: Inequality in the Labour Market*. Toronto: James Lorimer, 1983.

Phizacklea, Annie. *Unpacking the Fashion Industry: Gender, Racism and Class in Production*. New York: Routledge, 1990.

Pietilè, Hilkkä, and Jeanne Vickers. *Making Women Matter: The Role of the United Nations*. London: Zed Books, 1990.

Plant, Judith, ed. *Healing the Wounds: the Promise of Ecofeminism*. Toronto: Between the Lines, 1989.

Pobee, John, and Bärbel von Wartenberg-Potter. *New Eyes for Reading: Biblical and Theological Reflections by Women from the Third World*. Geneva: WCC Publications, 1986.

Polanyi, Karl. *The Great Transformation*. Boston: Beacon Press, 1957.

Pratt, Cran, and Roger Hutchinson. *Christian Faith and Economic Justice*. Burlington, ON: Trinity Press, 1988.

Prentice, Alison, Paula Bourne, Gail Cuthbert Brandt, Beth Light, Wendy Michinson and Naomi Black. *Canadian Women: A History*. Toronto: Harcourt, Brace, Jovanovich, 1988.

Prentice, Alison, and S. Trofimenkoff, eds. *The Neglected Majority*. Vol. 1. Toronto: McClelland and Stewart, 1977.

Primavesi, Anne. *From Apocalypse to Genesis*. Minneapolis: Fortress Press, 1991.

Public Service Alliance of Canada (PSAC). *Go Home ... And Stay There? A PSAC Response to Telework in the Federal Public Service*. Ottawa: PSAC, 1993.

Radford Ruether, Rosemary. *Liberation Theology: Human Hope Confronts Christian History and American Power*. Toronto: Paulist Press, 1972.

_____. *Gaia and God: An Ecofeminist Theology of Earth Healing*. San Francisco: Harper, 1992.

Radford Ruether, Rosemary, and Rosemary Skinner Keller, eds. *Women and Religion in America*. Vol. 1: *The Nineteenth Century*. New York: Harper & Row, 1981.

Rahner, Karl. *Foundations of Christian Faith*. New York: Crossroad, 1984.

Redclift, Nenneke, and Enzo Minigone, eds. *Beyond Employment*. London: Macmillan, 1985.

Redclift, Nenneke, and M. Thea Sinclair. *Working Women: International Perspectives on Labour and Gender Ideology*. London: Routledge, 1991.

Reeve, Ted, and Roger Hutchinson, eds. *Action Training in Canada: Reflections on Church-Based Education for Social Transformation*. Toronto: Centre for Research in Religion, Emmanuel College, 1997.

Reinicke, Wolfgang. *Global Public Policy: Governing without Government?* Washington, DC: Brookings Institute Press, 1998.

Rich, Adrienne. *Of Woman Born, Motherhood as Experience and Institution*. New York: Norton, 1976.

Riegelman Lubin, Carol, and Anne Winslow. *Social Justice for Women: The International Labor Organization*. London: Duke University Press, 1990.

Roach Pierson, Ruth. *"They're Still Women After All": The Second World War and Canadian Womanhood*. London: Croom Helm, 1986.

_____. *No Easy Road: Women in Canada: 1920s-1960s*. Toronto: New Hogtown Press, 1990.

Roach Pierson, Ruth, and Marjorie Griffin Cohen. *Canadian Women's Issues*. Vol. 2: *Bold Visions*. Toronto: James Lorimer, 1995.

Roach Pierson, Ruth, Marjorie Griffin Cohen, Paula Bourne and Philinda Masters. *Canadian Women's Issues*. Vol. 1: *Strong Voices*. Toronto: James Lorimer, 1993.

Robb, Carol, and Carl Casebolt. *Covenant for a New Creation: Ethics, Religion, and Public Policy*. Maryknoll, NY: Orbis Books, 1991.

Rogers, Barbara. *No Peace without Justice: Churches Confront the Mounting Racism of the 1980s*. Geneva: World Council of Churches, 1980.

Ross, David, and Peter Usher. *From the Roots Up: Economics as if Community Mattered*. Toronto: James Lorimer, 1986.

Rowbotham, Sheila. *Women in Movement: Feminism and Social Action*. New York: Routledge, 1992.

_____. *Homeworkers Worldwide*. London: Merlin Press, 1993.

Rowbotham, Sheila, and Swasti Mitter, eds. *Dignity and Daily Bread: New Forms of Economic Organizing among Poor Women in the Third World and the First*. New York: Routledge, 1994.

Sargent, Lydia, ed. *Women and Revolution*. Boston: South End Press, 1981.

Schenk, Christopher, and John Anderson, eds. *Technology Adjustment Research Programme*. Don Mills, ON: Ontario Federation of Labour, 1995.

Schneiders, Sandra. *Beyond Patching: Faith and Feminism in the Catholic Church*. New York: Paulist Press, 1991.

Schom-Moffatt, Patti, and Cynthia Telfer, eds. *The Women's Workbook*. Toronto: Between the Lines, 1983.

Schüssler Fiorenza, Elisabeth, and Anne Carr, eds. *Women, Work and Poverty*. Edinburgh: T & T Clark for *Concilium*, 1987.

Scott, Hilda. *Working Your Way to the Bottom: The Feminization of Poverty*. London: Pandora Press, 1984.

Seabrook, Jeremy. *The Myth of the Market: Promises and Illusions*. Bideford, Devon: Green Books, 1990.

Segundo, Juan Luis. *Grace and the Human Condition*. Maryknoll, NY: Orbis, 1973.

Sen, Amartya K. *Collective Choice and Social Welfare*. San Francisco: Holden-Day and Oliver & Boyd, 1970.

Seward, Shirley B. *Challenges of Labour Adjustment: The Case of Immigrant Women in the Clothing Industry*. Ottawa: Institute for Research on Public Policy, 1990.

Shiva, Vandana. *Staying Alive: Women, Ecology and Development*. London: Zed Books, 1988.

Shogan, Debra, ed. *A Reader in Feminist Ethics*. Toronto: Canadian Scholars' Press, 1993.

Silvera, Makeda. *Silenced: Talks with Working Class West Indian Women about Their Lives and Struggles as Domestic Workers in Canada*. Toronto: Sister Vision Press, 1989.

Smith, Dorothy. *The Everyday World as Problematic: A Feminist Sociology*. Boston: Northeastern University Press, 1987.

Social and Economic Policy Department of the Canadian Labour Congress. *Mr. Martin's Budget vs. the Alternative Federal Budget.* Ottawa: CLC, February 1999.

Soelle, Dorothee. *The Window of Vulnerability: A Political Spirituality.* Minneapolis: Fortress Press, 1990.

Soelle, Dorothee, with Shirley Cloyes. *To Work and to Love: A Theology of Creation.* Philadelphia: Fortress Press, 1984.

Sojourners. *Who Is My Neighbor? Economics as if Values Matter.* Washington: Sojourners, 1994.

Sparr, Pamela. *Mortgaging Women's Lives: Feminist Critiques of Structural Adjustment.* London: Zed Books, 1994.

Spretnak, Charlene. *States of Grace: The Recovery of Meaning in the Postmodern Age.* New York: Harper, 1991.

Standing Committee on External Affairs and International Trade. *Securing Our Global Future: Canada's Stake in the Unfinished Business of Third World Debt.* Ottawa, 1990.

Stanley, Liz, ed. *Feminist Praxis: Research, Theory, and Epistemology in Feminist Sociology.* New York: Routledge, 1990.

Statistics Canada. The Task Force on Immigration Practices and Procedures. *Domestic Workers on Employment Authorizations: Report.* Ottawa: Minister of Supply and Services Canada, April 1981.

————. *The Labour Force 1989: Report of the Task Force on Child Care.* Ottawa: Minister of Supply and Services Canada, 1986.

————. *Employment, Earnings and Hours: Catalogue 72-002.* Ottawa: Government of Canada, 1992.

Stivers, Robert, Christine Gudorf, Alice Frazer Evans and Robert Evans. *Christian Ethics: A Case Method Approach.* Maryknoll, NY: Orbis Books, 1990.

Strong-Boag, Veronica. *The New Day Recalled: Lives of Girls and Women in English Canada, 1919-1939.* Toronto: Copp Clark, 1988.

Strong-Boag, Veronica, and Anita Fellman, eds. *Re-thinking Canada: The Promise of Women's History.* Toronto: Copp Clark Pitman, 1986.

Swimme, Brian, and Thomas Berry. *The Universe Story.* San Francisco: Harper, 1992.

Szentes, Tamás. *The Transformation of the World Economy: New Directions and New Interests.* London: Zed Books, 1988.

Tanner, Kathryn. *The Politics of God: Christian Theologies and Social Justice.* Minneapolis: Fortress Press, 1992.

Teeple, Gary, ed. *Capitalism and the National Question*. Toronto: University of Toronto Press, 1972.

Thompson, Frank, and David Pollock. *The Iceberg and the Fire of Love: A Call to Ecological and Social Compassion*. Toronto: Anglican Book Centre, 1992.

Tobique Women as told to Janet Silman. *Enough Is Enough: Aboriginal Women Speak Out*. Toronto: Women's Press, 1987.

Traina, Cristina. *Feminist Ethics and Natural Law: The End of Anathemas*. Washington, DC: Georgetown University Press, 1999.

Turner, Joan, and Lois Emery. *Perspectives on Women in the 1980s*. Winnipeg: University of Manitoba Press, 1983.

United Nations. *Bulletin of Statistics on World Trade in Engineering Products, 1977*. New York, 1979.

United Nations Development Programme. *Human Development Report*. New York: Oxford University Press, 1999.

United States Department of Labour. *Technological Change and Its Labour Impact in Five Industries*. Bulletin 1961. Washington, DC: Bureau of Labour Statistics, 1977.

_____. Bureau of International Labor Affairs. *Wages, Benefits, Poverty Line, and Meeting Workers' Needs in the Apparel and Footwear Industries of Selected Countries*. Washington, DC, February 2000.

United States Senate. *Mergers and Industrial Concentration: Hearings Before the Subcommittee on Antitrust and Monopoly of the Senate Judiciary Committee*. Researcher: Howard Wachtel. Washington, DC, 12 May, 27 and 28 July and 21 September 1978.

Urban Dimensions Group, Inc. *Growth of the Contingent Workforce in Ontario: Structural Trends, Statistical Dimensions and Policy Implications*. A report prepared for the Ontario Women's Directorate, February 1989.

Van Houten, Gerry. *Corporate Canada: An Historical Outline*. Toronto: Progress Books, 1991.

Vannoy Adams, Michael. *The Multicultural Imagination: "Race," Color, and the Unconscious*. New York: Routledge, 1996.

Vetterling-Braggin, Mary, Frederick A. Elliston and Jane English, eds. *Feminism and Philosophy*. Totowa, NJ: Littlefield Adams, 1977.

Vickers, Jeanne. *Women and the World Economic Crisis*. Atlantic Highlands, NJ: Zed Books, 1991.

Vorst, Jesse, et al., eds. *Race, Class, Gender: Bonds and Barriers*. Toronto: Between the Lines, 1989.

Vosko, Leah. *The Last Thread: An Analysis of the Apparel Goods Provisions in the North American Free Trade Agreement and the Impact on Women*. Ottawa: Canadian Centre for Policy Alternatives, 1993.

Wachtel, Howard. *The Money Mandarins: The Making of a Supranational Economic Order*. New York: Pantheon Books, 1986.

Waring, Marilyn. *If Women Counted: A New Feminist Economics*. New York: Harper & Row, 1988.

Warner, Steven. *Fiber Science*. Englewood Cliffs, NJ: Prentice Hall, 1995.

Warnock, John. *Free Trade and the New Right Agenda*. Vancouver: New Star Books, 1988.

Watkins, Mel. *Madness and Ruin: Politics and the Economy in the Neoconservative Age*. Toronto: Between the Lines, 1992.

West Yorkshire Homeworking Group. *A Penny a Bag: Campaigning on Homework*. Batley: Yorkshire and Humberside Low Pay Unit, 1990.

Weston, Ann. *The NAFTA Papers: Implications for Canada, Mexico and Developing Countries*. Ottawa: The North-South Institute, 1994.

Wheatley, Phillis. *Poems on Various Subjects, Religious and Moral*. London: A. Bell, Bookfeller, Aldgate, 1773.

Wildung Harrison, Beverly. *Making the Connections: Essays in Feminist Social Ethics*. Edited by Carol Robb. Boston: Beacon Press, 1985.

Wilson James, Janet, ed. *Women in American Religion*. Philadelphia: University of Pennsylvania Press, 1980.

Wilson, S.J. *Women, the Family and the Economy*. Toronto: McGraw-Hill Ryerson, 1986.

Winter, Gibson. *Elements for a Social Ethic: Scientific Perspectives on Social Process*. New York: Macmillan, 1966.

Winter, Miriam Therese. *Woman Wisdom*. New York: Crossroad, 1991.

_____. *Woman Witness*. New York: Crossroad, 1992.

Wise, Cavel, ed. *The Post-NAFTA Political Economy: Mexico and the Western Hemisphere*. Baltimore: John Hopkins University, JAIS School of Advanced International Studies, 1997.

Women's Self Help Network. *Working Together for Change*. Vols. 1 and 2: *Training Manual and Final Report*. Campbell River, BC: Ptarmigan Press, 1984.

Women's World Congress for a Healthy Planet, Miami. *Action Agenda 21* (8-12 November 1991): 16-24. New York: Women's Environment and Development Organization, 1992.

World Conference of Church and Society: Official Report. Geneva: World Council of Churches, 1966.

Yalnizyan, Armine. *A Statistical Profile of Toronto's Labour Market 1976-1987*. Toronto: Social Planning Council, 1988.

―――――. *Lessons from the Dew Line: The Experience of Canadian Garment Workers*. Ottawa: Canadian Centre for Policy Alternatives, 1993.

Yalnizyan, Armine, T. Ran Ide and Arthur Cordell. *Shifting Time: Social Policy and the Future of Work*. Toronto: Between the Lines, 1994.

Young, Gay, Vidyamali Samarasinghe and Ken Kusterer. *Women at the Center: Development Issues and Practices for the 1990s*. West Hartford, CT: Kumarian Press, 1993.

Zweig, Michael, ed. *Religion and Economic Justice*. Philadelphia: Temple University Press, 1991.

Articles

Action Canada Network. "Action Bulletin: Special Budget Issue." 27 February 1995, 1-2.

Ainsworth, Jackie, et al. "Getting Organized...." In *Still Ain't Satisfied: Canadian Feminism Today*, edited by Maureen Fitzgerald, Connie Guberman and Margie Wolfe, 132-67. Toronto: Women's Press, 1982.

Allen, Sheila. "Locating Homework in an Analysis of the Ideological and Material Constraints on Women's Paid Work." In *Homework: Historical and Contemporary Perspectives on Paid Labor at Home*, edited by Eileen Boris and Cynthia Daniels, 272-91. Chicago: University of Illinois Press, 1989.

Amos, Valerie, and Pratibha Parmar. "Challenging Imperial Feminism." *Feminist Review* 17 (July 1984): 3-19.

Andrew, Caroline. "Women and the Welfare State." *Canadian Journal of Political Science* 17, 4 (December 1988): 667-83.

Anonymous Report. "Information Regarding the Tailoring Trade in a Small District of Toronto." Deputy Minister of Labour files, 1916-20, in Archives of Ontario. Referenced in Catherine Macleod, "Women in Production: The Toronto Dressmakers' Strike of 1931," in *Women at Work, Ontario, 1850-1930*, edited by Janice Acton, Penny Goldsmith and Bonnie Shepard, 316. Toronto: Canadian Women's Educational Press, 1974.

Arat-Koç, Sedef. "Importing Housewives: Non-Citizen Domestic Workers and the Crisis of the Domestic Sphere in Canada." In *Through the Kitchen Window: The Politics of Home and Family*, edited by Meg Luxton, Harriet Rosenberg and Sedef Arat-Koç, 81-104. Toronto: Garamond Press, 1990.

Arat-Koç, Sedef, and Fely Villasin. *Report and Recommendations on the Foreign Domestic Movement Program.* Toronto: Intercede, 1993.

Baca Zinn, Maxine, Lynn Weber Cannon, Elizabeth Higginbotham and Bonnie Thornton Dill. "The Costs of Exclusionary Practices in Women's Studies." *Signs: Journal of Women in Culture and Society* 11, 21 (Winter 1986): 290-303.

Bakker, Isabella. "Pay Equity and Economic Restructuring: The Polarization of Policy?" In *Just Wages: A Feminist Assessment of Pay Equity*, edited by Judy Fudge and Patricia McDermott, 254-80. Toronto: University of Toronto Press, 1991.

Banks, Brian. "One Billion Buyers, Easy Credit Terms." *Canadian Business* 67, 6 (June 1994): 33-36.

Barrett, Michèle, and Mary McIntosh. "Ethnocentrism and Socialist-Feminist Theory." *Feminist Review* 20 (June 1985): 23-47.

Basset, Penny. "Declining Female Labour Force Participation." *Perspectives: Labour and Income* 6, 2 (Summer 1994): 36-39.

Benería, Lourdes. "Gender and the Global Economy." In *Instability and Change in the World Economy*, edited by Arthur MacEwan, 241-58. New York: Monthly Review Press, 1989.

Benhabib, Seyla. "The Generalized and the Concrete Other." In *Ethics: A Feminist Reader*, edited by Elizabeth Frazer, Jennifer Hornsby and Sabina Lovibond, 267-300. Oxford: Blackwell, 1992.

Binder Wall, Naomi. "The Beautiful Strength of My Anger Put to Use." In *And Still We Rise: Feminist Political Mobilizing in Contemporary Canada*, edited by Linda Carty, 279-98. Toronto: Women's Press, 1993.

Black, Naomi. "The Canadian Women's Movement: The Second Wave." In *Changing Patterns: Women in Canada*, edited by Sandra Burt, Lorraine Code and Lindsay Dorney, 80-102. Toronto: McClelland and Stewart, 1988.

Boff, Leonardo. "The Contribution of Liberation Theology to a New Paradigm." In *Paradigm Change in Theology: A Symposium for the Future*, edited by Hans Küng and David Tracy, 408-23. New York: Crossroad, 1989.

Borowy, Jan, Shelly Gordon and Gayle Lebans. "Are These Clothes Clean? The Campaign for Fair Wages and Working Conditions for Homeworkers." In *And Still We Rise: Feminist Political Mobilizing in Contemporary Canada*, edited by Linda Carty, 299-330. Toronto: Women's Press, 1993.

Borowy, Jan, and Theresa Johnson. "Unions Confront Work Reorganization and the Rise of Precarious Employment: Home-Based Work in the Garment Industry and the Federal Public Service." In *Reshaping Work: Union Response to Technological Change*, edited by Christopher Schenk and John Anderson, 29-47. Don Mills, ON: Technology Adjustment Research Programme, Ontario Federation of Labour, 1995.

Bowles, Samuel, and Herbert Gintis. "The Economy Produces People: An Introduction to Post-Liberal Democracy." In *Religion and Economics*, edited by Michael Zweig, 221-44. Philadelphia: Temple University Press, 1991.

Brandt, Gail Cuthbert. "Weaving It Together: Life Cycle and the Industrial Experience of Female Cotton Workers in Quebec, 1910-1950." *Labour/Le Travail* 7 (Spring 1981): 113-26.

_____. "Pigeon-Holed and Forgotten: The Work of the Sub-Committee on the Post-War Problems of Women, 1943." *Social History* 15, 29 (1982): 239-59.

_____. "Women in the Quebec Cotton Industry, 1890-1950." *Material History Review* 31 (Spring 1990): 99-105.

_____. "Postmodern Patchwork: Some Recent Trends in the Writing of Women's History in Canada." *Canadian Historical Review* 72, 4 (December 1991): 441-70.

_____. "National Unity and the Politics of Political History." *Journal of the Canadian Historical Association* 3 (1992): 3-11.

Brooks, Neil. "We Can Save Social Programs." *Pro-Canada Dossier* 30 (March-April 1991): 11-12.

Brossard, Nicole. "Memory: Holocaust of Desire." *Trivia: A Journal of Ideas* 13 (Fall 1988): 42-47.

Brown, Rosemary. "Overcoming Sexism and Racism—How?" In *Racism in Canada*, edited by Ormond McKague, 163-78. Saskatoon: Fifth House Publishers, 1991.

Browne, Paul Leduc. "Under the Guise of Fairness, the Federal Budget Hurts Canadians in Need." Canadian Centre for Policy Alternatives, 22 February 1999. http://www.policyalternatives.ca.

Browne, Robert. "Alternatives to the International Monetary Fund." In *Beyond Bretton Woods: Alternatives to the Global Economic Order*, edited by John Cavanagh, Daphne Wysham and Marcos Arruda, 57-73. Boulder, CO: Pluto Press, with Institute for Policy Studies, Washington, and the Transnational Institute, Amsterdam, 1994.

Brubaker, Pamela K. "Economic Justice for Whom? Women Enter the Dialogue." In *Religion and Economics*, edited by Michael Zweig, 95-127. Philadelphia: Temple University Press, 1991.

Burt, Sandra. "Legislators, Women and Public Policy." In *Changing Patterns: Women in Canada*, edited by Sandra Burt, Lorraine Code and Lindsay Dorney, 129-56. Toronto: McClelland and Stewart, 1988.

Carr, Anne. "Feminist Theology in a New Paradigm." In *Paradigm Change in Theology: A Symposium for the Future*, edited by Hans Küng and David Tracy, 397-407. New York: Crossroad, 1989.

Cassidy, Richard. "The Ethics of Jesus, Christ-Centered Ethics and Lonergan's Method." In *Lonergan Workshop IV*, edited by F. Lawrence, 27-37. Chico, CA: Scholars Press, 1983.

Catty, James P. "Canada's Most Significant Merger." *CA Magazine* (September 1983): 48-51.

Christensen, Kathleen. "Independent Contracting." In *The New Era of Home-Based Work: Directions and Policies*, edited by Kathleen Christensen, 79-94. London: Westview Press, 1988.

_____. "Home-Based Clerical Work: No Simple Truth, No Single Reality." In *Homework: Historical and Contemporary Perspectives on Paid Labor at Home*, edited by Eileen Boris and Cynthia Daniels, 183-97. Chicago: University of Illinois Press, 1989.

Christiansen Ruffman, Linda. "Inherited Biases within Feminism: The 'Patricentric Syndrome' and the 'Either/Or Syndrome' in Sociology." In *Feminism: From Pressure to Politics*, edited by Angela Miles and Geraldine Finn, 123-46. Montreal: Black Rose Books, 1989.

"Clean Clothes Campaign." Amsterdam, The Netherlands, April 1993.

Clean Clothes Newsletter (Amsterdam, The Netherlands), 1 (November 1993) and 11 (August 1999).

Coalition for Fair Wages and Working Conditions for Homeworkers. "Backgrounders." Toronto, 1992.

_____. "Homeworkers Win Thousands of Dollars in Back Wages." *Newsletter* (June 1993): 2.

Cocks, Nancy. "The Wisdom of Doing Justice." In *Coalitions for Justice: The Story of Canada's Interchurch Coalitions*, edited by Christopher Lind and Joe Mihevc, 332-50. Ottawa: Novalis, 1994.

Code, Lorraine. "Credibility: A Double Standard." In *Feminist Perspectives: Philosophical Essays on Method and Morals*, edited by Lorraine Code, Sheila Mullett and Christine Overall, 64-88. Toronto: University of Toronto Press, 1988.

_____. "Feminist Theory." In *Changing Patterns: Women in Canada*, edited by Sandra Burt, Lorraine Code and Lindsay Dorney, 18-50. Toronto: McClelland and Stewart, 1988.

Cohen, Yolande. "Thoughts on Women and Power." In *Feminism: From Pressure to Politics*, edited by Angela Miles and Geraldine Finn, 353-74. Montreal: Black Rose Books, 1989.

Collier, Mary. "The Woman's Labour: 1739." In *The Augustan Reprint Society*, Publication No. 30, 5-17. Los Angeles: University of California William Andrews Clark Memorial Library, 1985.

Commission on the Status of Women. "Fourth World Conference on Women, Beijing, China: Draft Platform of Action." Catalogue 95-14681E 160695. New York: United Nations, 1995.

Coraggio, José Luis. "Human Capital: The World Bank's Approach to Education in Latin America." In *Beyond Bretton Woods: Alternatives to the Global Economic Order*, edited by John Cavanagh, Daphne Wysham and Marcos Arruda, 166-71. Boulder, CO: Pluto Press, with Institute for Policy Studies, Washington, and the Transnational Institute, Amsterdam, 1994.

Cormie, Lee. "On the Option for the Poor and Oppressed in Doing Social Ethics." *Toronto Journal of Theology* 7, 1 (1991): 19-34.

Crosby, David. "A Genuine Progress Indicator for Canada: An Alternative to Growth as a Measure of Progress." In *Alternative Federal Budget 1997 Papers*, edited by Canadian Centre for Policy Alternatives and Cho!ces: A Coalition for Social Justice. Ottawa: CCPA, 1997.

Crysdale, Cynthia. "Lonergan and Feminism." *Theological Studies* 53, 2 (June 1992): 234-56.

_____. "Horizons that Differ: Women and Men and the Flight from Understanding." *Cross Currents* 44, 3 (Fall 1994): 345-61.

_____. "Women and the Social Construction of Self-Appropriation." In *Lonergan and Feminism*, edited by Cynthia Crysdale. Toronto: University of Toronto Press, 1994.

Culpeper, Roy. "Agenda for Development." Response to Stephen Lewis' speech given at the Canadian Conference on United Nations Reform, Montreal, 23-25 March 1995.

Dagg, Alexandra. "Information on the Proposed Merger of Our Union."
    Fabric 10, 2 (March 1995): 1.
_____. "Manager's Report." *Fabric* 9, 4 (May 1995): 1.
Dagg, Alexandra, and Judy Fudge. "Sewing Pains: Homeworkers in the
    Garment Trade." *Our Times* (June 1992): 22-25.
"Declaration, Oaxtepec, Morelos, Mexico, 13 March 1994." Reported in
    "Popular Alternatives and Continental Alliances," *Correspondencia*
    16 (May 1994): 20-22.
"Declaration of Sentiments and Resolutions, Seneca Falls." In *Femi-
    nism: The Essential Historical Writings*, edited by Miriam Schnier,
    76-82. New York: Vintage, 1972.
Dillon, John. "Turning Mexico Inside Out." *Pro-Canada Dossier* 29
    (March-April 1991): 21-23.
Donner, Arthur. "Recession, Recovery, and Redistribution: The Three R's
    of the Canadian State Macro-policy in the 1980s." In *The New Era
    of Global Competition: State Policy and Market Power*, edited by
    Daniel Drache and Meric Gertler, 27-47. Montreal and Kingston:
    McGill-Queen's University Press, 1991.
Doran, Robert. "Theological Grounds for a World-Cultural Humanity."
    In *Creativity and Method: Essays in Honour of Bernard Lonergan*,
    edited by Matthew Lamb, 105-22. Milwaukee, WI: University
    Press, 1981.
_____. "Consciousness and Grace." *Method: Journal of Lonergan
    Studies* 11 (1993): 51-75.
Drache, Daniel. "Corporate Canada's Dream: Deal Makes Economic
    Continentalism a Political Reality." In *The Facts on Free Trade:
    Canada, Don't Trade It Away*, edited by Canadian Union of Public
    Employees, 35-39. Ottawa, 1988.
_____. "The Systematic Search for Flexibility: National Competitive-
    ness and New Work Relations." In *The New Era of Global Competi-
    tion: State Power and Market Power*, edited by Daniel Drache and
    Meric Gertler, 251-69. Montreal and Kingston: McGill-Queen's Uni-
    versity Press, 1991.
duRivage, Virginia, and David Jacobs, "Home-Based Work: Labor's
    Choices." In *Homework: Historical and Contemporary Perspectives
    on Paid Labor at Home*, edited by Eileen Boris and Cynthia Daniels,
    258-71. Chicago: University of Illinois Press, 1989.
Dworkin, Andrea. "The Politics of Intelligence." In *Ethics: A Feminist
    Reader*, edited by Elizabeth Frazer, Jennifer Hornsby and Sabina
    Lovibond, 100-31. Oxford: Blackwell, 1992.

Ecumenical Coalition for Economic Justice (ECEJ). "Ethical Reflections in the MAI." *Economic Justice Report* 9, 1 (March 1998).

————. "Not by Choice—The Growing Phenomena of Homework." *Economic Justice Report* 3, 1 (January 1992): 1-3.

————. "From the Double Day to the Endless Day." *Economic Justice Report* 3, 4 (December 1992): 1, 8-11.

————. "Fifty-one Alternatives to NAFTA." *Economic Justice Report* 4, 1 (April 1993): 1-8.

————. "The Global Garment Industry: Industrial Model for the Future." *Economic Justice Report* 5, 1 (April 1994): 1-3, 5-6, 8.

————. "Phase Out of Multifibre Arrangement Benefits Transnationals." *Economic Justice Report* 5, 1 (April 1994): 3-4.

————. "Jobs Are the Key to Social Security. Part One: Why and How Social Programs Will Be Cut, and Part Two: Matching Idle Hands with Unmet Needs." *Economic Justice Report* 5, 3 (October 1994).

————. "Social Policy Debate Raises Tough Questions." *Economic Justice Report* 5, 4 (December 1994).

————. "Jubilee 2000: Time for Debt Remission." *Economic Justice Report* 8, 4 (December 1997).

————. "Redistributing Wealth: A Jubilee Vision for a Global Vision." *Economic Justice Report* 10, 3 (October 1999).

Eteki, Marie-Louise. "Feminism and Democracy in Africa." *Match News* (Fall 1990): 1, 3-4.

Felix, David. "The Tobin Tax Proposal: Background, Issues and Prospects." A policy paper commissioned by the United Nations Development Program for the World Summit for Social Development: UNDP Human Development Report Office. New York: United Nations, 1994.

Findlay, Sue. "Problematizing Privilege: Another Look at Representation." In *And Still We Rise: Feminist Political Mobilizing in Contemporary Canada*, edited by Linda Carty, 207-24. Toronto: Women's Press, 1993.

Flax, Jane. "Women Do Theory." In *Women and Values: Readings in Recent Feminist Philosophy*, edited by Marilyn Pearsall, 2-7. Belmont, CA: Wadsworth Publishing, 1986.

Frager, Ruth. "No Proper Deal: Women Workers and the Canadian Labour Movement, 1870-1940." In *Union Sisters: Women in the Labour Movement*, edited by Linda Briskin and Lynda Yanz, 44-64. Toronto: Women's Press, 1983.

_____. "Sewing Solidarity: The Eaton's Strike of 1912." *Canadian Women's Studies* 7, 3 (Fall 1986): 96-98.

Fraser, Nancy. "What's Critical about Critical Theory? The Case of Habermas and Gender." In *Feminism as Critique: On the Politics of Gender*, edited by Seyla Benhabib and Drucilla Cornell, 31-55. Minneapolis: University of Minnesota Press, 1987.

Fudge, Judy, and Patricia McDermott. "Pay Equity in a Declining Economy: The Challenge Ahead." In *Just Wages: A Feminist Assessment of Pay Equity*, edited by Judy Fudge and Patricia McDermott, 281-88. Toronto: University of Toronto Press, 1991.

Gagnon, Madelaine. "My Body in Writing." In *Feminism: From Pressure to Politics*, edited by Angela Miles and Geraldine Finn, 379-88. Montreal: Black Rose Books, 1989.

Gannagé, Charlene. "Changing Dimensions of Control and Resistance: The Toronto Garment Industry." *Journal of Canadian Studies* 24, 4 (Winter 1989-90): 41-60.

GATT-Fly (Ecumenical Coalition for Economic Justice). "Free Trade in Services: The Multinationals' Agenda." *Pro-Canada Dossier* 21 (18 August 1989): 13-15.

Gilkey, Langdon. "The Paradigm Shift in Theology." In *Paradigm Change in Theology: A Symposium for the Future*, edited by Hans Küng and David Tracy, 367-83. New York: Crossroad, 1989.

Godard, Francis. "How Do Ways of Life Change?" In *Beyond Employment*, edited by Nanneka Redclift and Enzo Minigone. London: Macmillan, 1985.

Gorostiaga, Xabier. "The New Consensus: A Civilization Based on Harmony and Simplicity." Presented to a New Development Options Conference in Oslo, Sweden, 1995.

Gregory, Judith. "The Electronic Sweatshop." In *Perspectives on Women in the 1980s*, edited by Joan Turner and Lois Emery, 99-112. Winnipeg: University of Manitoba Press, 1983.

Griffin Cohen, Marjorie. "Women and Free Trade." In *The Free Trade Debates*, edited by Duncan Cameron. Toronto: James Lorimer, 1986.

_____. "Americanizing Services: U.S. Firms Eager to Run Our Institutions—For a Profit." In *The Facts on Free Trade: Canada, Don't Trade It Away*, edited by Canadian Union of Public Employees, 63-67. Ottawa, 1988.

————. "The Problem of Studying 'Economic Man.'" In *Feminism: From Pressure to Politics*, edited by Angela Miles and Geraldine Finn, 147-60. Montreal: Black Rose Books, 1989.

————. "Exports, Unemployment, and Regional Inequality: Economic Policy and Trade Theory." In *The New Era of Global Competition*, edited by Daniel Drache and Meric Gertler, 83-102. Montreal and Kingston: McGill-Queen's University Press, 1991.

————. "The Implications of Economic Restructuring for Women: The Canadian Situation." In *Engendering Macroeconomic Policy Reform*, edited by Isa Bakker. London: Zed Books, 1994.

Haddad, Jane, and Stephen Milton. "The Construction of Gender Roles in Social Policy: Mothers' Allowances and Day Care in Ontario Before World War II." *Canadian Women's Studies* 7, 4 (Winter 1986): 68-70.

Harder, Lois. "The Trouble With Democracy: Childcare Reform in Ontario and the Politics of Participation." In *And Still We Rise: Feminist Political Mobilizing in Contemporary Canada*, edited by Linda Carty, 243-57. Toronto: Women's Press, 1993.

Harding, Sandra. "The Instability of the Analytical Categories of Feminist Theory." In *Sex and Scientific Inquiry*, edited by Sandra Harding and Jean O'Barr, 283-302. Chicago: University of Chicago Press, 1975.

Hartmann, Heidi. "The Family as the Locus of Gender, Class and Political Struggle: The Example of Housework." In *Feminism and Methodology*, edited by Sandra Harding, 109-34. Indianapolis: Indiana University Press, 1987.

Hartsock, Nancy. "Feminist Theory and the Development of Revolutionary Strategy." In *Women and Values: Readings in Recent Feminist Philosophy*, edited by Marilyn Pearsall, 8-18. Belmont, CA: Wadsworth, 1986.

————. "The Feminist Standpoint: Developing the Ground for a Specifically Feminist Historical Materialism." In *Feminism and Methodology*, edited by Sandra Harding, 157-80. Indianapolis: Indiana University Press, 1987.

Himani Bannerji, Dionne Brand, Prabha Khosla and Makeda Silvera. "Conversation." *Women of Colour*, special issue of *Fireweed: A Feminist Quarterly* 16 (Spring 1983): 8-12, 14-15, as reprinted in *Canadian Women's Issues*, vol. 1: *Strong Voices*, edited by Ruth Roach Pierson, Marjorie Griffin Cohen, Paula Bourne and Philinda Masters, 235-38. Toronto: James Lorimer, 1993.

Hobbs, Margaret. "Equality and Difference: Feminism and the Defence of Women Workers during the Great Depression." *Labour/Le Travail* 32 (Fall 1993): 201-24.

Hogue, Jacqueline. "Madeleine Parent: une militante chevronnée." *Canadian Women's Studies* 7, 3 (Fall 1986): 103-104.

Holmstrom, Nancy. "Do Women Have a Distinct Nature?" In *Women and Values: Readings in Recent Feminist Philosophy*, edited by Marilyn Pearsall, 51-61. Belmont, CA: Wadsworth, 1986.

Hutchison, Roger. "Towards a 'Pedagogy for Allies of the Oppressed.'" *Studies in Religion/Sciences Religieuses* 13, 2 (Spring 1984): 145-50.

Intercede. "Domestics Sweep the World." *Wages for Housework Campaign Bulletin* 5, 1 (Spring 1981).

International Federation of Unions, "Organizing Homebased Workers." *Women at Work* (Winter 1994-95): 1-4.

International Ladies' Garment Workers' Union (ILGWU). "Special Edition on Union Merger." *Fabric* (24 March 1995): 1-4.

Johnson, Leo. "The Political Economy of Ontario Women in the Nineteenth Century." In *Women at Work, Ontario, 1850-1930*, edited by Janice Acton, Penny Goldsmith and Bonnie Shepard, 13-31. Toronto: Canadian Women's Educational Press, 1974.

Johnston, Wendy. "Introduction" to Madelaine Gagnon, "My Body in Writing." In *Feminism: From Pressure to Politics*, edited by Angela Miles and Geraldine Finn, 366-68. Montreal: Black Rose Books, 1989.

Jones, Susan. "New Legal Battle over Telework." *TECH Notes* 4 (April 1993): 4-5.

Kazi, Hamida. "The Beginning of a Debate Long Due: Some Observations on Ethnocentrism and Socialist-Feminist Theory." *Feminist Review* 22 (February 1986): 87-91.

Kelly Gadol, Joan. "The Social Relation of the Sexes." In *Feminism and Methodology*, edited by Sandra Harding, 15-28. Indianapolis: Indiana University Press, 1987.

Kidd, Dorothy. "Women's Organization: Learning from Yesterday." In *Women at Work, Ontario, 1850-1930*, edited by Janice Acton, Penny Goldsmith and Bonnie Shepard, 331-62. Toronto: Canadian Women's Educational Press, 1974.

Kline, Marlee. "Critique of the 'Feminist Standpoint.'" In *Race, Class, Gender: Bonds and Barriers*, edited by Jesse Vorst et al., 37-64. Toronto: Between the Lines, 1989.

Kollontai, Alexandra. "Sexual Relations and the Class Struggle." In *Ethics: A Feminist Reader*, edited by Elizabeth Frazer, Jennifer Hornsby and Sabina Lovibond, 303-18. Oxford: Blackwell, 1992.

Kopfensteiner, Thomas. "Globalization and the Autonomy of Moral Reasoning: An Essay in Fundamental Moral Theology." *Theological Studies* 54, 3 (1993): 485-511.

K[night] of L[abour]. "Where Labor Is Not a Prayer. *Walsh's Magazine* (Toronto, 1895-96): 112. Reprinted in "How the Sweatshop System Began: 'Homework' in Toronto." In *The Canadian Worker in the Twentieth Century*, edited by I. Abella and D. Millar, 154-56. Toronto: Oxford University Press, 1978.

Labour Behind the Label Coalition. "Wear Fair Action Kit." Toronto: Labour Behind the Label Coalition, 1998. http://www.web.net/˜msn, 1998.

Lamb, Matthew. "The Dialectics of Theory and Praxis within Paradigm Analysis." In *Paradigm Change in Theology: A Symposium for the Future*, edited by Hans Küng and David Tracy, 63-109. New York: Crossroad, 1989.

————. "Paradigms as Imperatives towards Critical Collaboration." In *Paradigm Change in Theology: A Symposium for the Future*, edited by Hans Küng and David Tracy, 453-60. New York: Crossroad, 1989.

Langille, David. "The Business Council on National Issues and the Canadian State." *Studies in Political Economy* 24 (Autumn 1987): 41-85.

Langille, David. "The BCNI Calls the Shots: Big Corporations Are Pulling the Canada-U.S. Trade Strings." In *The Facts on Free Trade: Canada, Don't Trade It Away*, edited by Canadian Union of Public Employees, 102-107. Ottawa, 1988.

Langille, David. "Exposing the Face of Corporate Rule." Toronto: Jesuit Centre for Social Faith and Justice, 1996.

Lawrence, Fred. "The Fragility of Consciousness: Lonergan and the Postmodern Other." *Theological Studies* 54 (1993): 55-94.

Leach, Belinda. "Flexible Work, Precarious Future: Some Lessons from the Canadian Clothing Industry." *Canadian Review of Sociology and Anthropology* 30, 1 (1993): 64-77.

Lee Bartky, Sandra. "Toward a Phenomenology of Feminist Consciousness." In *Feminism and Philosophy*, edited by Mary Vetterling-Braggin, Frederick A. Elliston and Jane English. Totowa, NJ: Littlefield Adams, 1977.

Lee, Marc. "Global Alternatives and Future Negotiations." Submission for the Ottawa-based Canadian Centre for Policy Alternatives to the Canadian Standing Committee on Foreign Affairs and International Trade, 26 April 1999.

Lonergan, Bernard. "Natural Right and Historical Mindedness." In *A Third Collection*. Edited by Frederick E. Crowe. New York: Paulist Press, 1985.

————. "The Ongoing Genesis of Methods." In *A Third Collection*. Edited by Frederick E. Crowe. New York: Paulist Press, 1985.

Lorde, Audre. "Age, Race, Class and Sex: Women Redefining Difference." In *Ethics: A Feminist Reader*, edited by Elizabeth Frazer, Jennifer Hornsby and Sabina Lovibond, 212-22. Oxford: Blackwell, 1992.

Loxley, John. "The Great Money Trick: The 1999-2000 Liberal Budget versus the Alternative Federal Budget." Department of Economics, University of Manitoba. http://www.policyalternatives.ca.

Lugones, Maria, and Elizabeth Spelman. "Have We Got a Theory for You! Feminist Theory, Cultural Imperialism and the Demand for 'The Woman's Voice.'" In *Women and Values: Readings in Recent Feminist Philosophy*, edited by Marilyn Pearsall, 19-31. Belmont, CA: Wadsworth, 1986.

Luxton, Meg. "The Home: A Contested Terrain." In *Still Ain't Satisfied: Canadian Feminism Today*, edited by Maureen Fitzgerald, Connie Guberman and Margie Wolfe, 112-22. Toronto: Women's Press, 1982.

Maart, Rozena. "Consciousness, Knowledge and Morality: The Absence of the Knowledge of White Consciousness in Contemporary Feminist Theory." In *A Reader in Feminist Ethics*, edited by Debra Shogan, 129-69. Toronto: Canadian Scholars' Press, 1993.

————. "Speaking Up, Speaking Out." In *A Reader in Feminist Ethics*, edited by Debra Shogan, 205-15. Toronto: Canadian Scholars' Press, 1993.

MacKinnon, Catherine. "Feminism, Marxism, Method, and the State: Toward Feminist Jurisprudence." In *Feminism and Methodology*, edited by Sandra Harding, 135-56. Indianapolis: Indiana University Press, 1987.

Macleod, Catherine. "Women in Production: The Toronto Dressmakers' Strike of 1931." In *Women at Work, Ontario, 1850-1930*, edited by Janice Acton, Penny Goldsmith and Bonnie Shepard, 309-30. Toronto: Canadian Women's Educational Press, 1974.

Maquila Solidarity Network. "Set-in Wins 'No Sweat Policy.'" *Maquila Network Update* 5, 2 (June 2000).

McDaniel, Susan. "The Changing Canadian Family: Women's Roles and the Impact of Feminism." In *Changing Patterns: Women in Canada*, edited by Sandra Burt, Lorraine Code and Lindsay Dorney, 103-28. Toronto: McClelland and Stewart, 1988.

McIntosh, Robert. "Sweated Labour: Female Needleworkers in Industrializing Canada." *Labour/Le Travail* 32 (Fall 1993): 105-38.

Metz, Johann Baptist. "Theology in the New Paradigm: Political Theology." In *Paradigm Change in Theology: A Symposium for the Future*, edited by Hans Küng and David Tracy, 355-66. New York: Crossroad, 1989.

Miles, Angela. "Ideological Hegemony in Political Discourse: Women's Specificity and Equality." In *Feminism: From Pressure to Politics*, edited by Angela Miles and Geraldine Finn, 271-86. Montreal: Black Rose Books, 1989.

Millar, D. "Women's Work." In *The Canadian Worker in the Twentieth Century*, edited by I. Abella and D. Millar, 154-56. Toronto: Oxford University Press, 1978.

Miller, Amata. "Global Economic Structures: Their Human Implications." In *Religion and Economics*, edited by Michael Zweig, 163-95. Philadelphia: Temple University Press, 1991.

Mitter, Swasti. "On Organizing Women in Casualized Work: A Global Overview." In *Dignity and Daily Bread: New Forms of Economic Organizing among Poor Women in the Third World and the First*, edited by Sheila Rowbotham and Swasti Mitter, 14-52. New York: Routledge, 1994.

Mohanty, Chandra. "Under Western Eyes: Feminist Scholarship and Colonial Discourses." *Feminist Review* 30 (Autumn 1988): 61-88.

Moody's International Manual. New York: Moody's Investors Service, December 1995. See "Bank of Canada," 1091-92; "Dylex Ltd.," 1243-44; "Government of Canada," 801-803; "Hudson's Bay Company," 1333-34; and "Singer Companies," 5132-33 and 6309.

Moore Lappé, Frances, and J. Baird Callicott. "Individual and Community in Society and Nature." In *Religion and Economics*, edited by Michael Zweig, 245-52. Philadelphia: Temple University Press, 1991.

Mullett, Sheila. "Shifting Perspectives: A New Approach to Ethics." In *Feminist Perspectives: Philosophical Essays on Method and Morals*, edited by Lorraine Code, Sheila Mullett and Christine Overall, 109-26. Toronto: University of Toronto Press, 1988.

Mummé, Carla Lipsig. "Renaissance of Homeworking in Developed Economies." *Industrial Relations* 38 (1983): 545-67.

———. "Women in the Clothing Trades." *Studies in Political Economy* 22 (1987): 41-71.

Muszynski, Alicya. "What Is Patriarchy?" In *Race, Class, Gender: Bonds and Barriers*, edited by Jesse Vorst et al., 65-86. Toronto: Between the Lines, 1989.

Nacpil-Alejandro, Lidy. "Some Notes on Economic Alternatives from a Feminist View." In *God's Image* 14, 1 (Spring 1995): 3-13.

"NAFTA Negotiating Text Exposes Hypocrisy of Mulroney Government." *Continental Trade Alert* 6, 3 (24 March 1992): 2.

Ng, Roxana. "Immigrant Women and Institutionalized Racism." In *Changing Patterns: Women in Canada*, edited by Sandra Burt, Lorraine Code and Lindsay Dorney, 184-203. Toronto: McClelland and Stewart, 1988.

Ng, Winnie. "Immigrant Women: The Silent Partners of the Women's Movement." In *Still Ain't Satisfied: Canadian Feminism Today*, edited by Maureen Fitzgerald, Connie Guberman and Margie Wolfe, 249-56. Toronto: Women's Press, 1982.

Nicholson, Linda. "Feminism and Marx." In *Feminism as Critique: On the Politics of Gender*, edited by Seyla Benhabib and Drucilla Cornell, 16-30. Minneapolis: University of Minnesota Press, 1987.

Nolan, Albert. "Taking Sides." *Scarboro Missions* (June 1985): 16-19.

Nourbese Philip, Marlene. "Gut Issues in Babylon: Racism and Anti-Racism in the Arts." *Fuse* 12, 5 (April-May 1989): 13-26.

O'Brien, Mary. "Feminist Praxis." In *Feminism: From Pressure to Politics*, edited by Angela Miles and Geraldine Finn, 327-44. Montreal: Black Rose Books, 1989.

O'Connor, June. "On Doing Religious Ethics." In *Women's Consciousness, Women's Conscience*, edited by Barbara Hilkert Andolsen, Christine Gudorf and Mary Pellauer, 265-84. San Francisco: Harper & Row, 1985.

O'Hara Graff, Ann. "The Struggle to Name Women's Experience: Assessment and Implications for Theological Construction." *Horizons* 20, 2 (Fall 1993): 215-33.

Oldfield, Margaret. "The Electronic Cottage—Boon or Bane for Mothers?" In *Proceedings of the Conference on Women, Work and Computerization, Helsinki, Finland, 30 June-2 July 1991*. Helsinki: Ministry of Social Affairs and Health, 1991.

Olson, Margrethe. "Corporate Culture and the Homeworker." In *The New Era of Home-Based Work: Directions and Policies*, edited by Kathleen Christensen, 126-34. London: Westview Press, 1988.

"Onward and Upward?" *Barron's*, 20 January 1992, 9-40.

Ordoñez, Juan Pablo. "No Human Being Is Disposable." Report. Washington: Project Dignity for Human Rights, 1995.

Panganiban, Ruth. "Women and Economics." *In God's Image* 14, 1 (Spring 1995): 13-16.

Parr, Joy. "Nature and Hierarchy: Reflections on Writing the History of Women and Children," *Atlantis* 11 (Fall 1985): 39-44.

Parsons, Susan. "Feminism and the Logic of Morality: A Consideration of Alternatives." In *Ethics: A Feminist Reader*, edited by Elizabeth Frazer, Jennifer Hornsby and Sabina Lovibond, 380-412. Oxford: Blackwell, 1992.

Parvey, Constance. "The Community Study: Its Mixed Messages for the Churches." In *Beyond Unity-in-Tension: Unity, Renewal, and the Community of Women and Men*, edited by Thomas Best. Geneva: WCC, 1988.

Pierson, Ruth Roach. "The History of Women and Paid Work." In *Women's Paid and Unpaid Work: Historical and Contemporary Perspectives*, edited by Paula Bourne, 17-34. Toronto: New Hogtown Press, 1985.

————. "Gender and the Unemployment Insurance Debates in Canada, 1934-1940." *Labour/Le Travail* 25 (1990): 77-103.

————. "The Mainstream Women's Movement and the Politics of Difference." In *Canadian Women's Issues*, vol. 1, by Ruth Roach Pierson, Marjorie Griffin Cohen, Paula Bourne and Philinda Masters, 186-263. Toronto: James Lorimer, 1993.

Pollack Petchesky, Rosalind. "Morality and Personhood: A Feminist Perspective." In *Ethics: A Feminist Reader*, edited by Elizabeth Frazer, Jennifer Hornsby and Sabina Lovibond, 413-39. Oxford: Blackwell, 1992.

Porter, Ann. "Women and Income Security in the Post-War Period: The Case of Unemployment Insurance, 1945-1962." *Labour/Le Travail* 31 (Spring 1993): 111-44.

Power Wilson, Andrea. "Gender Agenda: Women Overcoming Hurdles." *The Ontario Home Business Report: Working for People Working from Home* (February-April 1993): 28-30.

Prentice, Alison, et al. "Old and New Kinds of Work." In *Canadian Women: A History*, 123-28. Toronto: Harcourt, Brace, Jovanovich, 1988.

President's Corner, "Is a Devastating War in the Gulf and Perhaps Beyond Inevitable?" *The NECEF Report* 2, 3 (November-December 1990): 1-2. (NECEF is the Near East Cultural and Educational Foundation of Canada.)

"Profitable Overhaul: A Slimmer Eaton's Moves into High-Growth Fields." *Barron's*, 3 September 1984, 39.

Radford Ruether, Rosemary. "Spirit and Matter, Public and Private: The Challenge of Feminism to Traditional Dualisms." In *Embodied Love: Sensuality and Relationship as Feminist Values*, edited by Paula Cooey, Sharon Farmer and Mary Ellen Ross, 65-76. New York: Harper & Row, 1987.

_____. "Eschatology and Feminism." In *Lift Every Voice: Constructing Christian Theologies from the Underside*, edited by Susan Brooks Thistlethwaite and Mary Engel Potter, 11-124. New York: Harper & Row, 1990.

Ramazanoglu, Caroline. "Ethnocentrism and Socialist-Feminist Theory: A Response to Barrett and McIntosh." *Feminist Review* 22 (February 1986): 83-86.

Rivage, Virginia du, and David Jacobs. "Home-Based Work: Labor's Choices." In *Homework: Historical and Contemporary Perspectives on Paid Labor at Home* edited by Eileen Boris and Cynthia Daniels, 258-71. Chicago: University of Illinois Press, 1989.

Robb, Carol. "A Framework for Feminist Ethics." In *Women's Consciousness, Women's Conscience*, edited by Barbara Hilkert Andolsen, Christine Gudorf and Mary Pellauer, 211-34. San Francisco: Harper & Row, 1985.

Roberts, Nickie. "Sex, Class and Morality." In *Ethics: A Feminist Reader*, edited by Elizabeth Frazer, Jennifer Hornsby and Sabina Lovibond, 139-48. Oxford: Blackwell, 1992.

Rose, Hilary. "Hand, Brain, and Heart. A Feminist Epistemology for the Natural Sciences." In *Sex and Scientific Inquiry*, edited by Sandra Harding and Jean O'Barr, 265-82. Chicago: University of Chicago Press, 1987. Originally published in 1975.

Rose, Jaqueline. "Femininity and Its Discontents." In *Ethics: A Feminist Reader*, edited by Elizabeth Frazer, Jennifer Hornsby and Sabina Lovibond, 236-58. Oxford: Blackwell, 1992.

Safia Mirza, Heidi. "The Dilemma of Socialist Feminism: A Case for Black Feminism." *Feminist Review* 22 (February 1986): 103-105.

Sarvasy, Wendy, and Judith Van Allen. "Fighting the Feminization of Poverty: Socialist Feminist Analysis and Strategy." *Review of Radical Political Economics* 16 (1984): 98-110.

Shadd, Adrienne. "Institutionalized Racism and Canadian History: Notes of a Black Canadian." In *Racism in Canada*, edited by Ormond McKague, 1-6. Saskatoon: Fifth House, 1991.

Shields, Janice. "'Social Dumping' in Mexico under NAFTA." *Multinational Monitor*, 16, 4 (April 1995).

Shiva, Vandana. "Development, Ecology and Women." In *Healing the Wounds: The Promise of Ecofeminism*, edited by Judith Plant, 80-90. Toronto: Between the Lines, 1989.

Silman, Janet. "An Open Letter to Cranford Pratt and Roger Hutchinson." *Toronto Journal of Theology* 7, 1 (1991): 44-50.

Silvera, Makeda. "Immigrant Domestic Workers: Whose Dirty Laundry?" *Fireweed* 9 (1981): 53-58.

Sinclair, Scott. "Free Trade: A Dead-End Development Strategy for Mexico." *Pro-Canada Dossier* 27 (August 1990): 16-18.

Smith, Ruth. "Feminism and the Moral Subject." In *Women's Consciousness, Women's Conscience*, edited by Barbara Hilkert Andolsen, Christine Gudorf and Mary Pellauer, 235-50. San Francisco: Harper & Row, 1985.

Standing, Guy. "Global Feminization through Flexible Labour." *World Development* 17 (July 1989): 1077-95.

Stanford, Jim. "Economy Being Kept in Permanent Recession." Article adapted from a speech and published by the Canadian Centre for Policy Alternatives in *Monitor* 1, 10 (April 1995): 1.

Stanley, Liz, and Sue Wise. "Method, Methodology, and Epistemology in Feminist Research Processes." In *Feminist Praxis: Research, Theory, and Epistemology in Feminist Sociology*, edited by Liz Stanley, 20-60. London: Routledge, 1990.

Stinson, Jane. "Home Truths: Federal Government Teleworkers." *Our Times* 12, 1 (January 1993): 37-39.

Strong-Boag, Veronica. "Working Women and the State: The Case of Canada: 1889-1945." *Atlantis* 6 (Spring 1981): 1-9.

_____. "Discovering the Home: The Last 150 Years of Domestic Work in Canada." In *Women's Paid and Unpaid Work: Historical and Contemporary Perspectives*, edited by Paula Bourne, 35-60. Toronto: New Hogtown Press, 1985.

_____. "Writing about Women." In *Writing about Canada: A Handbook for Canadian Modern History*, edited by John Schultz, 175-200. Scarborough, ON: Prentice-Hall, 1990.

_____. "Ever a Crusader: Nellie McClung, First-Wave Feminist." In *Re-thinking Canada: The Promise of Women's History*, edited by Veronica Strong-Boag and Anita Fellman, 308-21. Toronto: Copp Clark Pitman, 1991.

_____. "Human Rights Law as Prism: Women's Organizations, Unions, and Ontario's Female Employees Fair Remuneration Act, 1951." *Canadian Historical Review* 72, 4 (December 1991): 532-57.

Swanson, Jean. "Competing to Be Poor." *Pro-Canada Dossier* 30 (March-April 1991): 10-11.

Tate, Jane. "Homework in West Yorkshire." In *Dignity and Daily Bread: New Forms of Economic Organizing among Poor Women in the Third World and the First*, edited by Sheila Rowbotham and Swasti Mitter, 193-217. New York: Routledge, 1994.

Tirado, Silvia. "Weaving Dreams, Constructing Realities: The Nineteenth of September National Union of Garment Workers in Mexico." In *Dignity and Daily Bread: New Forms of Economic Organizing among Poor Women in the Third World and the First*, edited by Sheila Rowbotham and Swasti Mitter, 100-13. New York: Routledge, 1994.

Toolan, David. "Nature Is a Heraclitean Fire: Reflection on Cosmology in an Ecological Age." *Studies in the Spirituality of Jesuits* 23, 5 (November 1991): 1-45.

Tracy, David. "Hermeneutical Reflections in the New Paradigm." In *Paradigm Change in Theology: A Symposium for the Future*, edited by Hans Küng and David Tracy, 34-62. New York: Crossroad, 1989.

U.S. Department of Labor. "Bureau of Labour Statistics: Bulletin 1961." In *Technological Change and Its Labour Impact in Five Industries*. Washington, DC, 1977.

Van Kirk, Sylvia. "The Role of Native Women in the Fur Trade Society of Western Canada, 1670-1830." In *Perspectives on Canadian Economic Development: Class, Staples, Gender and Elites*, edited by Gordon Laxer, 353-61. Toronto: Oxford University Press, 1991.

Vanier Institute. "Community Economic Development in Canada Today!" *Transition* (June 1990).

Wachtel, Howard. "Taming Global Money." In *Beyond Bretton Woods: Alternatives to the Global Economic Order*, edited by John Cavanagh, Daphne Wysham and Marcos Arruda, 74-81. Boulder, CO: Pluto Press, with Institute for Policy Studies, Washington, and the Transnational Institute, Amsterdam, 1994.

Wall, Naomi. "The Last Ten Years: A Personal/Political View." In *Still Ain't Satisfied: Canadian Feminism Today*, edited by Maureen Fitzgerald, Connie Guberman and Margie Wolfe, 15-29. Toronto: Women's Press, 1982.

Waring, Marilyn. "The Invisible Women." In *Public and Private Worlds: Women in Contemporary New Zealand*, edited by Shelagh Cox and Beverly James, 125-42. Wellington: Allen and Unwin New Zealand, 1987.

Webber, M., and S. Tonkin. "Technical Changes and the Rate of Profit in the Canadian Textile, Knitting and Clothing Industries." *Environment and Planning A* 20 (1988): 1487-1505.

Wentzel, Janice W. "The World's Women Unite in Diversity." *Canadian Woman Studies* 7, 1/2 (Spring/Summer 1986): 11-14.

Whitbeck, Caroline. "Theories of Sex Difference." In *Women and Values: Readings in Recent Feminist Philosophy*, edited by Marilyn Pearsall, 34-50. Belmont, CA: Wadsworth, 1986.

Wildung Harrison, Beverly. Review of *Feminism and Process Thought*. *Signs* (Spring 1982): 705-11.

————. "Restoring the Tapestry of Life: A Vocation of Feminist Theology." The Nelle Morton Lecture, 8 March 1984. In *The Drew Gateway* 54, 1 (1984): 39-48.

Wilson, Elizabeth. "Utopian Identities." In *Ethics: A Feminist Reader*, edited by Elizabeth Frazer, Jennifer Hornsby and Sabina Lovibond, 364-79. Oxford: Blackwell, 1992.

Women's Environment and Development Organization. "Does the Breast Cancer Epidemic Have Environmental Links?" *News and Views* 6, 1, (April 1993): 1, 9.

Yalnizyan, Armine. "Full Employment—Still a Viable Goal." In *Getting on Track: Social Democratic Strategies for Ontario*, edited by Daniel Drache. Montreal: McGill-Queen's University Press, 1992.

Yanz, Lynda. "Women's Maquila Network: Mexico to Central America." *Correspondencia* 16 (May 1994): 2-5.

Young, Iris. "Beyond the Unhappy Marriage: A Critique of Dual Systems Theory." In *Women and Revolution*, edited by Lydia Sargent, 43-70. Boston: South End Press, 1981.

Zweig, Michael. "Economics and Liberation Theology." In *Religion and Economics*, edited by Michael Zweig, 3-49. Philadelphia: Temple University Press, 1991.

Newspapers
Financial Post

11 November 1988. McKenna, Barrie. "Toronto Bay Store Serves as Prototype for Clothing Strategy," 4.

31 August 1990. "Mixed Review of Hudson Bay," 18.

28 September 1991. Evans, Mark. "Dylex Aiming to Raise $50M with Share Issue," 29.

22 November 1991. Evans, Mark. "Retailers Eye U.S. for Goods," 7.

12 December 1991. Evans, Mark. "Grim Outlook for Retailing," 5.

10 March 1992. Evans, Mark. "More Retail Carnage Foreseen," 3.

10 April 1992. Evans, Mark. "Dylex Confident of Profitability in '92," 20.

The Globe and Mail

20 September 1983. "Bay Boutique for Designers," F10.

6 May 1988. Howlett, Karen. "Hudson's Bay Unit Sell 'Just Kids' Clothing Division," B10.

10 November 1990. Kidd, Kenneth. "Retailers Skirt Shirt Benefit: $50-Million Break on Imports Ignored," B3.

9 January 1991. Galt, Virginia. "Federal Policies Common Thread in Protest: Garment Workers Demonstrate Over Job Losses as Bank Liquidates Upscale Firm," A6.

7 September 1991. Heinzl, John. "Big Loss for Dylex Despite More Sales," B7.

28 September 1991. Heinzl, John. "Dylex to Tap Stock Market," B5.

2 November 1991. Canadian Press. "Hudson's Bay Looks to U.S. Suppliers: Garment Makers Fear Loss of Business," B3.

30 November 1991. Heinzl, John. "Town and Country Chain to Close All 162 Stores: Dylex Decision to Cut Losses Affects 1,300 Employees," B1, 4.

7 December 1991. Heinzl, John. "Dylex Loss Deepens," B5.

12 December 1991. Heinzl, John. "865,312 Reasons for Sunday Shopping: Dylex Sends Ontario Premier Cheque to Show How Law has Boosted Sales," B1, 6.

10 March 1992. Heinzl, John. "Retailing Industry Still on Rocks: Survival Name of Game," B1, 10.

9 April 1992. Heinzl, John. "Dylex Posts $55.4-Million Loss: Discontinued Operations Account for Sizable Part of Year's Red Ink," B9.

10 April 1992. "Canadian Corporate Reports," B10.

5 May 1992. Heinzl, John. "Hudson's Bay to Buy 5 Robinsons Stores," B5.

15 May 1992. Chase, Steven "Bargain Harold's Goes Bi-the-Way: Dylex Buying 25 of Bankrupt Retailer's Sites to Expand Its BiWay Chain," B14.

29 May 1992. "Court Rules Against Homework Program," B5.

12 July 1992. Sweet, Lois. "Low Pay, Long Hours for Immigrant Piece Workers," A6.

15 August 1992. Bovard, James. "NAFTA's Protectionist Bent," B1, 3.

19 September 1992. Galt, Virginia. "Oh, Give Me a Home...," A1, A6.

22 September 1992. Stoffman, Daniel. "Immigration Adds Little to Economy," A17.

28 September 1992. "Lingerie a Strong Foundation for $20 Million-a-Year Firm," C1.

2 October 1992. Galt, Virginia. "$375 Jacket Stitched for $4, Conference Told: Protection for Homeworkers Promised as Union Seeks End to 'Exploitation,'" A1, A8.

26 October 1993. Little, Bruce, and Alan Freeman. "So, What's the Plan, Mr. Chrétien?" B1.

17 December 1993, "Homeworkers Receive Aid," A6.

1 January 1994. Saunders, John. "NAFTA: Day 1. Likely Winner on the Move," B1, 5.

1 January 1994. McKenna, Barrie. "NAFTA: Day 1. Threat Won't Force Change," B1, 5.

3 January 1994. "Support for NAFTA Hits All-Time High, Poll Says," A9.

15 February 1994. Rusk, James. "Garment Trade Conditions Protested," A16.

Inside U.S. Trade: An Exclusive Weekly Report on Major Government and Industry Trade Action
Special Reports

27 March 1992. "NAFTA Textiles Draft Reveals No Commitments on Tariffs, Quota Phaseout" and "NAFTA Text on Textiles," S1-5.

17 April 1992. "Senate Letter on NAFTA" and "U.S. Seeking Compromise with Canada on Rules of Origin for NAFTA Textiles," 17-18.

24 July 1992. "Canada Seeks to Block U.S. Market Access in NAFTA Textile Deal," 3.

14 August 1992. "Canada Accepts Three-Way Textile Deal, Falls Short on Wool Apparel Demands" and "Tariff-Rate Quotas in NAFTA Textile Deal," 4-5.

28 August 1992. "Textile Industry Likely to Press for Legislative Freeze on NAFTA Origin Rules," 1, 18-19.

4 September 1992. "Canadian Move to Lower Textile Tariffs Likely Despite Industry Opposition," 3.

5 March 1993. "Confidential White House Draft Details Options for NAFTA Labor Side Pact," S1-S10.

Kitchener-Waterloo Record

6 October 1992. "Home Sewers Exploited, Union Says," D1.

National Catholic Reporter

14 April 1995. Wirpsa, Leslie. "Women Risk Jobs to Denounce Maquilas," 8-9.

El Tiempo

17 March 1988. Ciudad Juarez, Mexico.

The Toronto Star

7 April 1982. Hepburn, Bob. "Almost 500 at Eaton's to be Laid Off," A3.

10 August 1982. "Recession Pinches Eaton's Too: Department Store Giant Says it Leads Rivals—in 'Race of Snails,'" E1.

9 November 1991. Landsberg, Michele. "Home Can Be a Sweatshop in Low-Paying Garment Trade," K1.

12 January 1992. Priest, Lisa. "Metro Workshop Told of 'Slave' Scandal," A2.

24 March 1992. "Trade Negotiators 'Stunned' by Leak," A1, 12.

7 April 1992. Ferguson, Jonathan. "Textile Firms Warn of Job Loss," A5.

26 August 1992. Girard, Daniel. "Sears Canada Issues Shares to Reduce Debt by $76 Million," F3.

6 September 1992. Girard, Daniel. "Risky Business," H1.

2 October 1992. Papp, Leslie. "Garment Industry Exploits 'Homeworkers,' Union Says," A2.

3 October 1992. Orwen, Patricia. "Rag Trade Future Unravelling Fast," A1, 8.

5 October 1992. Ontario Members of the Canadian Daily Newspaper Association and the Ontario Community Newspaper Association. "Adding to the Violence," A22.

7 October 1992. Papp, Leslie. "Pizza Order Clerks on Strike in Row Over 'Take-Home' Work," A2.

8 November 1992. McQuaig, Linda. "The Fraying of Our Social Safety Net," B1, 7.

8 November 1992. McQuaig, Linda. "U.S. Nurtures Idea the Poor Want to be Poor," B4.

9 November 1992. McQuaig, Linda. "Social Upheaval Taught Europe Value of Stability," A13: "Sweden's Cradle to Grave System."

10 November 1992. McQuaig, Linda. "You Get What You Pay for in Taxes," A1, and "A Matter of Priorities," A19.

11 November 1992. McQuaig, Linda. "Tory 'Stealth Policy' Slowly Kills Programs," A1, and "Moving toward the U.S. Model," A21.

12 November 1992. McQuaig, Linda. "How Much Do We Value Equality?" A1, and "What the Future Holds," A23.

29 November 1992. Hazel Henderson. "The Electronic Revolt," B1, 7.

18 December 1992. Keegan, William. "And Now the Real Irony: Capitalism Doesn't Work Either," A25.

18 December 1992. Fraser, Sylvia. "Freedom through Forgiveness," A27.

16 January 1993. Landsberg, Michele. "Unfair Media Biases Scrutinized by Women," J1.

19 January 1993. Landsberg, Michele. "To Valcourt, Raped, Beaten Women Aren't Refugees," C1.

25 January 1993. Moloney, Paul. "Pizza Pizza Franchisees Claim Company Exploits Them," C1.

30 January 1993. Thompson, Alan. "Persecuted Women May Be Accepted as Refugees," A1.

7 February 1993. Diebel, Linda. "Kissinger's 'Truly New World Order,'" B1.

7 February 1993. Ferguson, Jonathon. "The Winds of Trade," B1, 4.

11 February 1993. Ferguson, Jonathon. "Trade Pact a Step Back for Women, Rebick Says," A11.

15 February 1993. "Rape Victim [Kitty Nowdluk-Reynolds] Gets Apology from RCMP," A3.

7 March 1993. Wright, Lisa. "Protesters Swamp Eaton Centre: 1,000 Marchers Seek Justice for Workers on Strike," A7.

8 March 1993. Steed, Judy. "And the Revolution Goes On ... 90s Women Focus on a 'Fairer Share' of Power, Money," A1.

8 March 1993. Powell, Martin. "Marchers Call Firms Exploitative: Protest Precedes Women's Day," A10.

10 March 1993. Thompson, Alan. "Canada First in Recognizing Abused Women as Refugees," A2.

14 March 1993. Zerbisias, Antonia. "It's True: Dads Have No Time for Kids, Poll Shows," A14.

10 April 1993. Ferguson, Derek. "Mexican-Made Bras Don't Hold Up, Garment Workers Tell Trade Hearing," A6.

24 April 1993. Aarsteinsen, Barbara. "'Racist, Sexist' Slam Hits Heir to NAC Job," A6.

29 April 1993. Landsberg, Michele. "Anti-Immigrant Bigotry Sparks Attack on New Women's Leader," F1.

7 November 1993. Boyle, Theresa. "Moms of Victims Turn Grief to Action," A1, A6.

10 December 1993. Yakabuski, Konrad. "'Big Six' Bank Chiefs Take Home $6 Million," A1, A8.

10 December 1993. Yakabuski, Konrad. "At $800,000, Is this Man Underpaid?" D1.

16 December 1993. Papp, Leslie. "Home-Based Garment Workers Get Raise," A2.

17 December 1993. Payne, Steve. "Garment Workers Will Get Pay Hike," A14.

1 January 1994. McKenna, Barrie. "NAFTA: Day 1. Threat Won't Force Change," B1, 5.

7 January 1994. Landsberg, Michele. "Our Tolerance Focuses on White and Wealthy," B1.

4 February 1994. Toughill, Kelly. "A Gleeful Thorn in Their Side," A19.

15 February 1994. Van Alphen, Tony. "Help Urged for Garment Workers," A7.

21 February 1994. Murray, Maureen. "Business Handled Poorly, Alfred Sung Complains," B1.

6 March 1994. Zwolinski, Mark. "Women Mark Historic Year: Annual Event Organized by Women of Colour," A3.

23 March 1994. Camp, Dalton. "Politicians Blame Recession on Its Victims," A23.

28 March 1994. Murray, Maureen. "Let Free Trade Stretch Length of Americas, Organization of American States Head Says," D1.

29 March 1994. Murray, Maureen. "Banks to Topple Retail Empire," B1, 16.

30 March 1994. Murray, Maureen. "500 Out of Work as Judge Rules ETAC Bankrupt," C1.

30 March 1994. Walker, William. "NDP Puts Election Over New Policies," A1, 23.

2 April 1994. Murray, Maureen. "What Doused Rising Star ETAC Sales?" C1, 2.

23 May 1994. Crawford, Trish. "Fed-up Parents Unite to End School Violence," A1, 6.

25 May 1994. Monsebraaten, Laurie. "Poverty Stalking Young Families," A1, 6.

26 May 1994. Haliechuk, Rick. "Kay, Posluns Begin Court Battle for Control of Huge Dylex Empire," B1, 16.

26 May 1994. Murray, Maureen. "Hudson's Bay to Do Battle with Wal-Mart," B3.

21 June 1994. Monsebraaten, Laurie. "Rate of Child Poverty, Suicide 'Alarming,'" A1.

22 June 1994. Ferguson, Jonathan, and John Deverell. "Rate Hike Fuels Fear of New Recession," E1.

22 June 1994. Culpepper, Roy. "New Debt Crisis on Horizon," A19.

22 June 1994. "Chinese Textile Plant Death Toll Hits 52," A15.

24 June 1994. "Some Wealthy Show Knack for Avoiding Taxes," A12.

5 November 1994. Monsebraaten, Laurie. "Evolution of the Dole: Unemployment Insurance, A Capsule History," B1.

5 November 1994. Monsebraaten, Laurie. "Born Reluctantly, UI Turned into Ottawa's Main Social Policy Tool," B1, 6.

12 January 1995. Spears, John. "January Blowout: Troubled Dylex is Shutting Down 200 Stores," D1, 9.

24 January 1995. Deverell, John. "138 More Stores Will Be Closed, Dylex Reveals," D3.

25 January 1995. Deverell, John. "Dylex Gets $30 million Lifeline: Royal Bank Will Keep Retailer Afloat," B3.

27 January 1995. Chamberlain, Art. "20% Minimum Tax Urged on Big Profits," B1, 8.

29 January 1995. "How Tammy and Nancy Made Labour History," C1, 4.

31 January 1995. Deverell, John. "Dylex Set to Bargain for Survival: Troubled Retailer to Meet Landlords and Debt Holders," D3.

18 February 1995. McQuaig, Linda. "The Debt Obsession," C1, 4.

19 February 1995. McQuaig, Linda. "Who Cashes in on High Interest Rates," C4.

5 April 1995. Deverell, John. "Retail Woes Worsen: Survival Plan Removes Posluns from Ailing Dylex," C1, 3.

7 April 1995. Deverell, John. "Jubilant Bay Chief Celebrates Record Year," C1, 2.

10 April 1995. Deverell, John. "Eaton's Warehouse Revolution: Retailer Aims to Move Goods In and Out of Its Big Distribution Centre in a Day," E1, 3.

18 April 1995. Armstrong, Jane. "Tough Choices in 'Mean' Budget," A1, 12.

3 May 1995. McCarthy Shawn. "Tax Cut for Well-off Suggested," D1.

30 May 1995. McCarthy Shawn. "Nobel Winner Seeks Curb on Speculators," D3.

2 June 1995. Haliechuk, Rick. "Banks on Track to Record Profits," F1, 2.

5 July 1995. "What's a Billion? These People Know," B1.

1 February 1997. Scrivener, Leslie. "Church Bans Poster Naming Top Earners" and "Executive Salaries Called Unfair to Workers," A3 and K14.

The Toronto Sun

21 February 1994. Phooma, Rashida. "Still Fighting," S6.

Winnipeg Free Press

4 December 1991. Canadian Press. "Experts Foresee Reduction in Women's Clothing Stores," B27.

World Journal Daily News (Toronto Chinese Newspaper)
16 November 1991. "Life of Homeworkers—Suffering in Silence."

Speeches and Unpublished Material

Ecumenical Coalition for Economic Justice (ECEJ). "Notes on the Globalization of the Economic and Political System," Toronto, 31 March
1993. Unpublished

————. "Submission to the Ontario Ministry of Labour in Response to
the Consultation paper, 'Employment Standards Act and the Protection of Homeworkers,'" Toronto, 13 August 1993. Unpublished

Escalante, Ignacio Peón. "Savage Liberalism: A Case Study of the Clothing Industry in Mexico" (Mexico City, 1993). Translated by the
Ecumenical Coalition for Economic Justice, Toronto. Unpublished

GATT-Fly (Ecumenical Coalition for Economic Justice). "The Textile
and Clothing Industries in Canada: A Profile." Toronto, 1980.
Unpublished.

Griffin Cohen, Marjorie. "Feminism's Effect on Economics." Presented
to the Women's Studies Program, University of Toronto, 25 February 1985.

————. "The Razor's Edge Invisible: Feminism's Effect on Economics."
Presented to the Women's Studies Program, University of Toronto,
25 February 1985.

Handout at the OFL Convention, November 1991.

Homeworkers' Campaign Committee. "Homeworking Proposal: 'Homeworking: The Old and the New in Women's Employment.'"
Toronto, 1992. Unpublished.

International Ladies' Garment Workers' Union. "Challenging Employment Opportunity." Job description. Toronto, 1994.

————. Conference Notes. Port Elgin, ON, August 1992.

Kappler, Sheila. "Women and Justice in the Teachings of the Canadian
Catholic Bishops: Challenging the Categories." Ph.D. diss., University of St. Michael's College, Toronto, 1990.

Leach, Belinda. "Ideas about Work and Family: Outwork in Contemporary Ontario." Thesis, University of Toronto, Toronto, 1992.

Lewis, Stephen. "Agenda for Development." Speech given at the Canadian Conference on United Nations Reform, Montreal, 23-25
March 1995.

Lonergan, Bernard. "An Essay in Circulation Analysis: Revised Manuscript." Boston College, Spring 1983. Unpublished manuscripts, The Lonergan Research Institute, Toronto, ON.

McShane, Philip. "An Improbable Christian Vision and the Economic Rhythms of the Second Millennium Years." Unpublished manuscripts, The Lonergan Research Institute, Toronto, ON.

————. "Authentic Subjectivity and International Growth: Foundations." Unpublished manuscripts, The Lonergan Research Institute, Toronto, ON.

Mukherjee, Arun. "A House Divided: Black Women and American Feminist Theory." Unpublished paper, York University, Toronto.

National Action Committee on the Status of Women. "NAC Brief to the Sub-Committee on International Trade." Presented by Judy Rebick, Monique Simard and Hari Dimitrakopoulou-Ashton, 10 February 1993, 1-13.

National Apparel Bureau. Letter to the Hudson's Bay Company (Montreal, QC), 27 July 1993.

National Assembly of Religious Women. "Economics: Women's Cry for Change" (Kit). Chicago, 1988.

————. "Homeless Women: Creating Community, Creating Change" (Kit). Chicago, 1988.

National Interfaith Committee for Worker Justice. "Challenging Sweatshops: A Guide for the Religious Community" (Kit). Chicago, 1999.

Non-Governmental Organizations' Global Forum. "The Earth Charter." "Treaty on Alternative Economic Models." "Treaty on Consumption and Lifestyle." "Rio Framework Treaty on Non-Governmental Global Decision Making." "Draft Treaty on Racism." "Alternative Treaty on Trade and Sustainable Development." "Non-Governmental Treaty on Transnational Corporations: Democratic Regulation of TNC Conduct." Unpublished manuscripts, Rio de Janeiro, 11 June 1992.

O'Donovan, Theresa. "The Stubborn Argument of the Particular: Gregory Baum and Dorothy Smith." Ph.D. diss., University of St. Michael's College, Toronto, 1992.

————. "Towards a Feminist Theology of Work." In "On Human Work: A Feminist Critique of Laborem Exercens." Unpublished. Toronto, 1988.

Obedkoff, Vicki. "Crossing Over: A Feminist Theological Exploration of Co-dependency, the Recovery Movement and the Church." Ph.D. diss., Emmanuel College, Toronto, 1994.

Ontario Ministry of Labour. "The Employment Standards Act and the Protection of Homeworkers, Consultation Paper." Toronto, August 1993.

Pietilä, Hilkkä. "Daughters of Mother Earth." Unpublished papers, Finland, 1989.

––––––. "A Woman's Perspective: Some Outlines for Shaping a New Economics." Unpublished paper, Finland, 1991.

Public Service Alliance of Canada. "Homeworking (Telework) for Federal Public Workers." In the Conference on Homeworking Kit, "From the Double Day to the Endless Day." Toronto, 1992.

Schneiders, Sandra. Public lecture given at a Women Church Conference, Cincinnati, OH, 1988.

Silman, Janet. "A Women's View from Within: Indian Women as Moral Agents of Change in Canada." Ph.D. diss., Emmanuel College, Toronto, 1990.

Task Force on Immigration Practices and Procedures. *Domestic Workers on Employment Authorizations, Report.* April 1981, 35-45.

Tobin, James. Presentation given at a Canadian Centre for Policy Alternatives Seminar, National Arts Centre, Ottawa, 29 May 1995. Transcript: 5-6.

Townes, Emilie. "Critical Book Discussion: Kathryn Tanner, *The Politics of God: Christian Theologies and Social Justice* (Minneapolis: Fortress Press, 1992)." Presented at the Society of Christian Ethics' Thirty-fifth Annual Meeting, 7-9 January 1994, Chicago, IL.

Twohig-Moengangongo, Cora. "Feminist Consciousness and Bernard Lonergan's Notion of Dialectic." Ph.D. diss., Regis College, Toronto, 1992.

Unterberger, Alayne, and Ken Sturrock. "Health Status of Maquiladora Workers: What They Don't Know CAN Hurt Them." Unpublished Report, American Friends Service Committee, Philadelphia, 1998.

Wallach, Lori. "Impact of NAFTA on the U.S. Economy: NAFTA's Failure at 41 Months." Testimony by Public Citizen/Global Trade Watch before the International Trade Commission, 15 May 1997.

Waring, Marilyn. Public lecture sponsored by the Ontario Women's Directorate, Toronto 1990.

Poster

Langille, David. "Exposing the Face of Corporate Rule." Toronto: Jesuit Centre for Social Faith and Justice, 1996.

Videos

National Labor Committee. *Mickey Mouse Goes to Haiti*. 1996.

————. *Zoned for Slavery*. 1998.

Swimme, Brian. *The Order of the Universe*. No. 4 in a twelve-part video series: *Canticle to the Cosmos*. San Francisco, CA: New Story Project/Tides Foundation, 1990.

Index

Index

agency, 154, 194
Allen, Sheila, 182-83
anthropology, 154-56
Armstrong, Pat, 77
authenticity, 12, 235, 239, 247-48

Bank of Canada: and recession, 43;
the Great Sewing Exchange,
43-44
bargaining: broad-based, 11, 112,
117; weak position, 23; collective,
30, 99, 118, 124n. 11
Bartky, Sandra Lee, 183-84
Benhabib, Seyla, 185
Benjamin, Jessica, 193
Berry, Thomas, 158, 198
bias: kinds of, 140-46; and societal
decline, 147-50; legitimates false
conflicts, 216, 232; to be healed, 244
Borowy, Jan, 125nn. 17 and 21,
127n. 39, 128n. 56
Bowles, Samuel, 249
Boyd, Marion: grant, 99; interview
with, 104-108
Brandt, Gail Cuthbert, 167
brief, "Fair Wages...," 7-8, 103
Brown, Rosemary, 152
Brubaker, Pamela, 243
Burt, Sandra, 181
Business Council on National Issues
(BCNI in Canada), 32
Business Roundtable (USA), 32

capitalism, xxvi: expansion of, 18;
phases, 18-44; developed/unde-
veloped capitalist economies
(DCEs, UCEs), 30, 36
child/dependent care, 7, 10, 118,
159, 183-88, 195, 282
Clean Clothes Campaign: postcards,
100-102, 111, 117-18; in Europe,
215
Coalition for Fair Wages and Working
Conditions for Homeworkers
(Homework Coalition): time
frame, xxvi; brief, 7-10; beginnings of, 90; campaign, 91-92;
and labour law, 97-100; postcard
campaign, 100-10; homeworking
conference, 101-102; underlying
issues, 108-22; voluntary compliance, 256
Code, Lorraine, 154
Cohen, Marjorie Griffin, 251-52, 258
computer-aided: design (CAD), 40,
66; manufacturing (CAM), 40,
66; modular manufacturing,
66-67
consciousness: split, 77, 79-80, 145,
149; feminist consciousness and
horizon, 136-39; critical, 144-50;
social, 194, 262, 279; common
sense, 144-50; and anthropology,
153; and patriarchy, 156-58; communal, 160; immediacy and

349

Series Published by Wilfrid Laurier University Press for the Canadian Corporation for Studies in Religion / Corporation Canadienne des Sciences Religieuses

Editions SR

Comparative Ethics Series / Collection d'Éthique Comparée

Dissertations SR

Studies in Christianity and Judaism / Études sur le christianisme et le judaïsme

3. *Society, the Sacred, and Scripture in Ancient Judaism: A Sociology of Knowledge*
   Jack N. Lightstone / 1988 / xiv + 126 pp.
4. *Law in Religious Communities in the Roman Period: The Debate Over* Torah
   and Nomos *in Post-Biblical Judaism and Early Christianity*
   Peter Richardson and Stephen Westerholm with A. I. Baumgarten, Michael Pettem
   and Cecilia Wassén / 1991 / x + 164 pp.
5. *Dangerous Food: 1 Corinthians 8-10 in Its Context*
   Peter D. Gooch / 1993 / xviii + 178 pp.
6. *The Rhetoric of the Babylonian Talmud, Its Social Meaning and Context*
   Jack N. Lightstone / 1994 / xiv + 317 pp.
7. *Whose Historical Jesus?*
   Edited by William E. Arnal and Michel Desjardins / 1997 / vi + 337 pp.
8. *Religious Rivalries and the Struggle for Success in Caesarea Maritima*
   Edited by Terence L. Donaldson / 2000 / xiv + 402 pp.
9. *Text and Artifact in the Religions of Mediterranean Antiquity*
   Edited by Stephen G. Wilson and Michel Desjardins / 2000 / xvi + 616 pp.

The Study of Religion in Canada /
Sciences Religieuses au Canada

1. *Religious Studies in Alberta: A State-of-the-Art Review*
   Ronald W. Neufeldt / 1983 / xiv + 145 pp.
2. *Les sciences religieuses au Québec depuis 1972*
   Louis Rousseau et Michel Despland / 1988 / 158 p.
3. *Religious Studies in Ontario: A State-of-the-Art Review*
   Harold Remus, William Closson James and Daniel Fraikin / 1992 / xviii + 422 pp.
4. *Religious Studies in Manitoba and Saskatchewan: A State-of-the-Art Review*
   John M. Badertscher, Gordon Harland and Roland E. Miller / 1993 / vi + 166 pp.
5. *The Study of Religion in British Columbia: A State-of-the-Art Review*
   Brian J. Fraser / 1995 / x + 127 pp.

Studies in Women and Religion /
Études sur les femmes et la religion

1. *Femmes et religions**
   Sous la direction de Denise Veillette / 1995 / xviii + 466 p.
   Only available from Les Presses de l'Université Laval
2. *The Work of Their Hands: Mennonite Women's Societies in Canada*
   Gloria Neufeld Redekop / 1996 / xvi + 172 pp.
3. *Profiles of Anabaptist Women: Sixteenth-Century Reforming Pioneers*
   Edited by C. Arnold Snyder and Linda A. Huebert Hecht / 1996 / xxii + 438 pp.
4. *Voices and Echoes: Canadian Women's Spirituality*
   Edited by Jo-Anne Elder and Colin O'Connell / 1997 / xxviii + 237 pp.
5. *Obedience, Suspicion and the Gospel of Mark: A Mennonite-Feminist Exploration of Biblical Authority*
   Lydia Neufeld Harder / 1998 / xiv + 168 pp.
6. *Clothed in Integrity: Weaving Just Cultural Relations and the Garment Industry*
   Barbara Paleczny / 2000 / xxxiv + 352 pp.

SR Supplements

1. *Footnotes to a Theology: The Karl Barth Colloquium of 1972*
   Edited and Introduced by Martin Rumscheidt / 1974 / viii + 151 pp. / OUT OF PRINT
2. *Martin Heidegger's Philosophy of Religion*
   John R. Williams / 1977 / x + 190 pp. / OUT OF PRINT

3. *Mystics and Scholars: The Calgary Conference on Mysticism 1976*
   Edited by Harold Coward and Terence Penelhum / 1977 / viii + 121 pp. / OUT OF PRINT
4. *God's Intention for Man: Essays in Christian Anthropology*
   William O. Fennell / 1977 / xii + 56 pp. / OUT OF PRINT
5. *"Language" in Indian Philosophy and Religion*
   Edited and Introduced by Harold G. Coward / 1978 / x + 98 pp. / OUT OF PRINT
6. *Beyond Mysticism*
   James R. Horne / 1978 / vi + 158 pp. / OUT OF PRINT
7. *The Religious Dimension of Socrates' Thought*
   James Beckman / 1979 / xii + 276 pp. / OUT OF PRINT
8. *Native Religious Traditions*
   Edited by Earle H. Waugh and K. Dad Prithipaul / 1979 / xii + 244 pp. / OUT OF PRINT
9. *Developments in Buddhist Thought: Canadian Contributions to Buddhist Studies*
   Edited by Roy C. Amore / 1979 / iv + 196 pp.
10. *The Bodhisattva Doctrine in Buddhism*
    Edited and Introduced by Leslie S. Kawamura / 1981 / xxii + 274 pp. / OUT OF PRINT
11. *Political Theology in the Canadian Context*
    Edited by Benjamin G. Smillie / 1982 / xii + 260 pp.
12. *Truth and Compassion: Essays on Judaism and Religion in Memory of Rabbi Dr. Solomon Frank*
    Edited by Howard Joseph, Jack N. Lightstone and Michael D. Oppenheim
    1983 / vi + 217 pp.
13. *Craving and Salvation: A Study in Buddhist Soteriology*
    Bruce Matthews / 1983 / xiv + 138 pp. / OUT OF PRINT
14. *The Moral Mystic*
    James R. Horne / 1983 / x + 134 pp.
15. *Ignatian Spirituality in a Secular Age*
    Edited by George P. Schner / 1984 / viii + 128 pp. / OUT OF PRINT
16. *Studies in the Book of Job*
    Edited by Walter E. Aufrecht / 1985 / xii + 76 pp.
17. *Christ and Modernity: Christian Self-Understanding in a Technological Age*
    David J. Hawkin / 1985 / x + 181 pp.
18. *Young Man Shinran: A Reappraisal of Shinran's Life*
    Takamichi Takahatake / 1987 / xvi + 228 pp. / OUT OF PRINT
19. *Modernity and Religion*
    Edited by William Nicholls / 1987 / vi + 191 pp.
20. *The Social Uplifters: Presbyterian Progressives and the Social Gospel in Canada, 1875-1915*
    Brian J. Fraser / 1988 / xvi + 212 pp. / OUT OF PRINT

Series discontinued

Available from:

Wilfrid Laurier University Press

Waterloo, Ontario, Canada   N2L 3C5
Telephone: (519) 884-0710, ext. 6124
Fax: (519) 725-1399
E-mail: press@wlu.ca
World Wide Web: http://www.wlu.ca/~wwwpress/